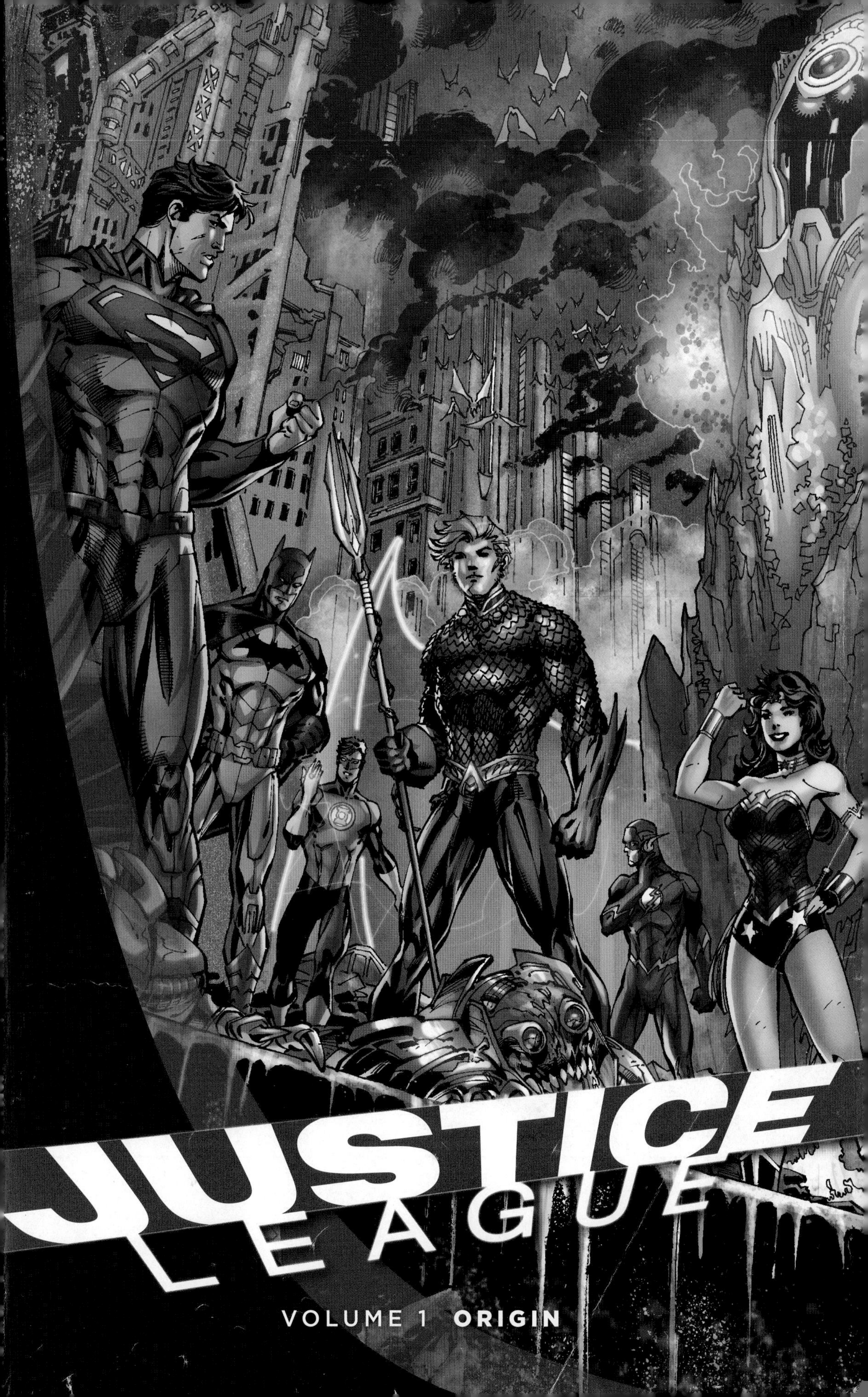
JUSTICE
LEAGUE
VOLUME 1 ORIGIN

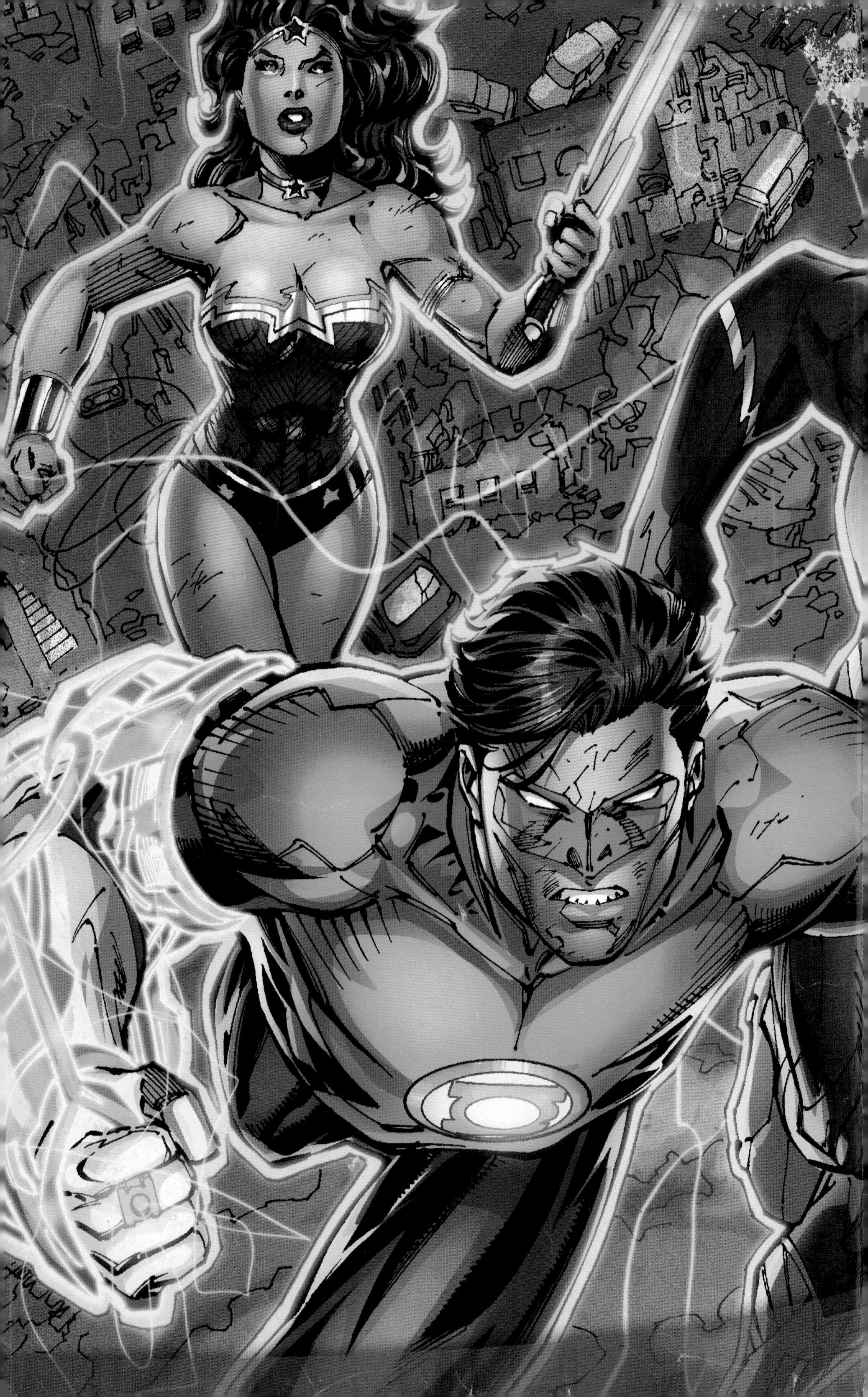

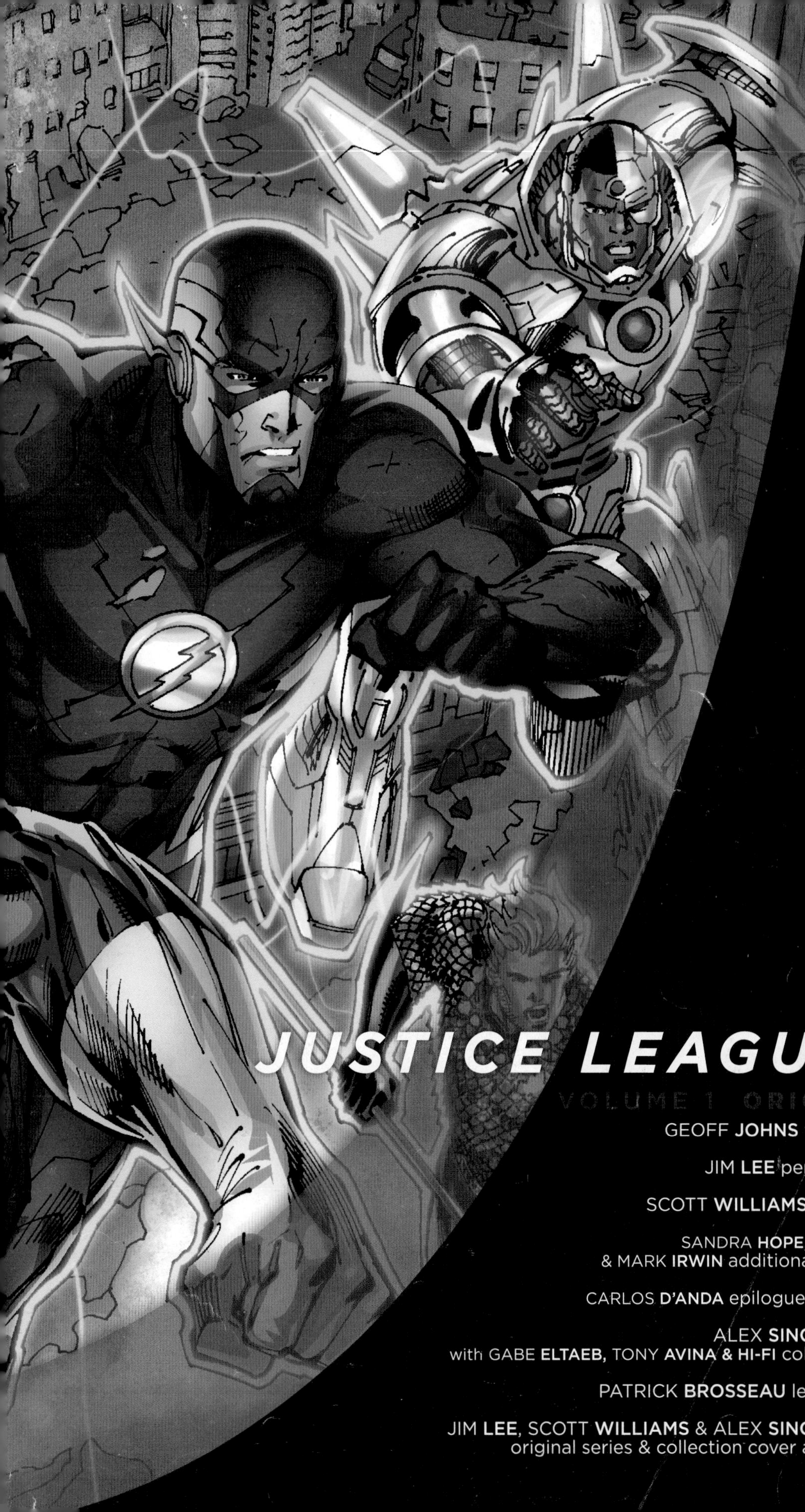

JUSTICE LEAGUE

VOLUME 1: ORIGIN

GEOFF **JOHNS** writer

JIM **LEE** penciller

SCOTT **WILLIAMS** inker

SANDRA **HOPE, BATT**
& MARK **IRWIN** additional inks

CARLOS **D'ANDA** epilogue artist

ALEX **SINCLAIR**
with GABE **ELTAEB**, TONY **AVINA** & **HI-FI** colorists

PATRICK **BROSSEAU** letterer

JIM **LEE**, SCOTT **WILLIAMS** & ALEX **SINCLAIR**
original series & collection cover artists

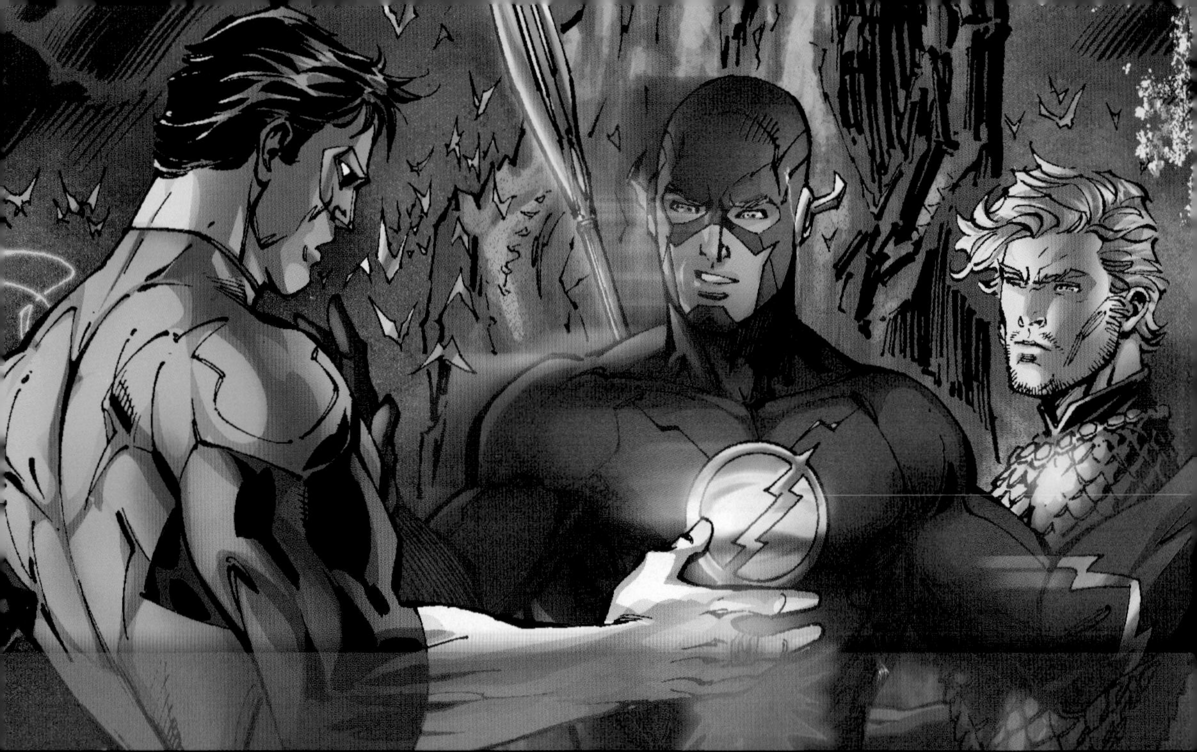

EDDIE BERGANZA BRIAN CUNNINGHAM Editors - Original Series
REX OGLE Associate Editor - Original Series DARREN SHAN Assistant Editor - Original Series
PETER HAMBOUSSI Editor ROBBIN BROSTERMAN Design Director - Books
ROBBIE BIEDERMAN Publication Design

EDDIE BERGANZA Executive Editor
BOB HARRAS VP - Editor-in-Chief

DIANE NELSON President DAN DIDIO and JIM LEE Co-Publishers
GEOFF JOHNS Chief Creative Officer
JOHN ROOD Executive VP - Sales, Marketing and Business Development
AMY GENKINS Senior VP - Business and Legal Affairs NAIRI GARDINER Senior VP - Finance
JEFF BOISON VP - Publishing Operations MARK CHIARELLO VP - Art Direction and Design
JOHN CUNNINGHAM VP - Marketing TERRI CUNNINGHAM VP - Talent Relations and Services
ALISON GILL Senior VP - Manufacturing and Operations DAVID HYDE VP - Publicity
HANK KANALZ Senior VP - Digital JAY KOGAN VP - Business and Legal Affairs, Publishing
JACK MAHAN VP - Business Affairs, Talent NICK NAPOLITANO VP - Manufacturing Administration
SUE POHJA VP - Book Sales COURTNEY SIMMONS Senior VP - Publicity
BOB WAYNE Senior VP - Sales

JUSTICE LEAGUE VOLUME 1: ORIGIN
Published by DC Comics. Cover and compilation Copyright © 2012 DC Comics.

DC Comics, 1700 Broadway, New York, NY 10019
A Warner Bros. Entertainment Company
Printed by RR Donnelley, Salem, VA, USA. 3/30/12. First Printing.

HC ISBN: 978-1-4012-3461-4
SC ISBN: 978-1-4012-3788-2

Library of Congress Cataloging-in-Publication Data
Johns, Geoff, 1973-
Justice League volume 1 : origin / Geoff Johns, Jim Lee, Scott Williams.
p. cm.
"Originally published in single magazine form in JUSTICE LEAGUE 1-6"—T.p. verso.
ISBN 978-1-4012-3461-4 (hardcover : alk. paper)
1. Graphic novels. I. Lee, Jim, 1964- II. Williams, Scott. III. Title.
PN6728.J87J65 2012
741.5'973—dc23
2011051844

SUSTAINABLE FORESTRY INITIATIVE
Certified Chain of Custody
At Least 25% Certified Forest Content
www.sfiprogram.org
SFI-01042
APPLIES TO TEXT STOCK ONLY

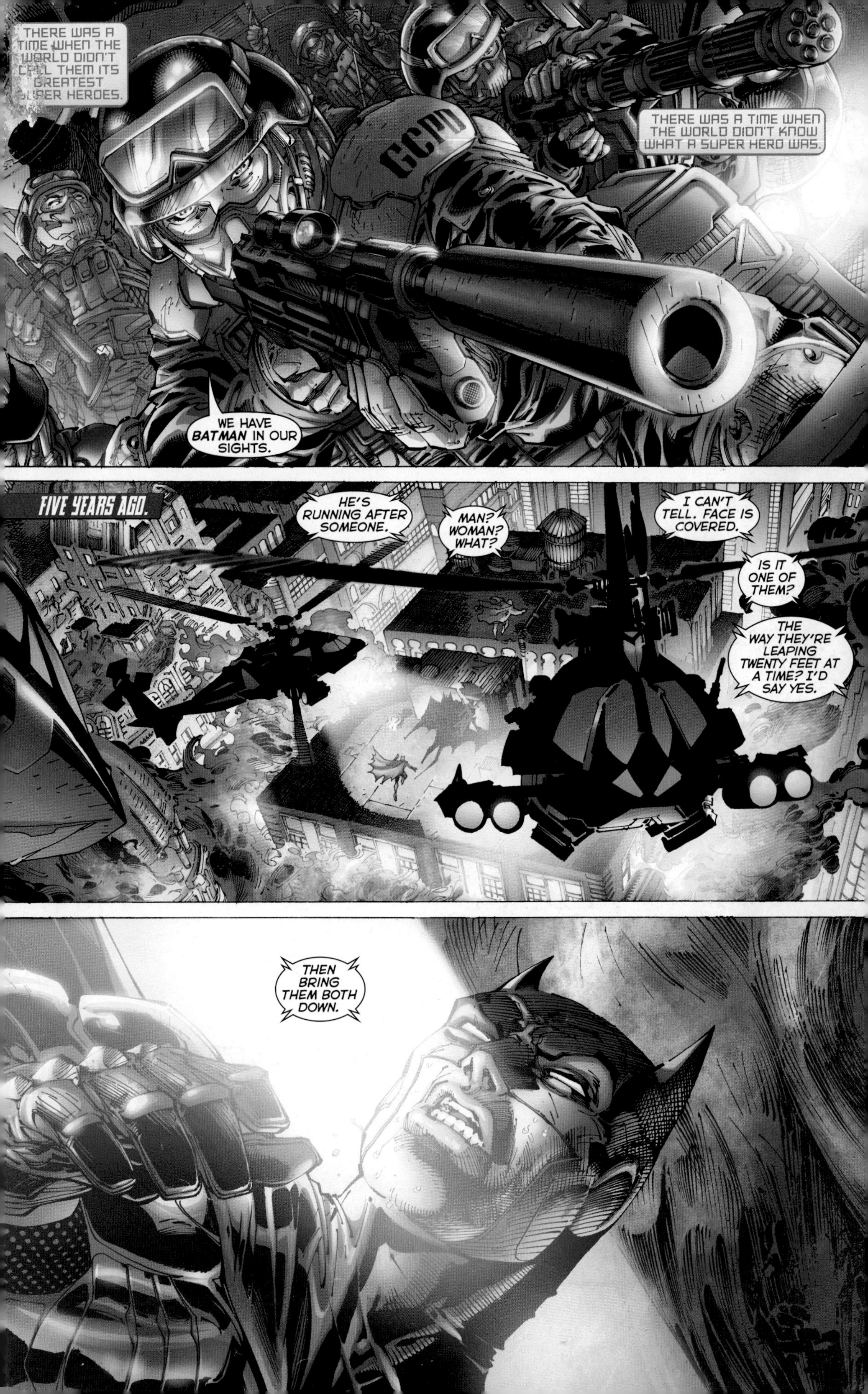
THERE WAS A TIME WHEN THE WORLD DIDN'T CALL THEM ITS GREATEST SUPER HEROES.
THERE WAS A TIME WHEN THE WORLD DIDN'T KNOW WHAT A SUPER HERO WAS.
GCPD
WE HAVE BATMAN IN OUR SIGHTS.
FIVE YEARS AGO.
HE'S RUNNING AFTER SOMEONE.
MAN? WOMAN? WHAT?
I CAN'T TELL. FACE IS COVERED.
IS IT ONE OF THEM?
THE WAY THEY'RE LEAPING TWENTY FEET AT A TIME? I'D SAY YES.
THEN BRING THEM BOTH DOWN.

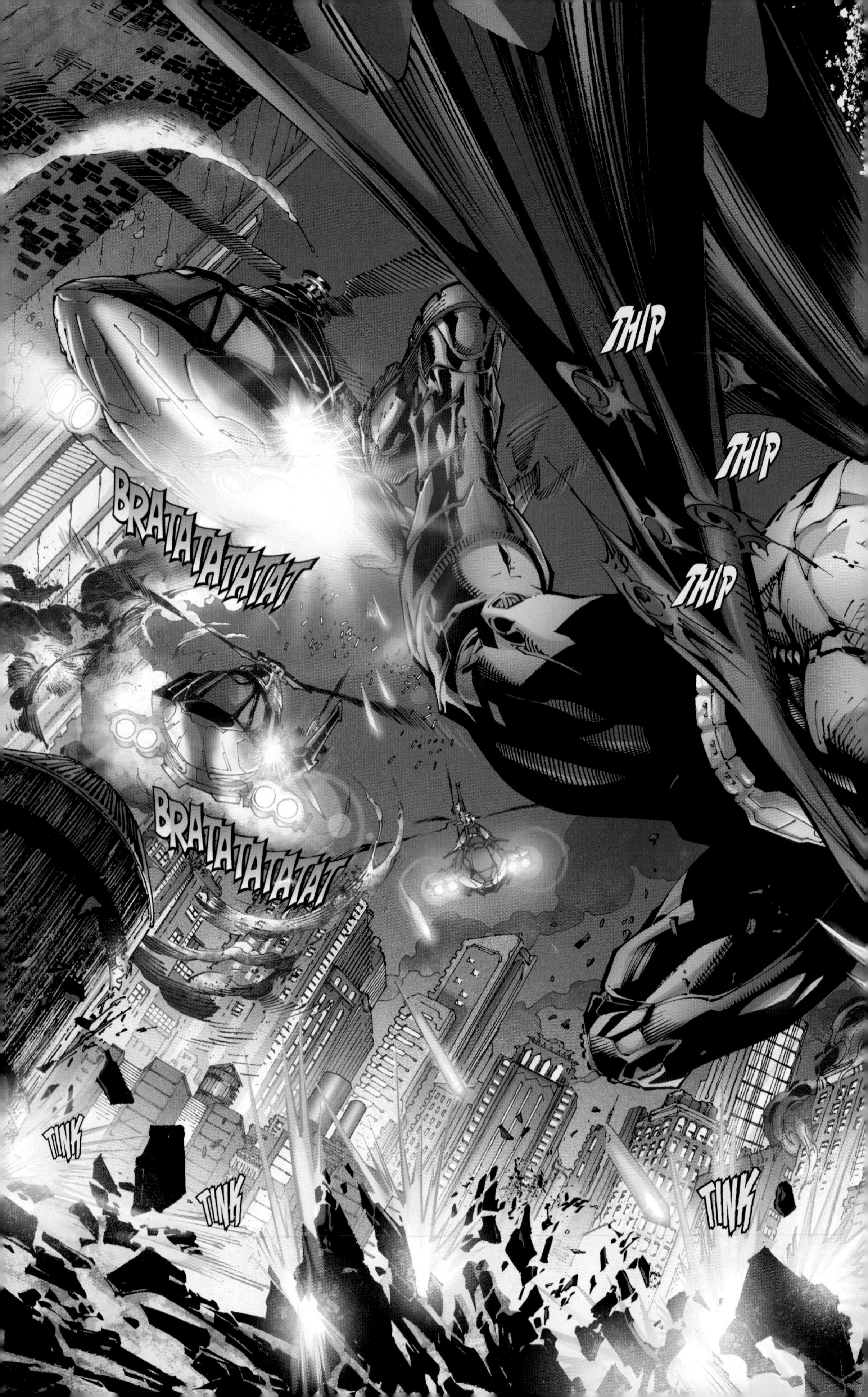
THIP
THIP
THIP
BRATATATATAT
BRATATATATAT
TINK
TINK
TINK

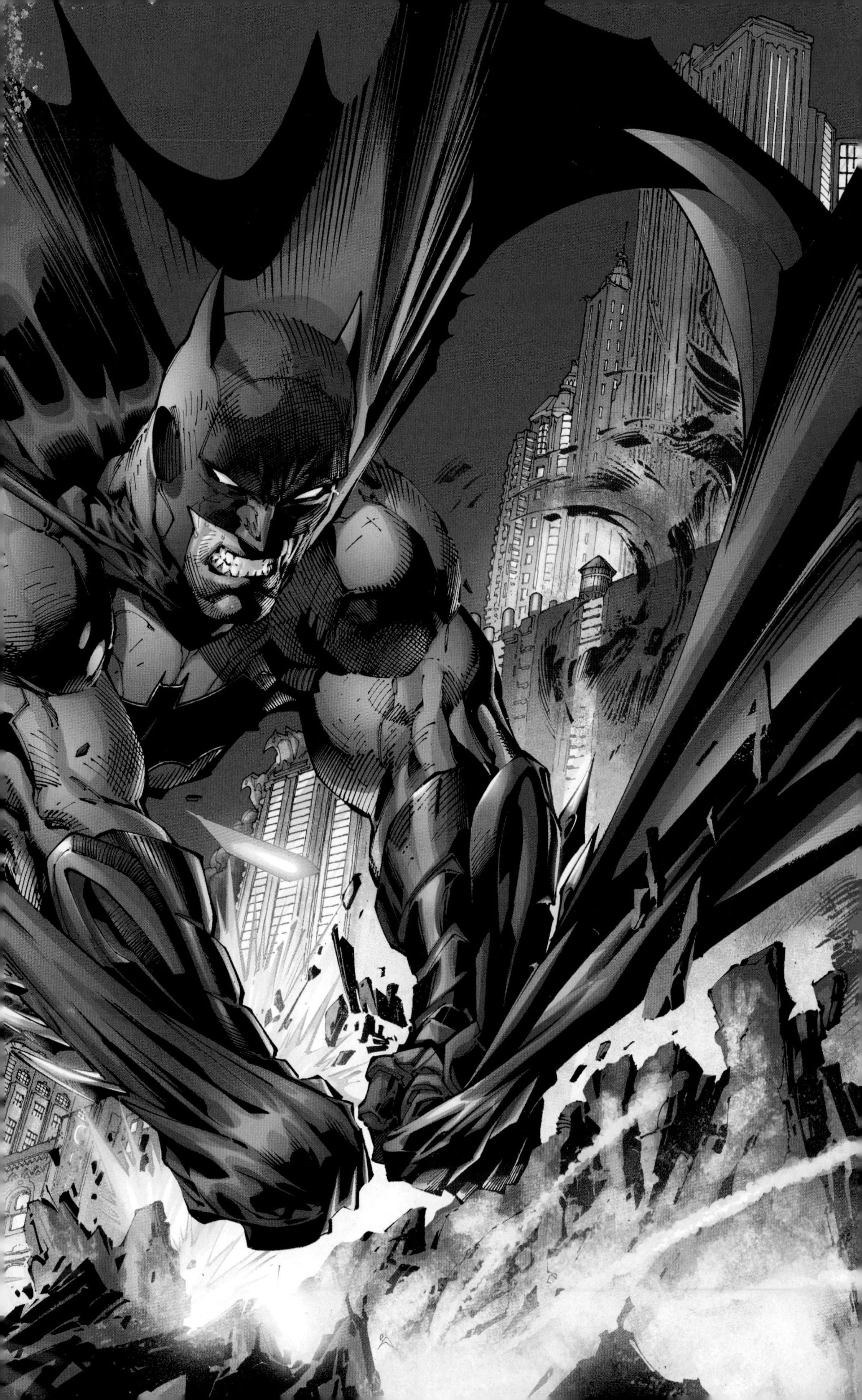

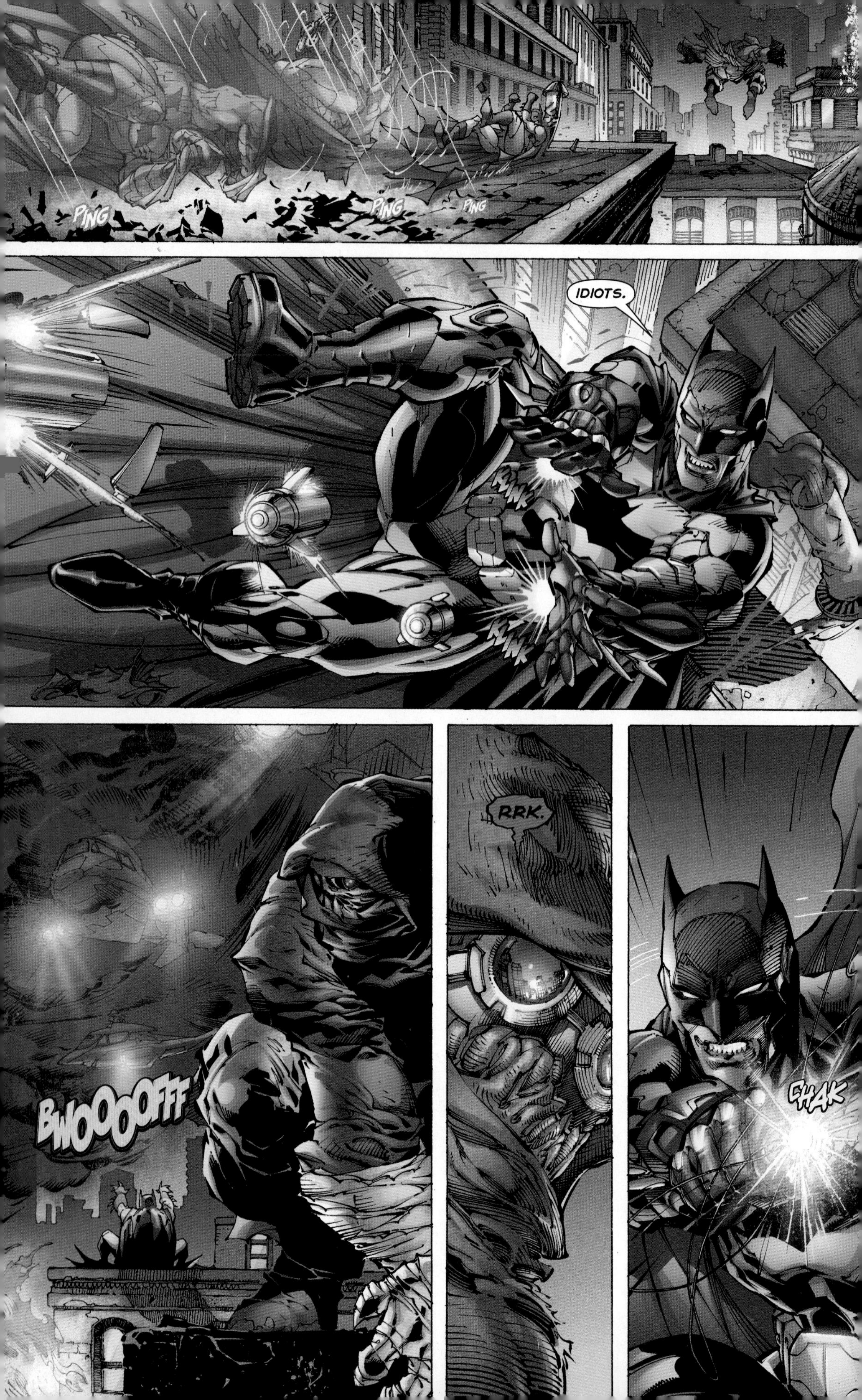
PING
PING
PING
IDIOTS.
KLINK
KLINK
BWOOOOFFF
RRK.
CHAK

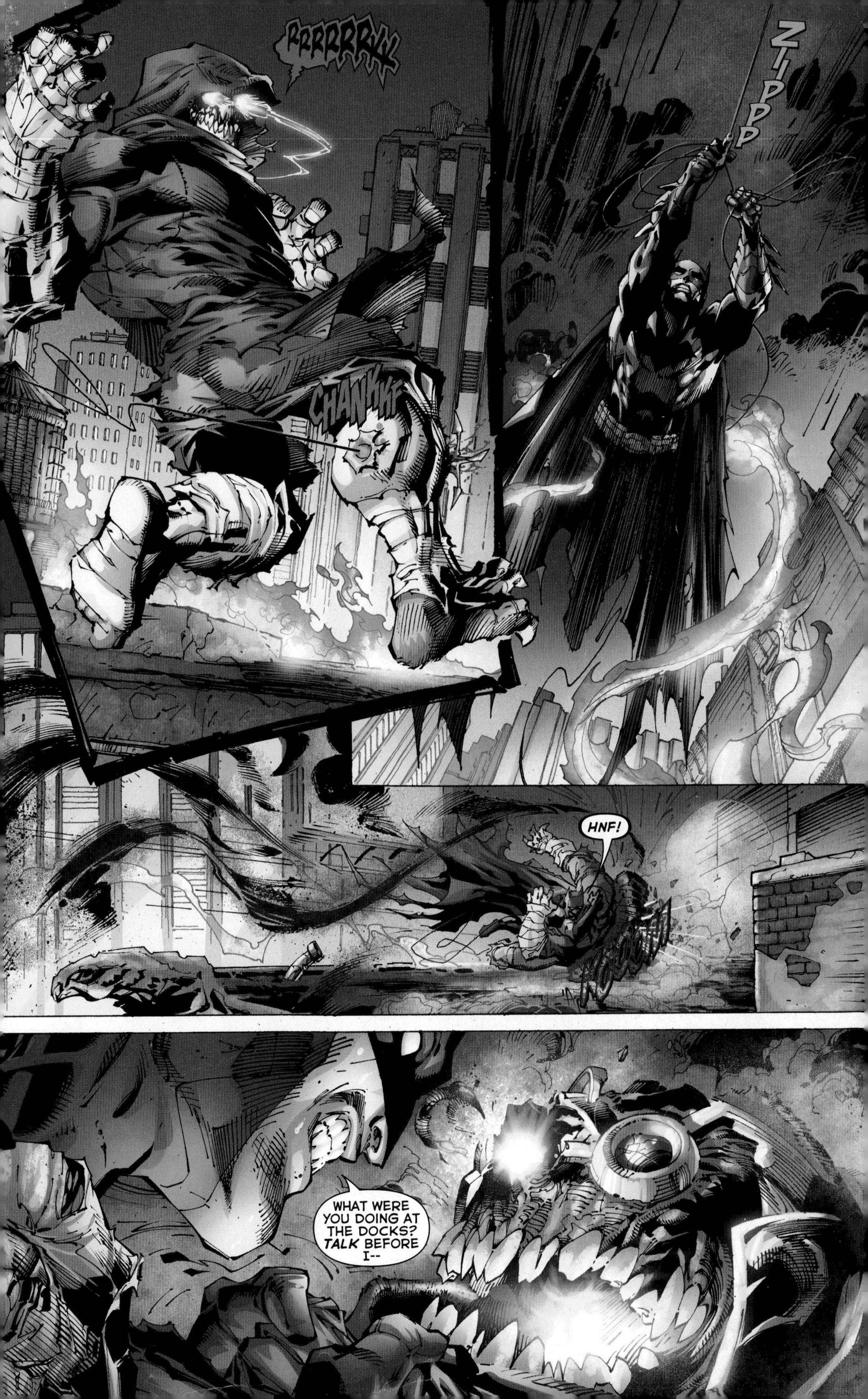
RRRRRRYAL
ZIIPPP
CHANKKK
HNF!
WHAT WERE YOU DOING AT THE DOCKS? *TALK* BEFORE I--

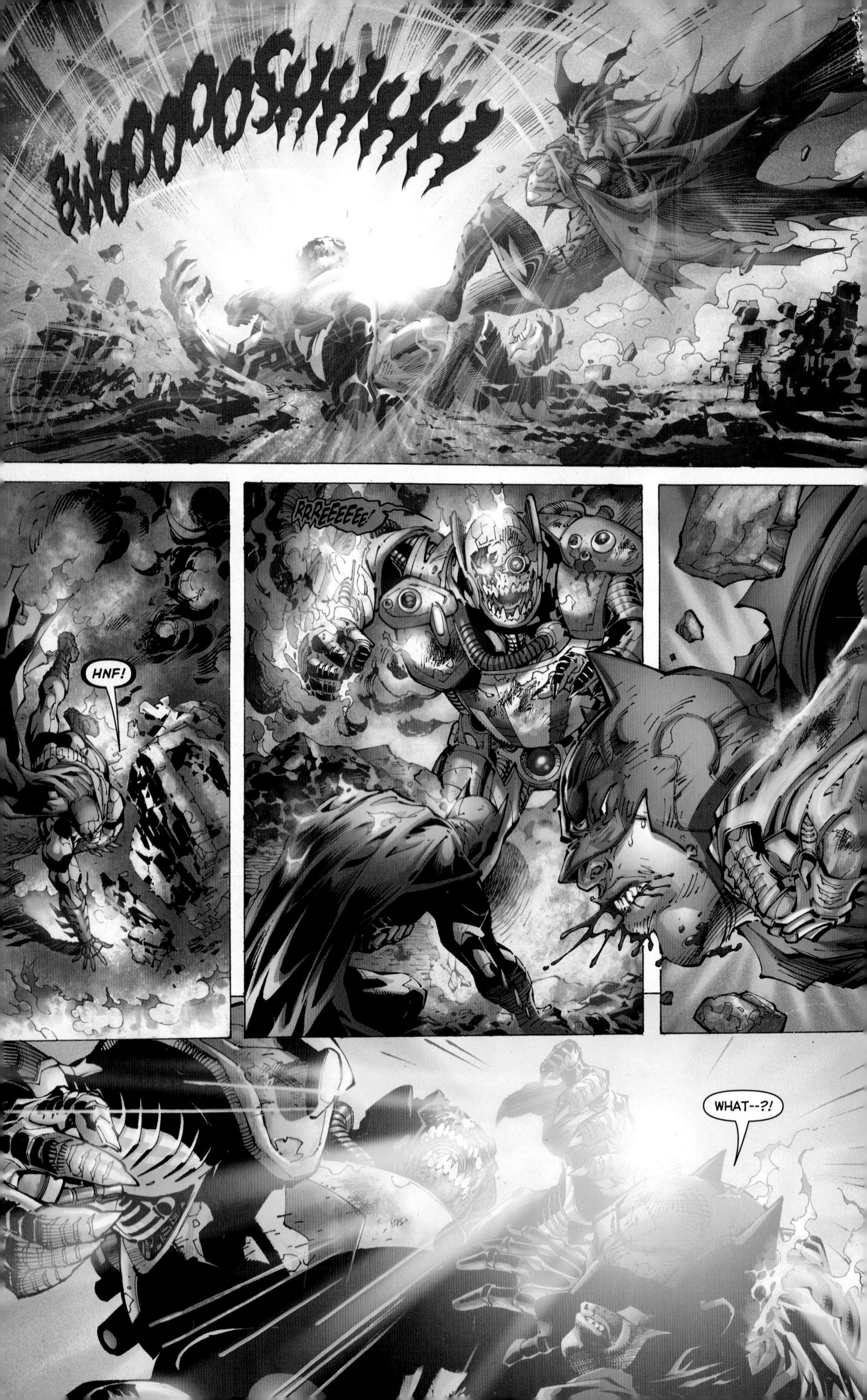
BWOOOOSHHHH
HNF!
BRRREEEEEE!
WHAT--?!

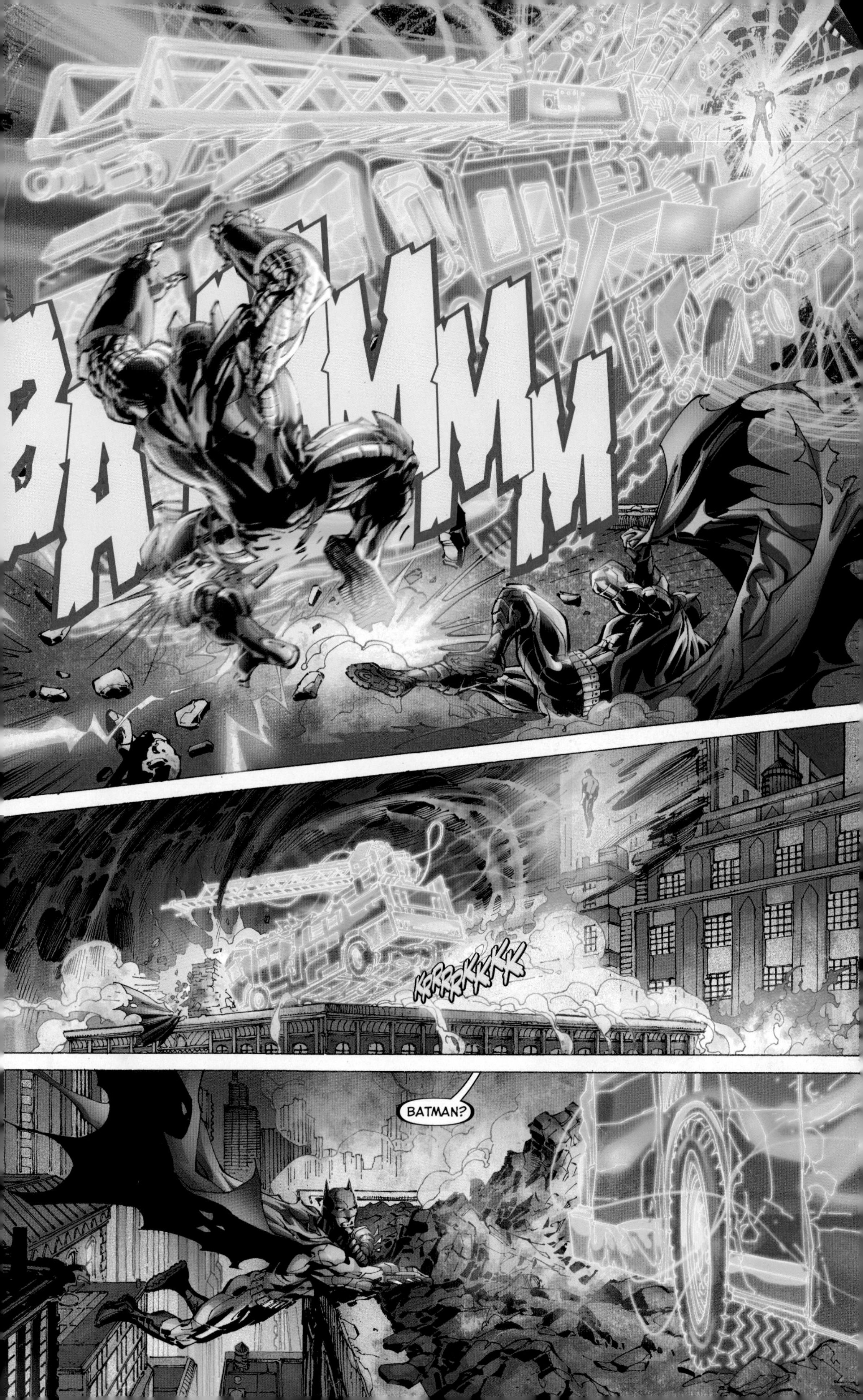
BAMMMM
KRRRKKKK
BATMAN?

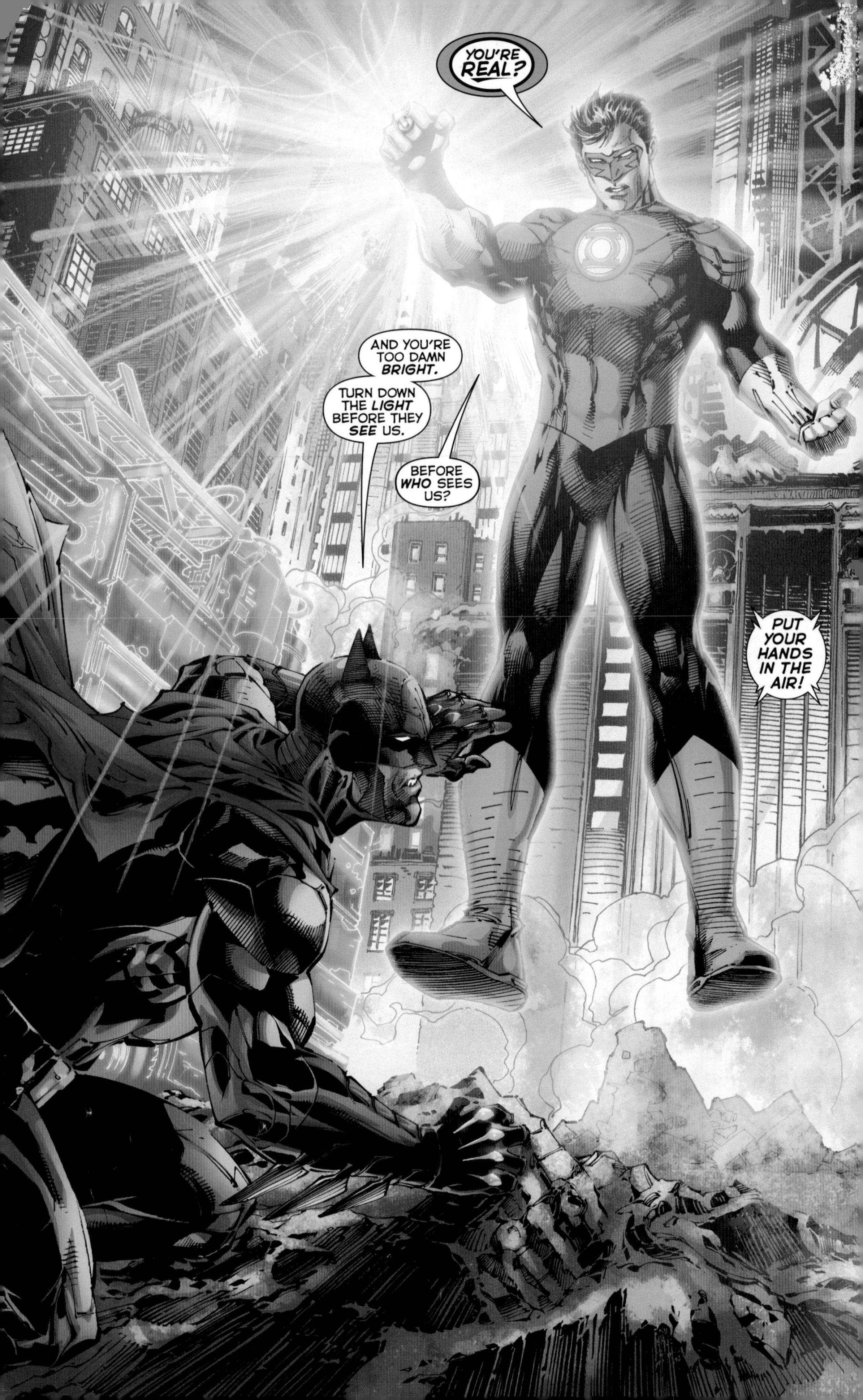
YOU'RE REAL?
AND YOU'RE TOO DAMN BRIGHT.
TURN DOWN THE LIGHT BEFORE THEY SEE US.
BEFORE WHO SEES US?
PUT YOUR HANDS IN THE AIR!

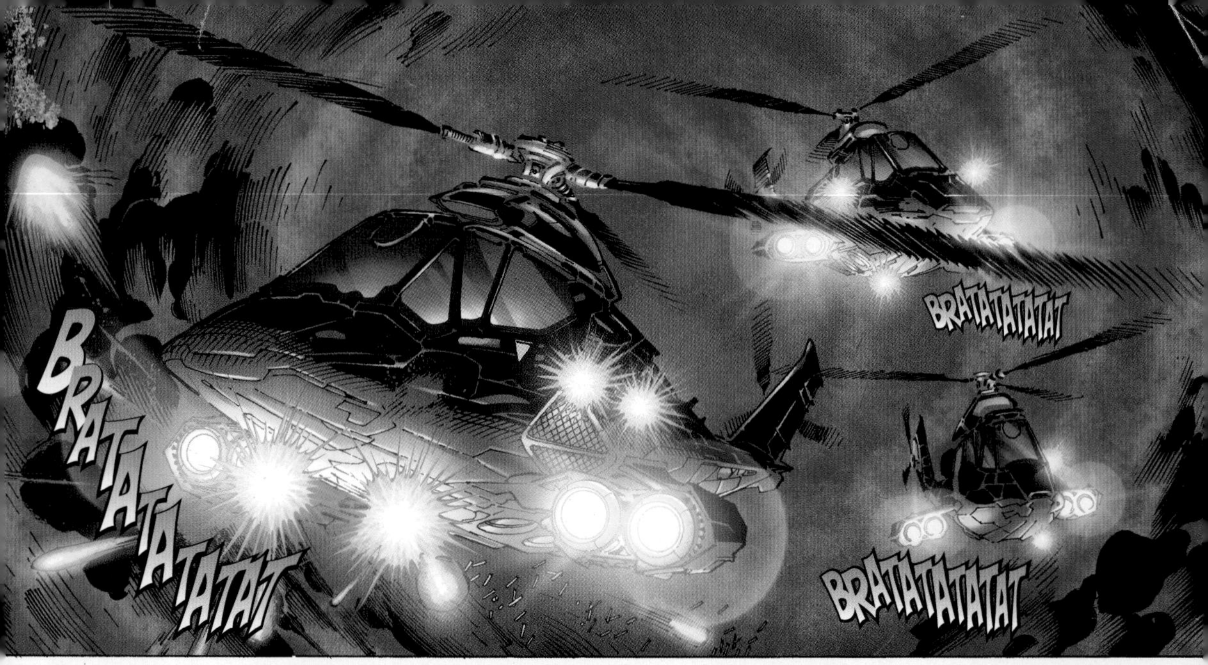
BRATATATATAT
BRATATATATAT
BRATATATATAT

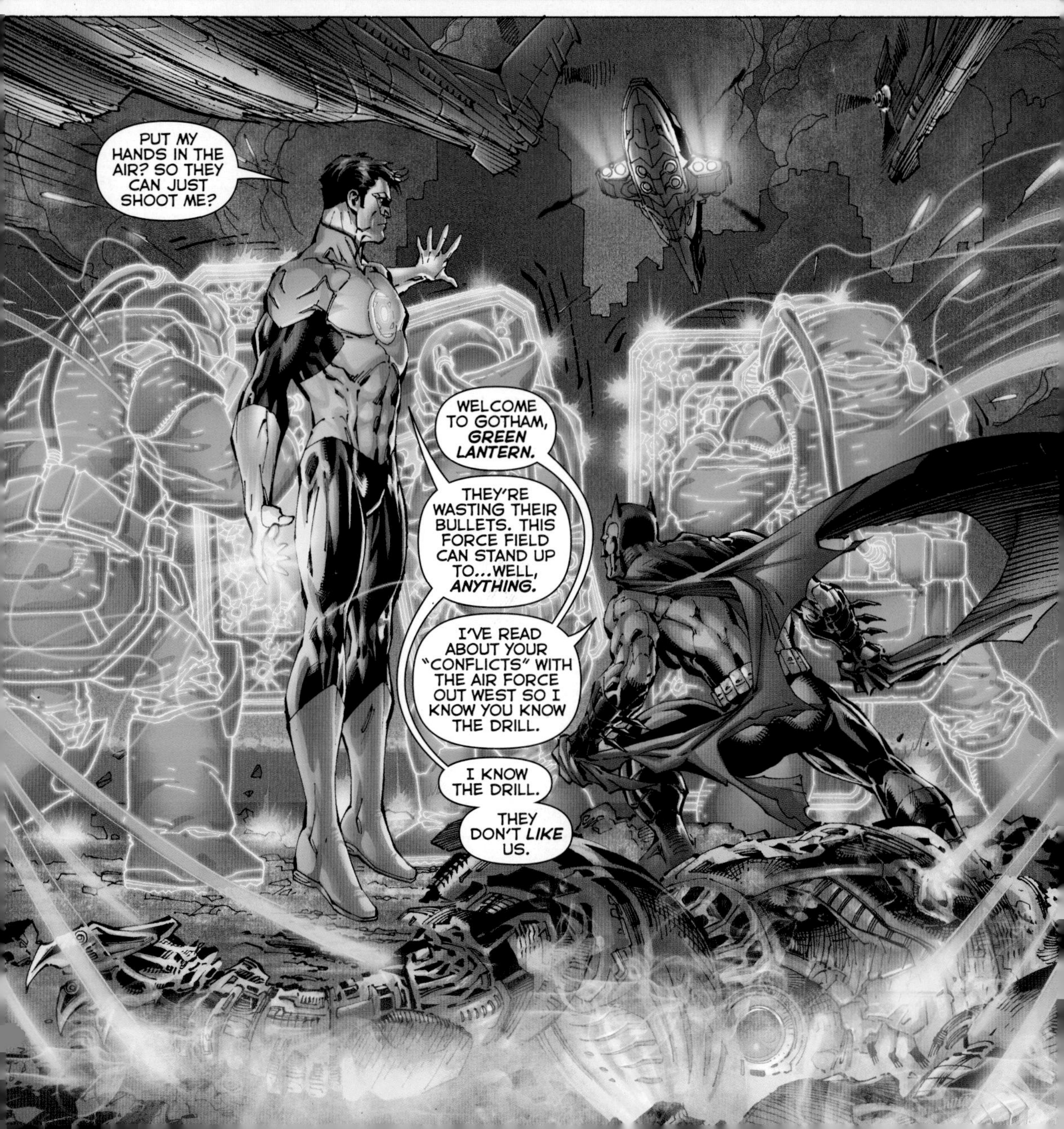
PUT MY HANDS IN THE AIR? SO THEY CAN JUST SHOOT ME?
WELCOME TO GOTHAM, GREEN LANTERN.
THEY'RE WASTING THEIR BULLETS. THIS FORCE FIELD CAN STAND UP TO...WELL, ANYTHING.
I'VE READ ABOUT YOUR "CONFLICTS" WITH THE AIR FORCE OUT WEST SO I KNOW YOU KNOW THE DRILL.
I KNOW THE DRILL.
THEY DON'T LIKE US.

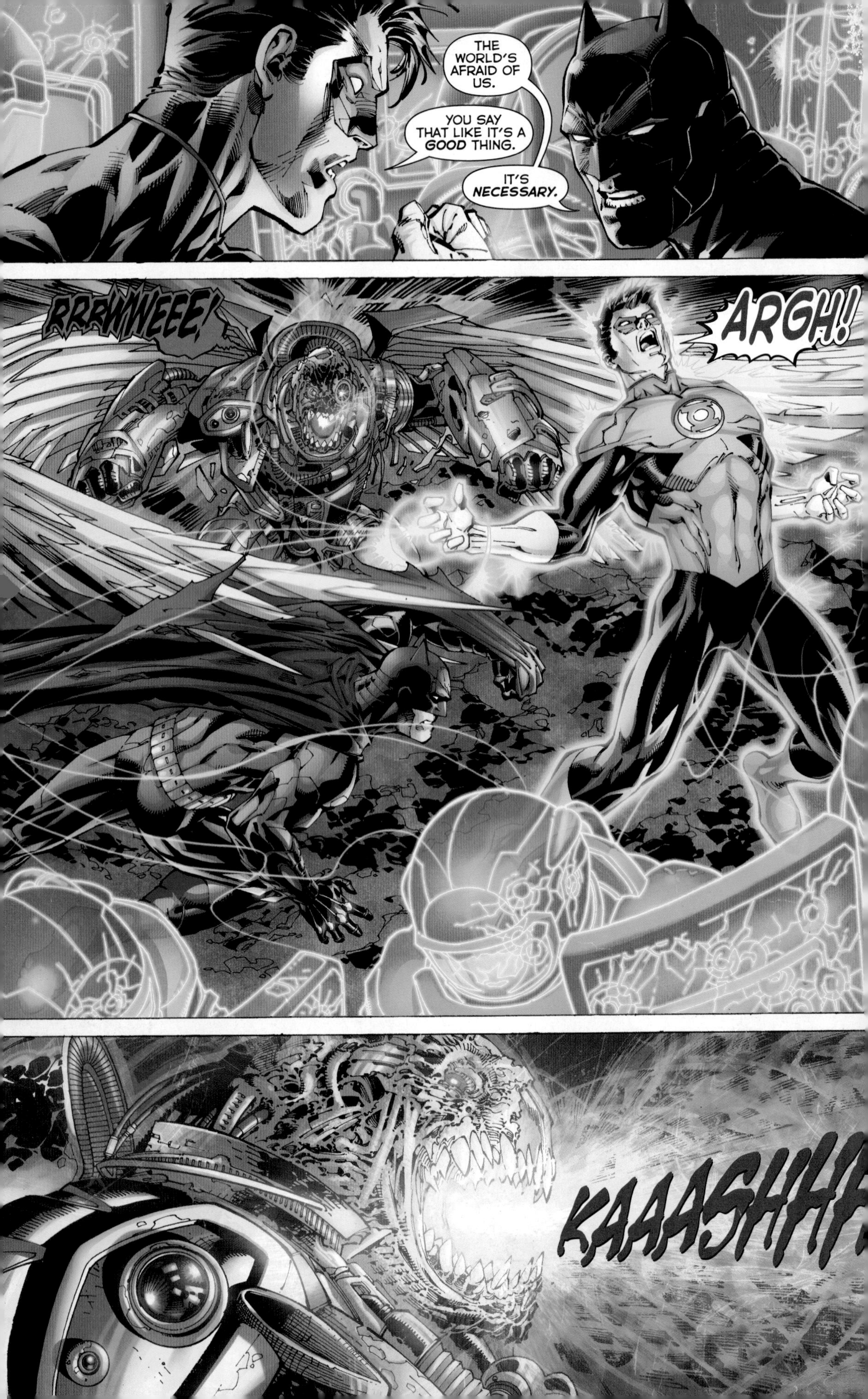
THE WORLD'S AFRAID OF US.
YOU SAY THAT LIKE IT'S A GOOD THING.
IT'S NECESSARY.
RRRWWEEE!
ARGH!
KAAASHH

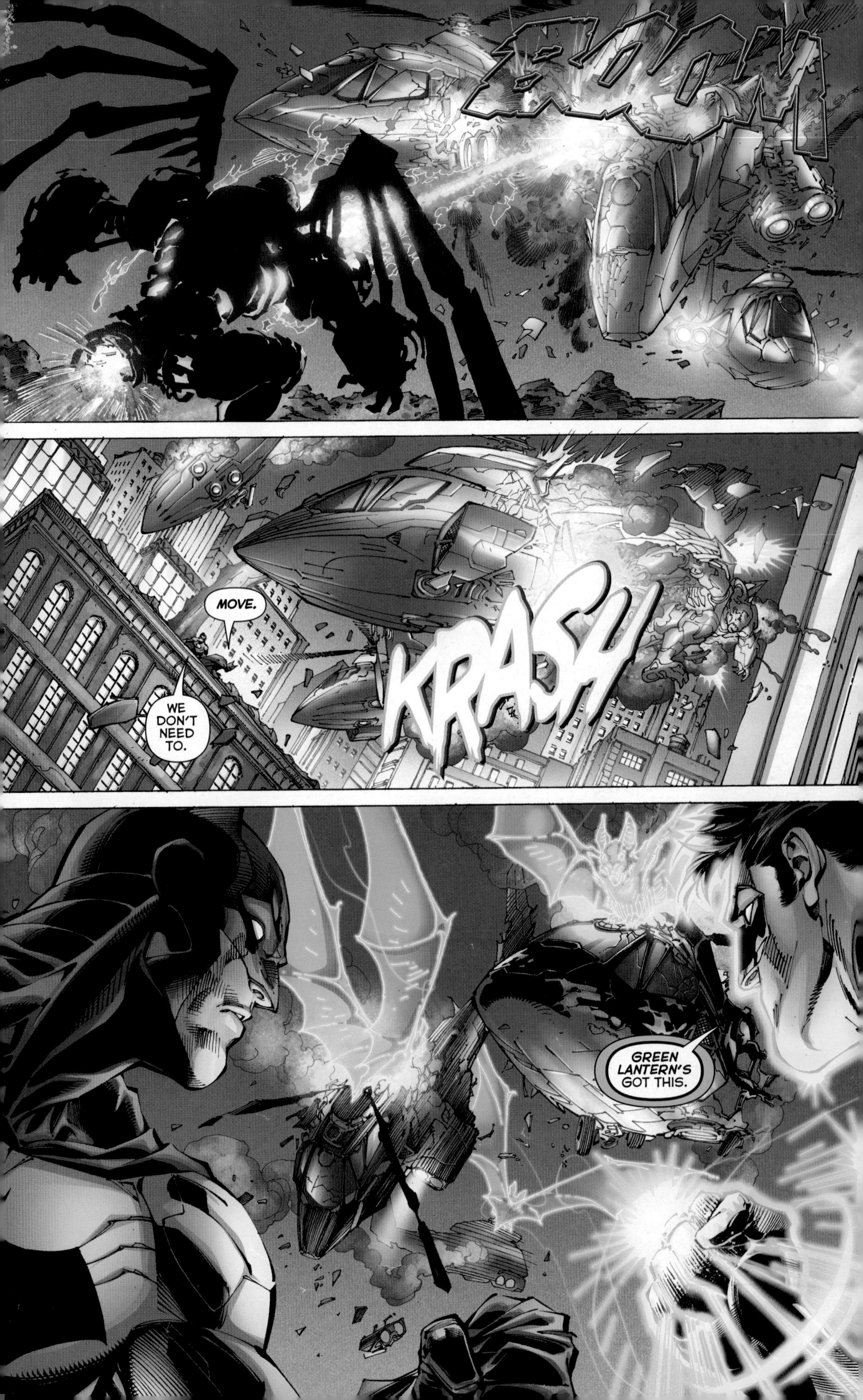
BOOM
MOVE.
WE DON'T NEED TO.
KRASH
GREEN LANTERN'S GOT THIS.

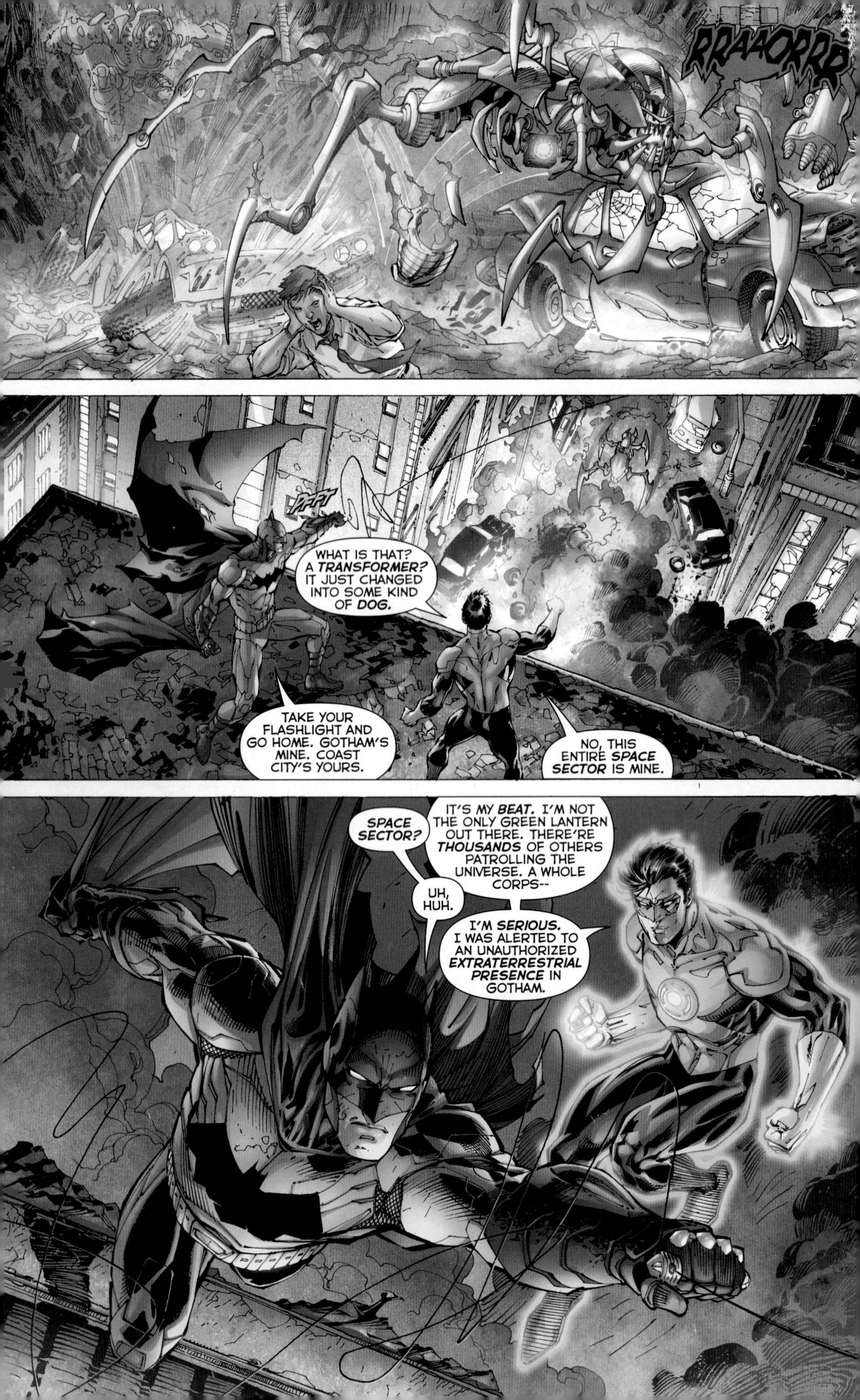
RRAAORRR
PPFFT
WHAT IS THAT? A TRANSFORMER? IT JUST CHANGED INTO SOME KIND OF DOG.
TAKE YOUR FLASHLIGHT AND GO HOME. GOTHAM'S MINE. COAST CITY'S YOURS.
NO, THIS ENTIRE SPACE SECTOR IS MINE.
SPACE SECTOR?
IT'S MY BEAT. I'M NOT THE ONLY GREEN LANTERN OUT THERE. THERE'RE THOUSANDS OF OTHERS PATROLLING THE UNIVERSE. A WHOLE CORPS--
UH, HUH.
I'M SERIOUS. I WAS ALERTED TO AN UNAUTHORIZED EXTRATERRESTRIAL PRESENCE IN GOTHAM.

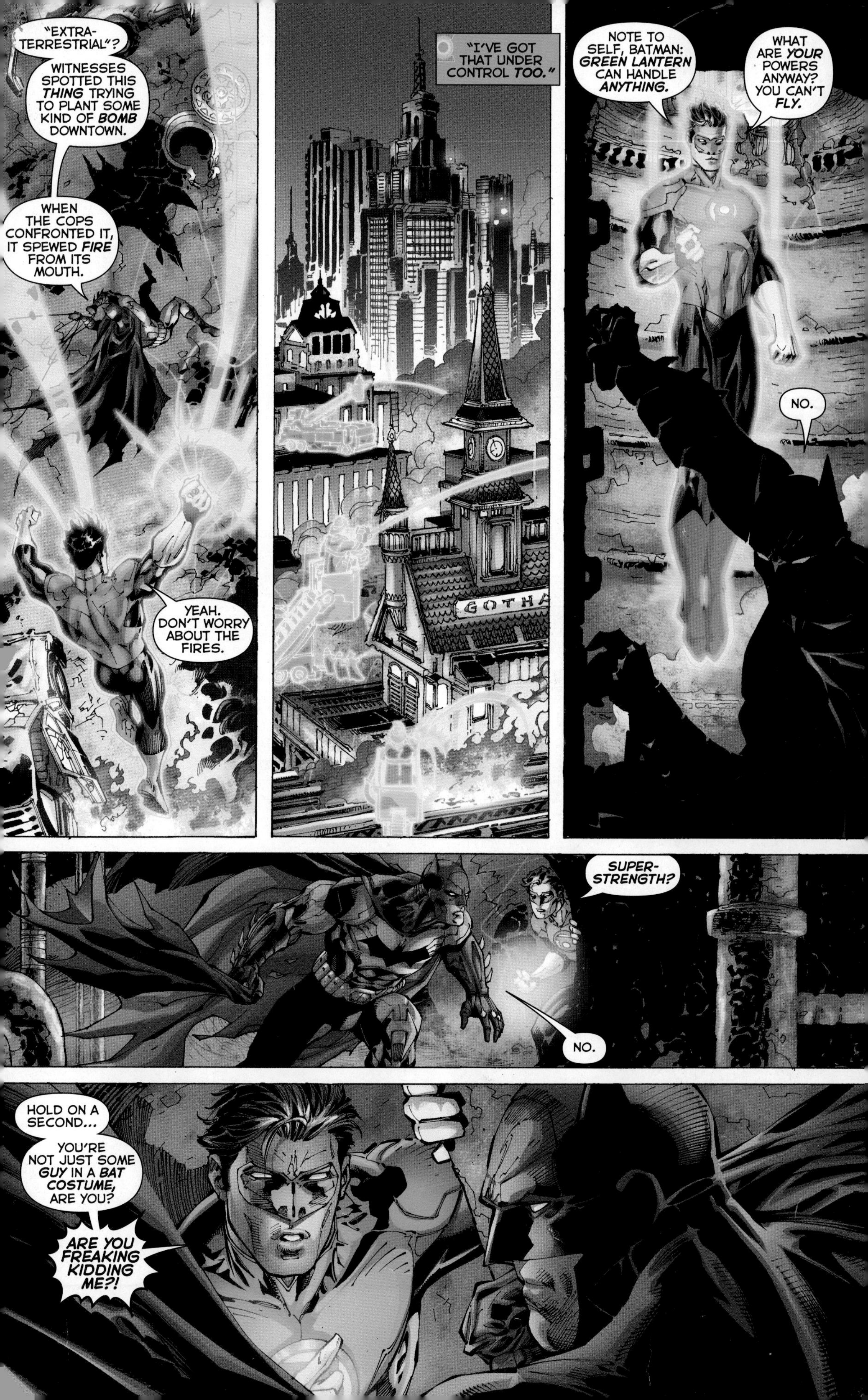
"EXTRA-TERRESTRIAL"?
WITNESSES SPOTTED THIS *THING* TRYING TO PLANT SOME KIND OF *BOMB* DOWNTOWN.
WHEN THE COPS CONFRONTED IT, IT SPEWED *FIRE* FROM ITS MOUTH.
YEAH. DON'T WORRY ABOUT THE FIRES.
"I'VE GOT THAT UNDER CONTROL *TOO.*"
GOTHA
NOTE TO SELF, BATMAN: *GREEN LANTERN* CAN HANDLE *ANYTHING.*
WHAT ARE *YOUR* POWERS ANYWAY? YOU CAN'T *FLY.*
NO.
SUPER-STRENGTH?
NO.
HOLD ON A SECOND...
YOU'RE NOT JUST SOME *GUY* IN A *BAT COSTUME,* ARE YOU?
ARE YOU FREAKING KIDDING ME?!

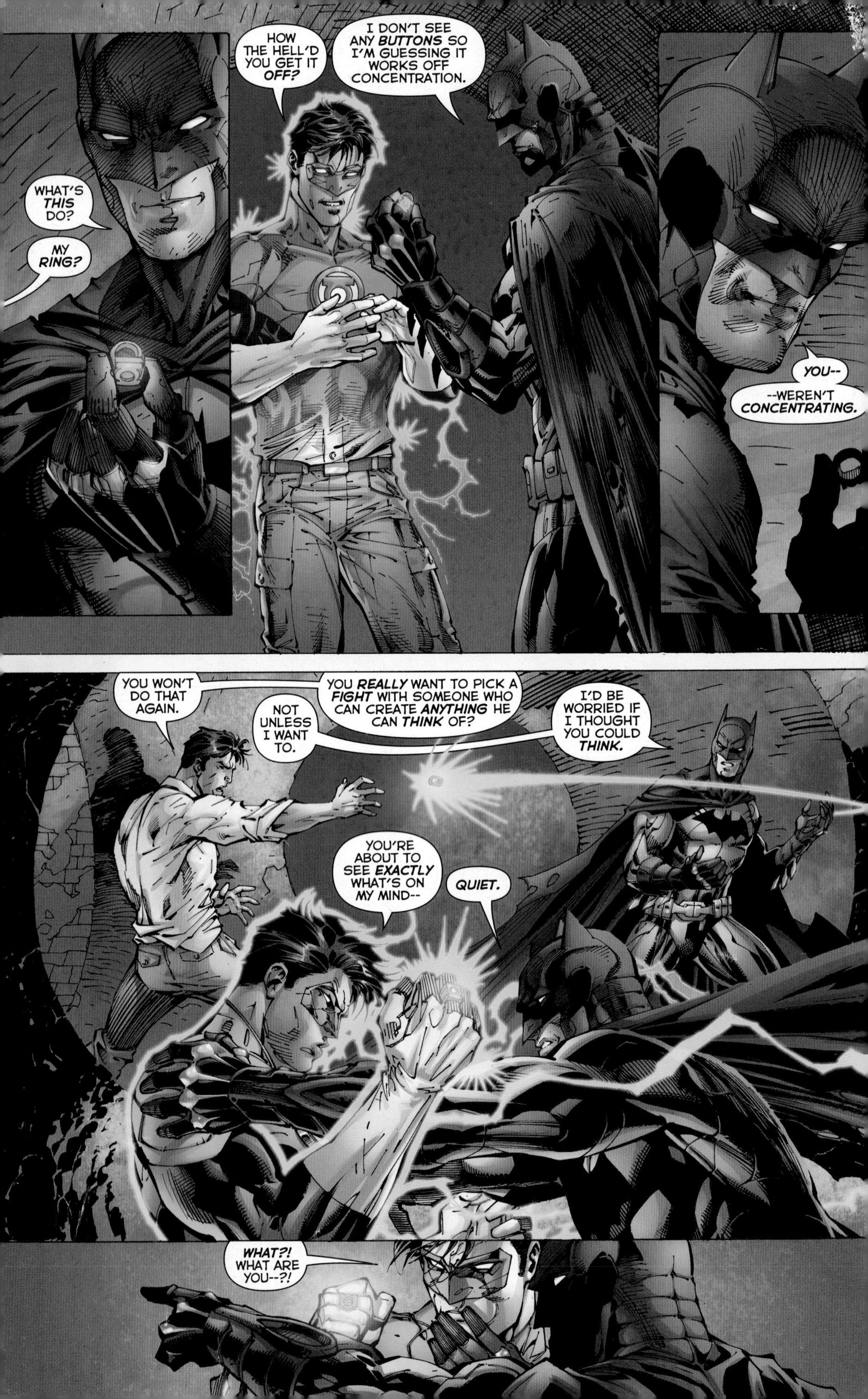

WHAT'S THIS DO?
MY RING?
HOW THE HELL'D YOU GET IT OFF?
I DON'T SEE ANY BUTTONS SO I'M GUESSING IT WORKS OFF CONCENTRATION.
YOU--
--WEREN'T CONCENTRATING.
YOU WON'T DO THAT AGAIN.
NOT UNLESS I WANT TO.
YOU REALLY WANT TO PICK A FIGHT WITH SOMEONE WHO CAN CREATE ANYTHING HE CAN THINK OF?
I'D BE WORRIED IF I THOUGHT YOU COULD THINK.
YOU'RE ABOUT TO SEE EXACTLY WHAT'S ON MY MIND--
QUIET.
WHAT?! WHAT ARE YOU--?!

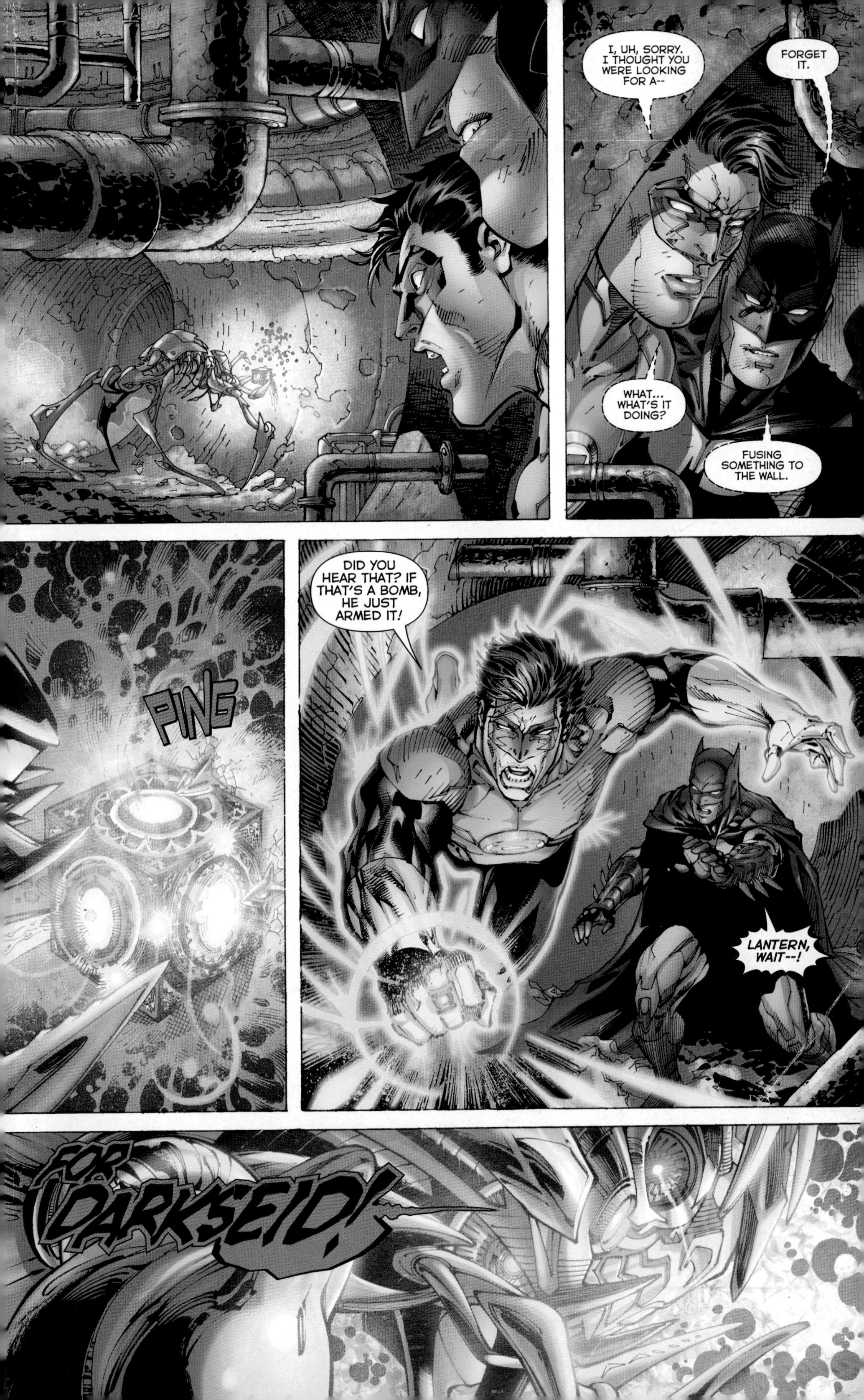
I, UH, SORRY. I THOUGHT YOU WERE LOOKING FOR A--
FORGET IT.
WHAT... WHAT'S IT DOING?
FUSING SOMETHING TO THE WALL.
PING
DID YOU HEAR THAT? IF THAT'S A BOMB, HE JUST ARMED IT!
LANTERN, WAIT--!
FOR DARKSEID!

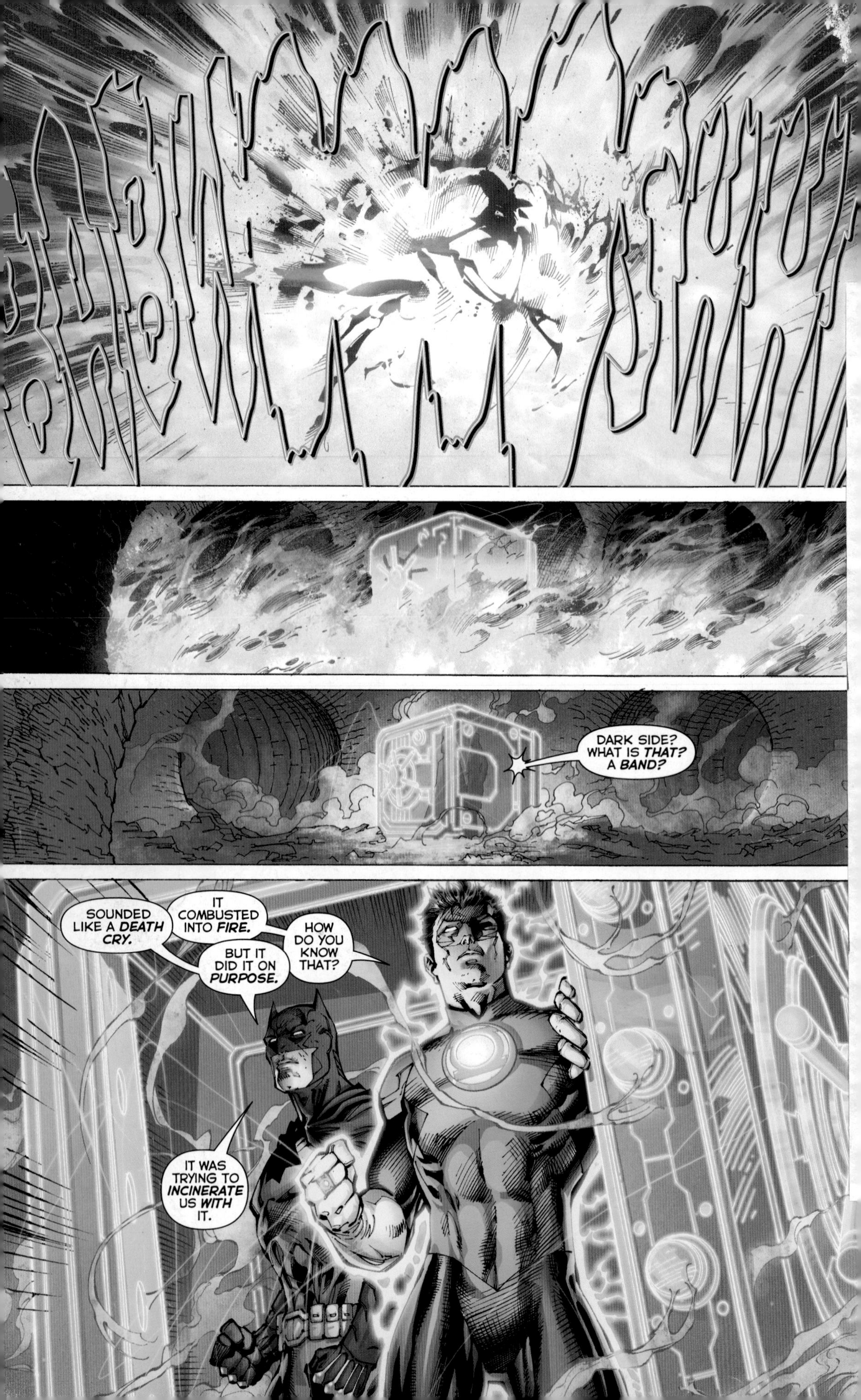
DARK SIDE? WHAT IS THAT? A BAND?
SOUNDED LIKE A DEATH CRY.
IT COMBUSTED INTO FIRE.
BUT IT DID IT ON PURPOSE.
HOW DO YOU KNOW THAT?
IT WAS TRYING TO INCINERATE US WITH IT.

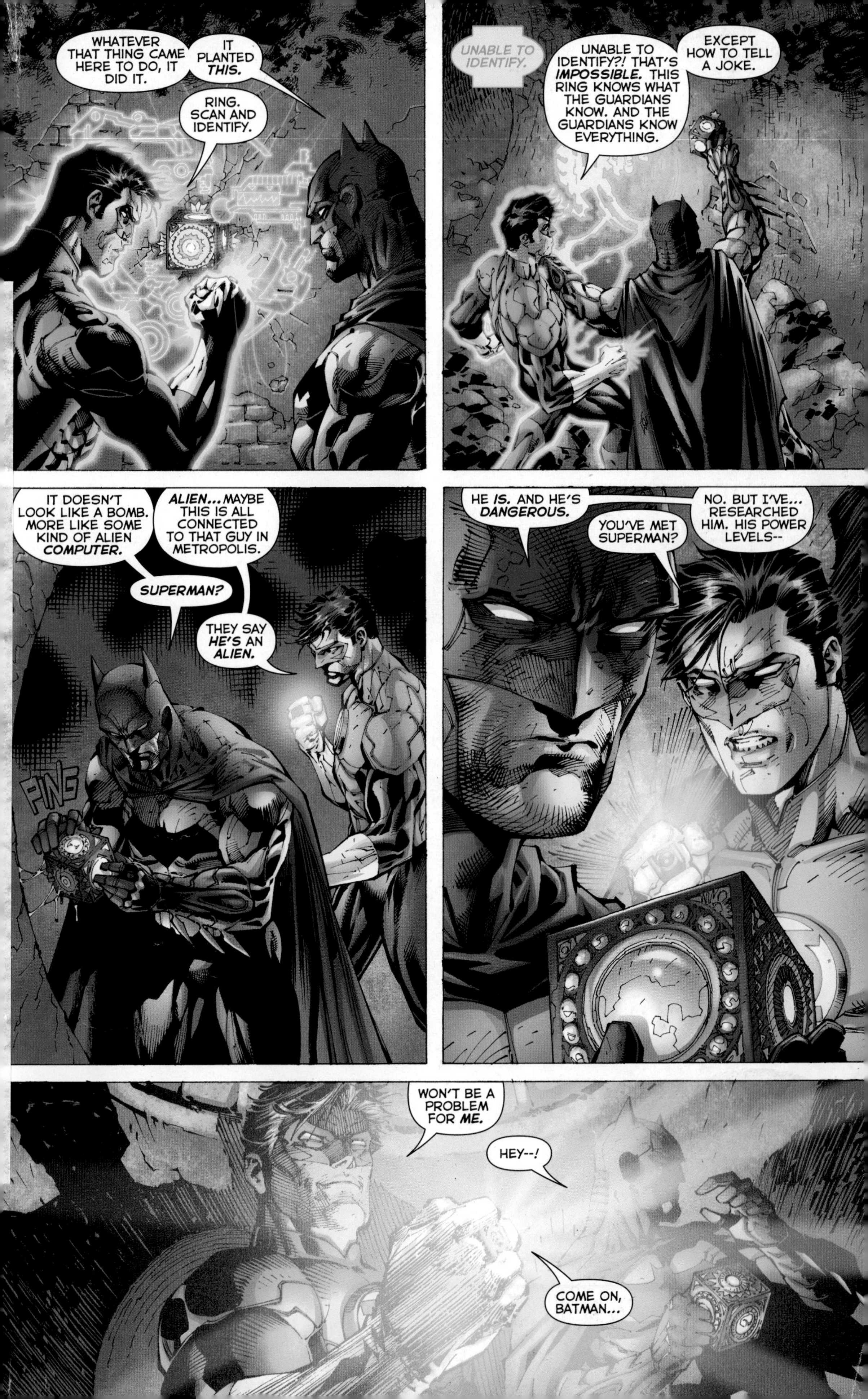
WHATEVER THAT THING CAME HERE TO DO, IT DID IT.
IT PLANTED THIS.
RING. SCAN AND IDENTIFY.
UNABLE TO IDENTIFY.
UNABLE TO IDENTIFY?! THAT'S IMPOSSIBLE. THIS RING KNOWS WHAT THE GUARDIANS KNOW. AND THE GUARDIANS KNOW EVERYTHING.
EXCEPT HOW TO TELL A JOKE.
IT DOESN'T LOOK LIKE A BOMB. MORE LIKE SOME KIND OF ALIEN COMPUTER.
ALIEN... MAYBE THIS IS ALL CONNECTED TO THAT GUY IN METROPOLIS.
SUPERMAN?
THEY SAY HE'S AN ALIEN.
PING
HE IS. AND HE'S DANGEROUS.
YOU'VE MET SUPERMAN?
NO. BUT I'VE... RESEARCHED HIM. HIS POWER LEVELS--
WON'T BE A PROBLEM FOR ME.
HEY--!
COME ON, BATMAN...

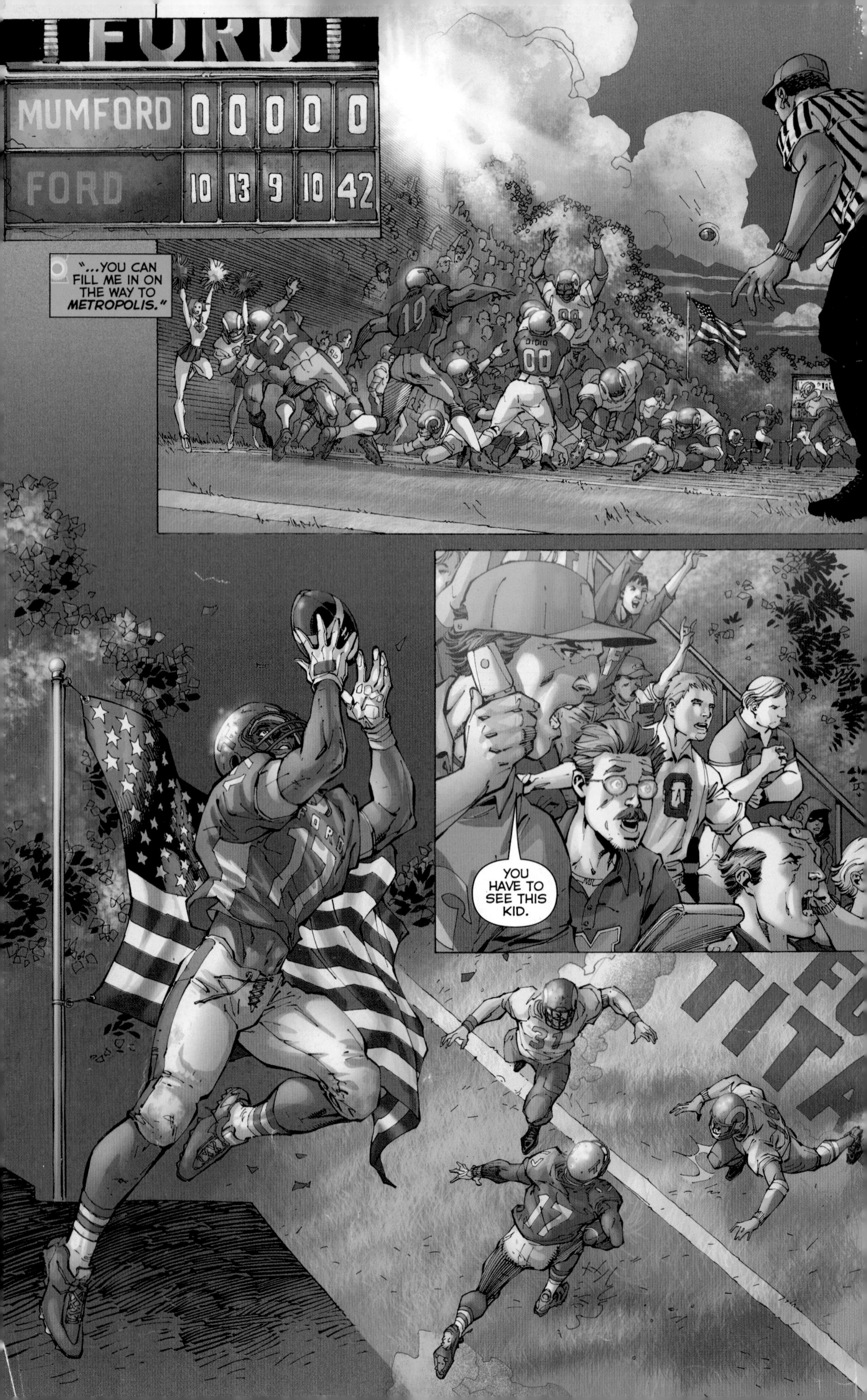

FORD
MUMFORD 0 0 0 0 0
FORD 10 13 9 10 42
"...YOU CAN FILL ME IN ON THE WAY TO METROPOLIS."
YOU HAVE TO SEE THIS KID.

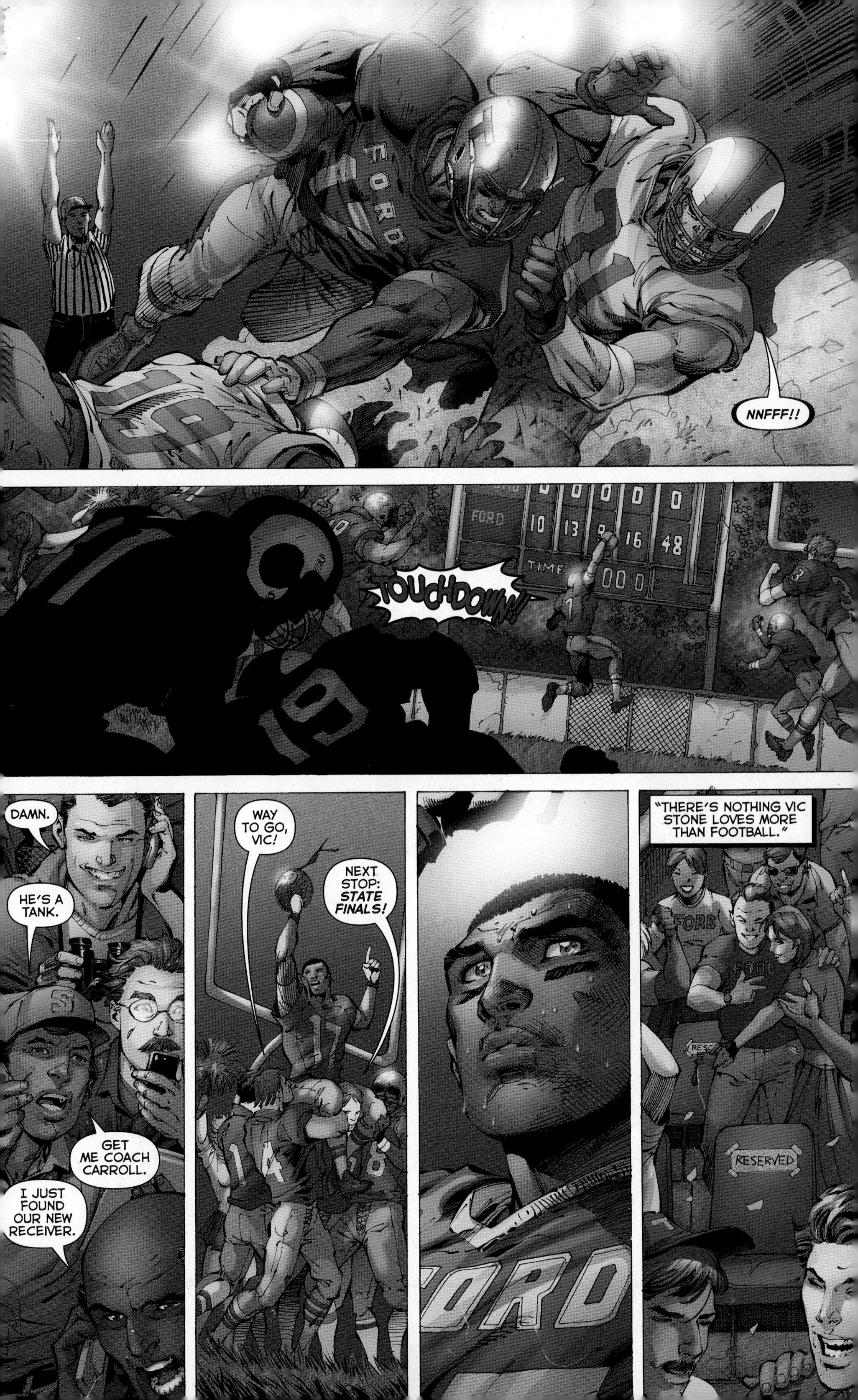
NNFFF!!
TOUCHDOWN!!
DAMN.
HE'S A TANK.
GET ME COACH CARROLL.
I JUST FOUND OUR NEW RECEIVER.
WAY TO GO, VIC!
NEXT STOP: STATE FINALS!
"THERE'S NOTHING VIC STONE LOVES MORE THAN FOOTBALL."
RESERVED

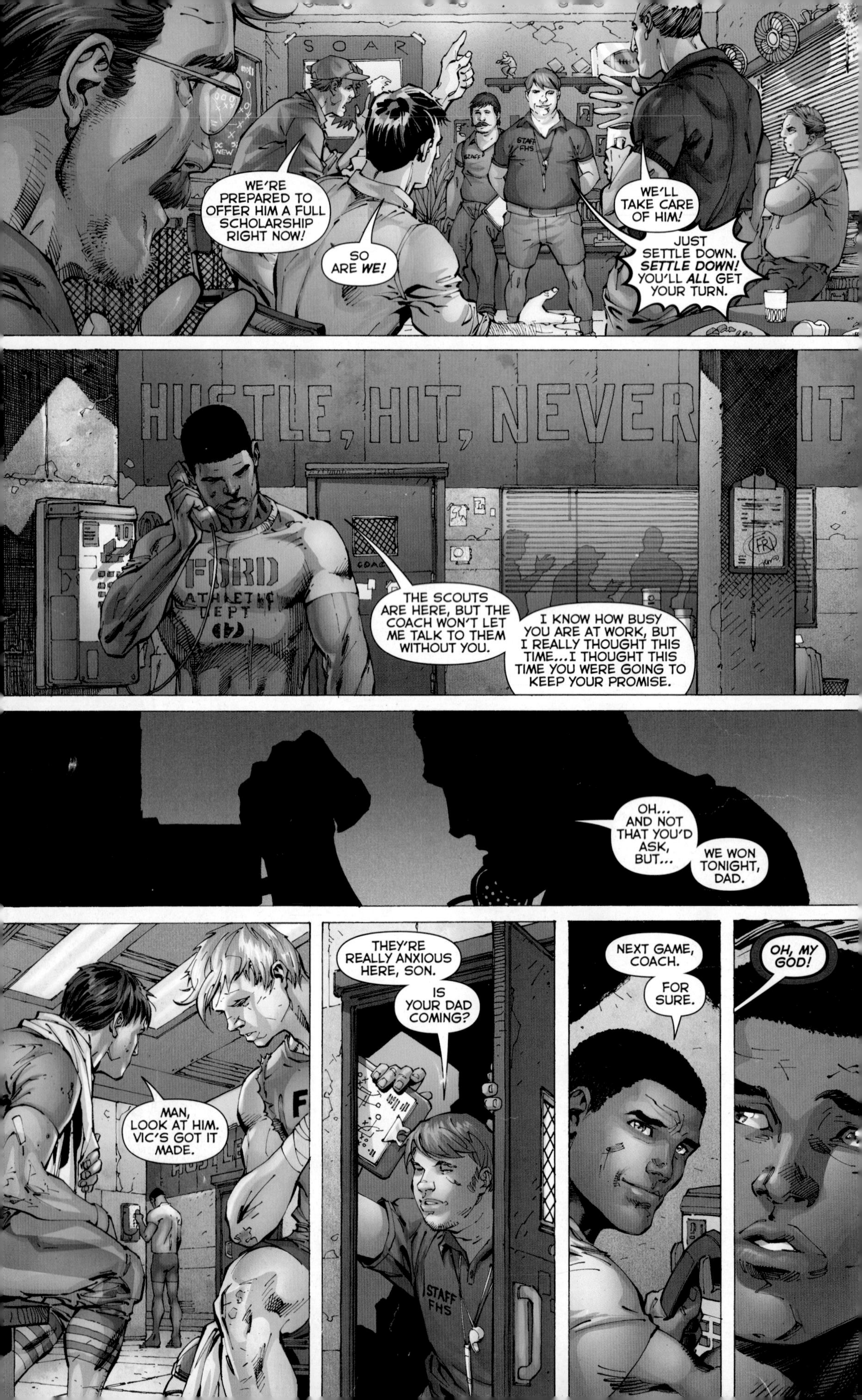
SOAR
WE'RE PREPARED TO OFFER HIM A FULL SCHOLARSHIP RIGHT NOW!
SO ARE WE!
WE'LL TAKE CARE OF HIM!
JUST SETTLE DOWN. SETTLE DOWN! YOU'LL ALL GET YOUR TURN.
HUSTLE, HIT, NEVER
FORD ATHLETIC DEPT
THE SCOUTS ARE HERE, BUT THE COACH WON'T LET ME TALK TO THEM WITHOUT YOU.
I KNOW HOW BUSY YOU ARE AT WORK, BUT I REALLY THOUGHT THIS TIME...I THOUGHT THIS TIME YOU WERE GOING TO KEEP YOUR PROMISE.
OH... AND NOT THAT YOU'D ASK, BUT...
WE WON TONIGHT, DAD.
MAN, LOOK AT HIM. VIC'S GOT IT MADE.
THEY'RE REALLY ANXIOUS HERE, SON.
IS YOUR DAD COMING?
STAFF FHS
NEXT GAME, COACH.
FOR SURE.
OH, MY GOD!

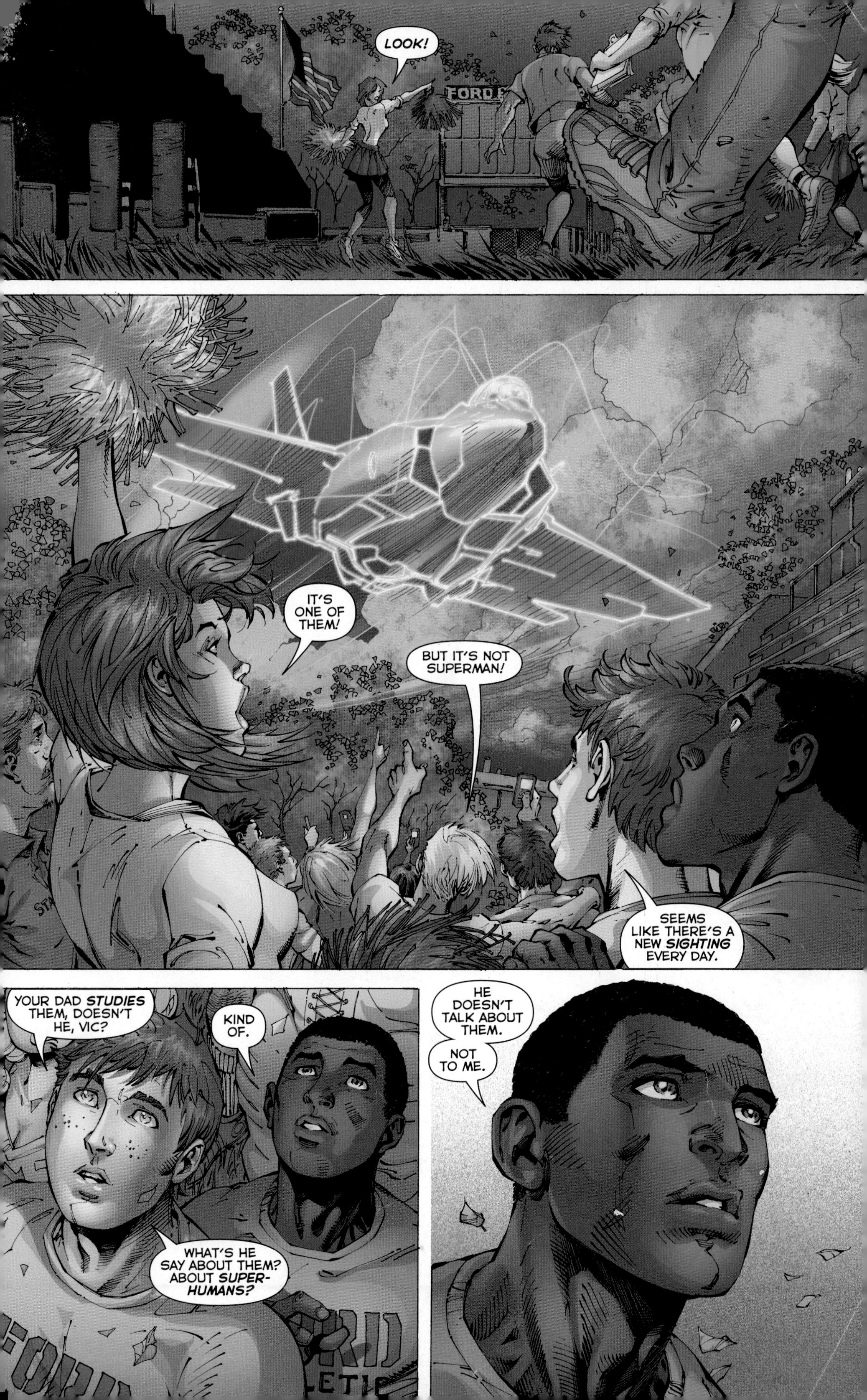
LOOK!
FORD
IT'S ONE OF THEM!
BUT IT'S NOT SUPERMAN!
SEEMS LIKE THERE'S A NEW SIGHTING EVERY DAY.
YOUR DAD STUDIES THEM, DOESN'T HE, VIC?
KIND OF.
WHAT'S HE SAY ABOUT THEM? ABOUT SUPER-HUMANS?
HE DOESN'T TALK ABOUT THEM.
NOT TO ME.

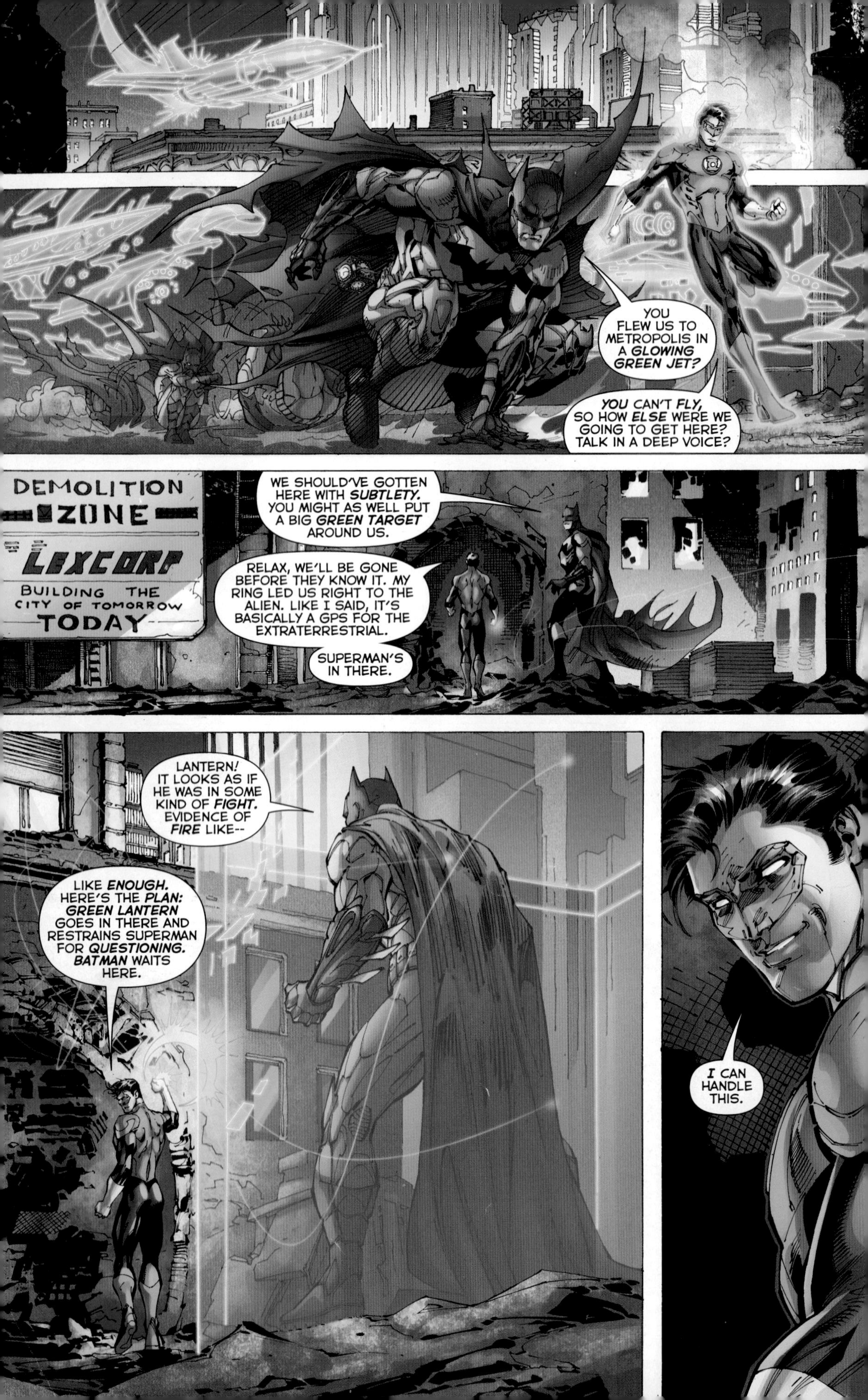
YOU FLEW US TO METROPOLIS IN A *GLOWING GREEN JET?*
YOU CAN'T *FLY,* SO HOW *ELSE* WERE WE GOING TO GET HERE? TALK IN A DEEP VOICE?
DEMOLITION ZONE
LEXCORP
BUILDING THE CITY OF TOMORROW TODAY
WE SHOULD'VE GOTTEN HERE WITH *SUBTLETY.* YOU MIGHT AS WELL PUT A BIG *GREEN TARGET* AROUND US.
RELAX, WE'LL BE GONE BEFORE THEY KNOW IT. MY RING LED US RIGHT TO THE ALIEN. LIKE I SAID, IT'S BASICALLY A GPS FOR THE EXTRATERRESTRIAL.
SUPERMAN'S IN THERE.
LANTERN! IT LOOKS AS IF HE WAS IN SOME KIND OF *FIGHT.* EVIDENCE OF *FIRE* LIKE--
LIKE *ENOUGH.* HERE'S THE *PLAN: GREEN LANTERN* GOES IN THERE AND RESTRAINS SUPERMAN FOR *QUESTIONING. BATMAN* WAITS HERE.
I CAN HANDLE THIS.

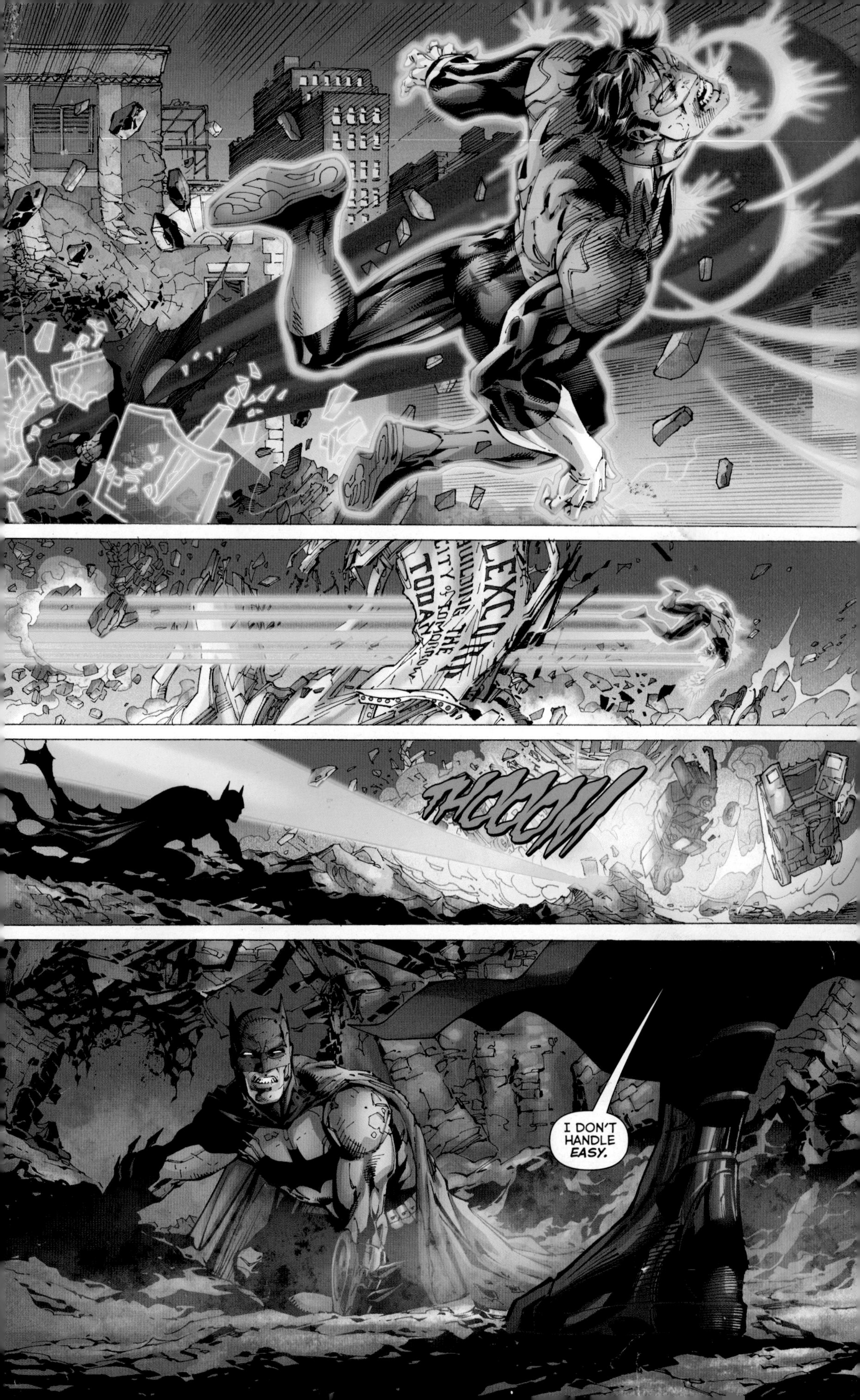
THOOOM
I DON'T HANDLE *EASY*.

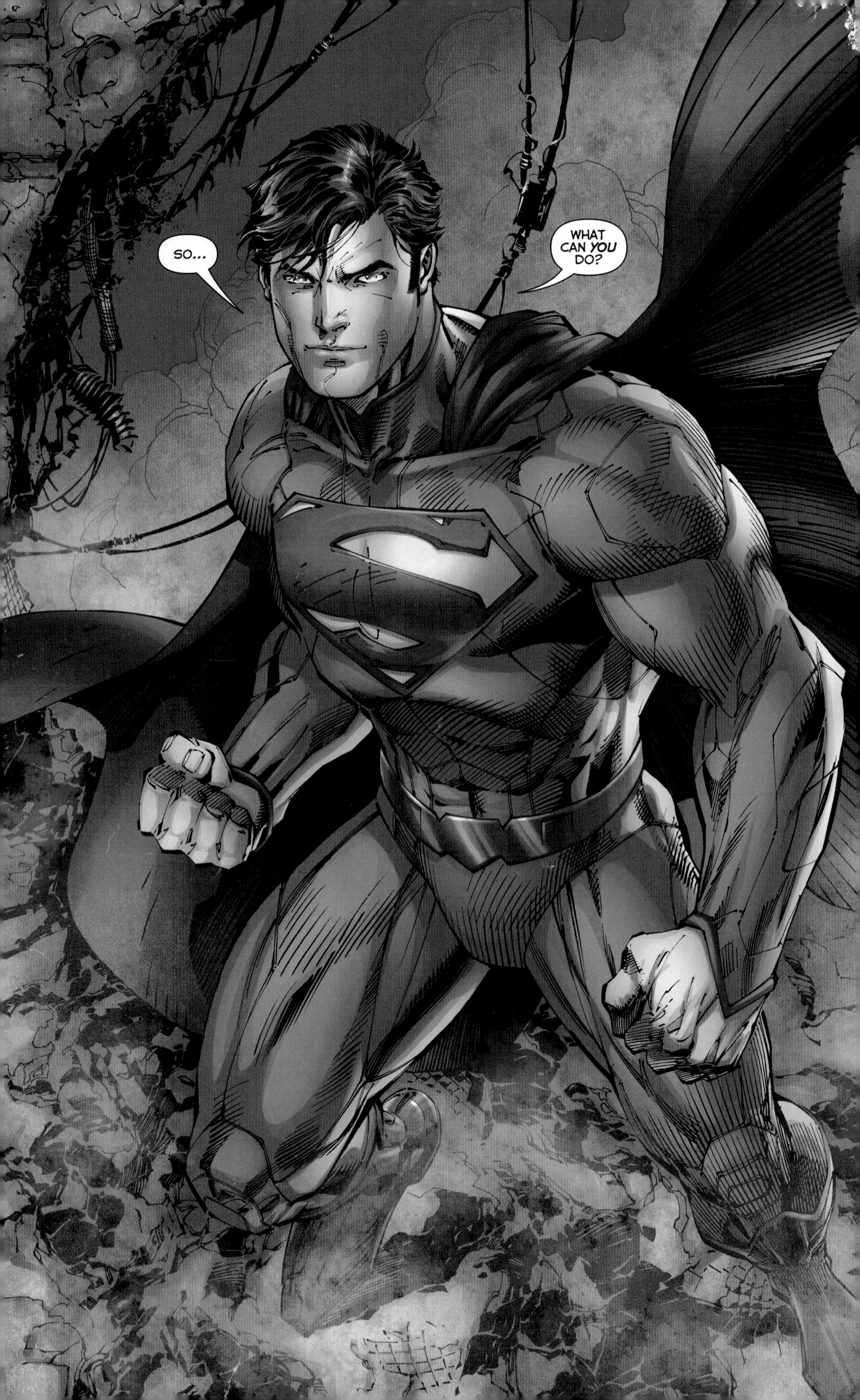
SO...
WHAT CAN YOU DO?

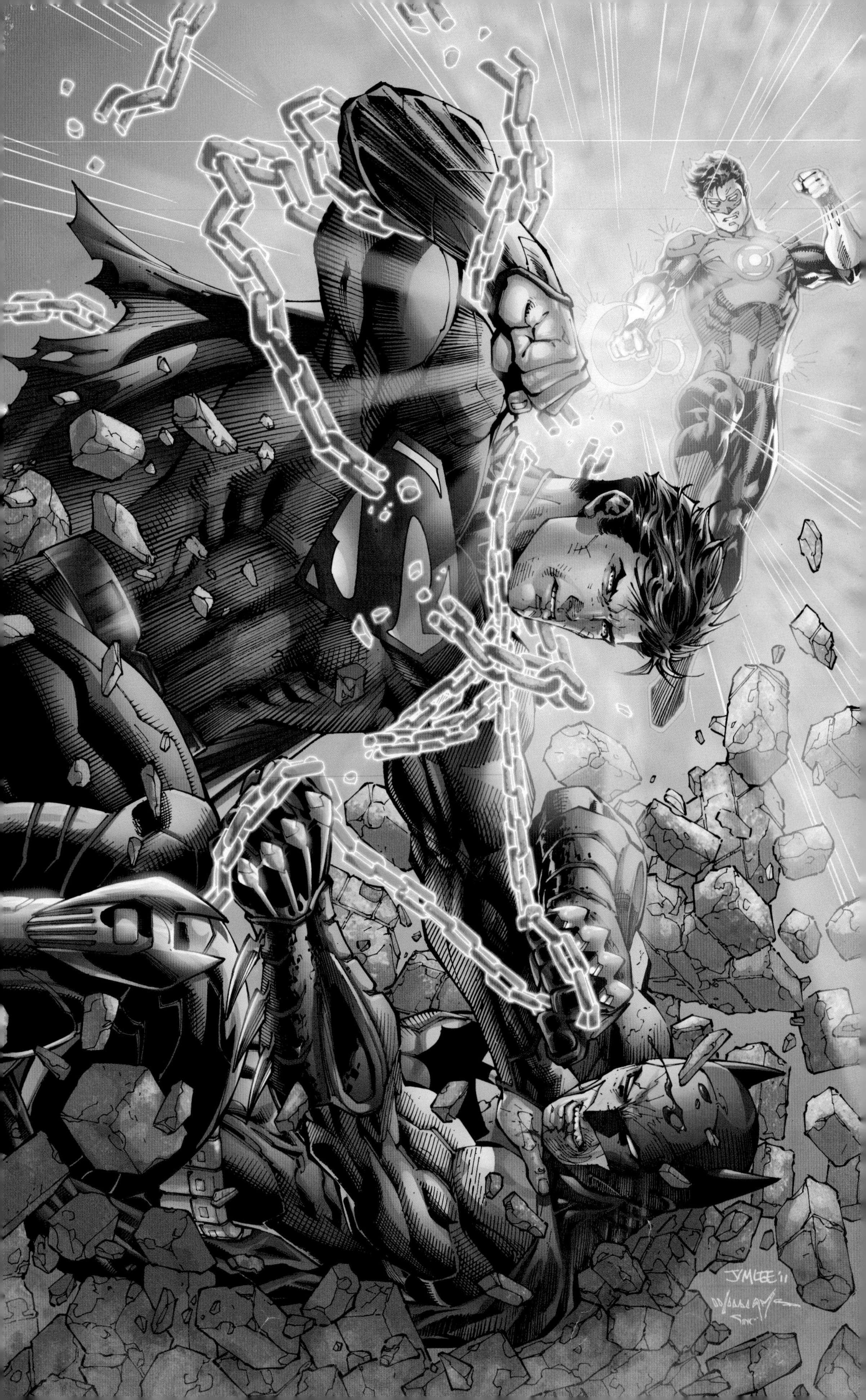

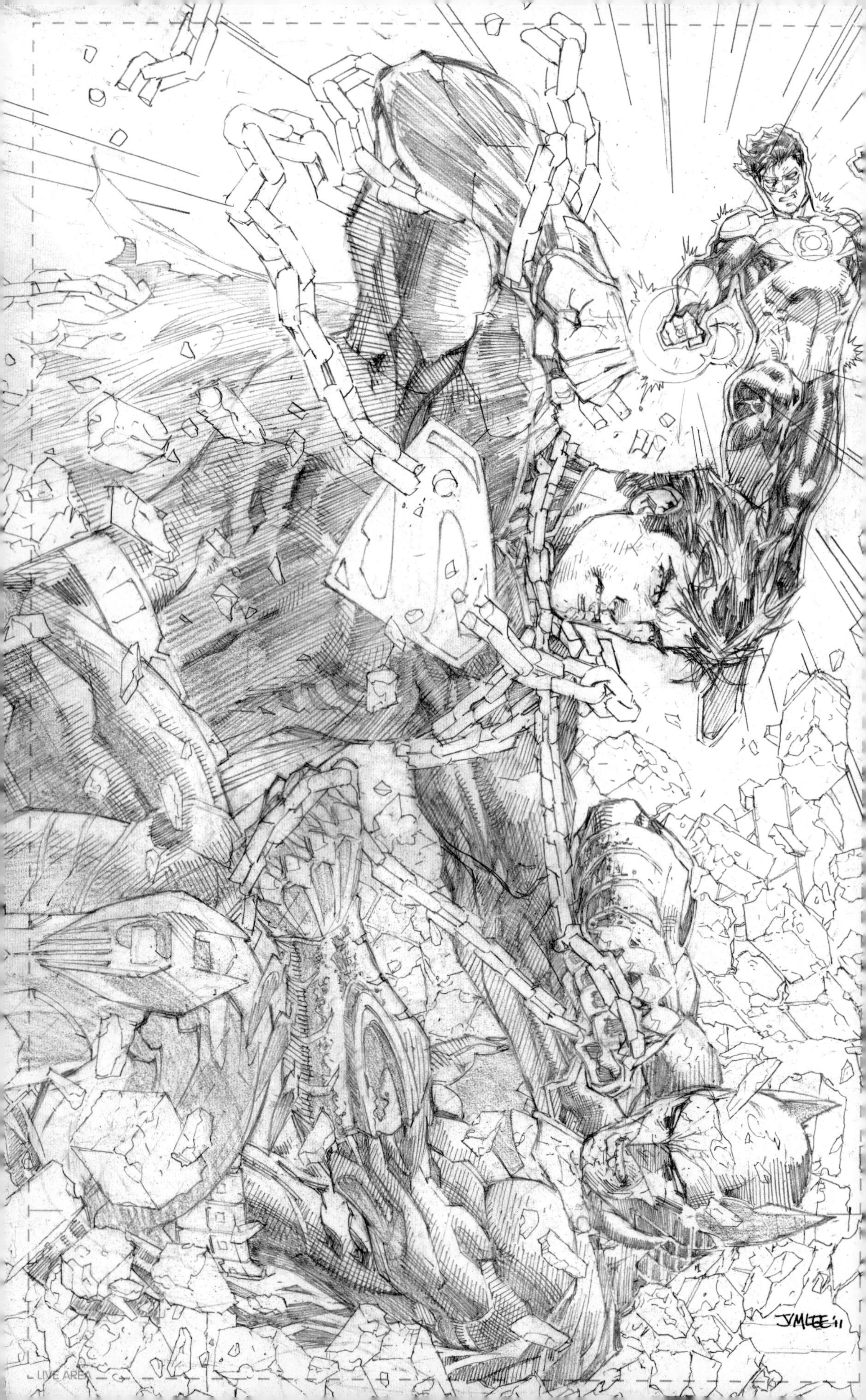
JIMLEE '11
LIVE AREA

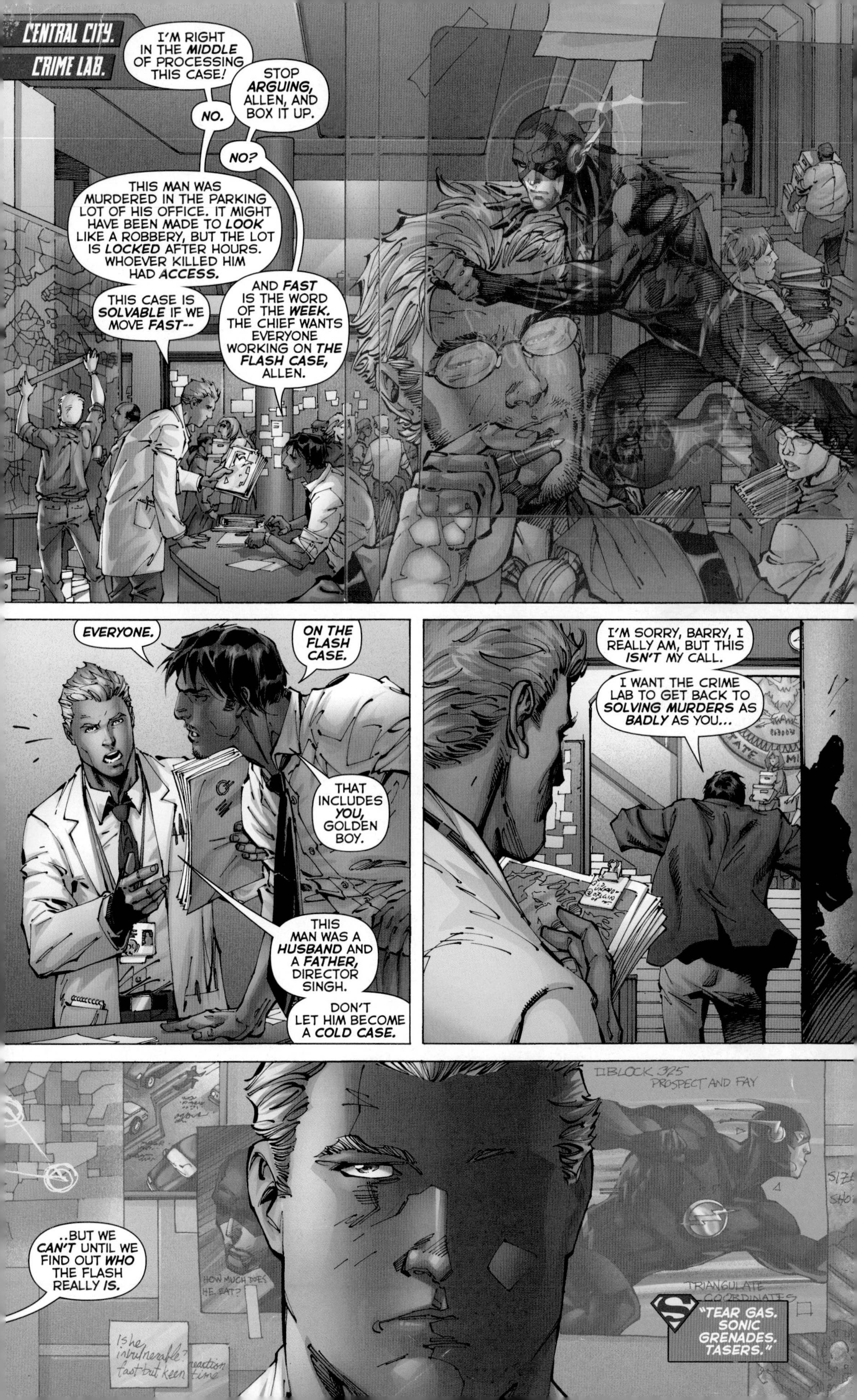
CENTRAL CITY.
CRIME LAB.
I'M RIGHT IN THE MIDDLE OF PROCESSING THIS CASE!
STOP ARGUING, ALLEN, AND BOX IT UP.
NO.
NO?
THIS MAN WAS MURDERED IN THE PARKING LOT OF HIS OFFICE. IT MIGHT HAVE BEEN MADE TO LOOK LIKE A ROBBERY, BUT THE LOT IS LOCKED AFTER HOURS. WHOEVER KILLED HIM HAD ACCESS.
THIS CASE IS SOLVABLE IF WE MOVE FAST--
AND FAST IS THE WORD OF THE WEEK. THE CHIEF WANTS EVERYONE WORKING ON THE FLASH CASE, ALLEN.
EVERYONE.
ON THE FLASH CASE.
THAT INCLUDES YOU, GOLDEN BOY.
THIS MAN WAS A HUSBAND AND A FATHER, DIRECTOR SINGH.
DON'T LET HIM BECOME A COLD CASE.
I'M SORRY, BARRY, I REALLY AM, BUT THIS ISN'T MY CALL.
I WANT THE CRIME LAB TO GET BACK TO SOLVING MURDERS AS BADLY AS YOU...
..BUT WE CAN'T UNTIL WE FIND OUT WHO THE FLASH REALLY IS.
BLOCK 325 PROSPECT AND FAY
HOW MUCH DOES HE EAT?
Is he invulnerable? fast but keen reaction time
TRIANGULATE COORDINATES
"TEAR GAS. SONIC GRENADES. TASERS."

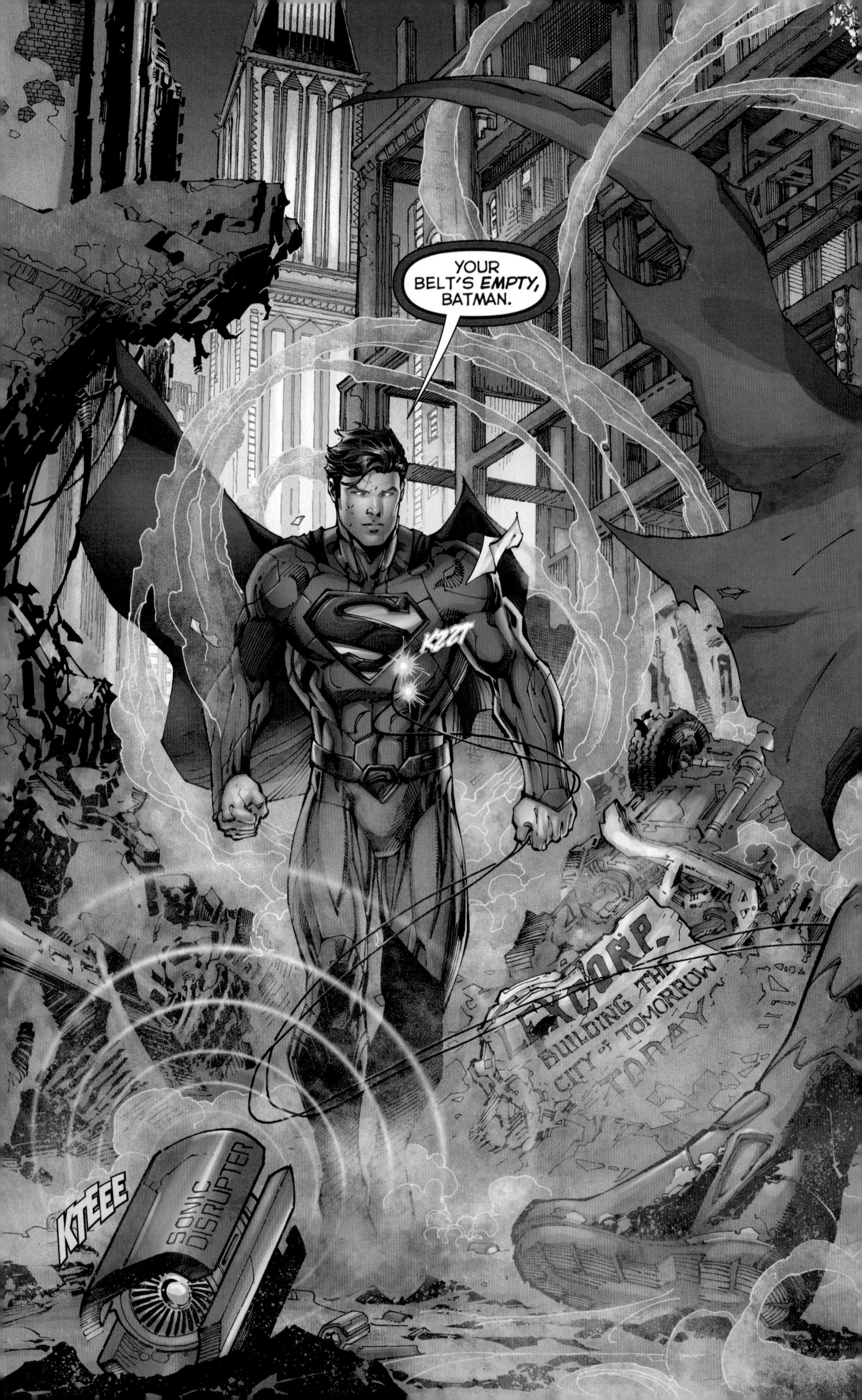
YOUR BELT'S EMPTY, BATMAN.
KZZT
LEXCORP.
BUILDING THE CITY of TOMORROW TODAY
SONIC DISRUPTER
KTEEE

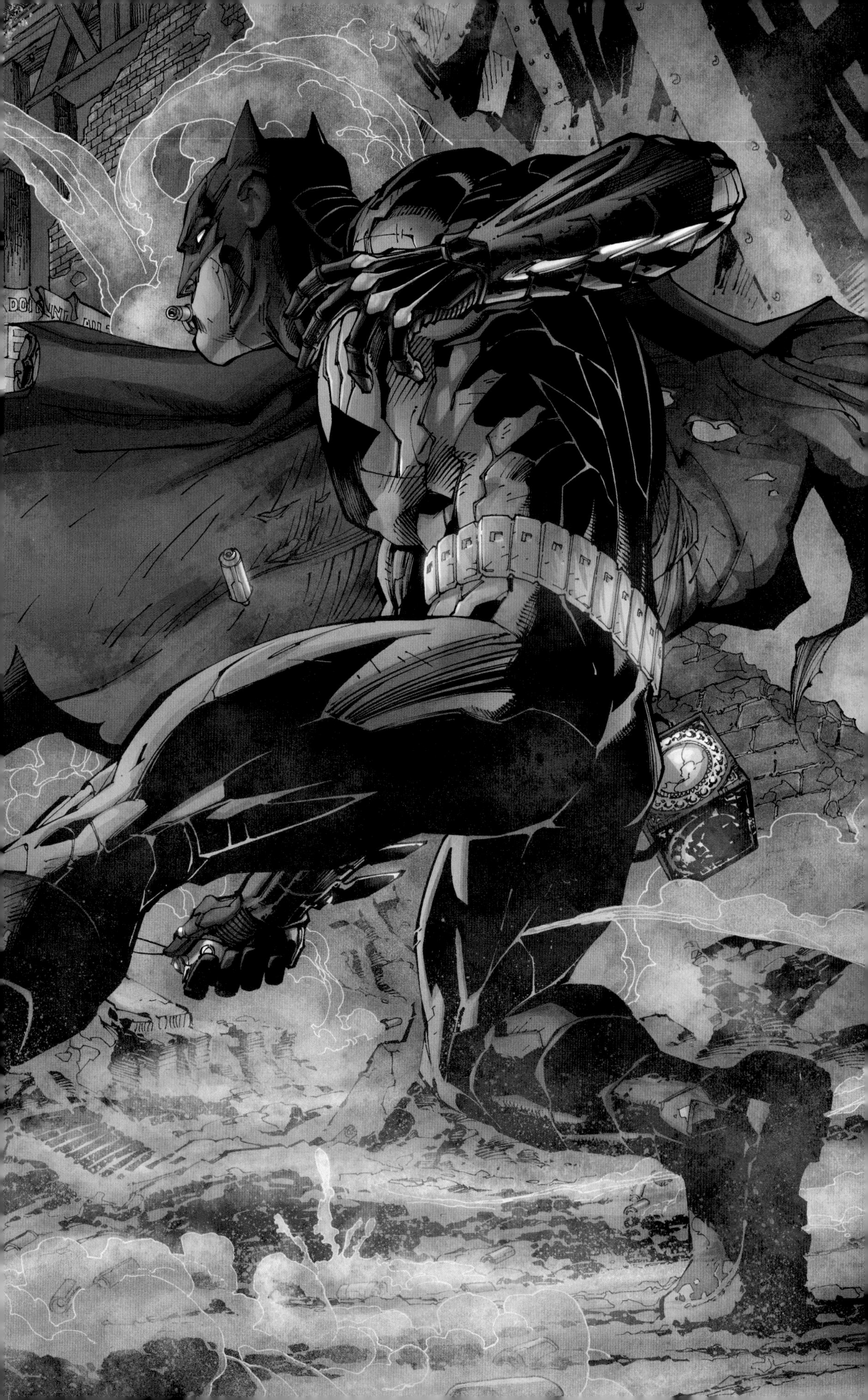

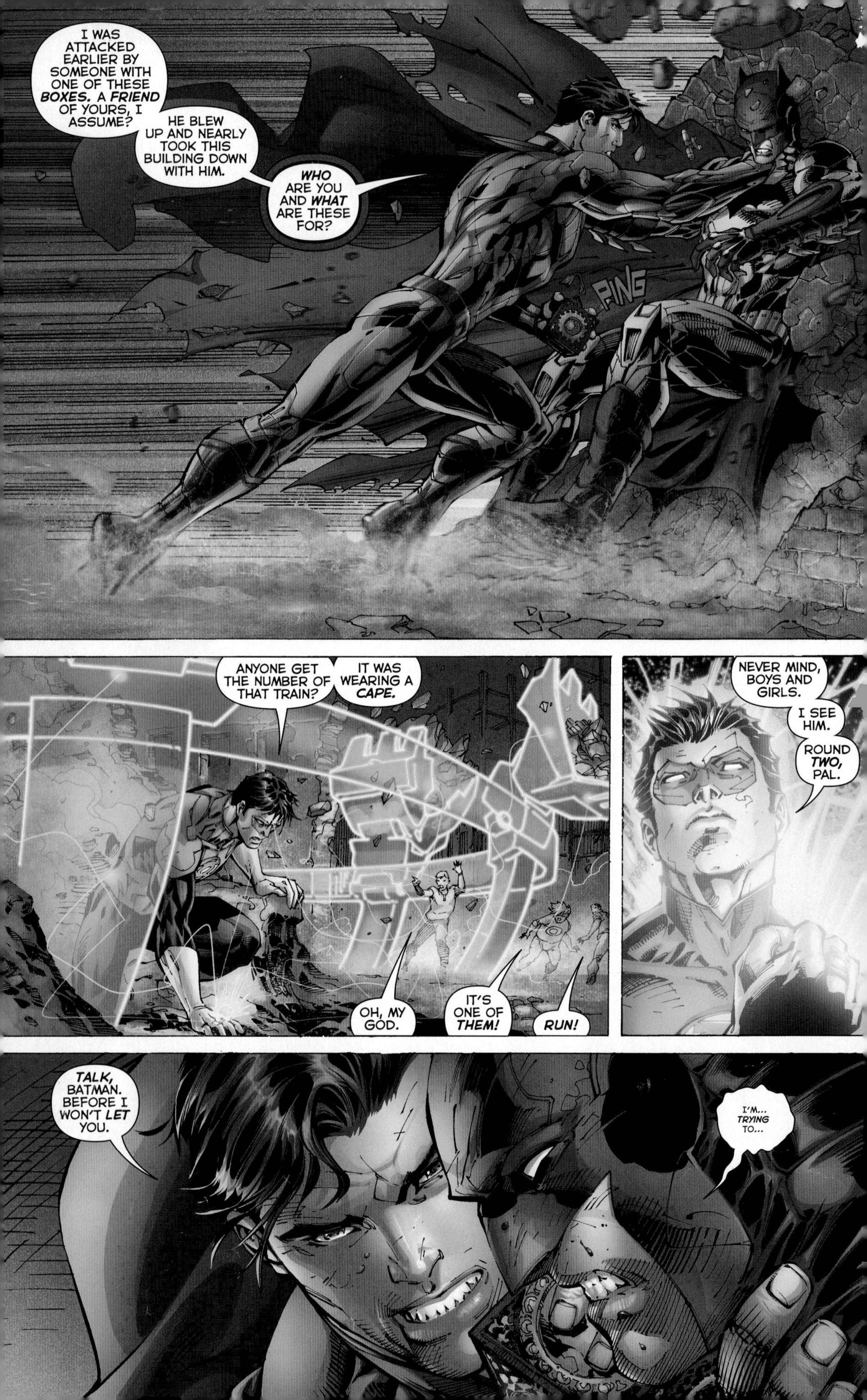

I WAS ATTACKED EARLIER BY SOMEONE WITH ONE OF THESE *BOXES.* A *FRIEND* OF YOURS, I ASSUME?
HE BLEW UP AND NEARLY TOOK THIS BUILDING DOWN WITH HIM.
WHO ARE YOU AND *WHAT* ARE THESE FOR?
PING
ANYONE GET THE NUMBER OF THAT TRAIN?
IT WAS WEARING A *CAPE.*
OH, MY GOD.
IT'S ONE OF *THEM!*
RUN!
NEVER MIND, BOYS AND GIRLS.
I SEE HIM.
ROUND *TWO,* PAL.
TALK, BATMAN. BEFORE I WON'T *LET* YOU.
I'M... *TRYING* TO...

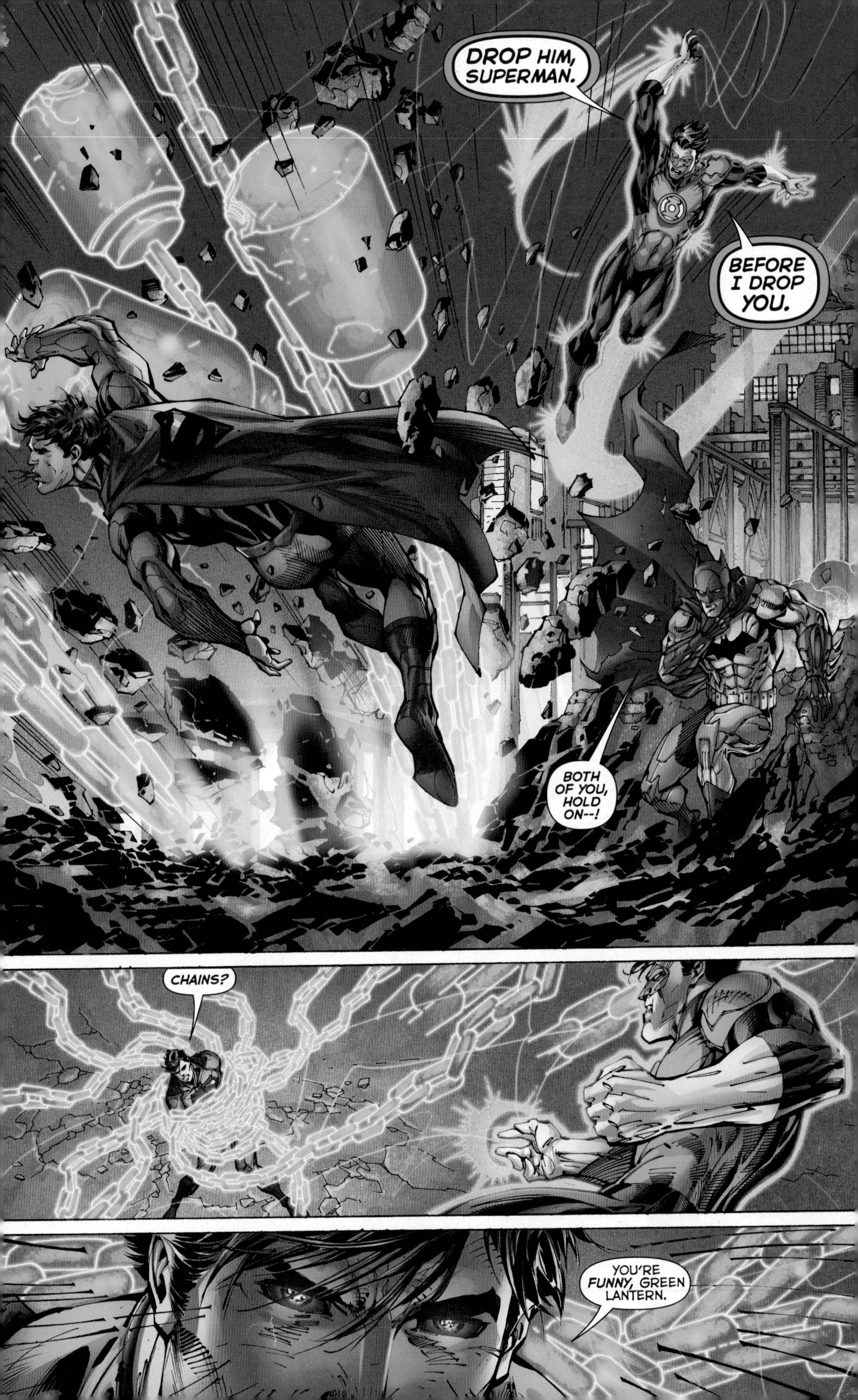
DROP HIM, SUPERMAN.
BEFORE I DROP YOU.
BOTH OF YOU, HOLD ON--!
CHAINS?
YOU'RE FUNNY, GREEN LANTERN.

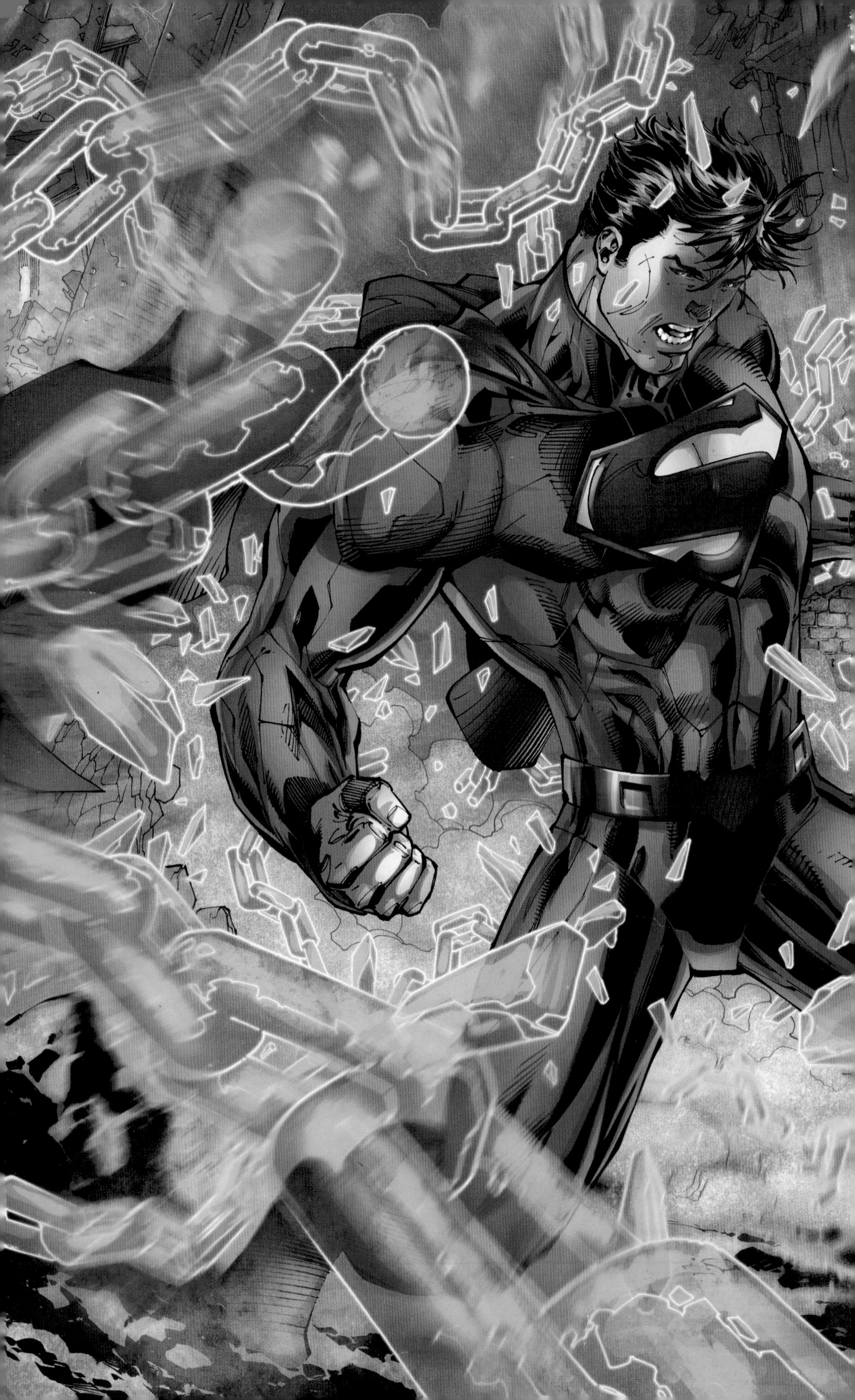

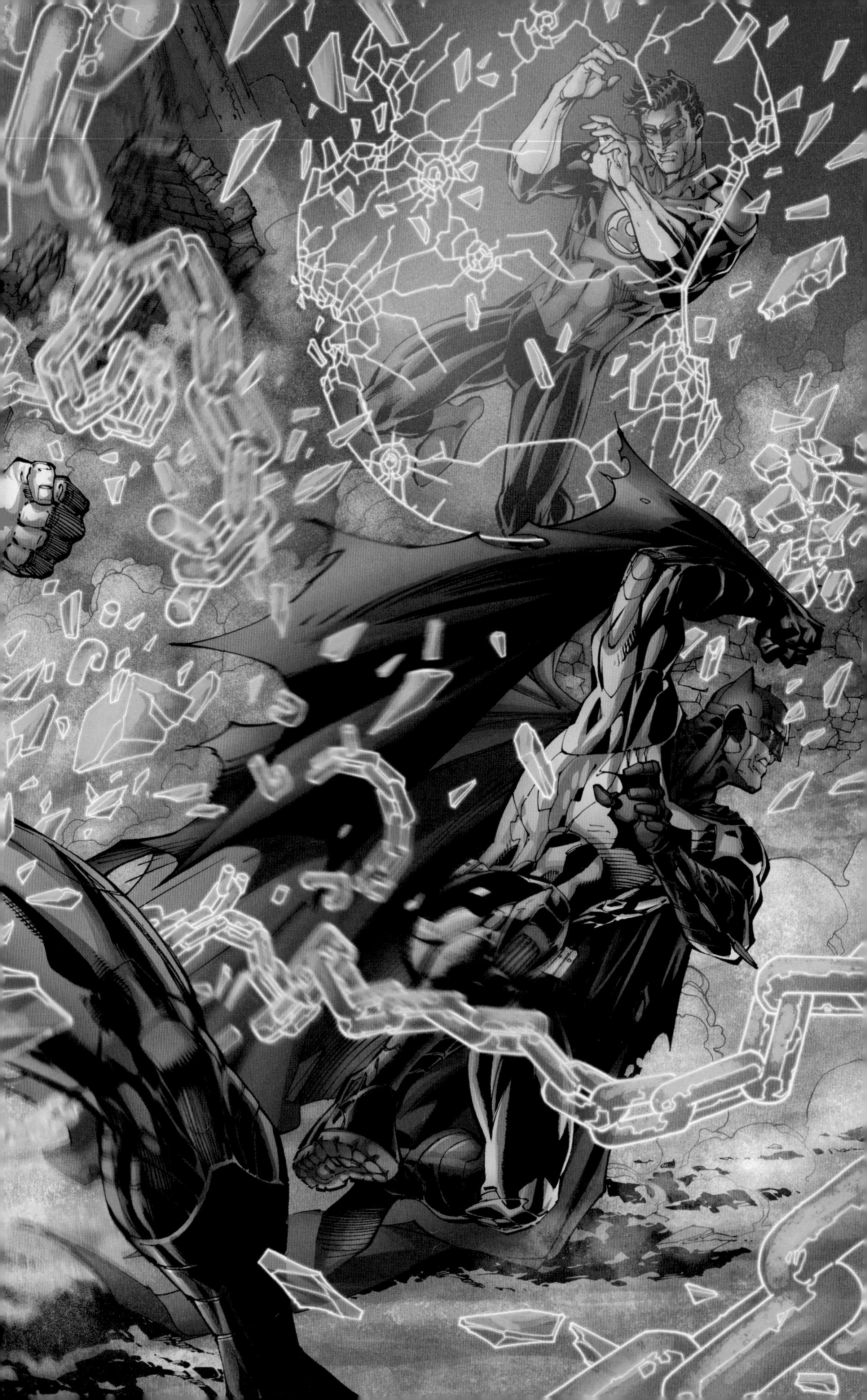

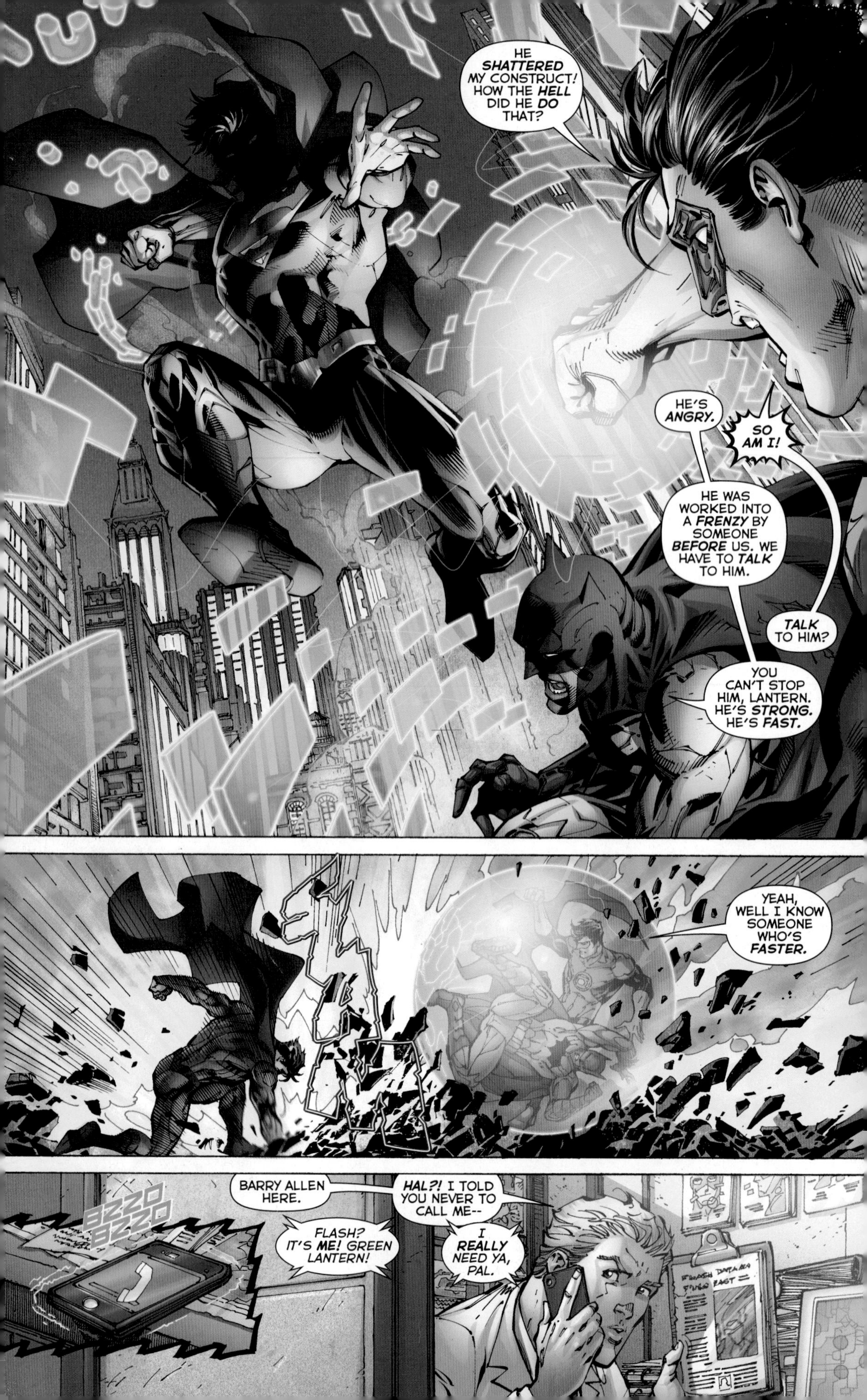
HE SHATTERED MY CONSTRUCT! HOW THE HELL DID HE DO THAT?
HE'S ANGRY.
SO AM I!
HE WAS WORKED INTO A FRENZY BY SOMEONE BEFORE US. WE HAVE TO TALK TO HIM.
TALK TO HIM?
YOU CAN'T STOP HIM, LANTERN. HE'S STRONG. HE'S FAST.
YEAH, WELL I KNOW SOMEONE WHO'S FASTER.
BZZO BZZO
BARRY ALLEN HERE.
FLASH? IT'S ME! GREEN LANTERN!
HAL?! I TOLD YOU NEVER TO CALL ME--
I REALLY NEED YA, PAL.

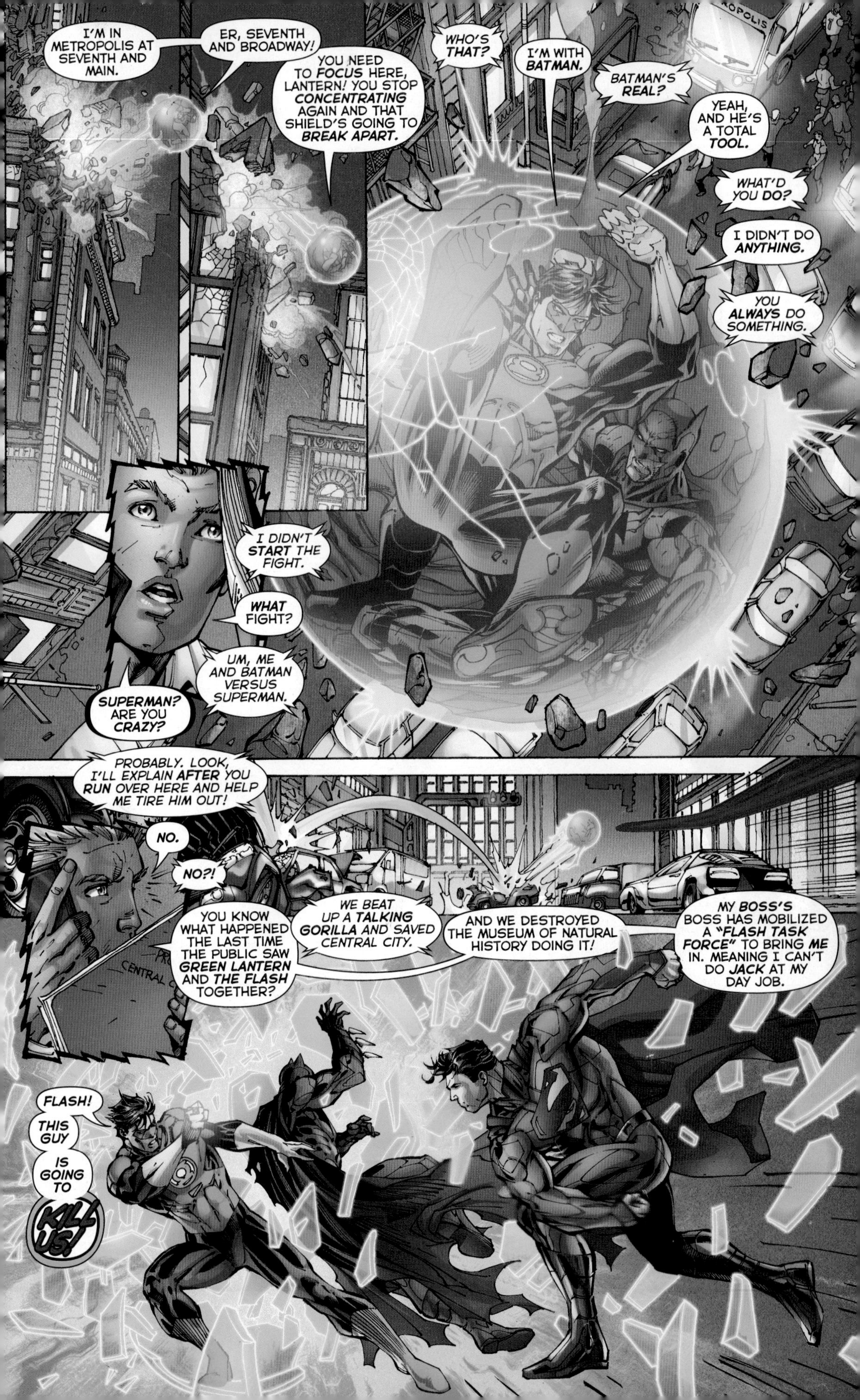

I'M IN METROPOLIS AT SEVENTH AND MAIN.
ER, SEVENTH AND BROADWAY!
YOU NEED TO FOCUS HERE, LANTERN! YOU STOP CONCENTRATING AGAIN AND THAT SHIELD'S GOING TO BREAK APART.
WHO'S THAT?
I'M WITH BATMAN.
BATMAN'S REAL?
YEAH, AND HE'S A TOTAL TOOL.
WHAT'D YOU DO?
I DIDN'T DO ANYTHING.
YOU ALWAYS DO SOMETHING.
I DIDN'T START THE FIGHT.
WHAT FIGHT?
UM, ME AND BATMAN VERSUS SUPERMAN.
SUPERMAN? ARE YOU CRAZY?
PROBABLY. LOOK, I'LL EXPLAIN AFTER YOU RUN OVER HERE AND HELP ME TIRE HIM OUT!
NO.
NO?!
YOU KNOW WHAT HAPPENED THE LAST TIME THE PUBLIC SAW GREEN LANTERN AND THE FLASH TOGETHER?
WE BEAT UP A TALKING GORILLA AND SAVED CENTRAL CITY.
AND WE DESTROYED THE MUSEUM OF NATURAL HISTORY DOING IT!
MY BOSS'S BOSS HAS MOBILIZED A "FLASH TASK FORCE" TO BRING ME IN. MEANING I CAN'T DO JACK AT MY DAY JOB.
FLASH! THIS GUY IS GOING TO KILL US!

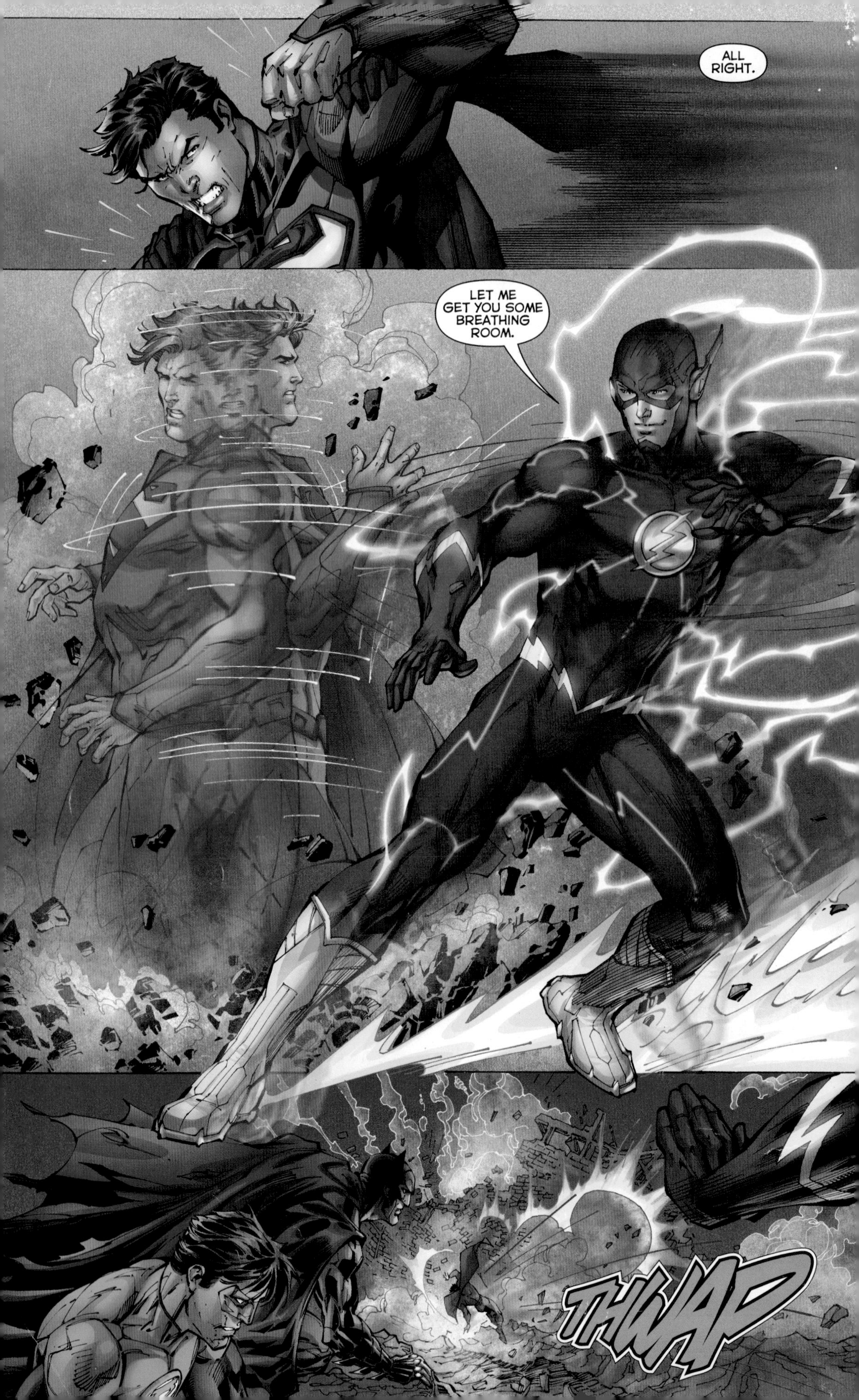
ALL RIGHT.
LET ME GET YOU SOME BREATHING ROOM.
THWAP

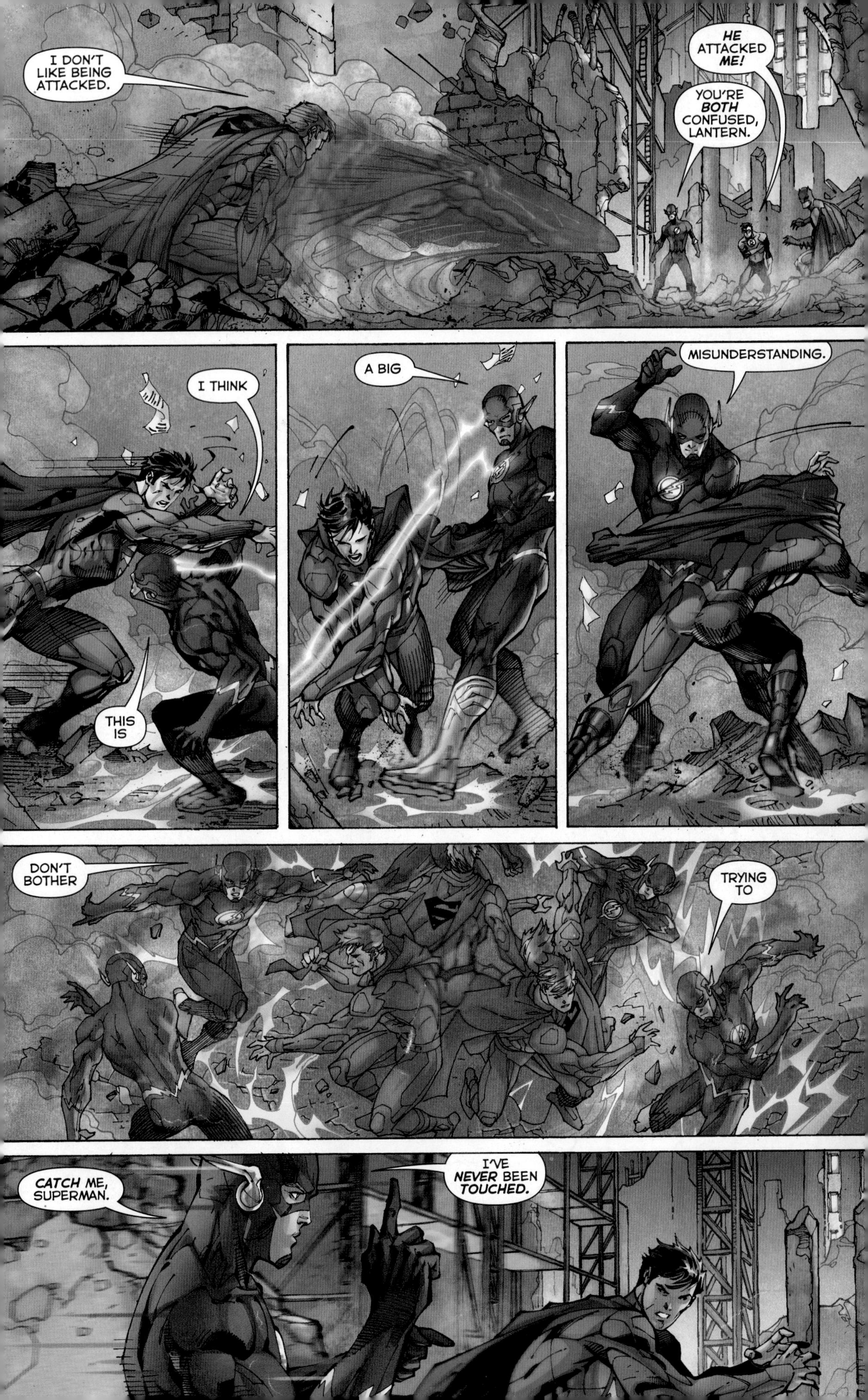

I DON'T LIKE BEING ATTACKED.
HE ATTACKED *ME!*
YOU'RE *BOTH* CONFUSED, LANTERN.
I THINK
THIS IS
A BIG
MISUNDERSTANDING.
DON'T BOTHER
TRYING TO
CATCH ME, SUPERMAN.
I'VE *NEVER* BEEN *TOUCHED.*

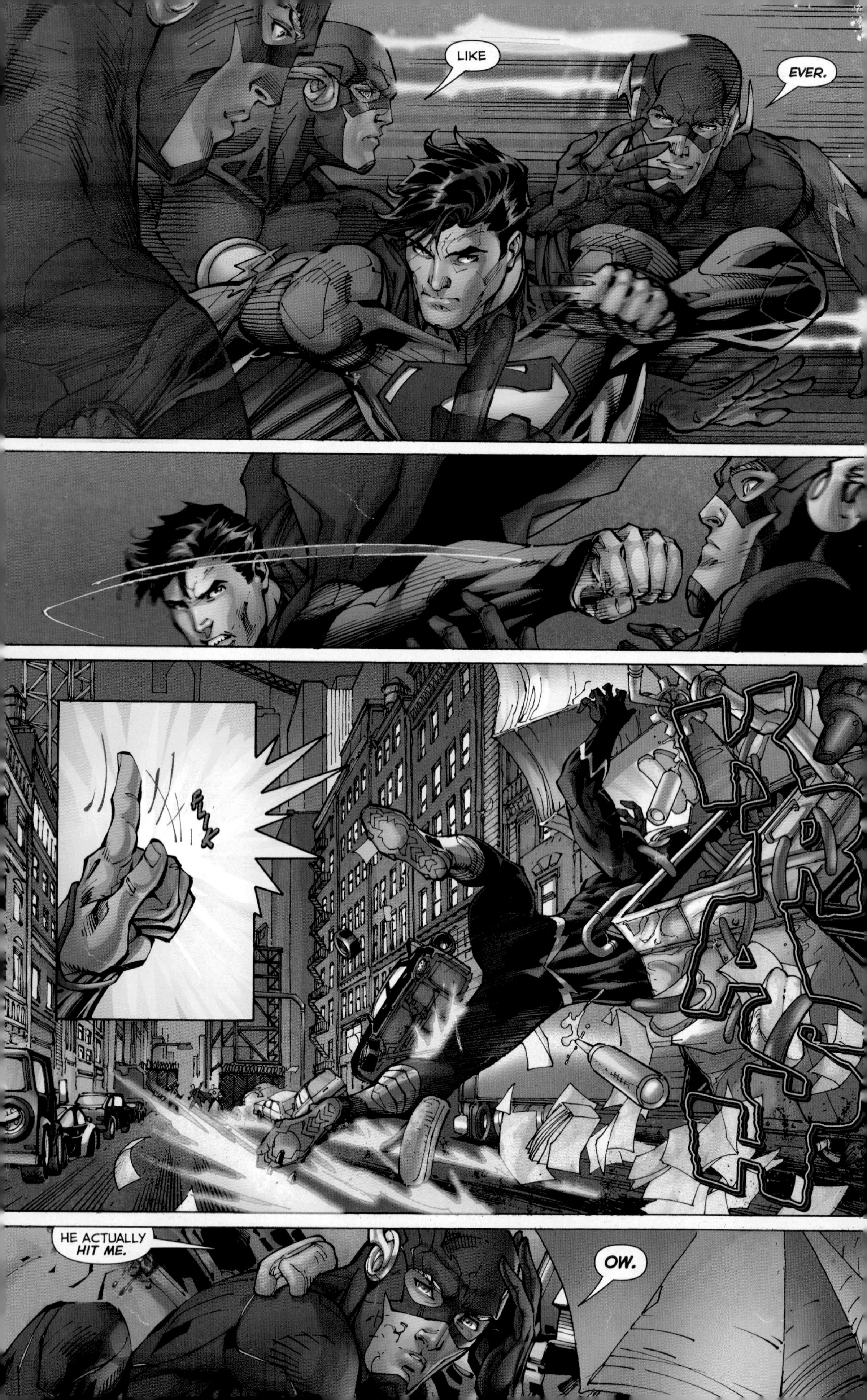
LIKE
EVER.
FLIK
HE ACTUALLY HIT ME.
OW.

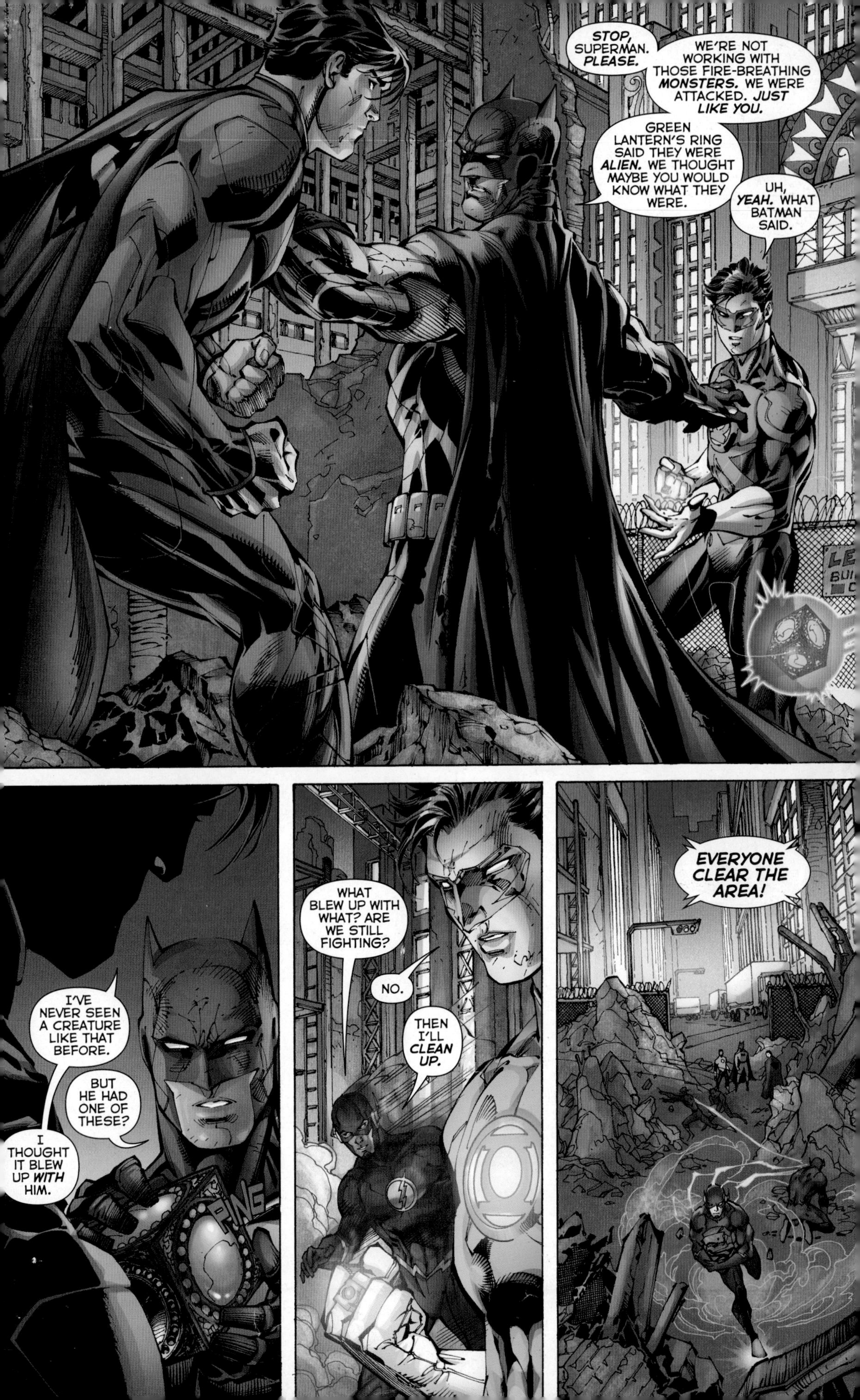
STOP, SUPERMAN. PLEASE.
WE'RE NOT WORKING WITH THOSE FIRE-BREATHING MONSTERS. WE WERE ATTACKED. JUST LIKE YOU.
GREEN LANTERN'S RING SAID THEY WERE ALIEN. WE THOUGHT MAYBE YOU WOULD KNOW WHAT THEY WERE.
UH, YEAH. WHAT BATMAN SAID.
I'VE NEVER SEEN A CREATURE LIKE THAT BEFORE.
BUT HE HAD ONE OF THESE?
I THOUGHT IT BLEW UP WITH HIM.
WHAT BLEW UP WITH WHAT? ARE WE STILL FIGHTING?
NO.
THEN I'LL CLEAN UP.
EVERYONE CLEAR THE AREA!

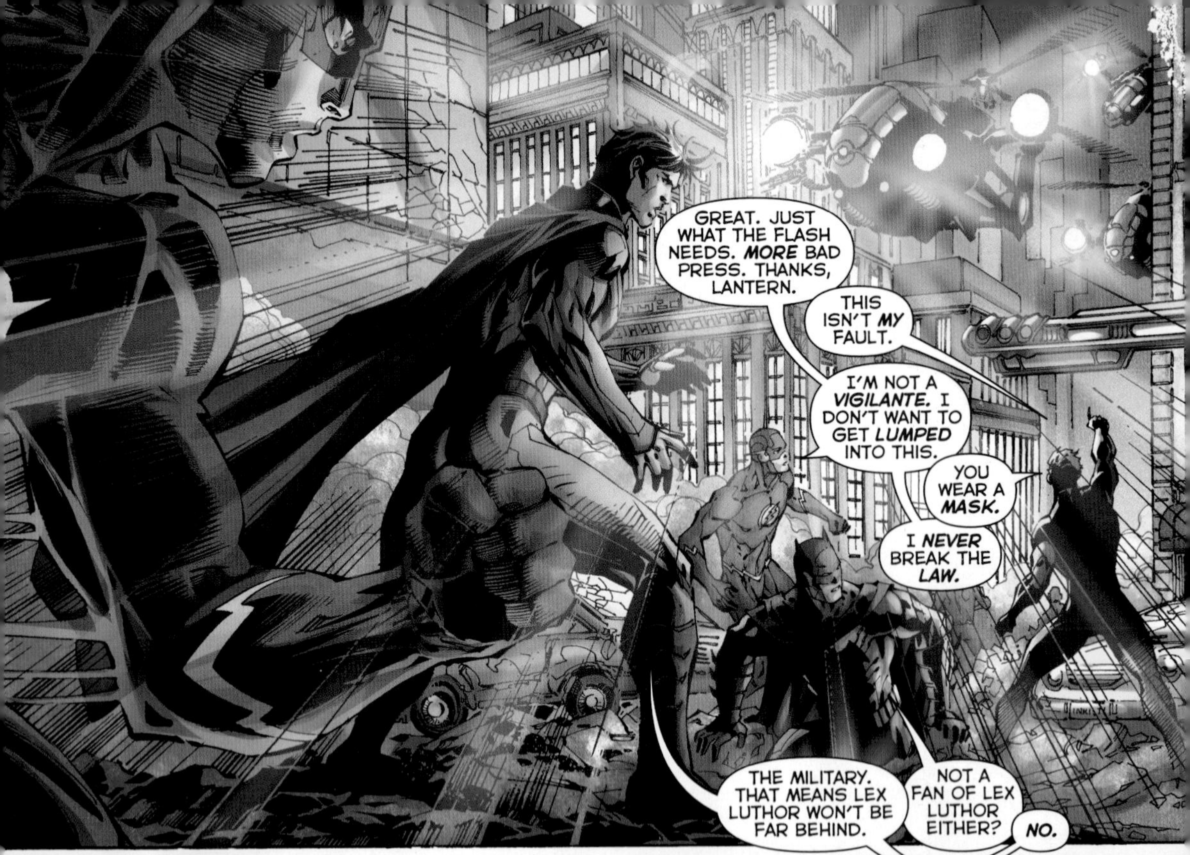
GREAT. JUST WHAT THE FLASH NEEDS. MORE BAD PRESS. THANKS, LANTERN.
THIS ISN'T MY FAULT.
I'M NOT A VIGILANTE. I DON'T WANT TO GET LUMPED INTO THIS.
YOU WEAR A MASK.
I NEVER BREAK THE LAW.
THE MILITARY. THAT MEANS LEX LUTHOR WON'T BE FAR BEHIND.
NOT A FAN OF LEX LUTHOR EITHER?
NO.

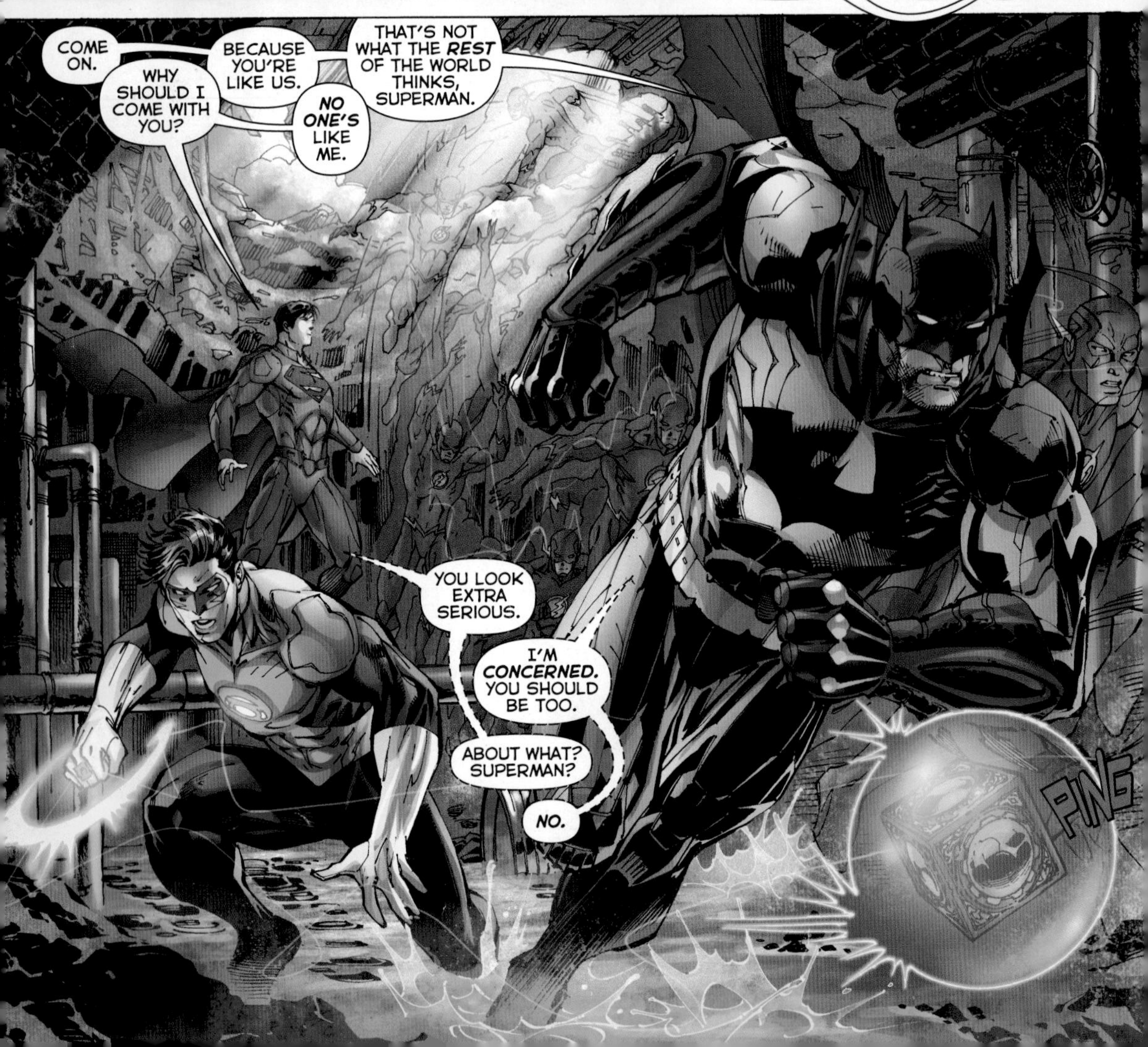
COME ON.
WHY SHOULD I COME WITH YOU?
BECAUSE YOU'RE LIKE US.
NO ONE'S LIKE ME.
THAT'S NOT WHAT THE REST OF THE WORLD THINKS, SUPERMAN.
YOU LOOK EXTRA SERIOUS.
I'M CONCERNED. YOU SHOULD BE TOO.
ABOUT WHAT? SUPERMAN?
NO.
PING

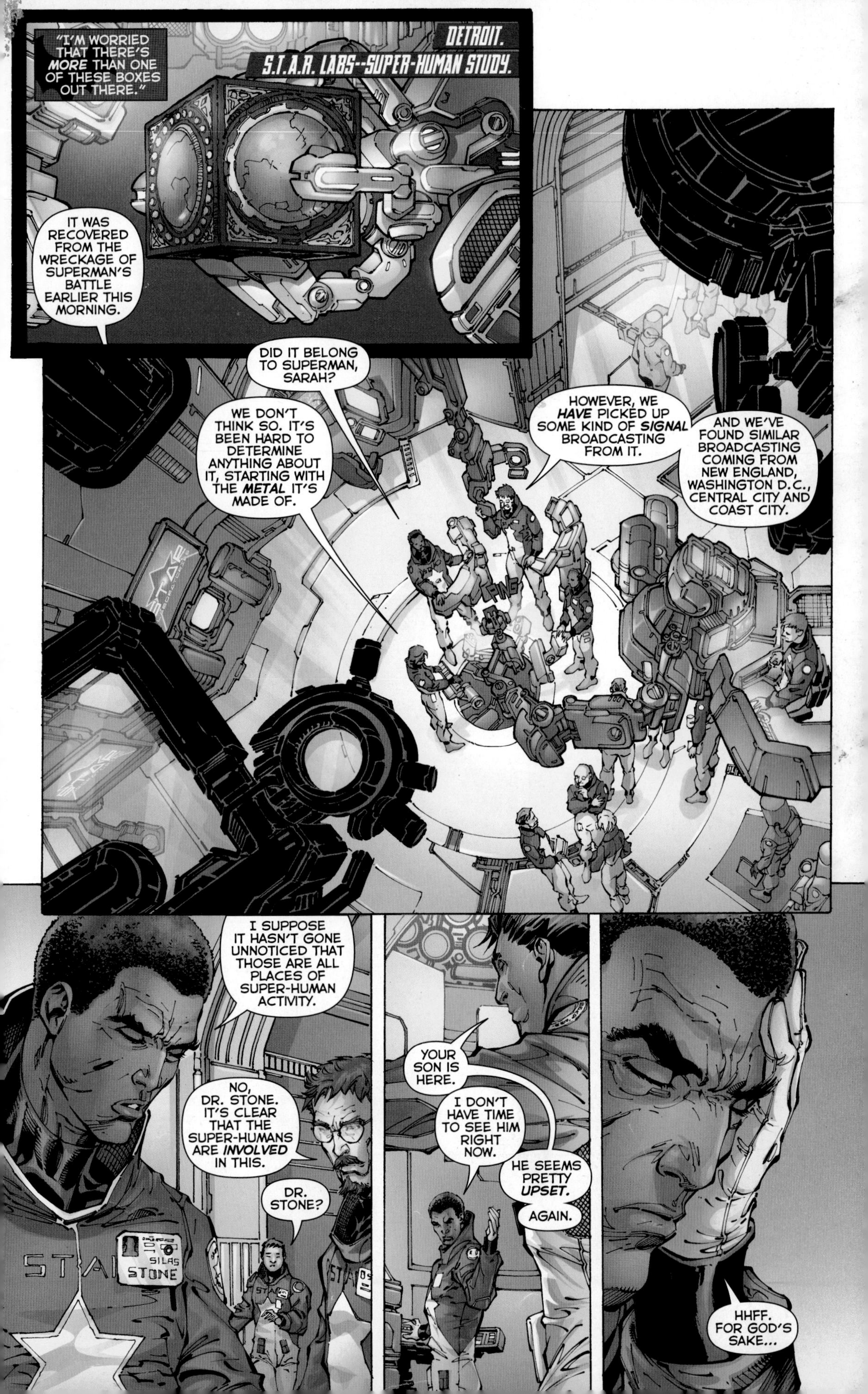
"I'M WORRIED THAT THERE'S MORE THAN ONE OF THESE BOXES OUT THERE."
DETROIT.
S.T.A.R. LABS--SUPER-HUMAN STUDY.
IT WAS RECOVERED FROM THE WRECKAGE OF SUPERMAN'S BATTLE EARLIER THIS MORNING.
DID IT BELONG TO SUPERMAN, SARAH?
WE DON'T THINK SO. IT'S BEEN HARD TO DETERMINE ANYTHING ABOUT IT, STARTING WITH THE METAL IT'S MADE OF.
HOWEVER, WE HAVE PICKED UP SOME KIND OF SIGNAL BROADCASTING FROM IT.
AND WE'VE FOUND SIMILAR BROADCASTING COMING FROM NEW ENGLAND, WASHINGTON D.C., CENTRAL CITY AND COAST CITY.
I SUPPOSE IT HASN'T GONE UNNOTICED THAT THOSE ARE ALL PLACES OF SUPER-HUMAN ACTIVITY.
NO, DR. STONE. IT'S CLEAR THAT THE SUPER-HUMANS ARE INVOLVED IN THIS.
DR. STONE?
SILAS STONE
YOUR SON IS HERE.
I DON'T HAVE TIME TO SEE HIM RIGHT NOW.
HE SEEMS PRETTY UPSET.
AGAIN.
HHFF. FOR GOD'S SAKE...

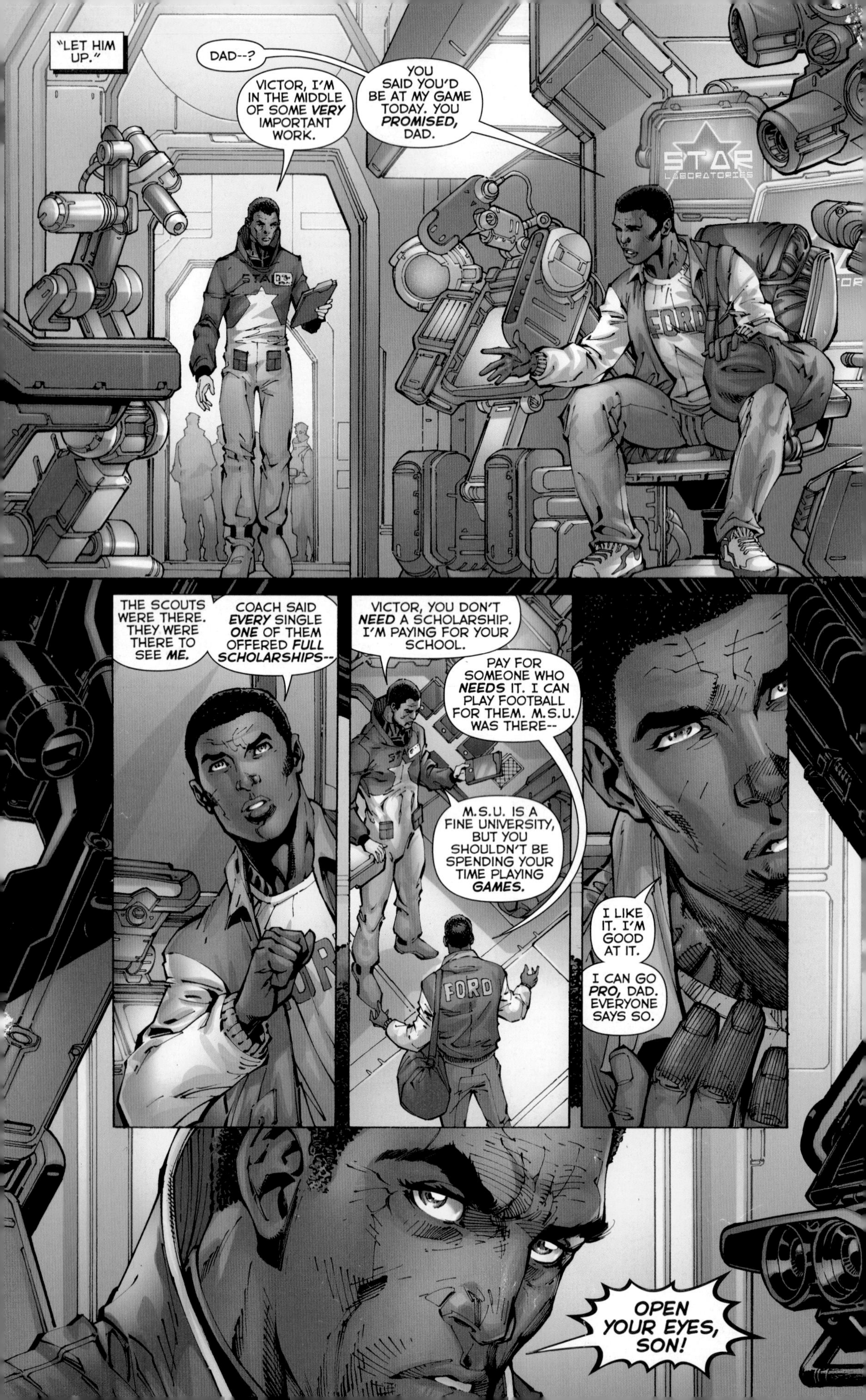
"LET HIM UP."
DAD--?
VICTOR, I'M IN THE MIDDLE OF SOME VERY IMPORTANT WORK.
YOU SAID YOU'D BE AT MY GAME TODAY. YOU PROMISED, DAD.
STAR LABORATORIES
FORD
THE SCOUTS WERE THERE. THEY WERE THERE TO SEE ME.
COACH SAID EVERY SINGLE ONE OF THEM OFFERED FULL SCHOLARSHIPS--
VICTOR, YOU DON'T NEED A SCHOLARSHIP. I'M PAYING FOR YOUR SCHOOL.
PAY FOR SOMEONE WHO NEEDS IT. I CAN PLAY FOOTBALL FOR THEM. M.S.U. WAS THERE--
M.S.U. IS A FINE UNIVERSITY, BUT YOU SHOULDN'T BE SPENDING YOUR TIME PLAYING GAMES.
FORD
I LIKE IT. I'M GOOD AT IT.
I CAN GO PRO, DAD. EVERYONE SAYS SO.
OPEN YOUR EYES, SON!

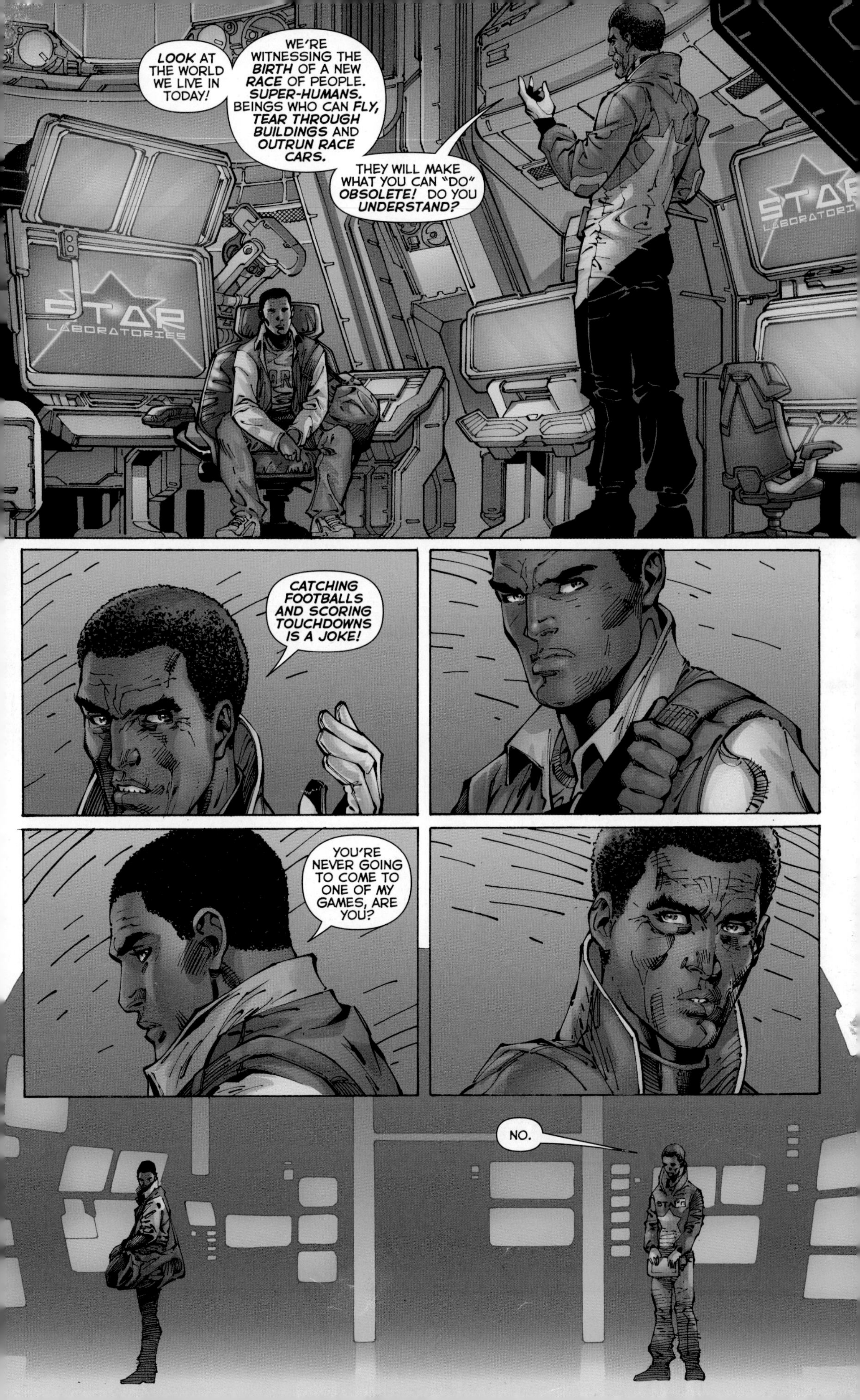
LOOK AT THE WORLD WE LIVE IN TODAY!
WE'RE WITNESSING THE BIRTH OF A NEW RACE OF PEOPLE. SUPER-HUMANS. BEINGS WHO CAN FLY, TEAR THROUGH BUILDINGS AND OUTRUN RACE CARS.
THEY WILL MAKE WHAT YOU CAN "DO" OBSOLETE! DO YOU UNDERSTAND?
STAR LABORATORIES
CATCHING FOOTBALLS AND SCORING TOUCHDOWNS IS A JOKE!
YOU'RE NEVER GOING TO COME TO ONE OF MY GAMES, ARE YOU?
NO.

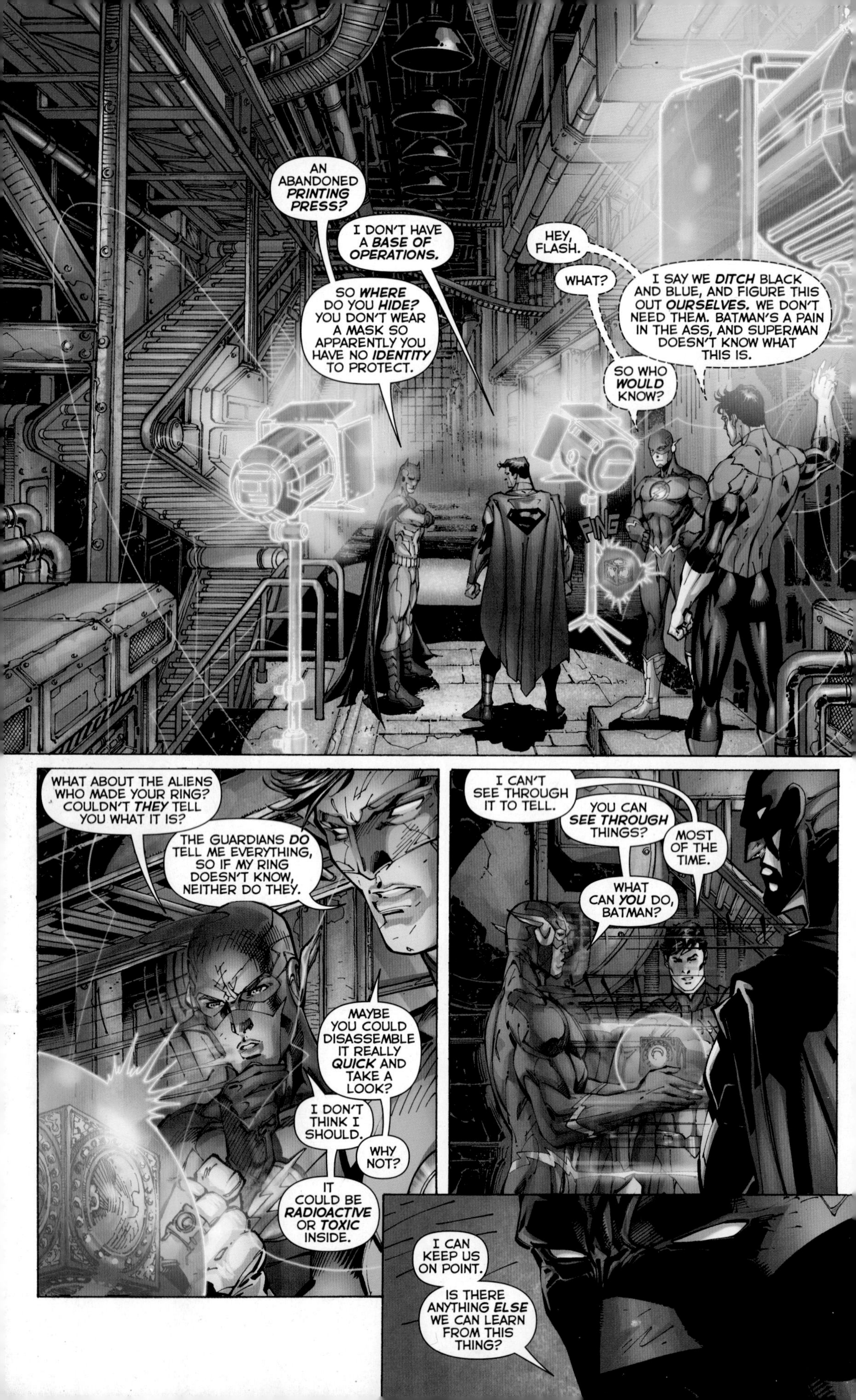
AN ABANDONED PRINTING PRESS?
I DON'T HAVE A BASE OF OPERATIONS.
SO WHERE DO YOU HIDE? YOU DON'T WEAR A MASK SO APPARENTLY YOU HAVE NO IDENTITY TO PROTECT.
HEY, FLASH.
WHAT?
I SAY WE DITCH BLACK AND BLUE, AND FIGURE THIS OUT OURSELVES. WE DON'T NEED THEM. BATMAN'S A PAIN IN THE ASS, AND SUPERMAN DOESN'T KNOW WHAT THIS IS.
SO WHO WOULD KNOW?
PING
WHAT ABOUT THE ALIENS WHO MADE YOUR RING? COULDN'T THEY TELL YOU WHAT IT IS?
THE GUARDIANS DO TELL ME EVERYTHING, SO IF MY RING DOESN'T KNOW, NEITHER DO THEY.
MAYBE YOU COULD DISASSEMBLE IT REALLY QUICK AND TAKE A LOOK?
I DON'T THINK I SHOULD.
WHY NOT?
IT COULD BE RADIOACTIVE OR TOXIC INSIDE.
I CAN'T SEE THROUGH IT TO TELL.
YOU CAN SEE THROUGH THINGS?
MOST OF THE TIME.
WHAT CAN YOU DO, BATMAN?
I CAN KEEP US ON POINT.
IS THERE ANYTHING ELSE WE CAN LEARN FROM THIS THING?

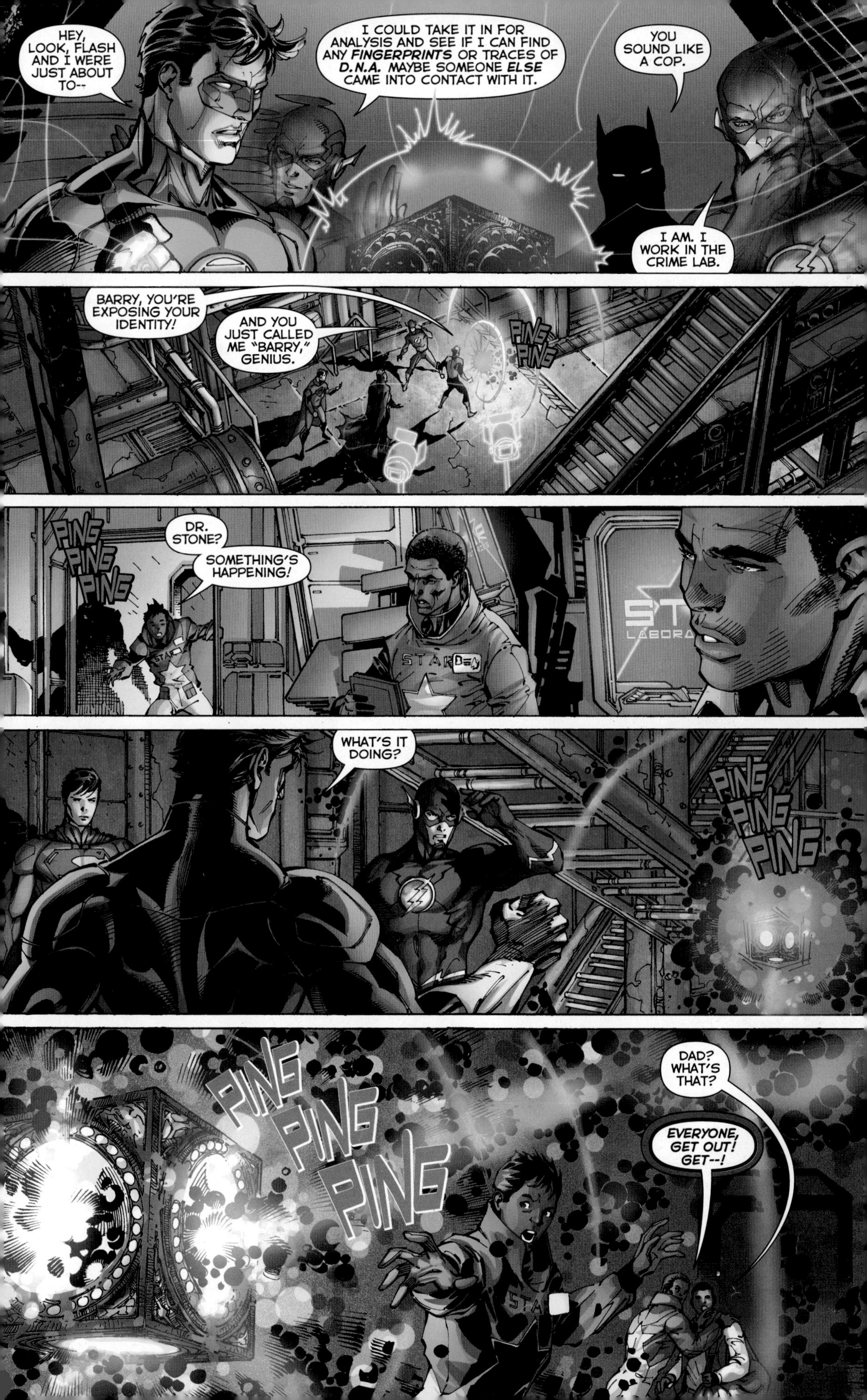
HEY, LOOK, FLASH AND I WERE JUST ABOUT TO--
I COULD TAKE IT IN FOR ANALYSIS AND SEE IF I CAN FIND ANY FINGERPRINTS OR TRACES OF D.N.A. MAYBE SOMEONE ELSE CAME INTO CONTACT WITH IT.
YOU SOUND LIKE A COP.
I AM. I WORK IN THE CRIME LAB.
BARRY, YOU'RE EXPOSING YOUR IDENTITY!
AND YOU JUST CALLED ME "BARRY," GENIUS.
PING PING
PING PING PING
DR. STONE?
SOMETHING'S HAPPENING!
WHAT'S IT DOING?
PING PING PING
PING PING PING
DAD? WHAT'S THAT?
EVERYONE, GET OUT! GET--!

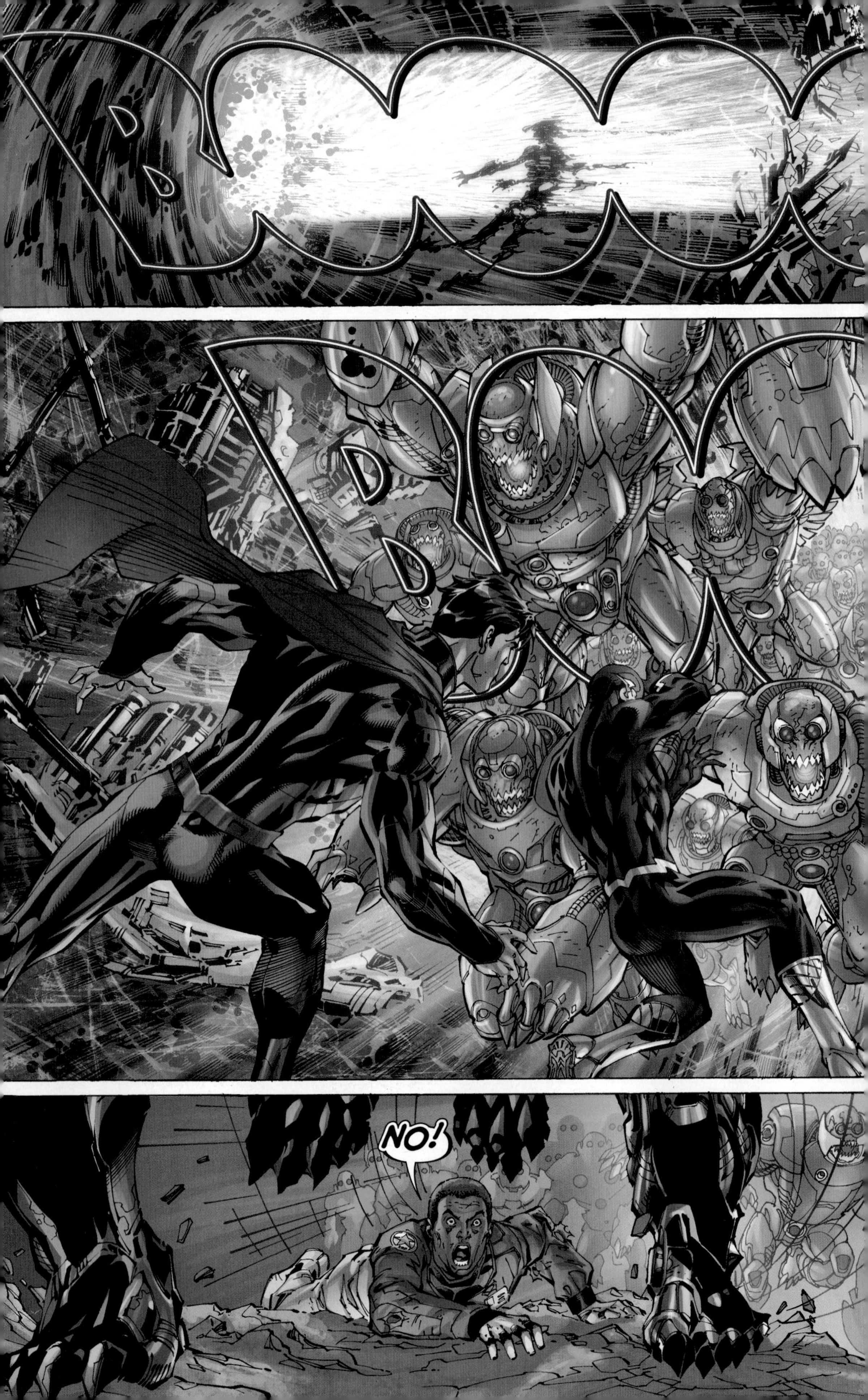
NO!

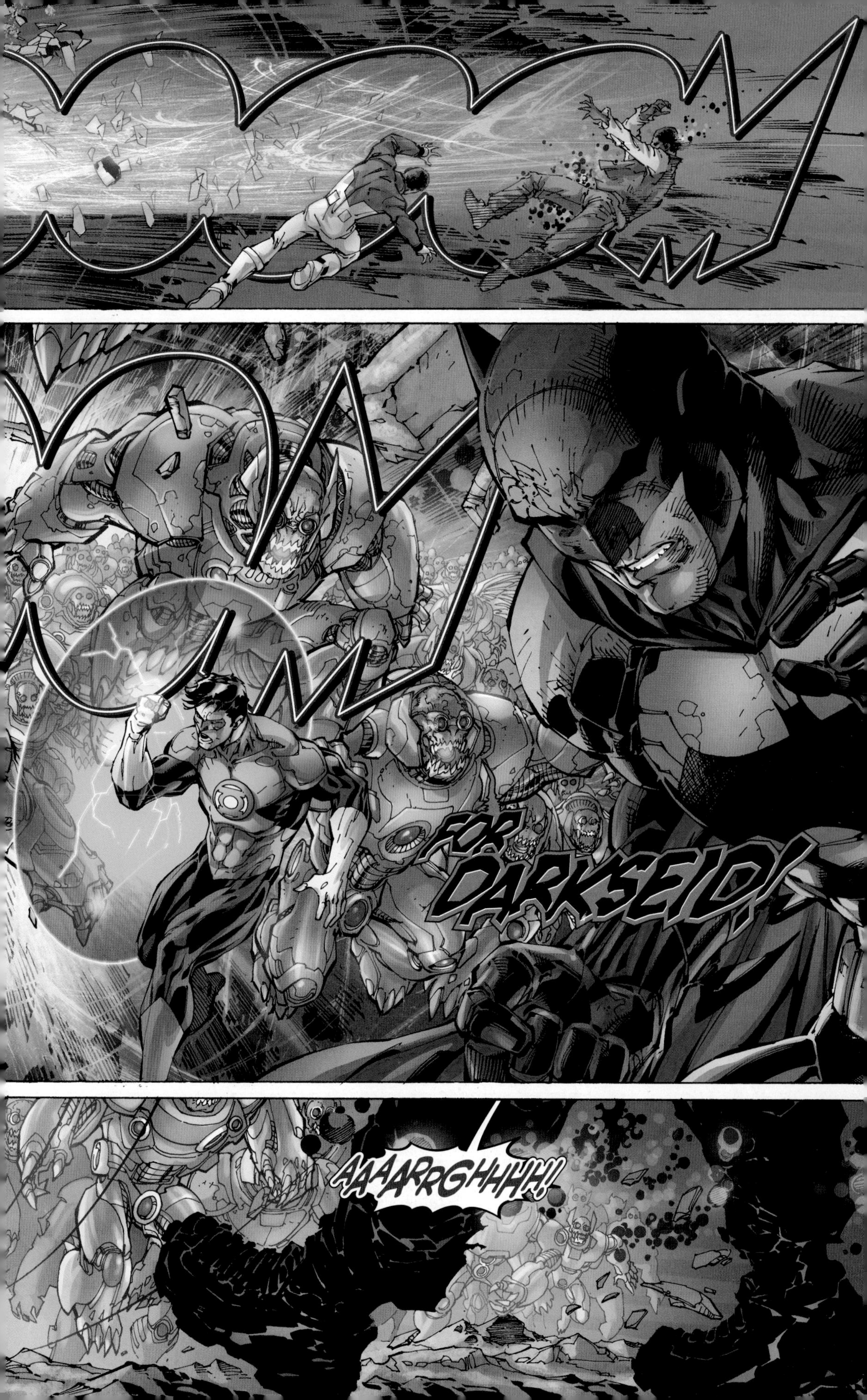
FOR DARKSEID!
AAAARRGHHHH!

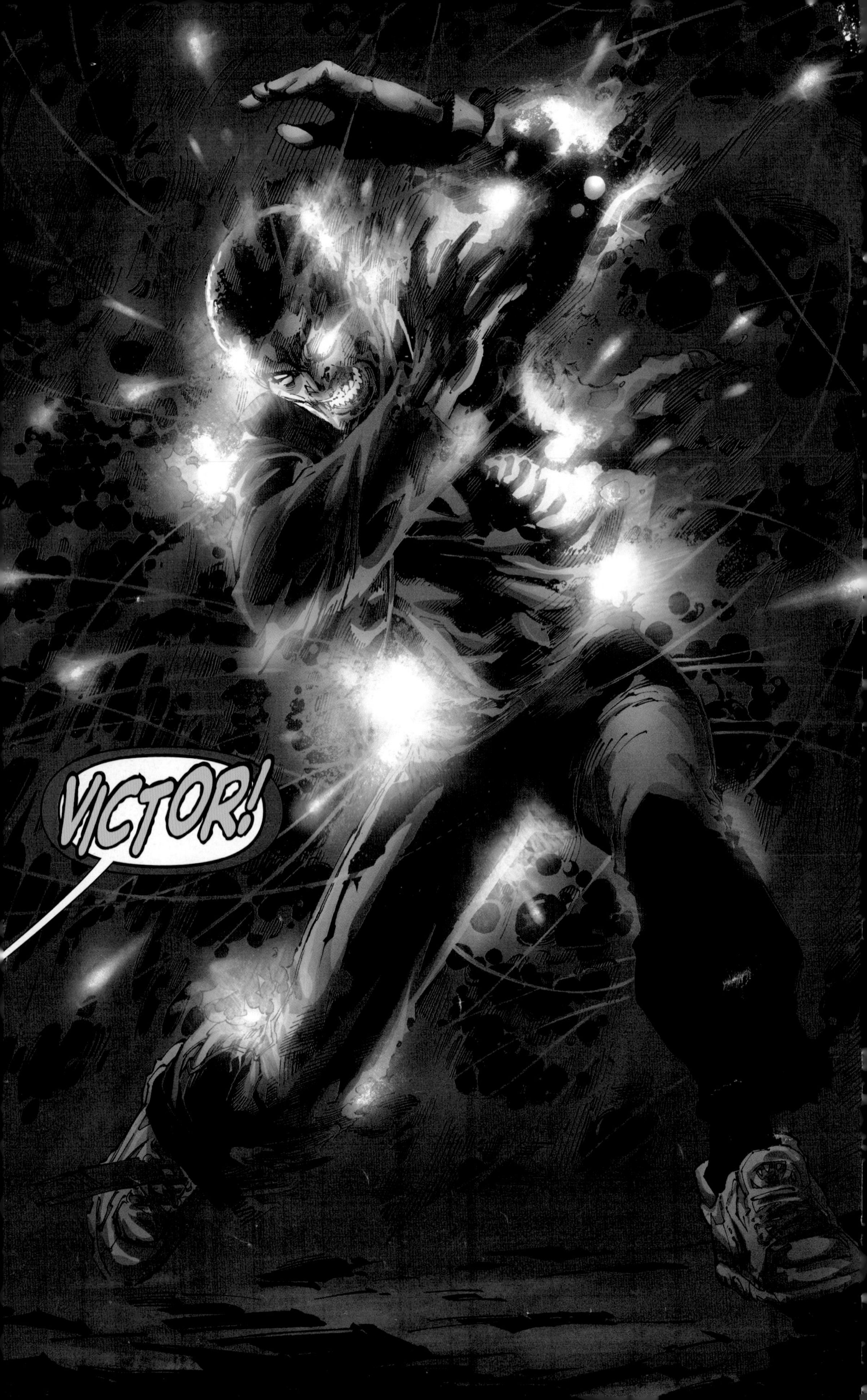
VICTOR!

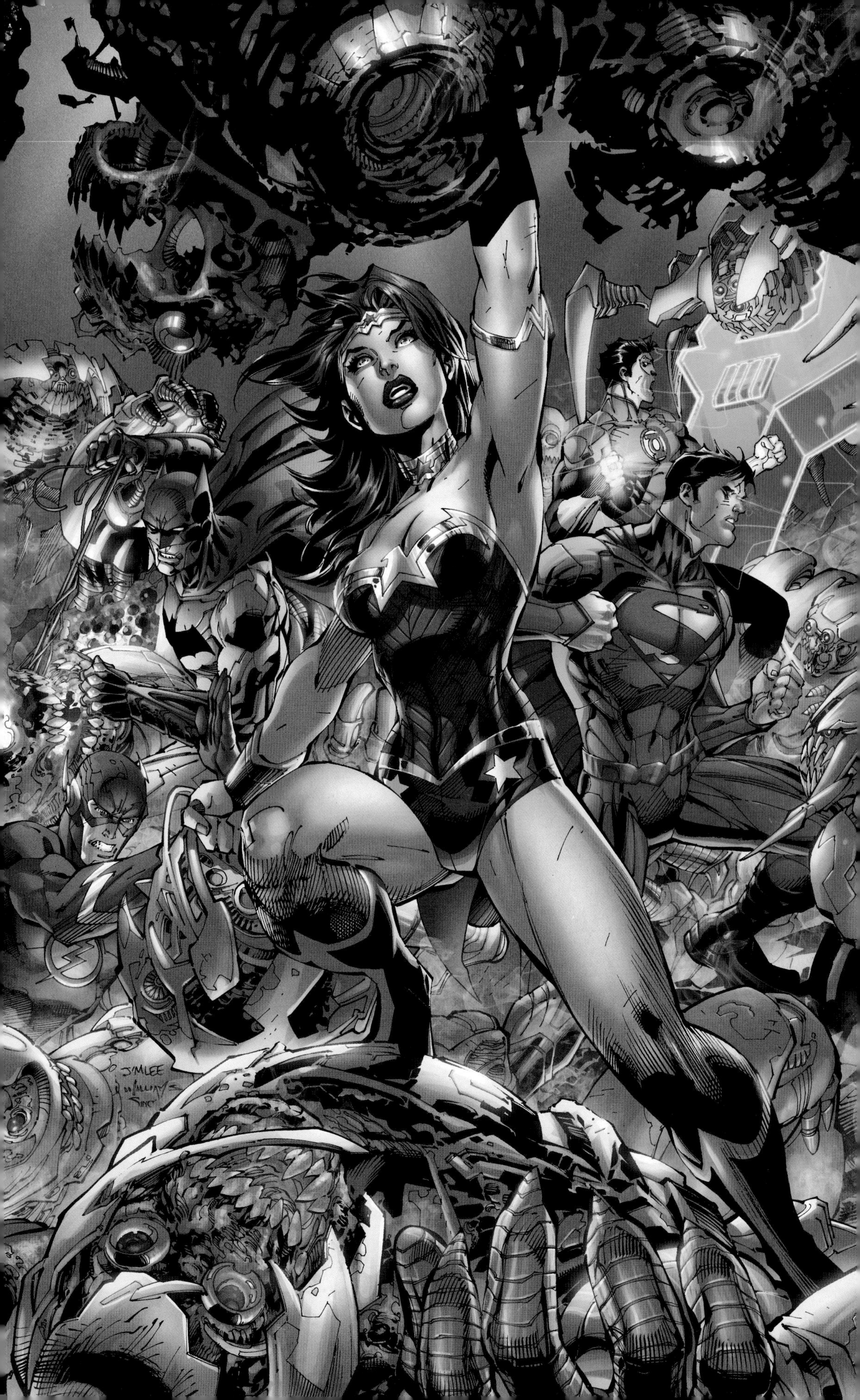

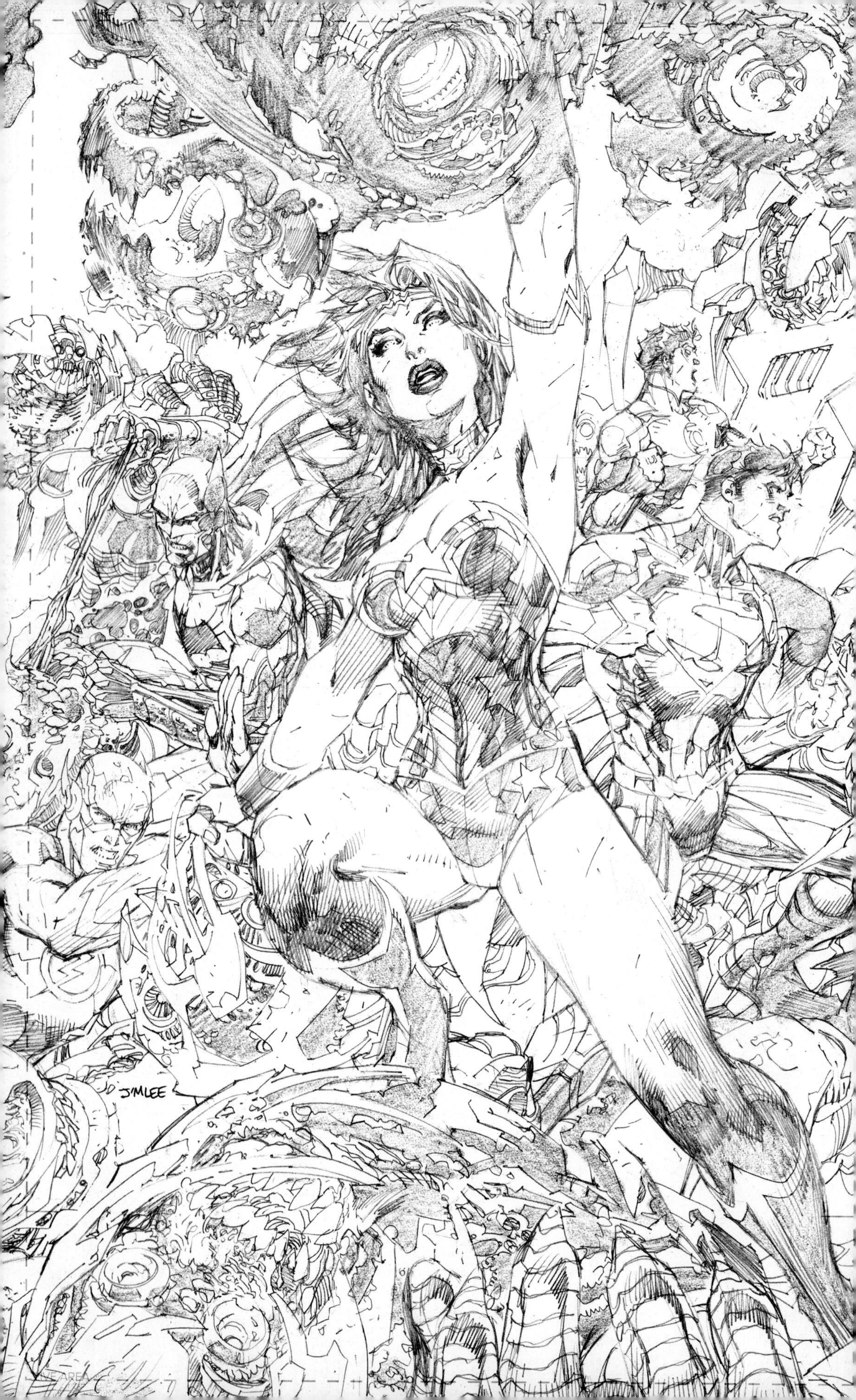

JIMLEE

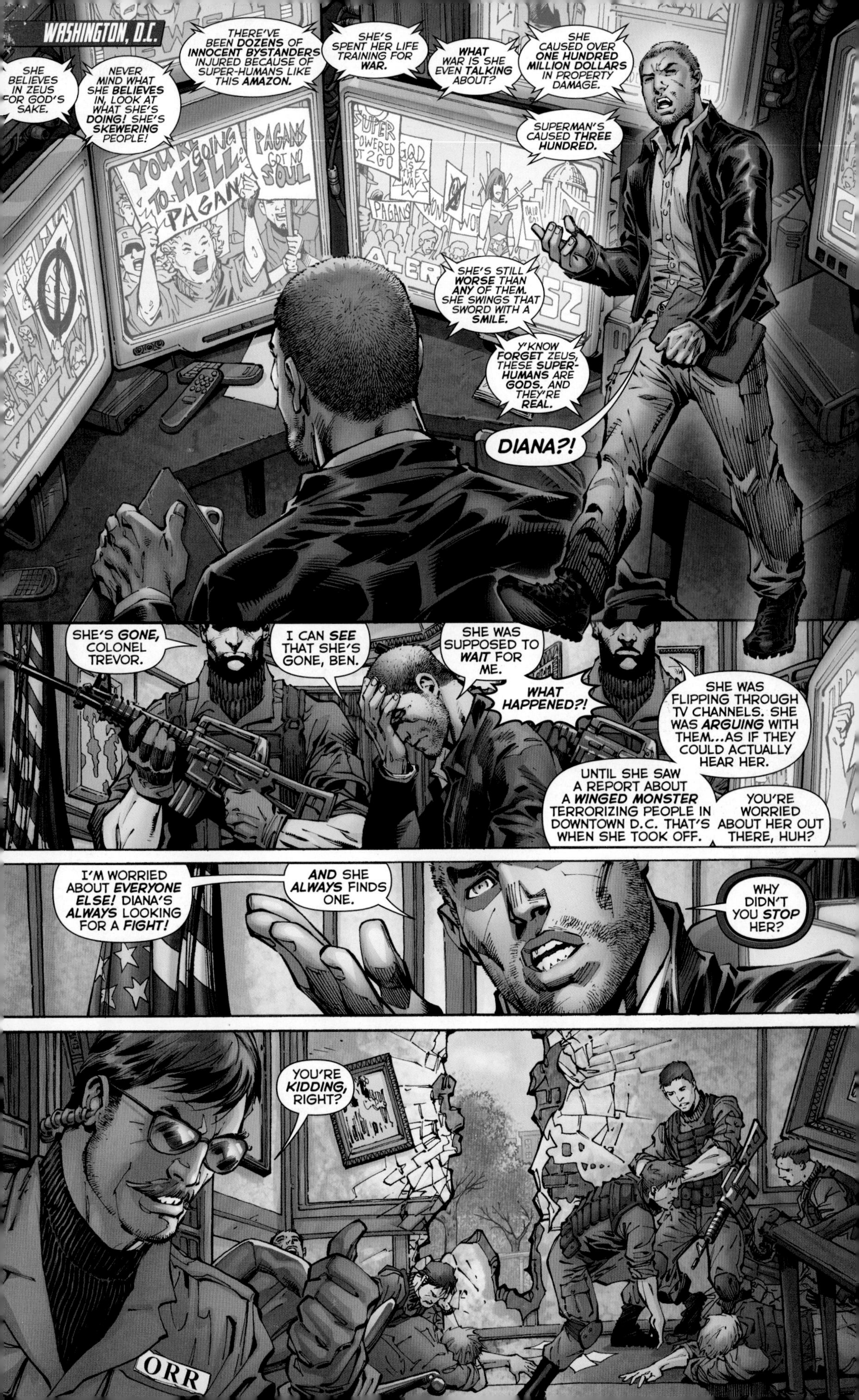
WASHINGTON, D.C.
SHE BELIEVES IN ZEUS FOR GOD'S SAKE.
NEVER MIND WHAT SHE BELIEVES IN, LOOK AT WHAT SHE'S DOING! SHE'S SKEWERING PEOPLE!
THERE'VE BEEN DOZENS OF INNOCENT BYSTANDERS INJURED BECAUSE OF SUPER-HUMANS LIKE THIS AMAZON.
SHE'S SPENT HER LIFE TRAINING FOR WAR.
WHAT WAR IS SHE EVEN TALKING ABOUT?
SHE CAUSED OVER ONE HUNDRED MILLION DOLLARS IN PROPERTY DAMAGE.
SUPERMAN'S CAUSED THREE HUNDRED.
PAGANS GOT NO SOUL
SHE'S STILL WORSE THAN ANY OF THEM. SHE SWINGS THAT SWORD WITH A SMILE.
Y'KNOW FORGET ZEUS, THESE SUPER-HUMANS ARE GODS. AND THEY'RE REAL.
DIANA?!
SHE'S GONE, COLONEL TREVOR.
I CAN SEE THAT SHE'S GONE, BEN.
SHE WAS SUPPOSED TO WAIT FOR ME.
WHAT HAPPENED?!
SHE WAS FLIPPING THROUGH TV CHANNELS. SHE WAS ARGUING WITH THEM...AS IF THEY COULD ACTUALLY HEAR HER.
UNTIL SHE SAW A REPORT ABOUT A WINGED MONSTER TERRORIZING PEOPLE IN DOWNTOWN D.C. THAT'S WHEN SHE TOOK OFF.
YOU'RE WORRIED ABOUT HER OUT THERE, HUH?
I'M WORRIED ABOUT EVERYONE ELSE! DIANA'S ALWAYS LOOKING FOR A FIGHT!
AND SHE ALWAYS FINDS ONE.
WHY DIDN'T YOU STOP HER?
YOU'RE KIDDING, RIGHT?
ORR

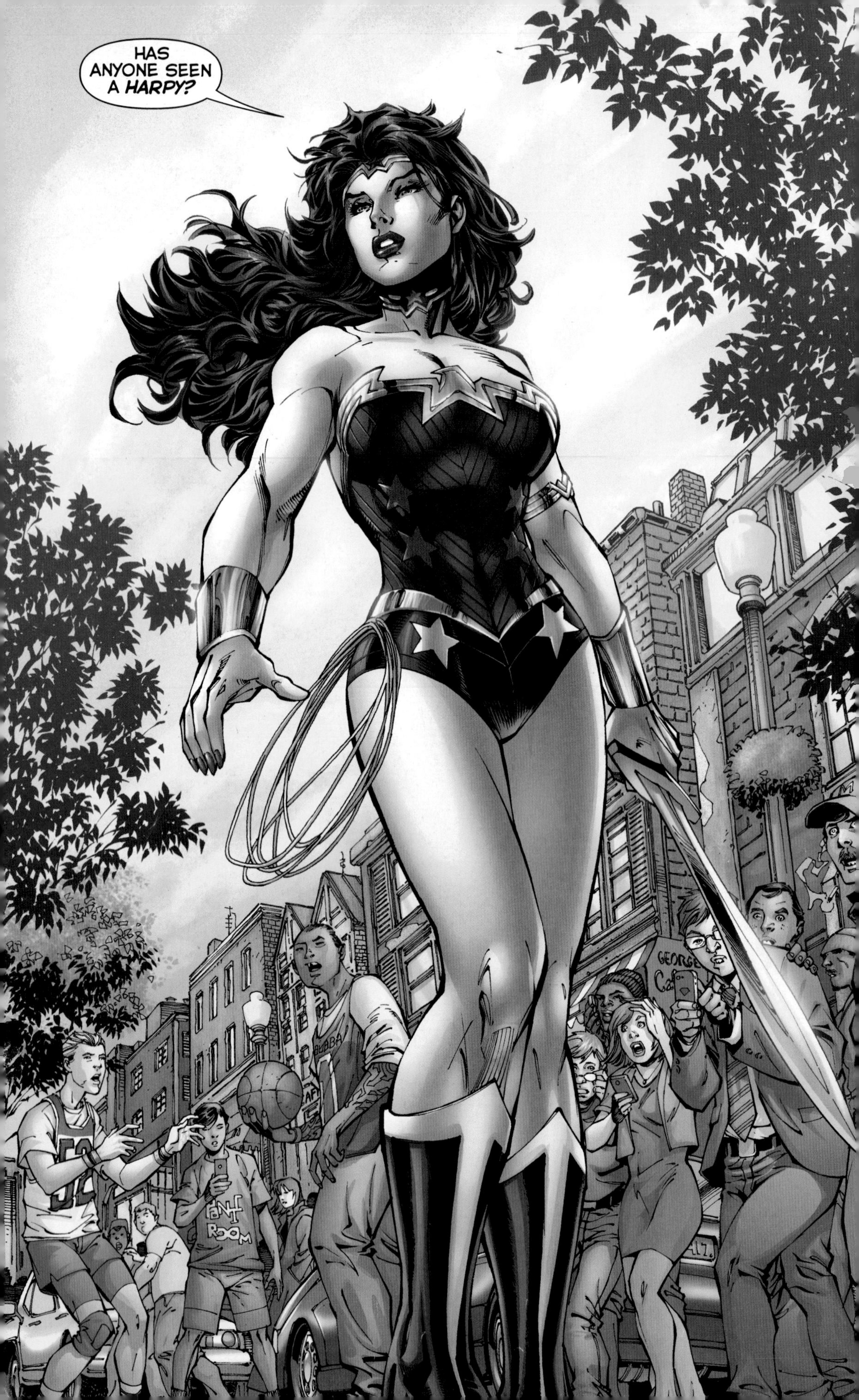
HAS ANYONE SEEN A *HARPY?*

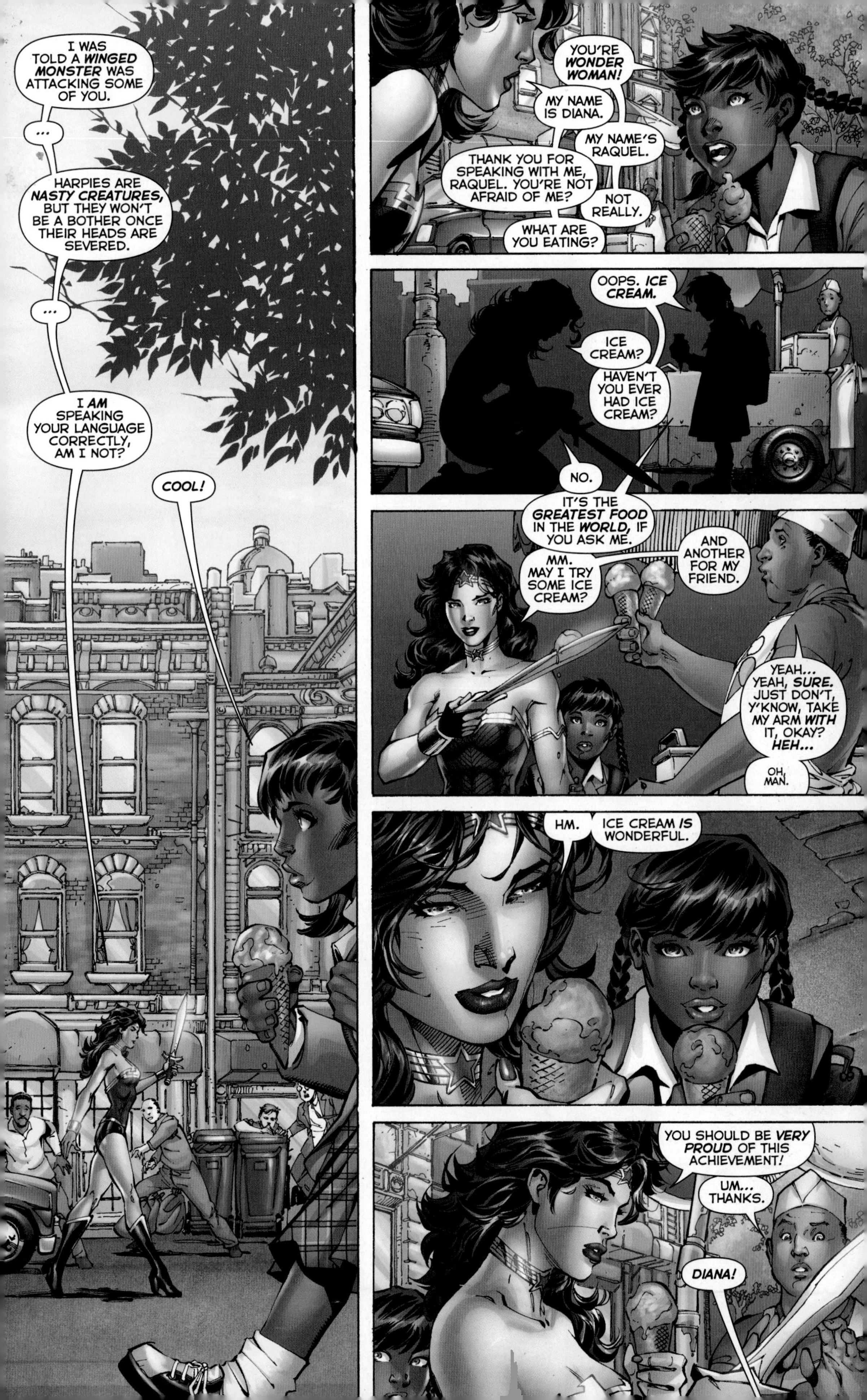

I WAS TOLD A WINGED MONSTER WAS ATTACKING SOME OF YOU.
...
HARPIES ARE NASTY CREATURES, BUT THEY WON'T BE A BOTHER ONCE THEIR HEADS ARE SEVERED.
...
I AM SPEAKING YOUR LANGUAGE CORRECTLY, AM I NOT?
COOL!
YOU'RE WONDER WOMAN!
MY NAME IS DIANA.
MY NAME'S RAQUEL.
THANK YOU FOR SPEAKING WITH ME, RAQUEL. YOU'RE NOT AFRAID OF ME?
NOT REALLY.
WHAT ARE YOU EATING?
OOPS. ICE CREAM.
ICE CREAM?
HAVEN'T YOU EVER HAD ICE CREAM?
NO.
IT'S THE GREATEST FOOD IN THE WORLD, IF YOU ASK ME.
MM. MAY I TRY SOME ICE CREAM?
AND ANOTHER FOR MY FRIEND.
YEAH... YEAH, SURE. JUST DON'T, Y'KNOW, TAKE MY ARM WITH IT, OKAY? HEH...
OH, MAN.
HM.
ICE CREAM IS WONDERFUL.
YOU SHOULD BE VERY PROUD OF THIS ACHIEVEMENT!
UM... THANKS.
DIANA!

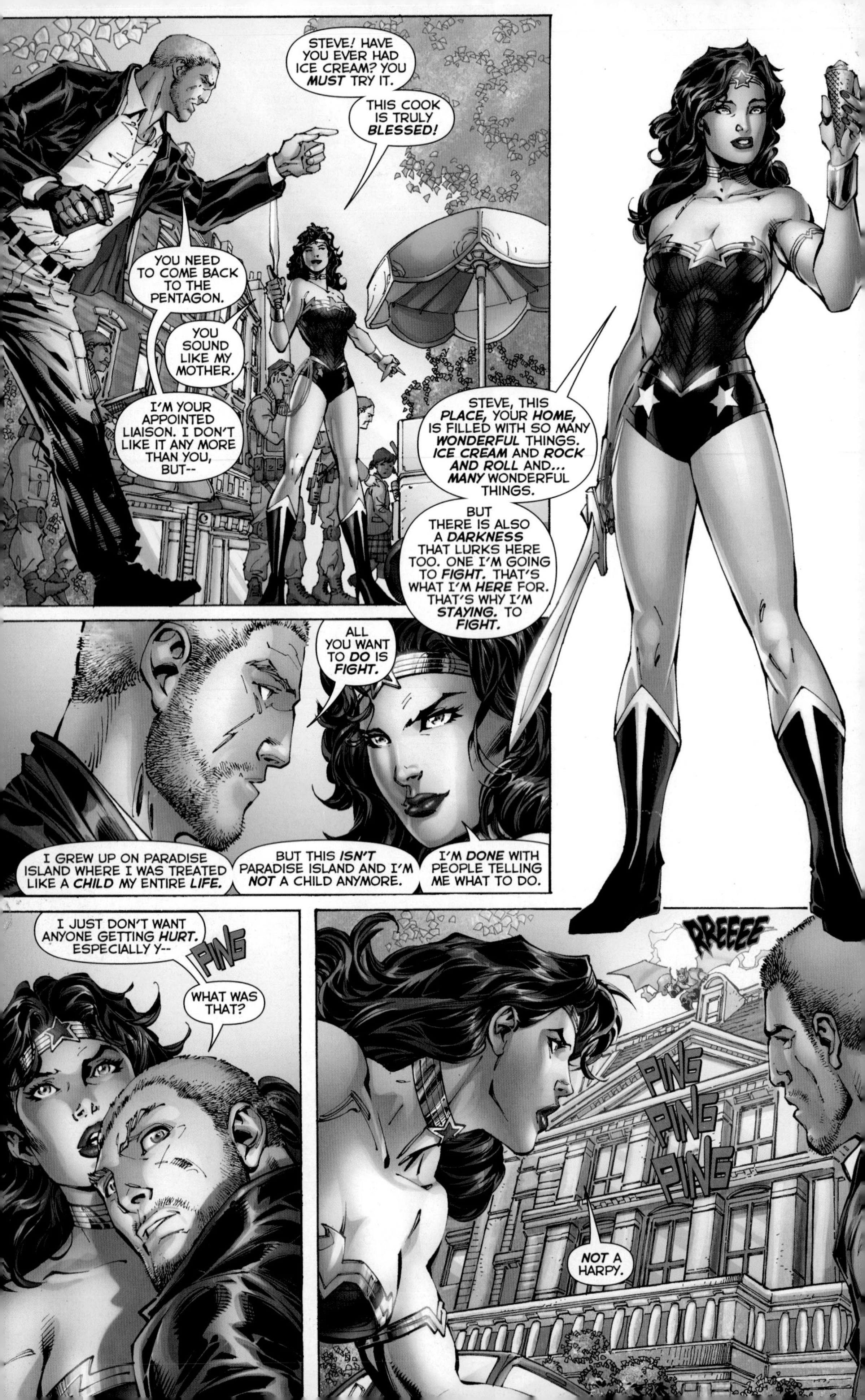
STEVE! HAVE YOU EVER HAD ICE CREAM? YOU MUST TRY IT.
THIS COOK IS TRULY BLESSED!
YOU NEED TO COME BACK TO THE PENTAGON.
YOU SOUND LIKE MY MOTHER.
I'M YOUR APPOINTED LIAISON. I DON'T LIKE IT ANY MORE THAN YOU, BUT--
STEVE, THIS PLACE, YOUR HOME, IS FILLED WITH SO MANY WONDERFUL THINGS. ICE CREAM AND ROCK AND ROLL AND... MANY WONDERFUL THINGS.
BUT THERE IS ALSO A DARKNESS THAT LURKS HERE TOO. ONE I'M GOING TO FIGHT. THAT'S WHAT I'M HERE FOR. THAT'S WHY I'M STAYING. TO FIGHT.
ALL YOU WANT TO DO IS FIGHT.
I GREW UP ON PARADISE ISLAND WHERE I WAS TREATED LIKE A CHILD MY ENTIRE LIFE.
BUT THIS ISN'T PARADISE ISLAND AND I'M NOT A CHILD ANYMORE.
I'M DONE WITH PEOPLE TELLING ME WHAT TO DO.
I JUST DON'T WANT ANYONE GETTING HURT. ESPECIALLY Y--
PING
WHAT WAS THAT?
RREEEE
PING
PING
PING
NOT A HARPY.

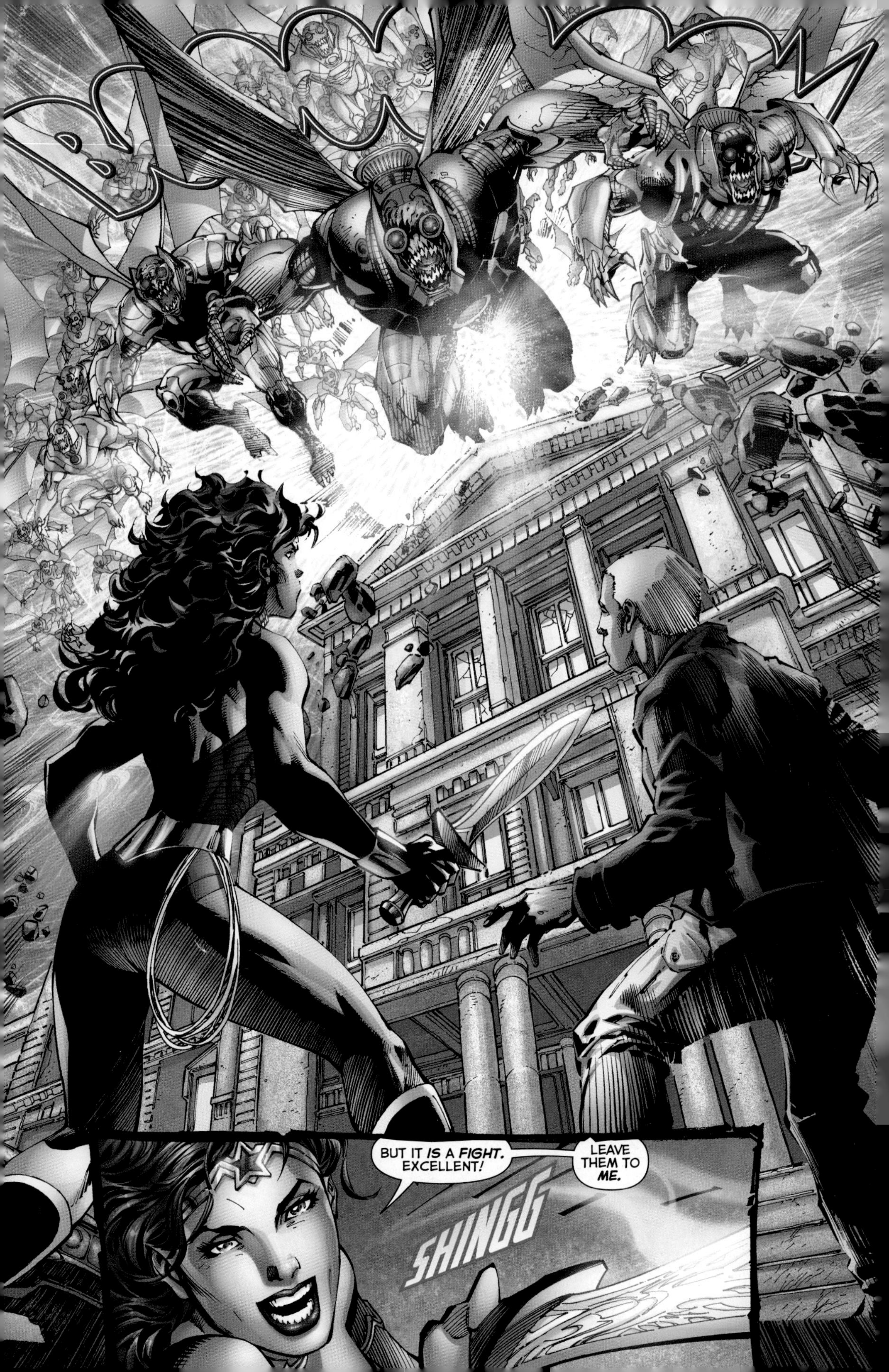
BOOOOM
BUT IT IS A FIGHT. EXCELLENT!
LEAVE THEM TO ME.
SHINGG

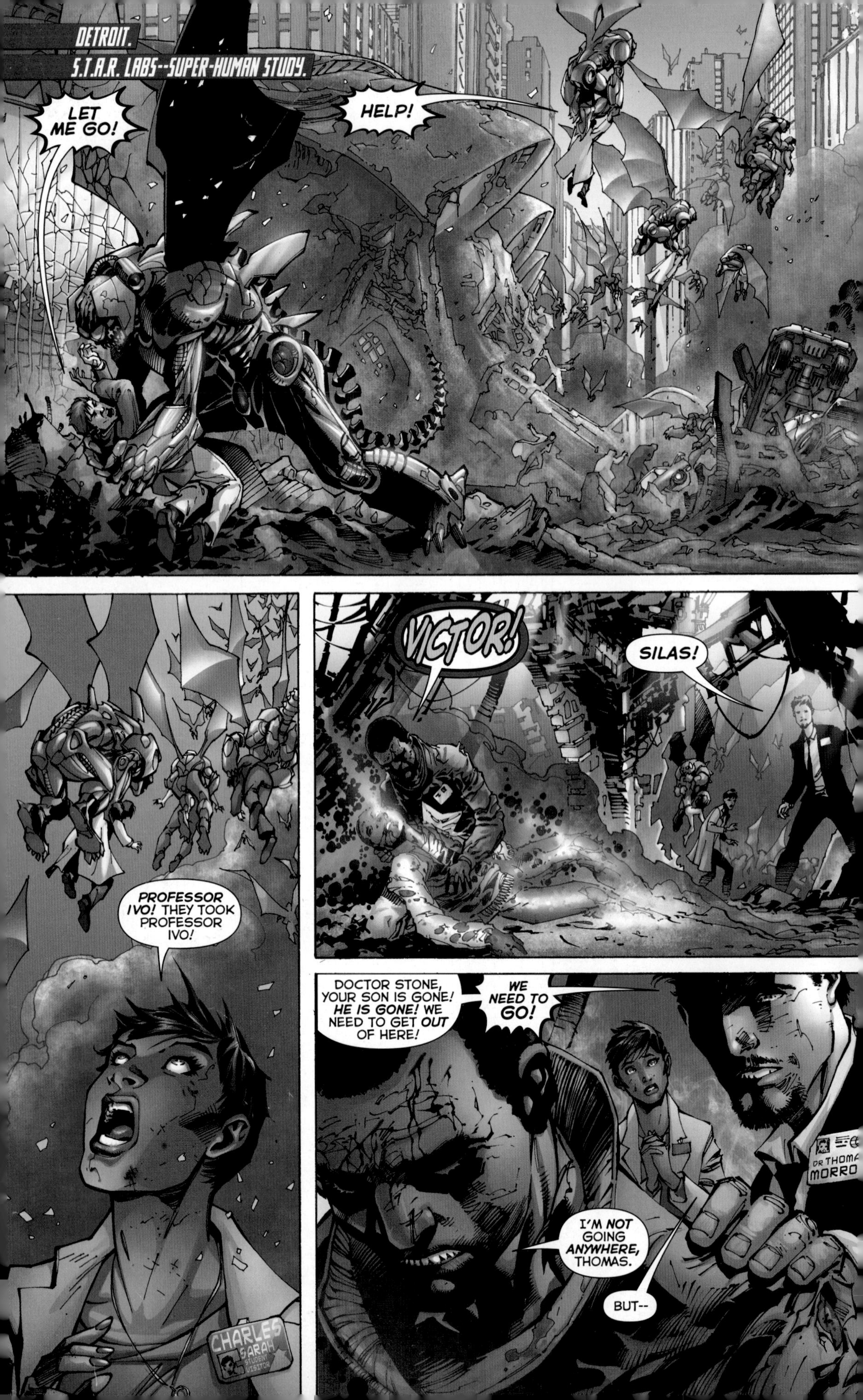
DETROIT.
S.T.A.R. LABS--SUPER-HUMAN STUDY.
LET ME GO!
HELP!
PROFESSOR IVO! THEY TOOK PROFESSOR IVO!
CHARLES
SARAH
STUDENT VISITOR
VICTOR!
SILAS!
DOCTOR STONE, YOUR SON IS GONE! HE IS GONE! WE NEED TO GET OUT OF HERE!
WE NEED TO GO!
DR THOMA
MORRO
I'M NOT GOING ANYWHERE, THOMAS.
BUT--

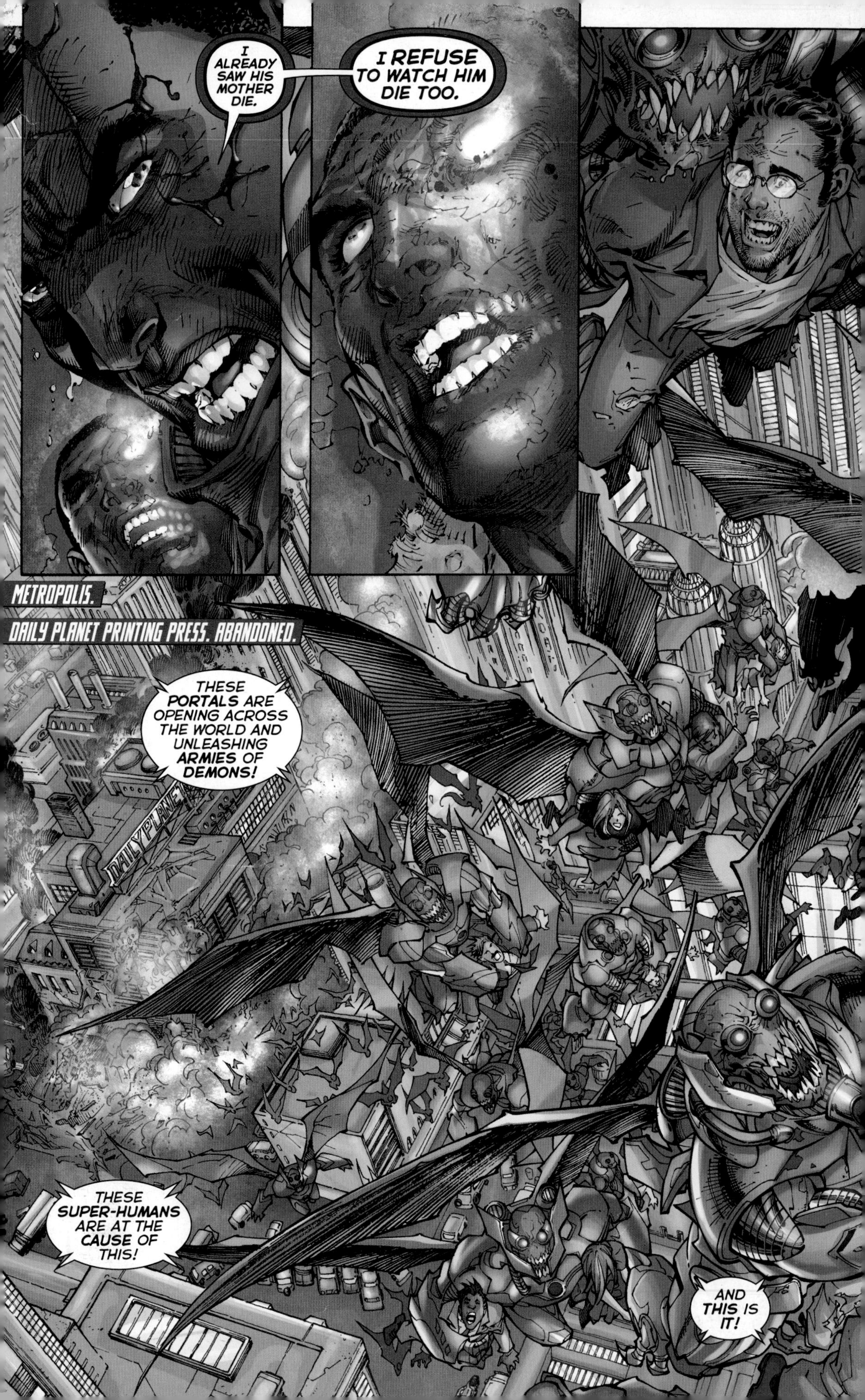
I ALREADY SAW HIS MOTHER DIE.
I REFUSE TO WATCH HIM DIE TOO.
METROPOLIS.
DAILY PLANET PRINTING PRESS. ABANDONED.
THESE PORTALS ARE OPENING ACROSS THE WORLD AND UNLEASHING ARMIES OF DEMONS!
DAILY PLANET
THESE SUPER-HUMANS ARE AT THE CAUSE OF THIS!
AND THIS IS IT!

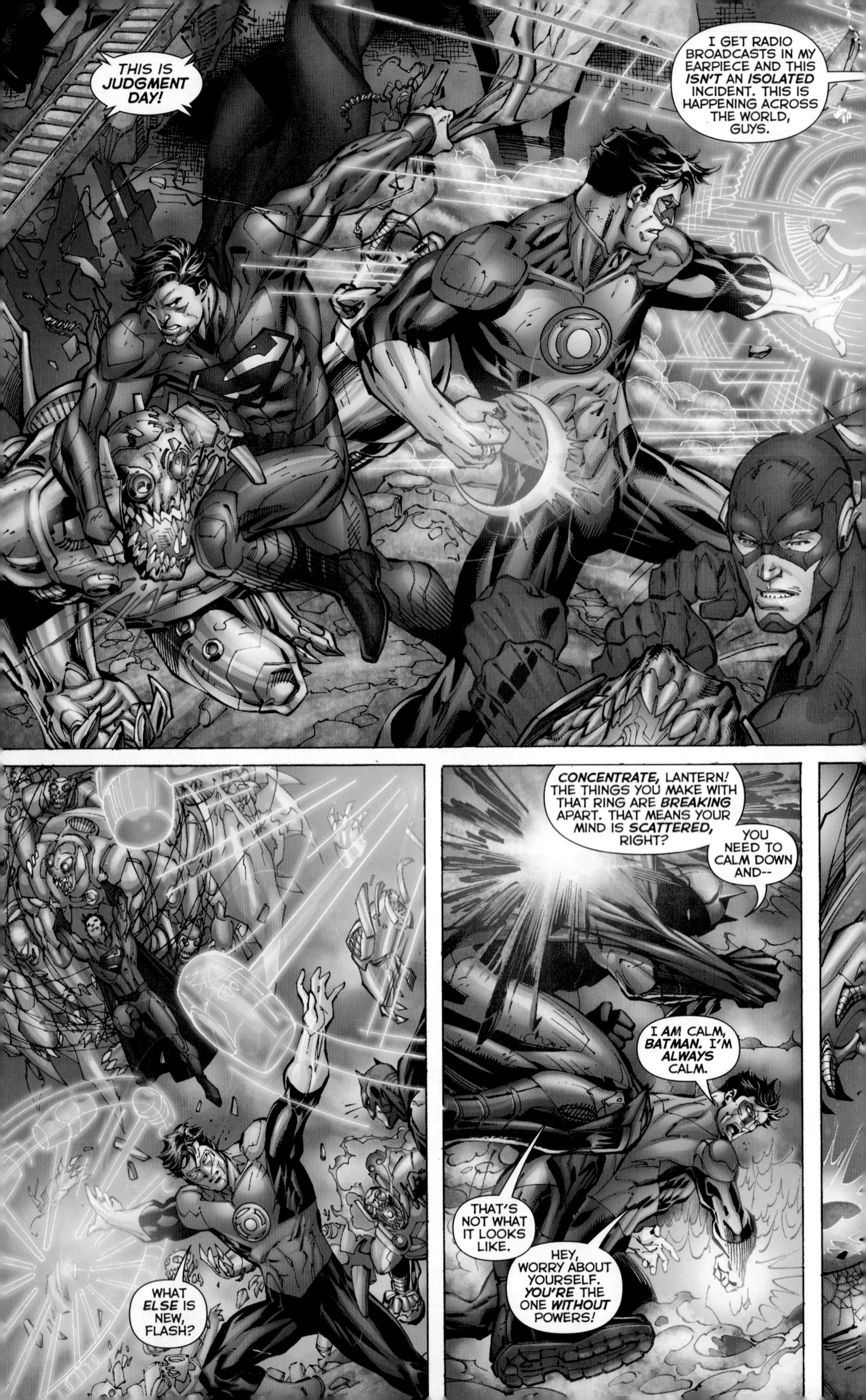
THIS IS JUDGMENT DAY!
I GET RADIO BROADCASTS IN MY EARPIECE AND THIS ISN'T AN ISOLATED INCIDENT. THIS IS HAPPENING ACROSS THE WORLD, GUYS.
WHAT ELSE IS NEW, FLASH?
CONCENTRATE, LANTERN! THE THINGS YOU MAKE WITH THAT RING ARE BREAKING APART. THAT MEANS YOUR MIND IS SCATTERED, RIGHT?
YOU NEED TO CALM DOWN AND--
I AM CALM, BATMAN. I'M ALWAYS CALM.
THAT'S NOT WHAT IT LOOKS LIKE.
HEY, WORRY ABOUT YOURSELF. YOU'RE THE ONE WITHOUT POWERS!

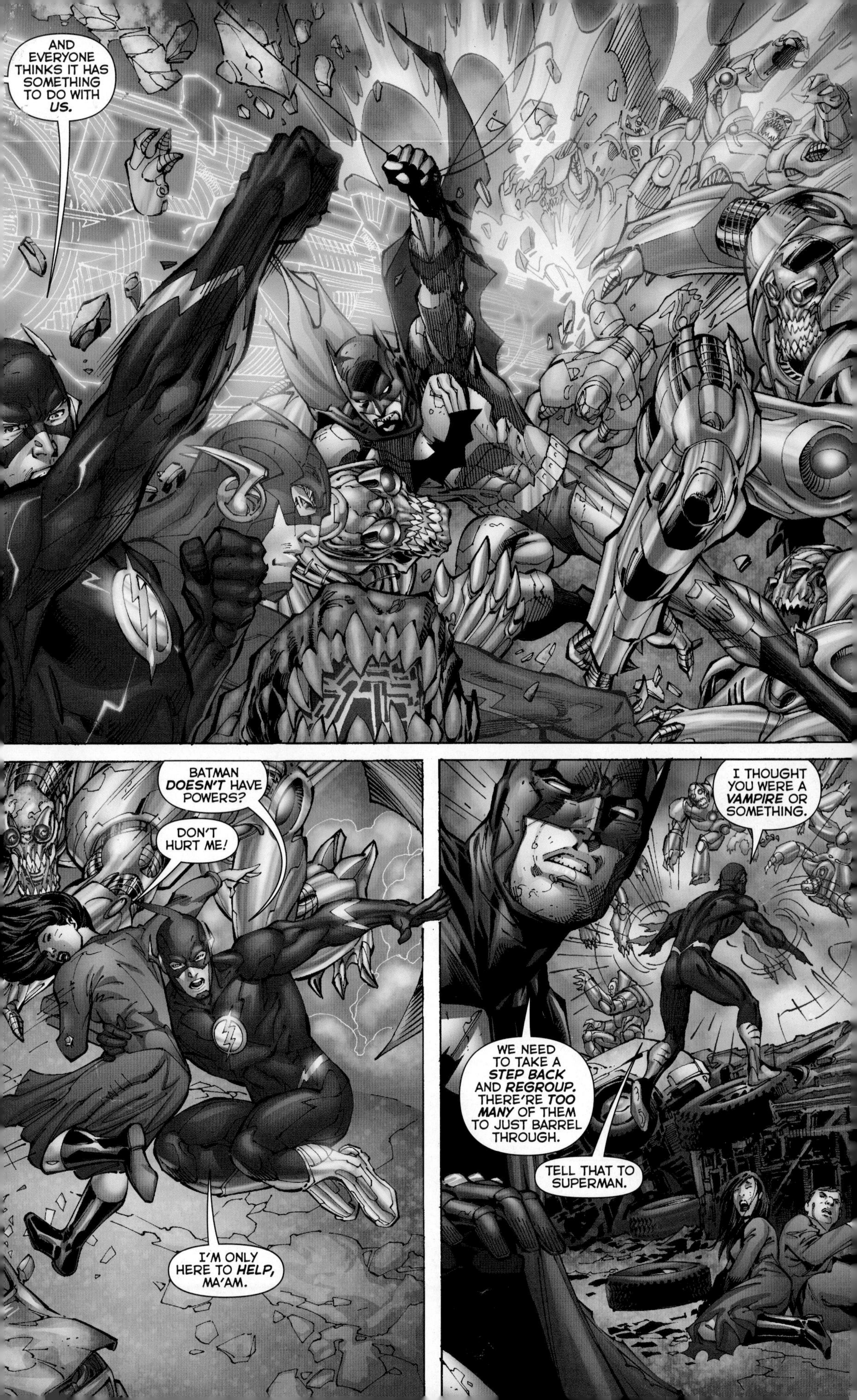
AND EVERYONE THINKS IT HAS SOMETHING TO DO WITH US.
BATMAN DOESN'T HAVE POWERS?
DON'T HURT ME!
I'M ONLY HERE TO HELP, MA'AM.
I THOUGHT YOU WERE A VAMPIRE OR SOMETHING.
WE NEED TO TAKE A STEP BACK AND REGROUP. THERE'RE TOO MANY OF THEM TO JUST BARREL THROUGH.
TELL THAT TO SUPERMAN.

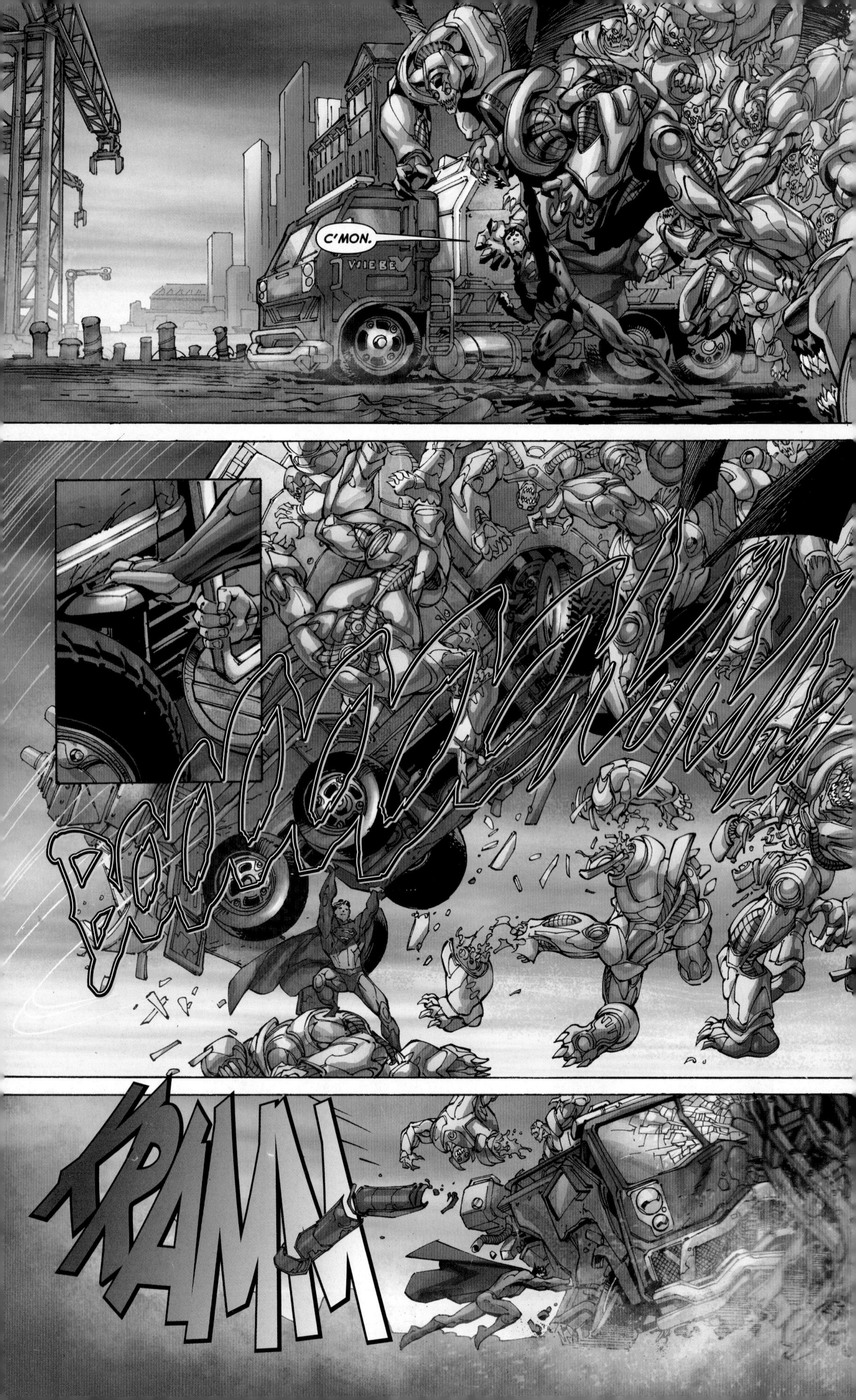
C'MON.
WIEBE

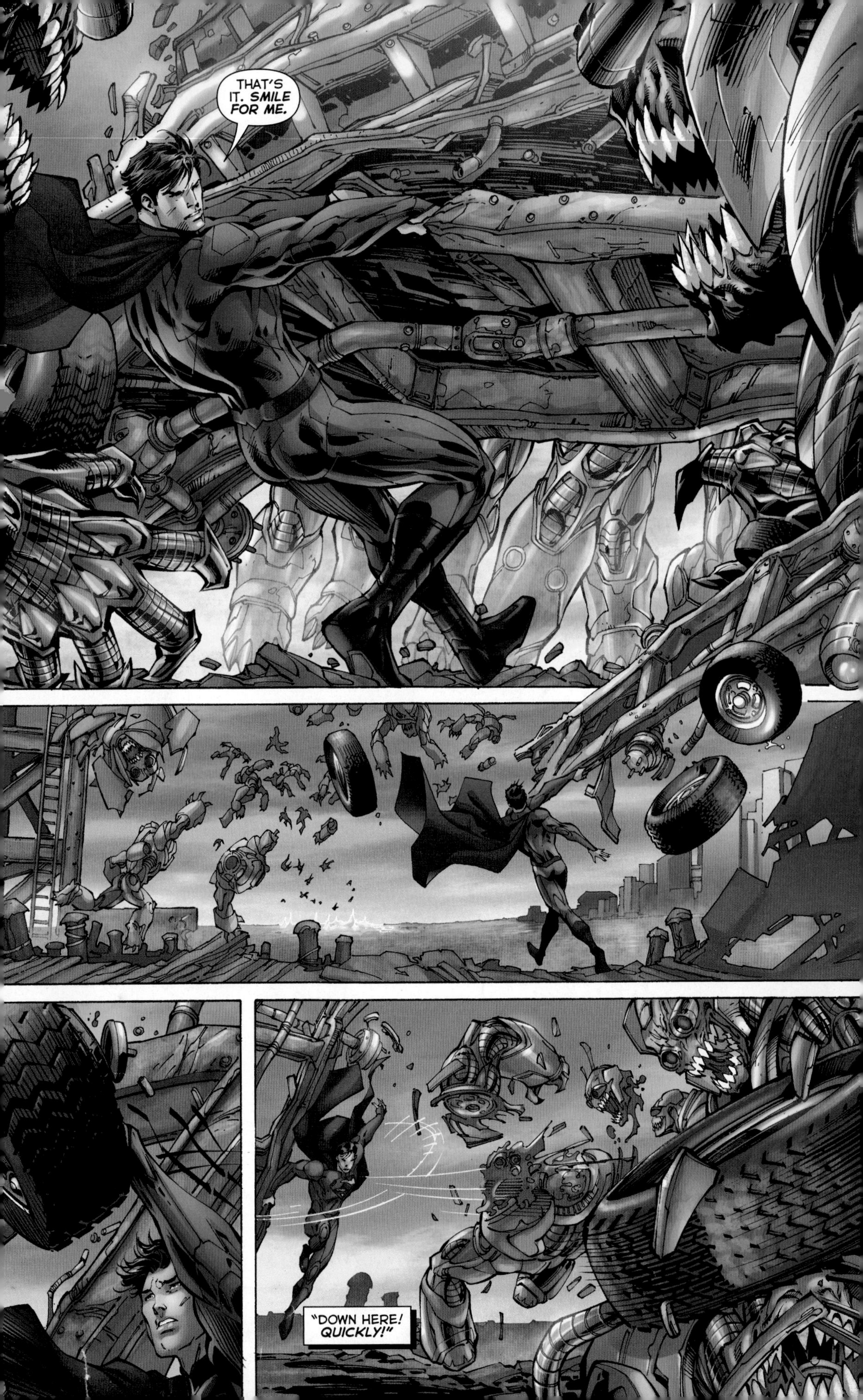
THAT'S IT. SMILE FOR ME.
"DOWN HERE! QUICKLY!"

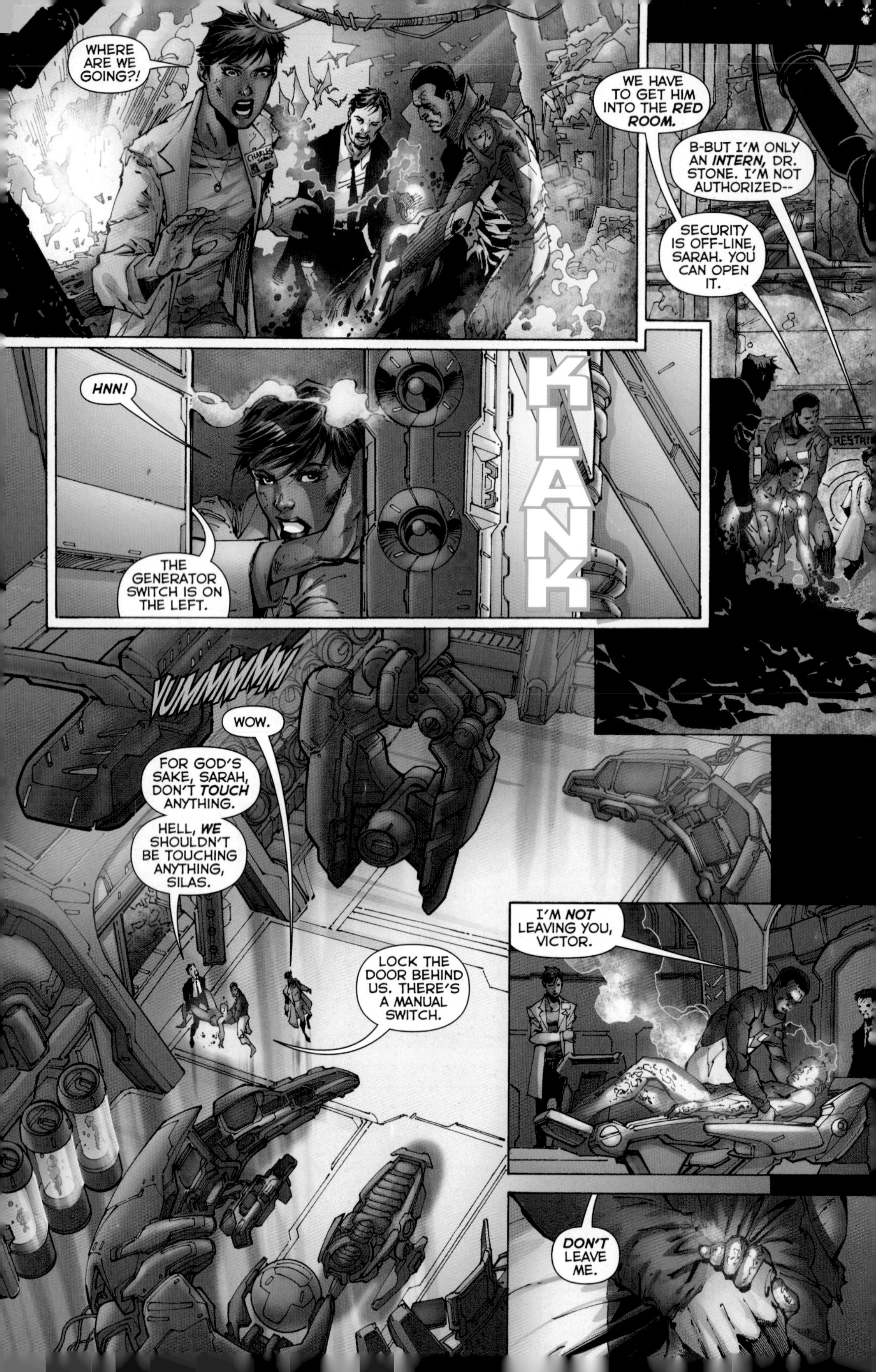
WHERE ARE WE GOING?!
WE HAVE TO GET HIM INTO THE *RED ROOM.*
B-BUT I'M ONLY AN *INTERN,* DR. STONE. I'M NOT AUTHORIZED--
SECURITY IS OFF-LINE, SARAH. YOU CAN OPEN IT.
HNN!
THE GENERATOR SWITCH IS ON THE LEFT.
KLANK
VUMMMMM
WOW.
FOR GOD'S SAKE, SARAH, DON'T *TOUCH* ANYTHING.
HELL, *WE* SHOULDN'T BE TOUCHING ANYTHING, SILAS.
LOCK THE DOOR BEHIND US. THERE'S A MANUAL SWITCH.
I'M *NOT* LEAVING YOU, VICTOR.
DON'T LEAVE ME.

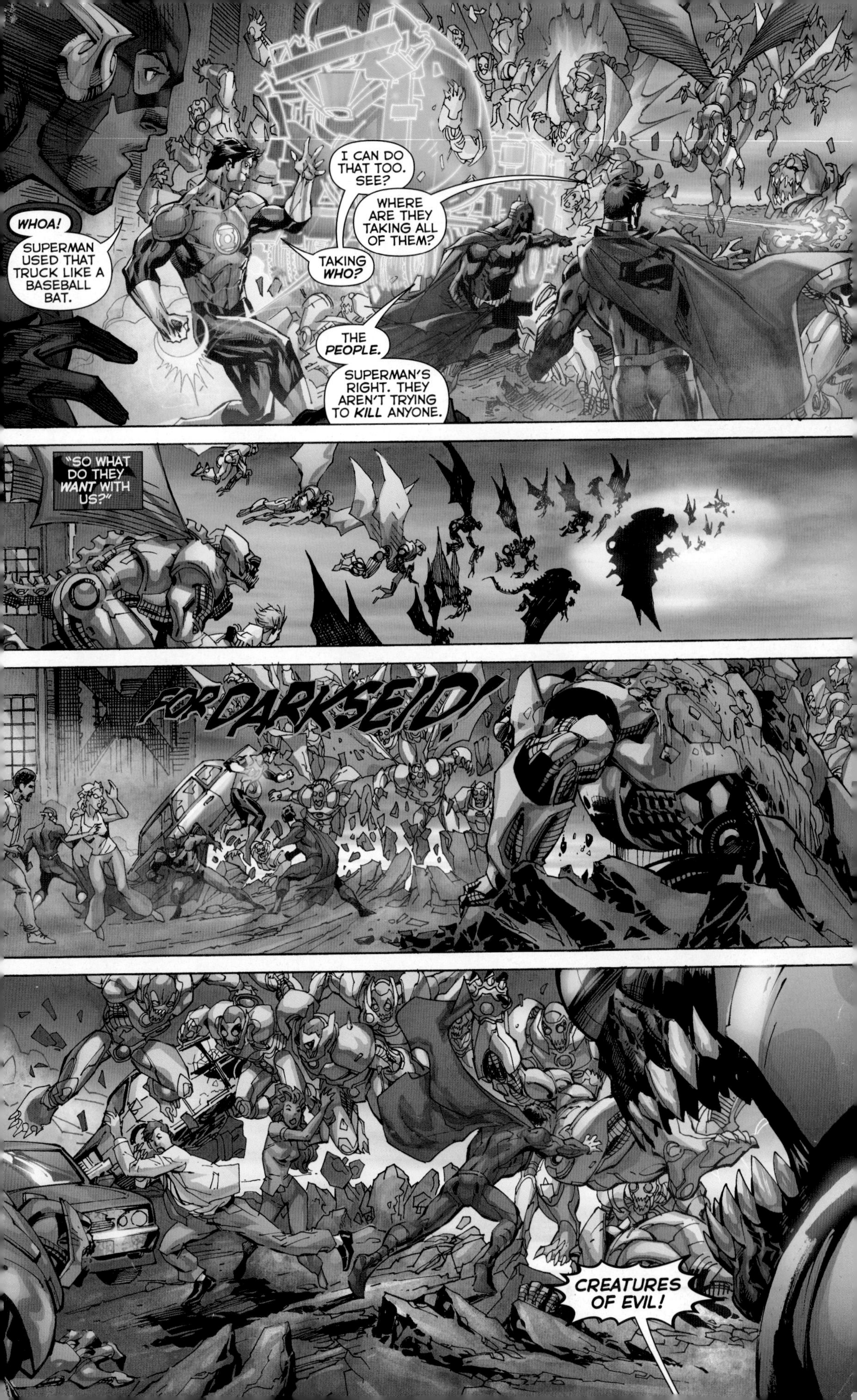
WHOA!
SUPERMAN USED THAT TRUCK LIKE A BASEBALL BAT.
I CAN DO THAT TOO. SEE?
TAKING WHO?
WHERE ARE THEY TAKING ALL OF THEM?
THE PEOPLE.
SUPERMAN'S RIGHT. THEY AREN'T TRYING TO KILL ANYONE.
"SO WHAT DO THEY WANT WITH US?"
FOR DARKSEID!
CREATURES OF EVIL!

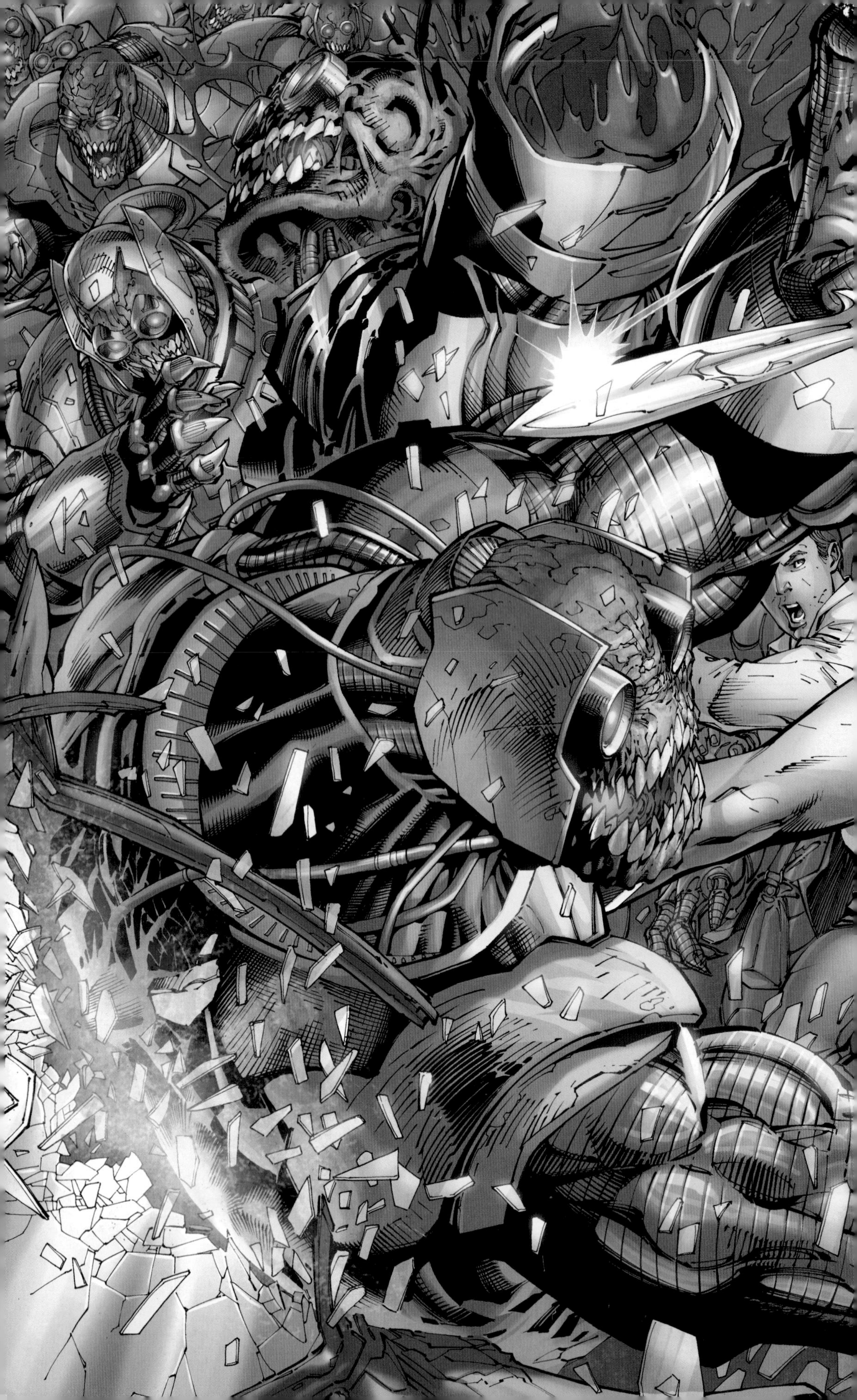

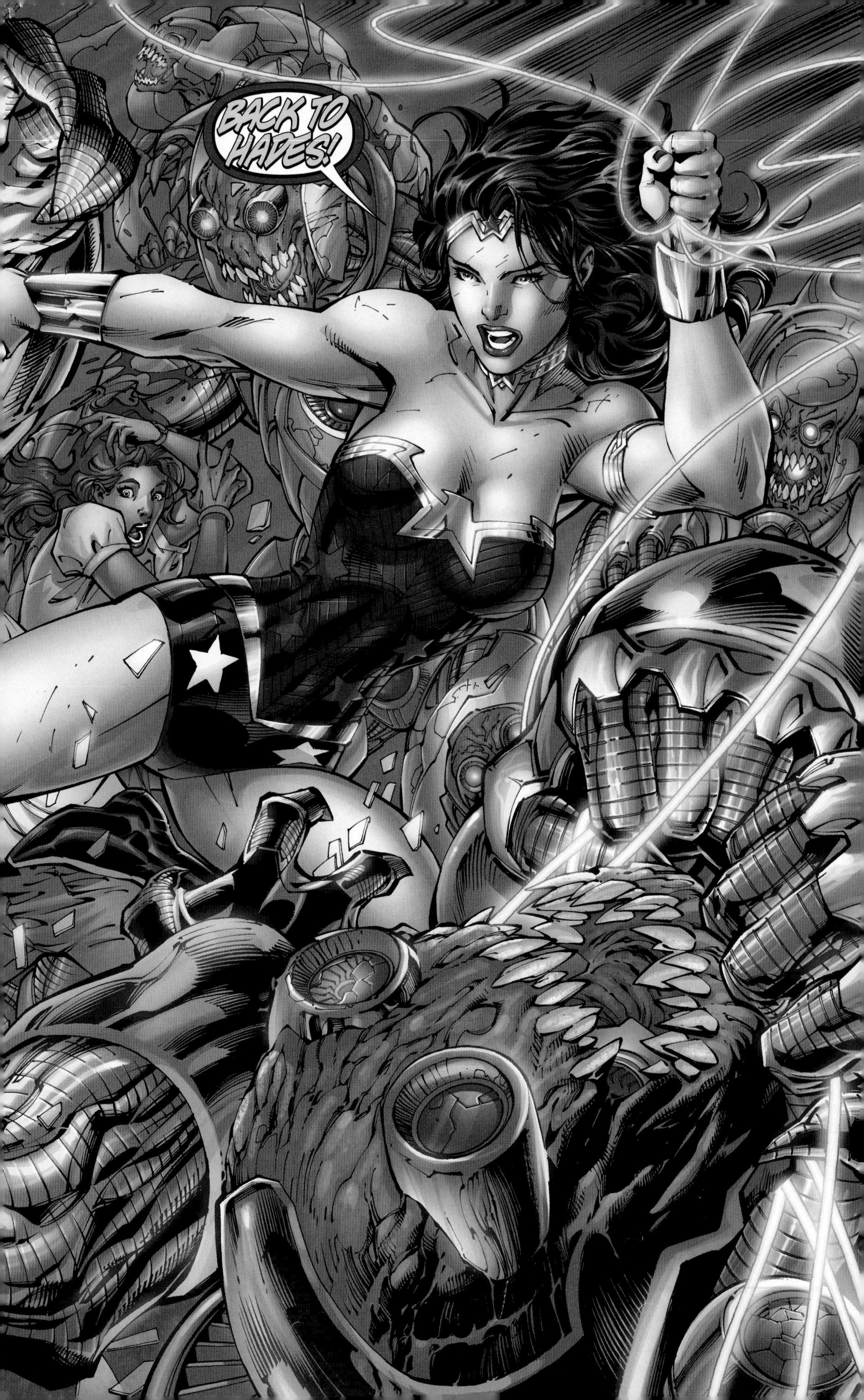
BACK TO HADES!

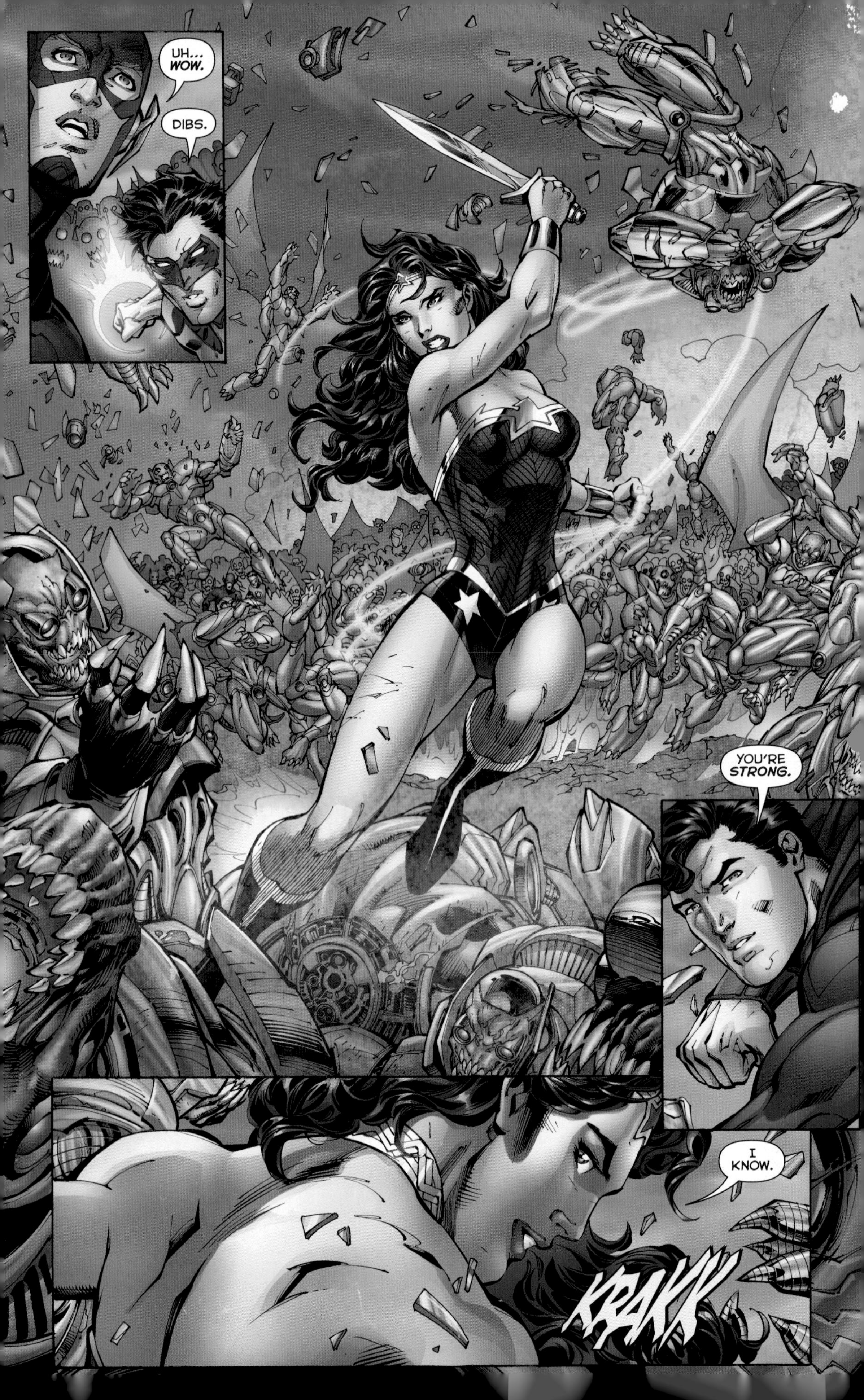
UH... WOW.
DIBS.
YOU'RE STRONG.
I KNOW.
KRAKK

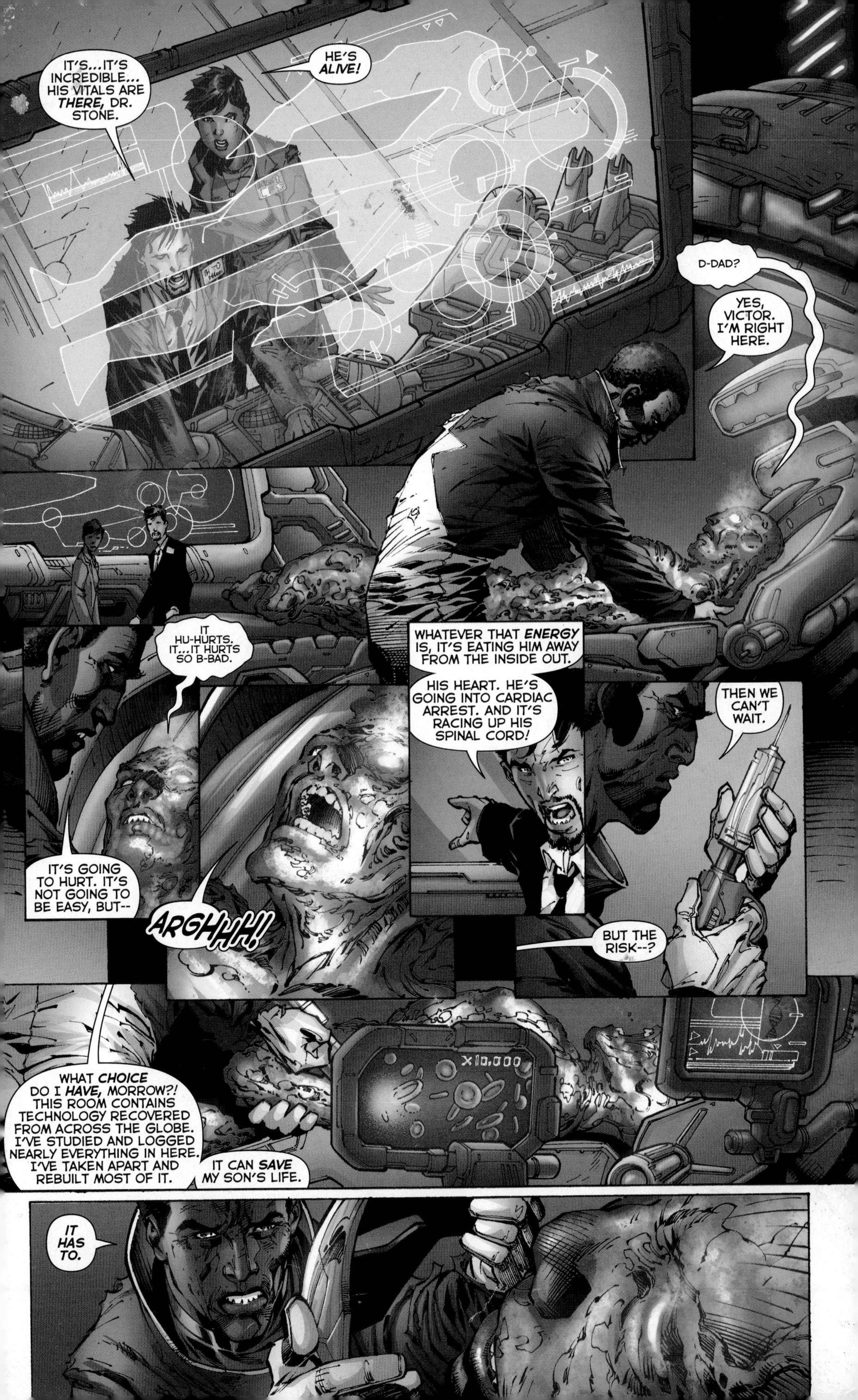
IT'S...IT'S INCREDIBLE... HIS VITALS ARE THERE, DR. STONE.
HE'S ALIVE!
D-DAD?
YES, VICTOR. I'M RIGHT HERE.
IT HU-HURTS. IT...IT HURTS SO B-BAD.
IT'S GOING TO HURT. IT'S NOT GOING TO BE EASY, BUT--
ARGHHH!
WHATEVER THAT ENERGY IS, IT'S EATING HIM AWAY FROM THE INSIDE OUT.
HIS HEART. HE'S GOING INTO CARDIAC ARREST. AND IT'S RACING UP HIS SPINAL CORD!
THEN WE CAN'T WAIT.
BUT THE RISK--?
X10,000
WHAT CHOICE DO I HAVE, MORROW?! THIS ROOM CONTAINS TECHNOLOGY RECOVERED FROM ACROSS THE GLOBE. I'VE STUDIED AND LOGGED NEARLY EVERYTHING IN HERE. I'VE TAKEN APART AND REBUILT MOST OF IT.
IT CAN SAVE MY SON'S LIFE.
IT HAS TO.

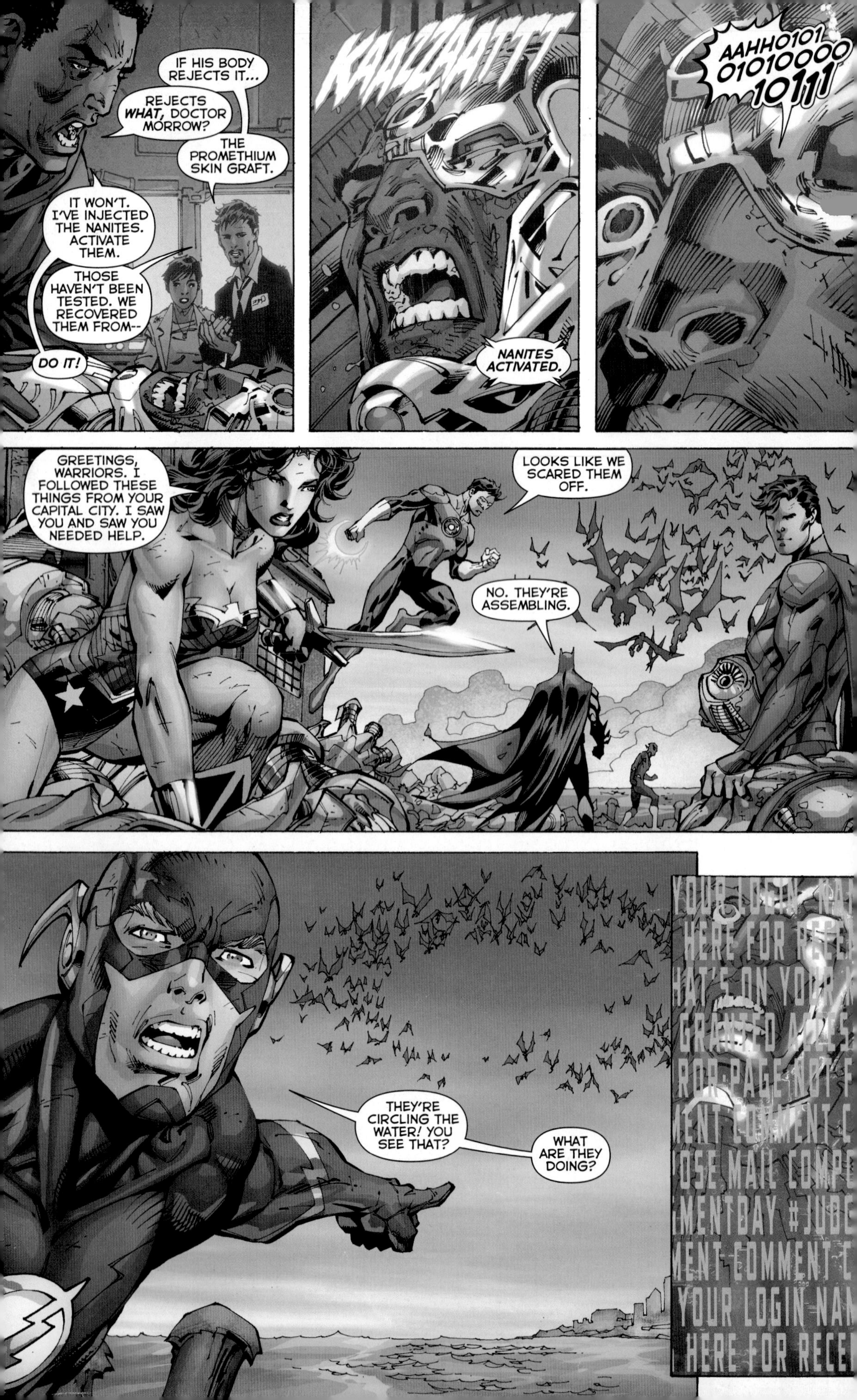
IF HIS BODY REJECTS IT...
REJECTS WHAT, DOCTOR MORROW?
THE PROMETHIUM SKIN GRAFT.
IT WON'T. I'VE INJECTED THE NANITES. ACTIVATE THEM.
THOSE HAVEN'T BEEN TESTED. WE RECOVERED THEM FROM--
DO IT!
KAAZZAATTT
NANITES ACTIVATED.
AAHH0101 01010000 10111
GREETINGS, WARRIORS. I FOLLOWED THESE THINGS FROM YOUR CAPITAL CITY. I SAW YOU AND SAW YOU NEEDED HELP.
LOOKS LIKE WE SCARED THEM OFF.
NO. THEY'RE ASSEMBLING.
THEY'RE CIRCLING THE WATER! YOU SEE THAT?
WHAT ARE THEY DOING?

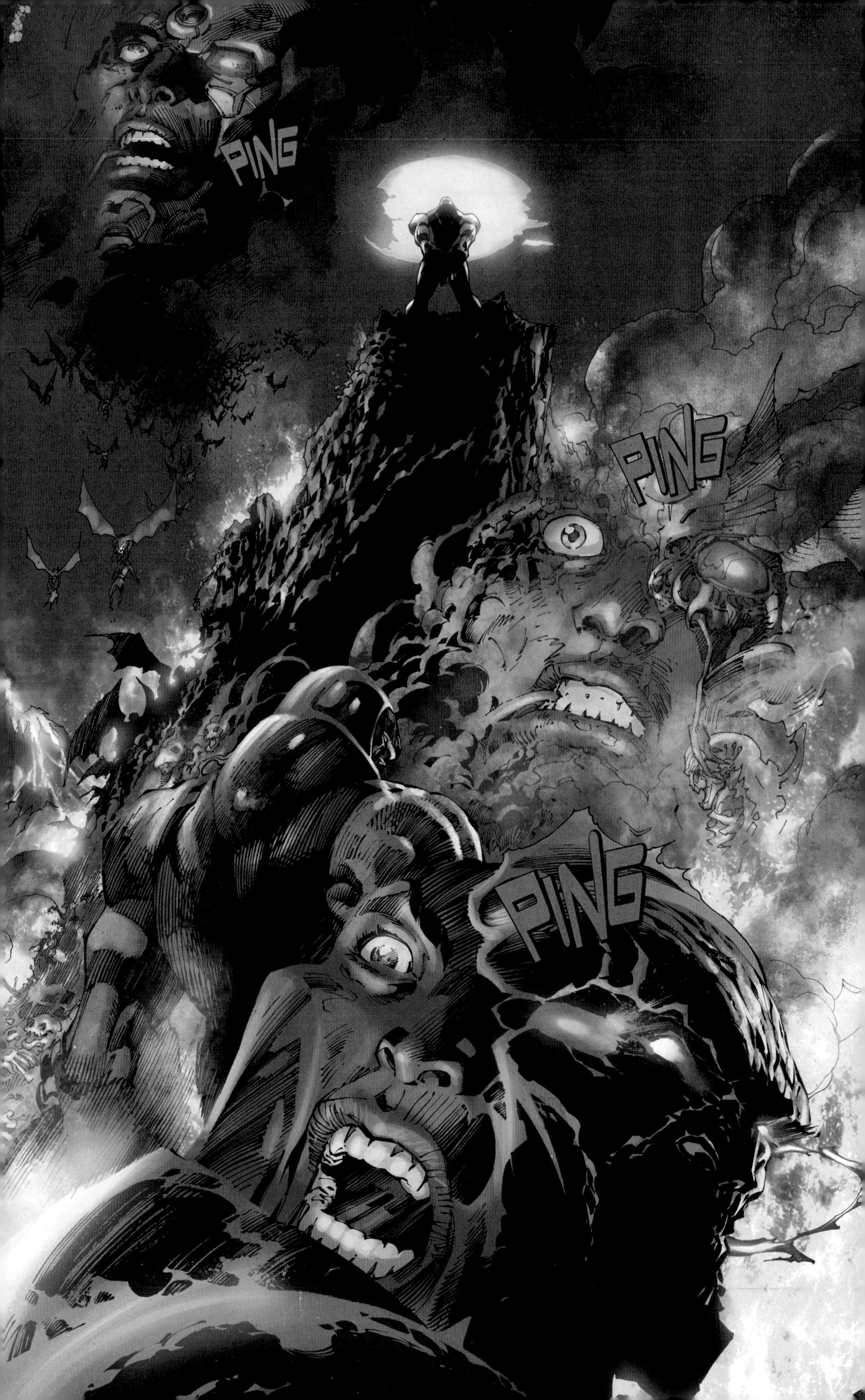
PING
PING
PING

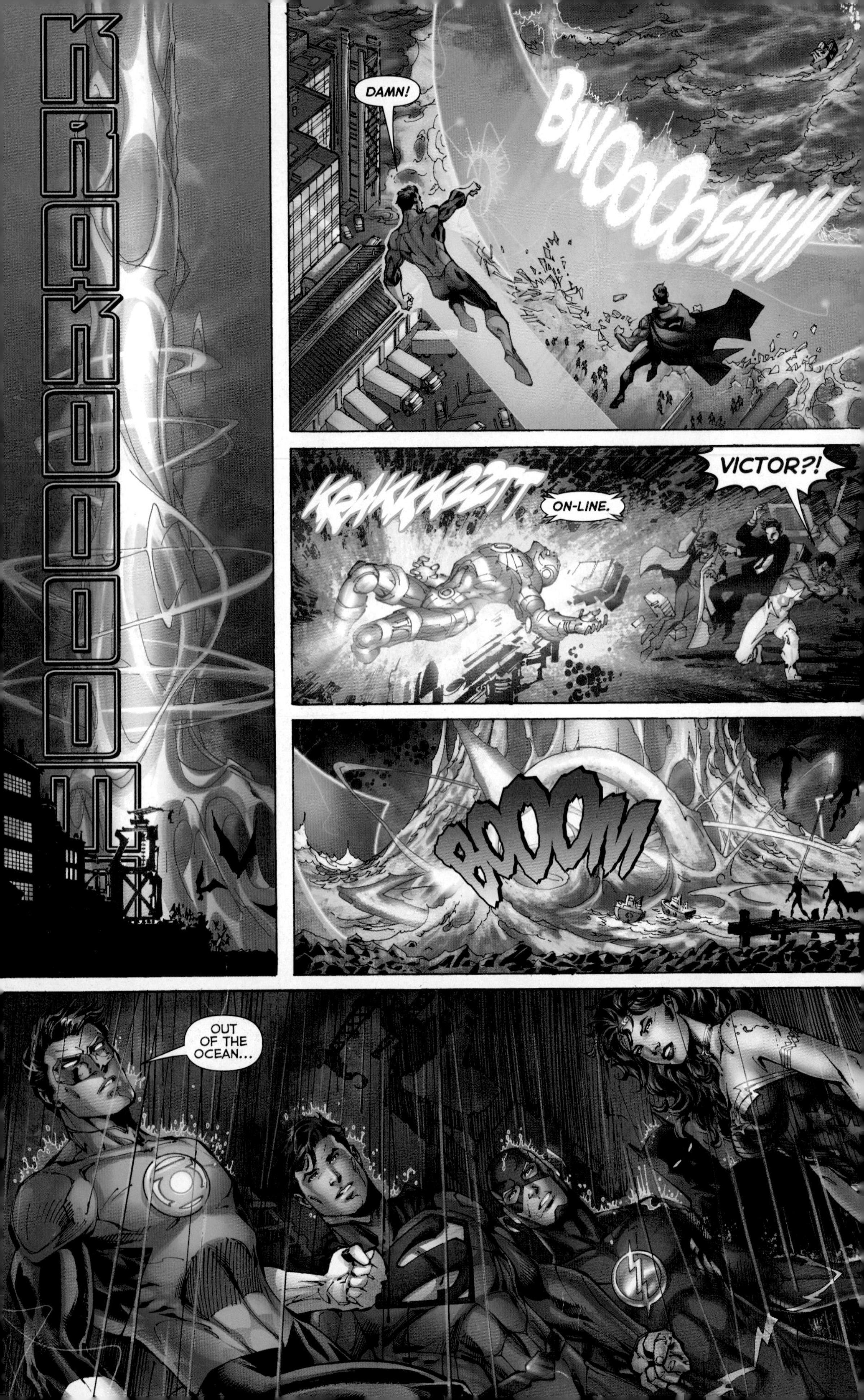

DAMN!
ON-LINE.
VICTOR?!
BOOOM
OUT OF THE OCEAN...

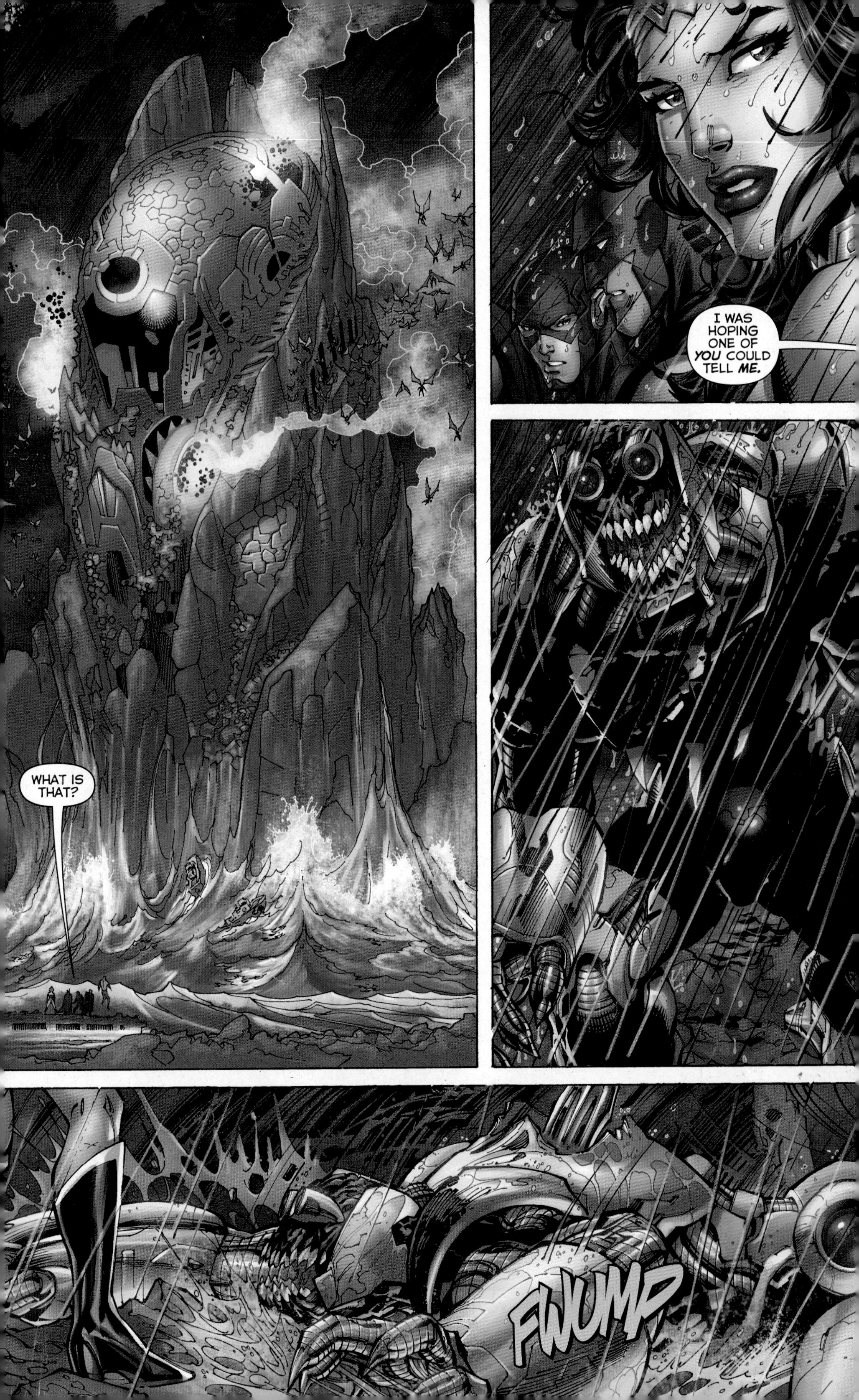
WHAT IS THAT?
I WAS HOPING ONE OF YOU COULD TELL ME.
FWUMP

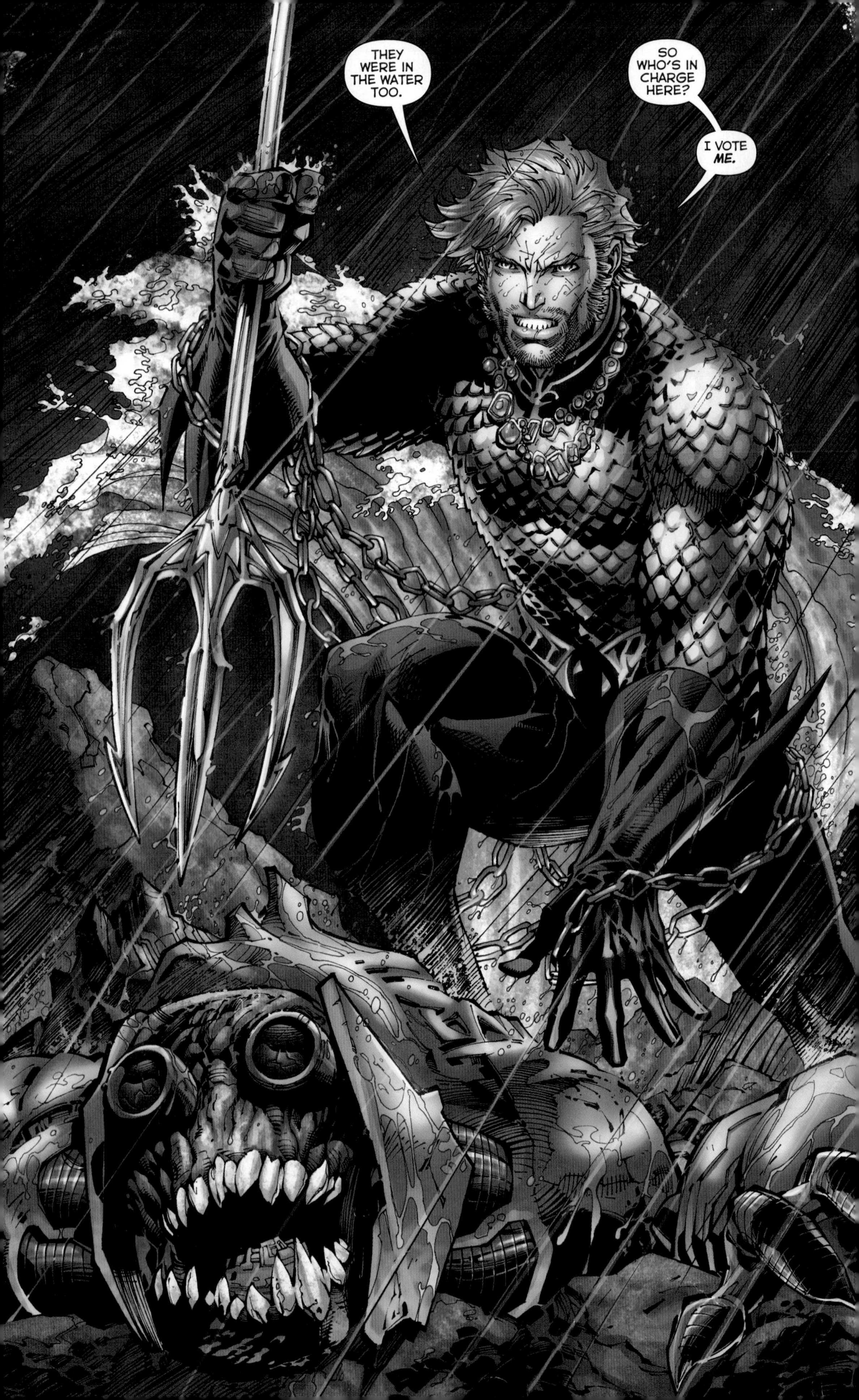
THEY WERE IN THE WATER TOO.
SO WHO'S IN CHARGE HERE?
I VOTE *ME.*

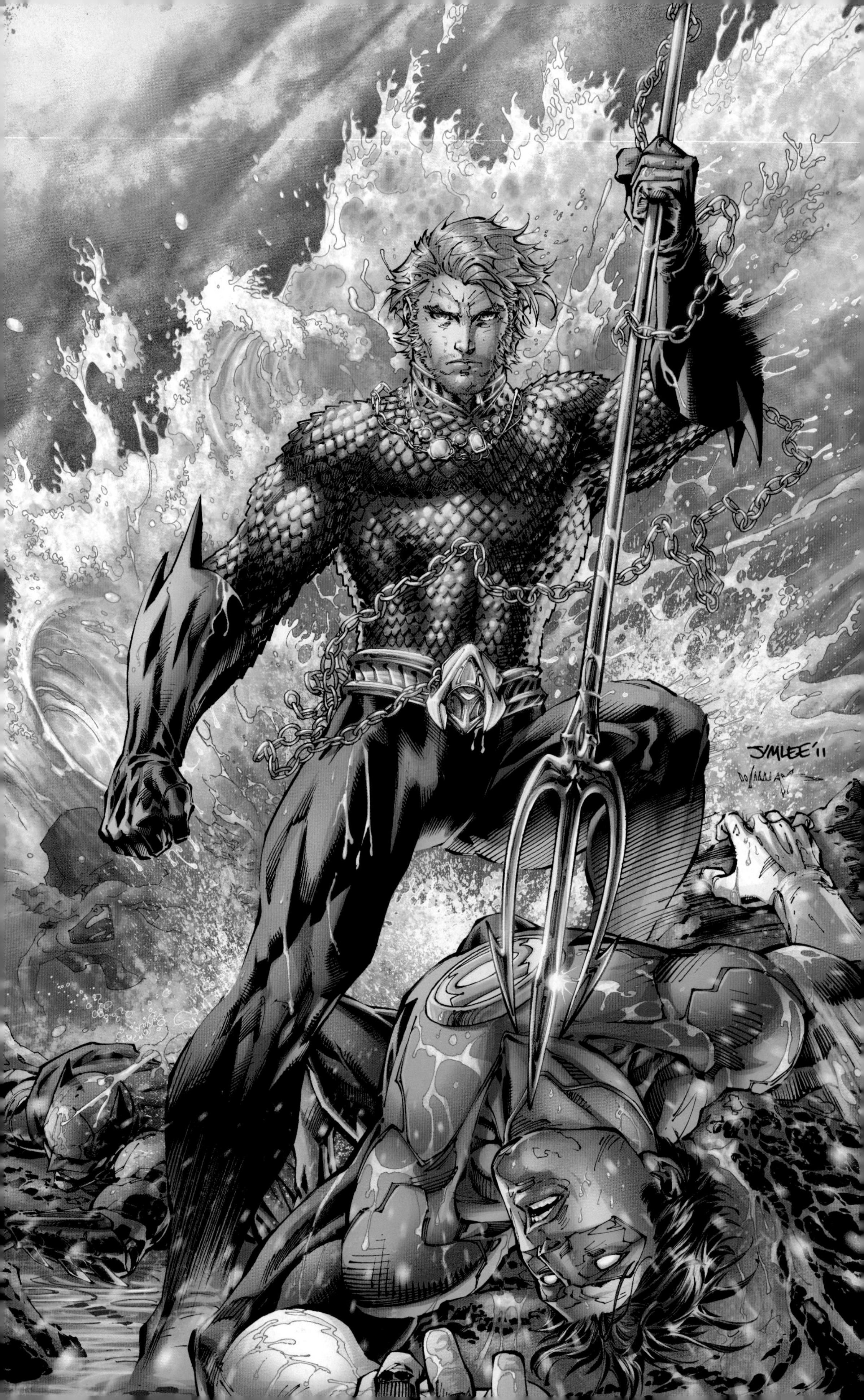

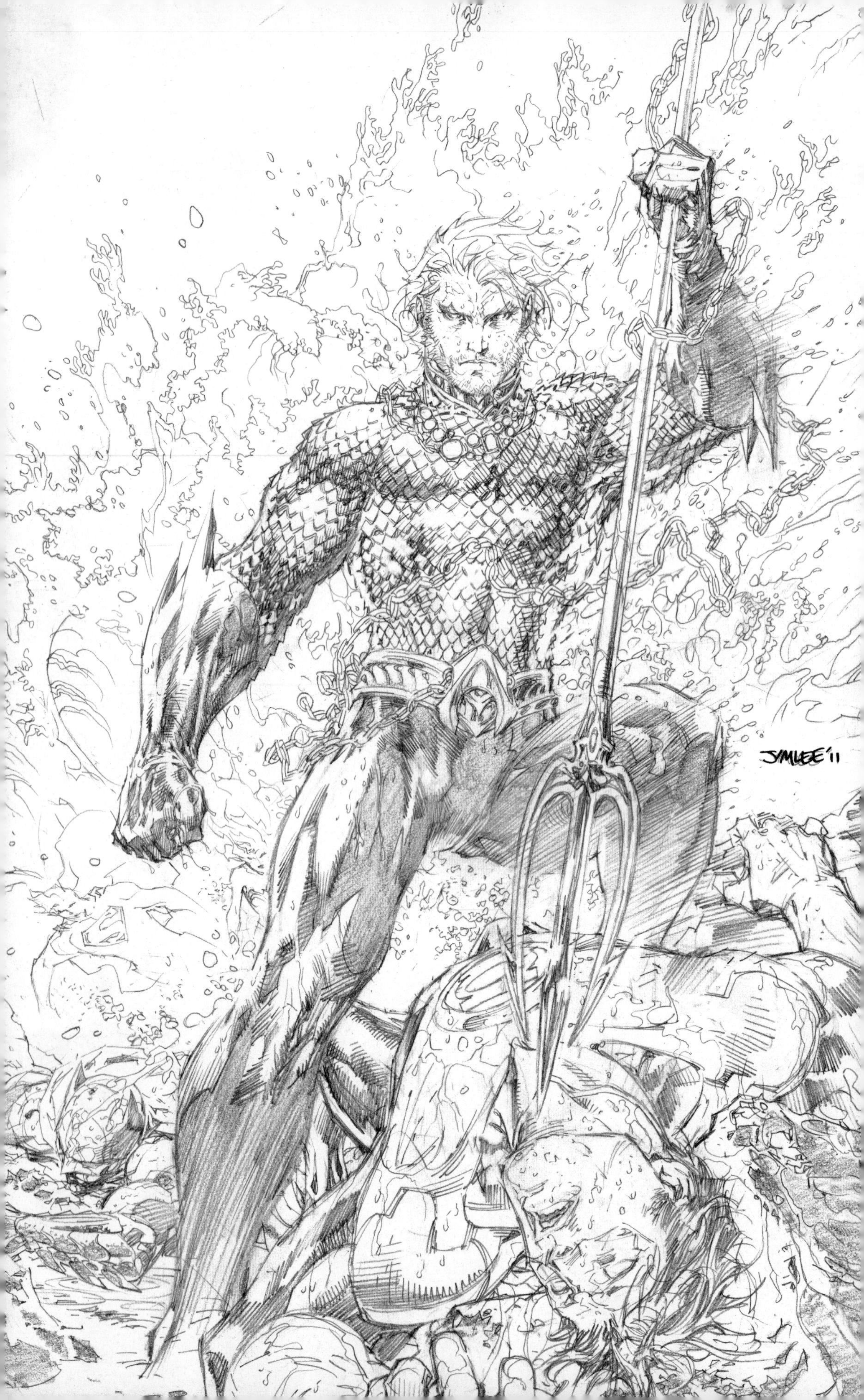
JIMLEE '11

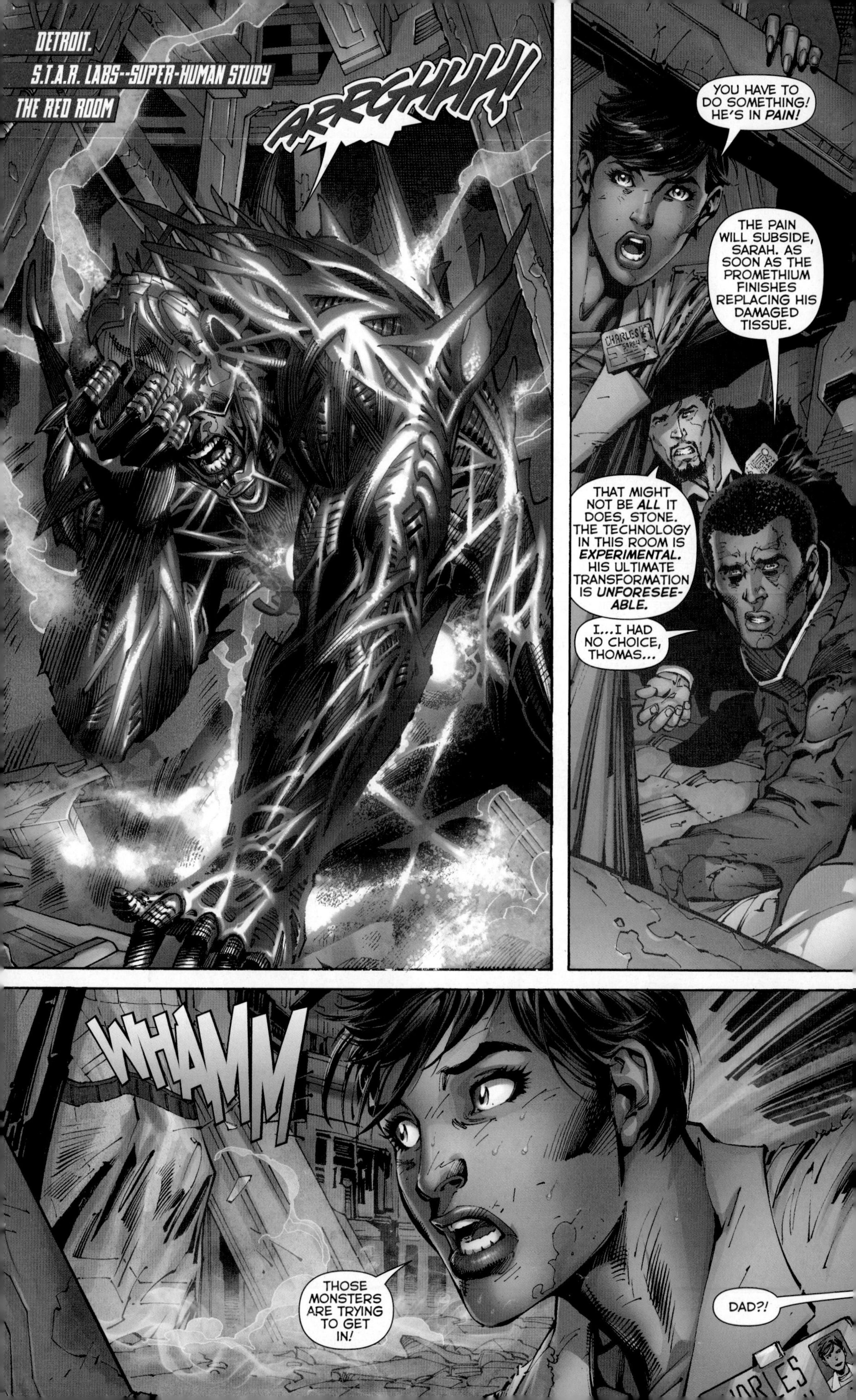
DETROIT.
S.T.A.R. LABS--SUPER-HUMAN STUDY
THE RED ROOM
ARRGHHH!
YOU HAVE TO DO SOMETHING! HE'S IN PAIN!
THE PAIN WILL SUBSIDE, SARAH. AS SOON AS THE PROMETHIUM FINISHES REPLACING HIS DAMAGED TISSUE.
THAT MIGHT NOT BE ALL IT DOES, STONE. THE TECHNOLOGY IN THIS ROOM IS EXPERIMENTAL. HIS ULTIMATE TRANSFORMATION IS UNFORESEE-ABLE.
I...I HAD NO CHOICE, THOMAS...
WHAMM
THOSE MONSTERS ARE TRYING TO GET IN!
DAD?!

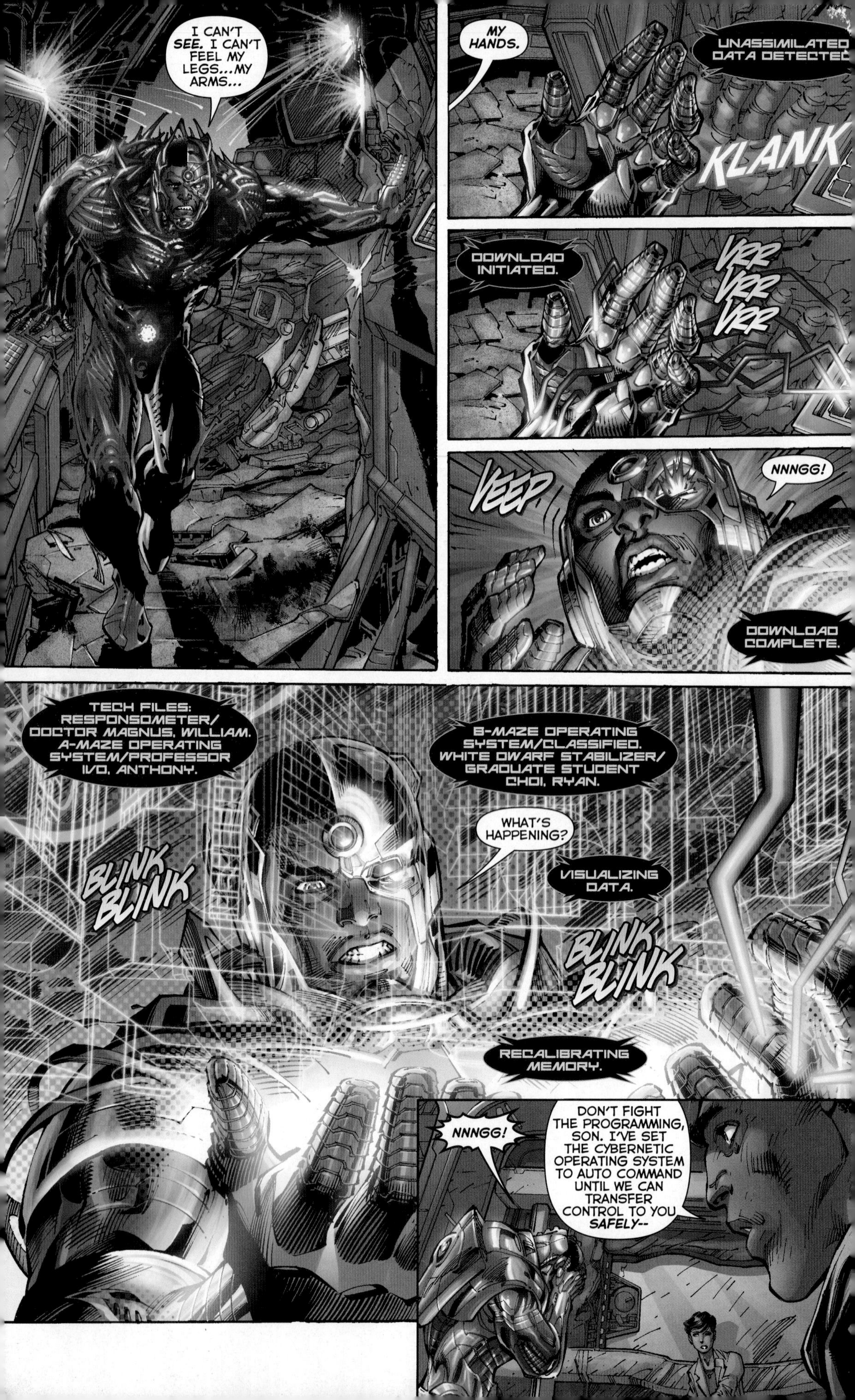
I CAN'T SEE. I CAN'T FEEL MY LEGS...MY ARMS...
MY HANDS.
UNASSIMILATED DATA DETECTED
KLANK
DOWNLOAD INITIATED.
VRR VRR VRR
VEEP
NNNGG!
DOWNLOAD COMPLETE.
TECH FILES: RESPONSOMETER/ DOCTOR MAGNUS, WILLIAM. A-MAZE OPERATING SYSTEM/PROFESSOR IVO, ANTHONY.
B-MAZE OPERATING SYSTEM/CLASSIFIED. WHITE DWARF STABILIZER/ GRADUATE STUDENT CHOI, RYAN.
WHAT'S HAPPENING?
VISUALIZING DATA.
BLINK BLINK
BLINK BLINK
RECALIBRATING MEMORY.
NNNGG!
DON'T FIGHT THE PROGRAMMING, SON. I'VE SET THE CYBERNETIC OPERATING SYSTEM TO AUTO COMMAND UNTIL WE CAN TRANSFER CONTROL TO YOU *SAFELY*--

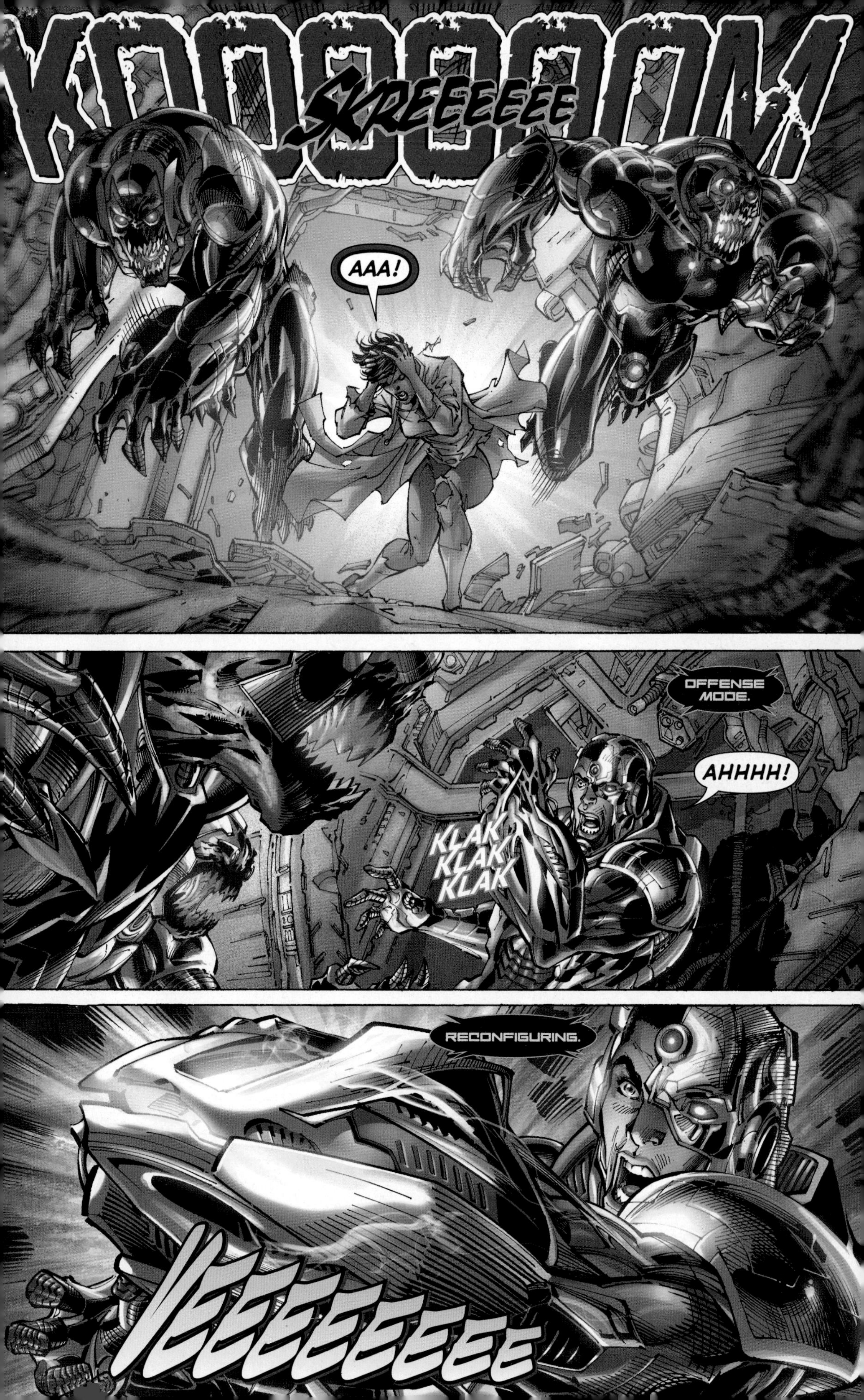
KOOOOOM!
SKREEEEEEE
AAA!
OFFENSE MODE.
AHHHH!
KLAK KLAK KLAK
RECONFIGURING.
VEEEEEEEE

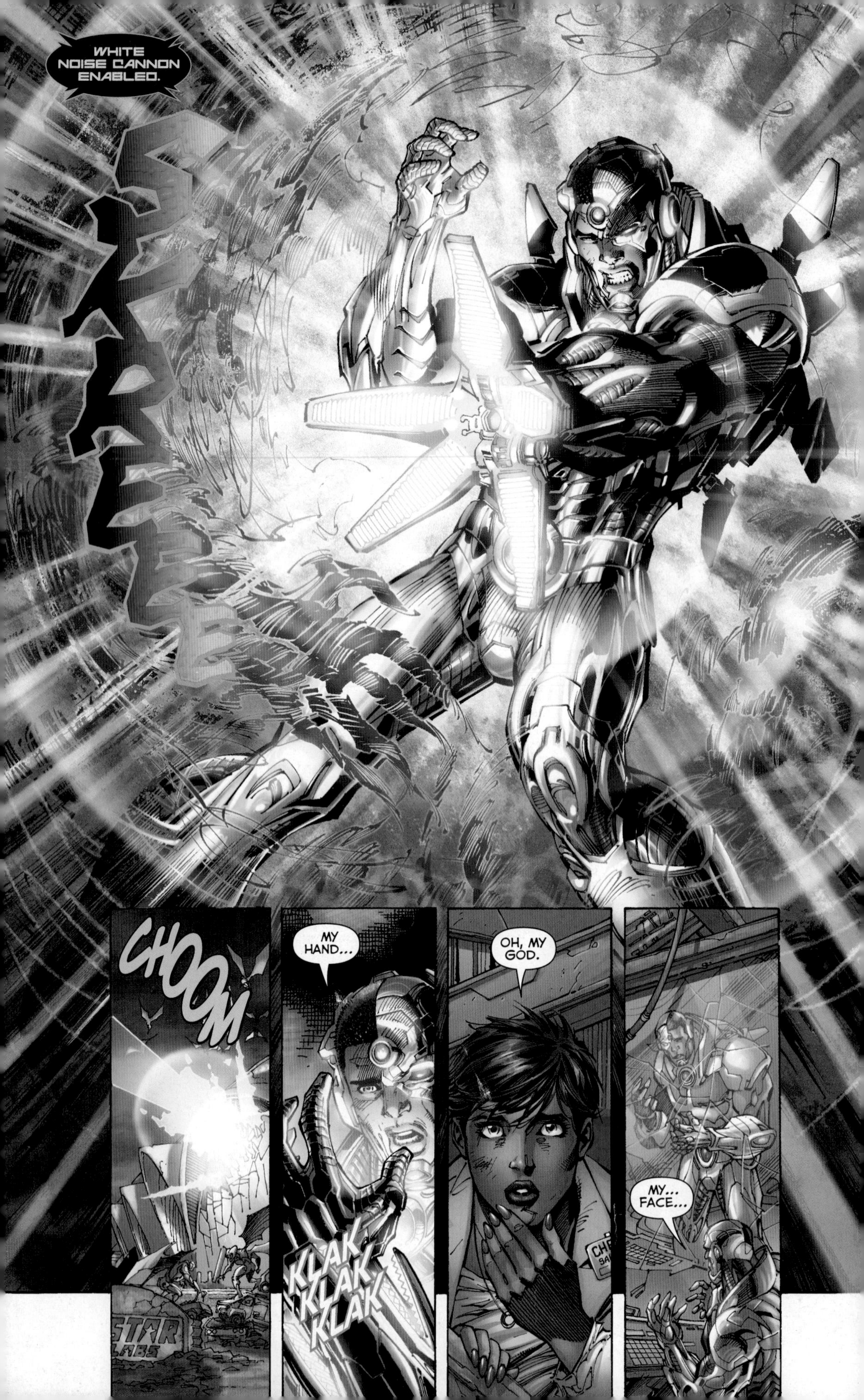
WHITE NOISE CANNON ENABLED.
CHOOM
STAR LABS
MY HAND...
KLAK KLAK KLAK
OH, MY GOD.
MY... FACE...

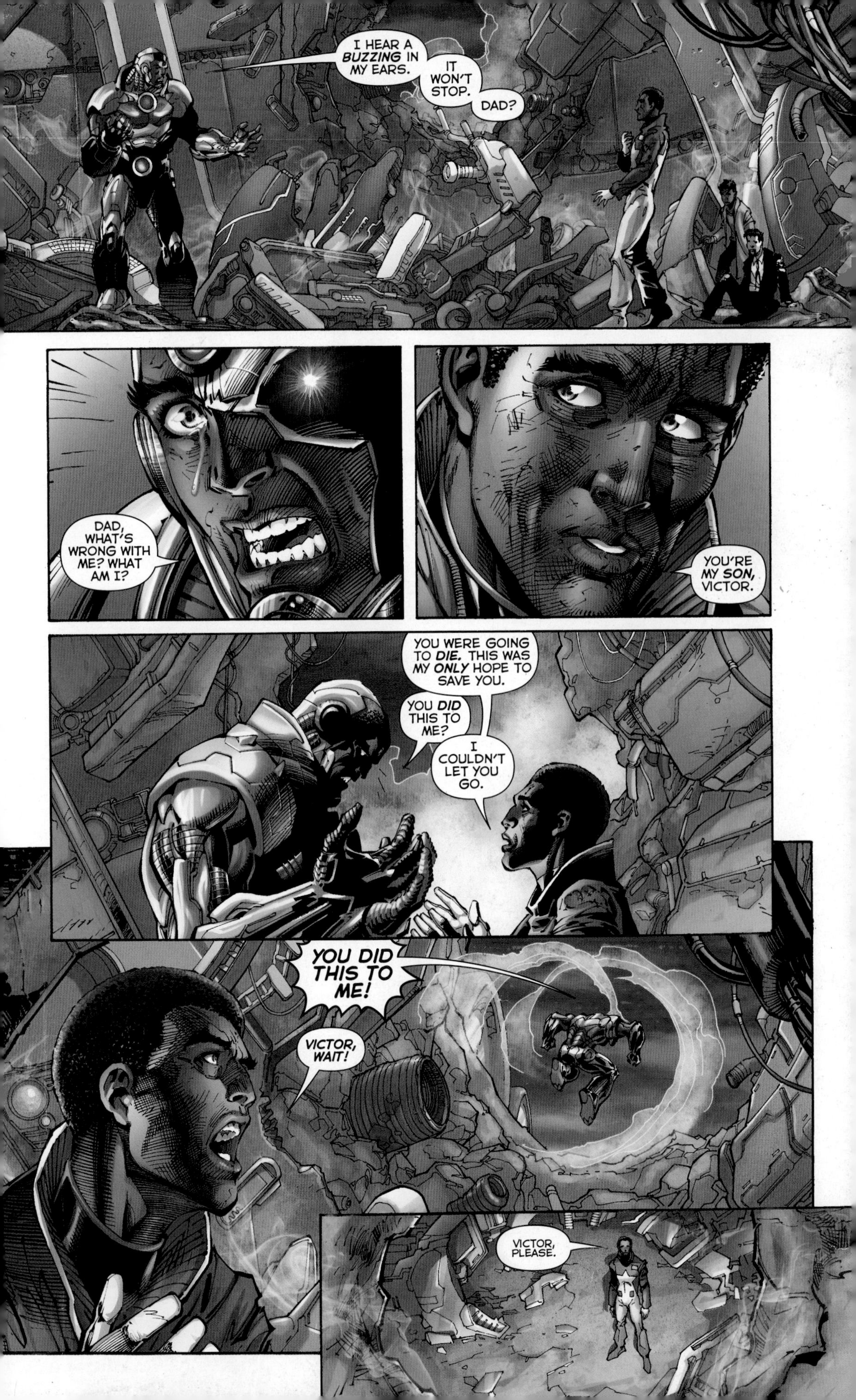

I HEAR A *BUZZING* IN MY EARS.
IT WON'T STOP.
DAD?
DAD, WHAT'S WRONG WITH ME? WHAT AM I?
YOU'RE MY *SON,* VICTOR.
YOU WERE GOING TO *DIE.* THIS WAS MY *ONLY* HOPE TO SAVE YOU.
YOU *DID* THIS TO ME?
I COULDN'T LET YOU GO.
YOU DID THIS TO ME!
VICTOR, WAIT!
VICTOR, PLEASE.

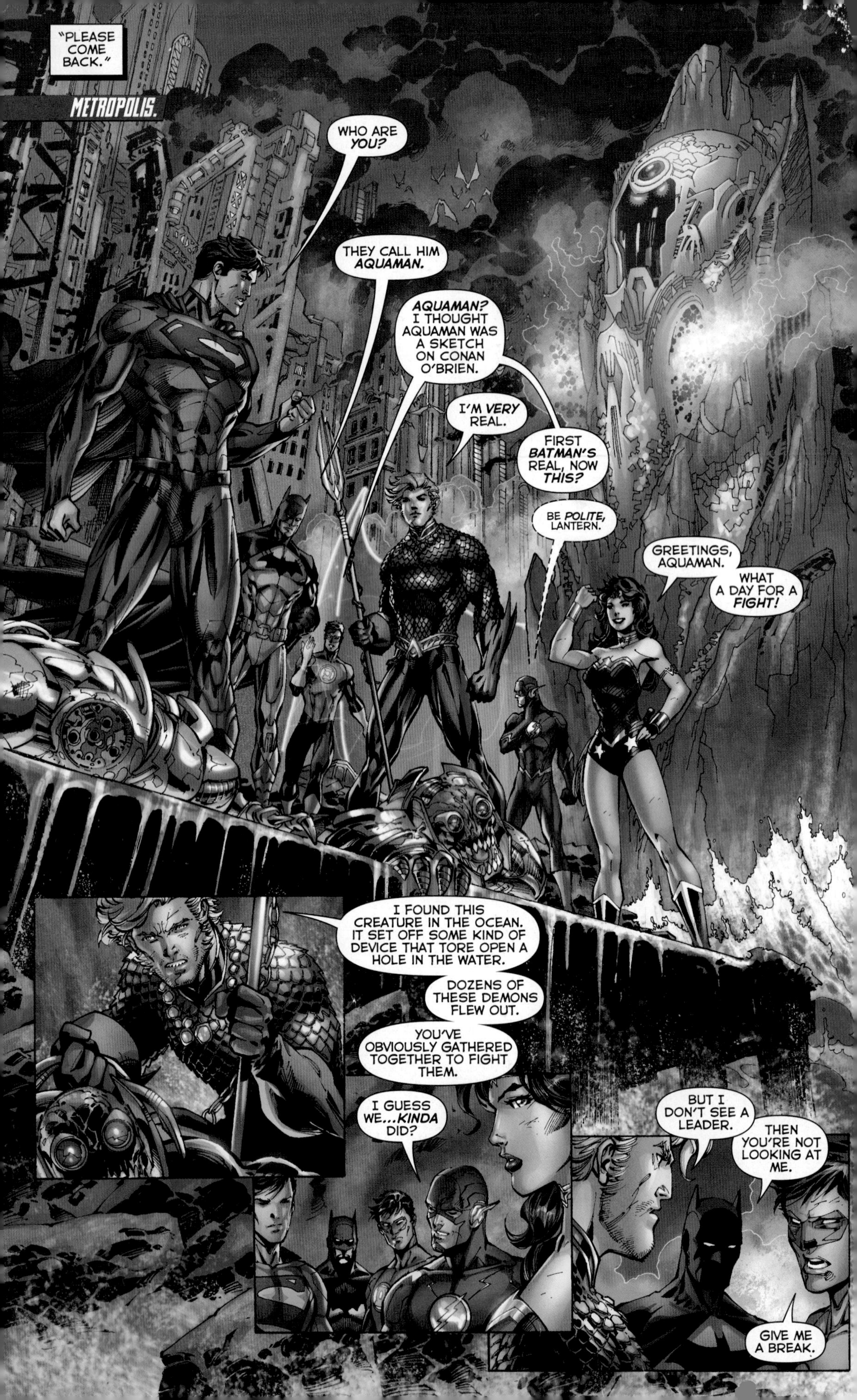
"PLEASE COME BACK."
METROPOLIS.
WHO ARE YOU?
THEY CALL HIM AQUAMAN.
AQUAMAN? I THOUGHT AQUAMAN WAS A SKETCH ON CONAN O'BRIEN.
I'M VERY REAL.
FIRST BATMAN'S REAL, NOW THIS?
BE POLITE, LANTERN.
GREETINGS, AQUAMAN.
WHAT A DAY FOR A FIGHT!
I FOUND THIS CREATURE IN THE OCEAN. IT SET OFF SOME KIND OF DEVICE THAT TORE OPEN A HOLE IN THE WATER.
DOZENS OF THESE DEMONS FLEW OUT.
YOU'VE OBVIOUSLY GATHERED TOGETHER TO FIGHT THEM.
I GUESS WE...KINDA DID?
BUT I DON'T SEE A LEADER.
THEN YOU'RE NOT LOOKING AT ME.
GIVE ME A BREAK.

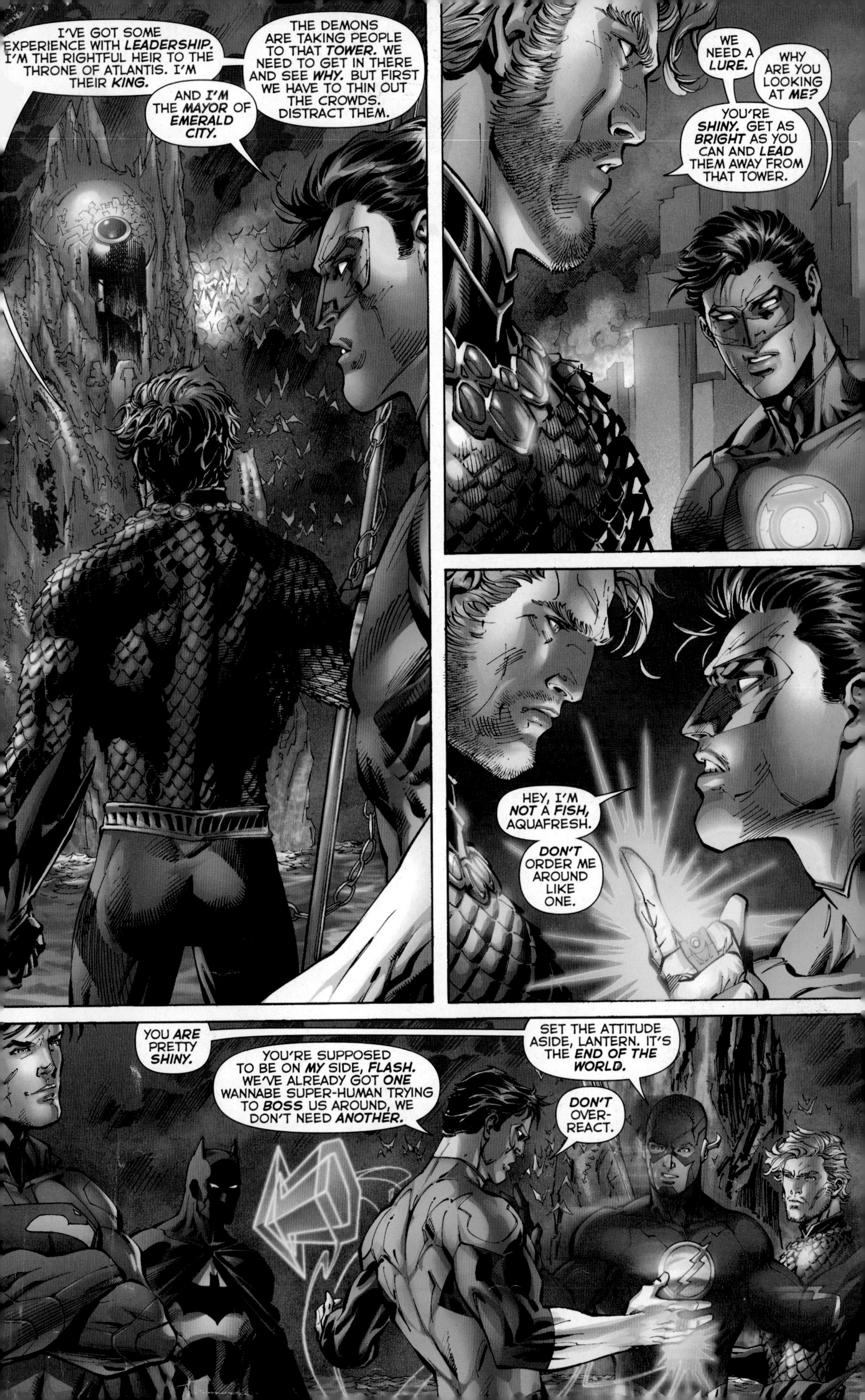
I'VE GOT SOME EXPERIENCE WITH LEADERSHIP. I'M THE RIGHTFUL HEIR TO THE THRONE OF ATLANTIS. I'M THEIR KING.
THE DEMONS ARE TAKING PEOPLE TO THAT TOWER. WE NEED TO GET IN THERE AND SEE WHY. BUT FIRST WE HAVE TO THIN OUT THE CROWDS. DISTRACT THEM.
AND I'M THE MAYOR OF EMERALD CITY.
WE NEED A LURE.
WHY ARE YOU LOOKING AT ME?
YOU'RE SHINY. GET AS BRIGHT AS YOU CAN AND LEAD THEM AWAY FROM THAT TOWER.
HEY, I'M NOT A FISH, AQUAFRESH.
DON'T ORDER ME AROUND LIKE ONE.
YOU ARE PRETTY SHINY.
YOU'RE SUPPOSED TO BE ON MY SIDE, FLASH. WE'VE ALREADY GOT ONE WANNABE SUPER-HUMAN TRYING TO BOSS US AROUND, WE DON'T NEED ANOTHER.
SET THE ATTITUDE ASIDE, LANTERN. IT'S THE END OF THE WORLD.
DON'T OVER-REACT.

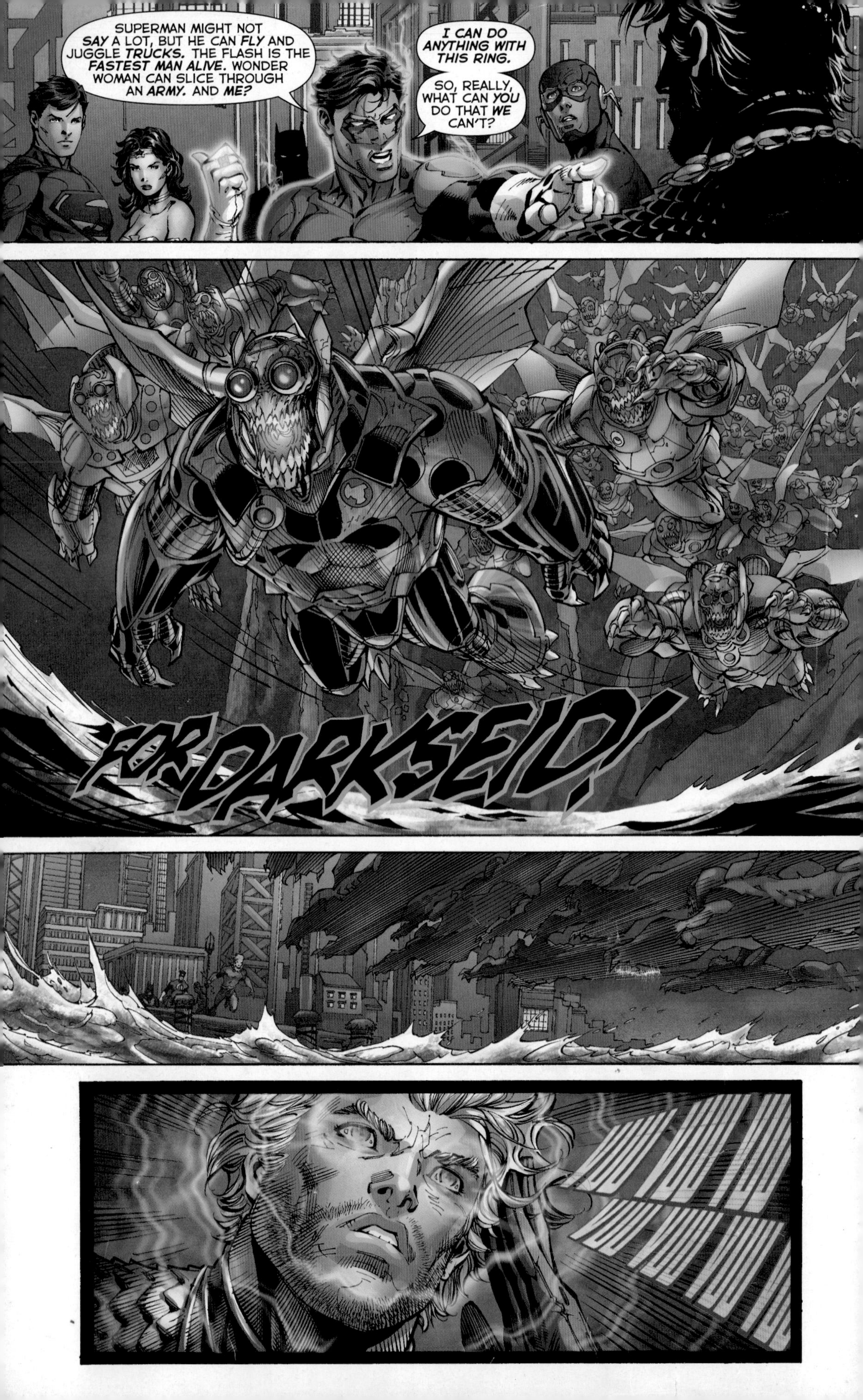
SUPERMAN MIGHT NOT SAY A LOT, BUT HE CAN FLY AND JUGGLE TRUCKS. THE FLASH IS THE FASTEST MAN ALIVE. WONDER WOMAN CAN SLICE THROUGH AN ARMY. AND ME?
I CAN DO ANYTHING WITH THIS RING.
SO, REALLY, WHAT CAN YOU DO THAT WE CAN'T?
FOR DARKSEID!

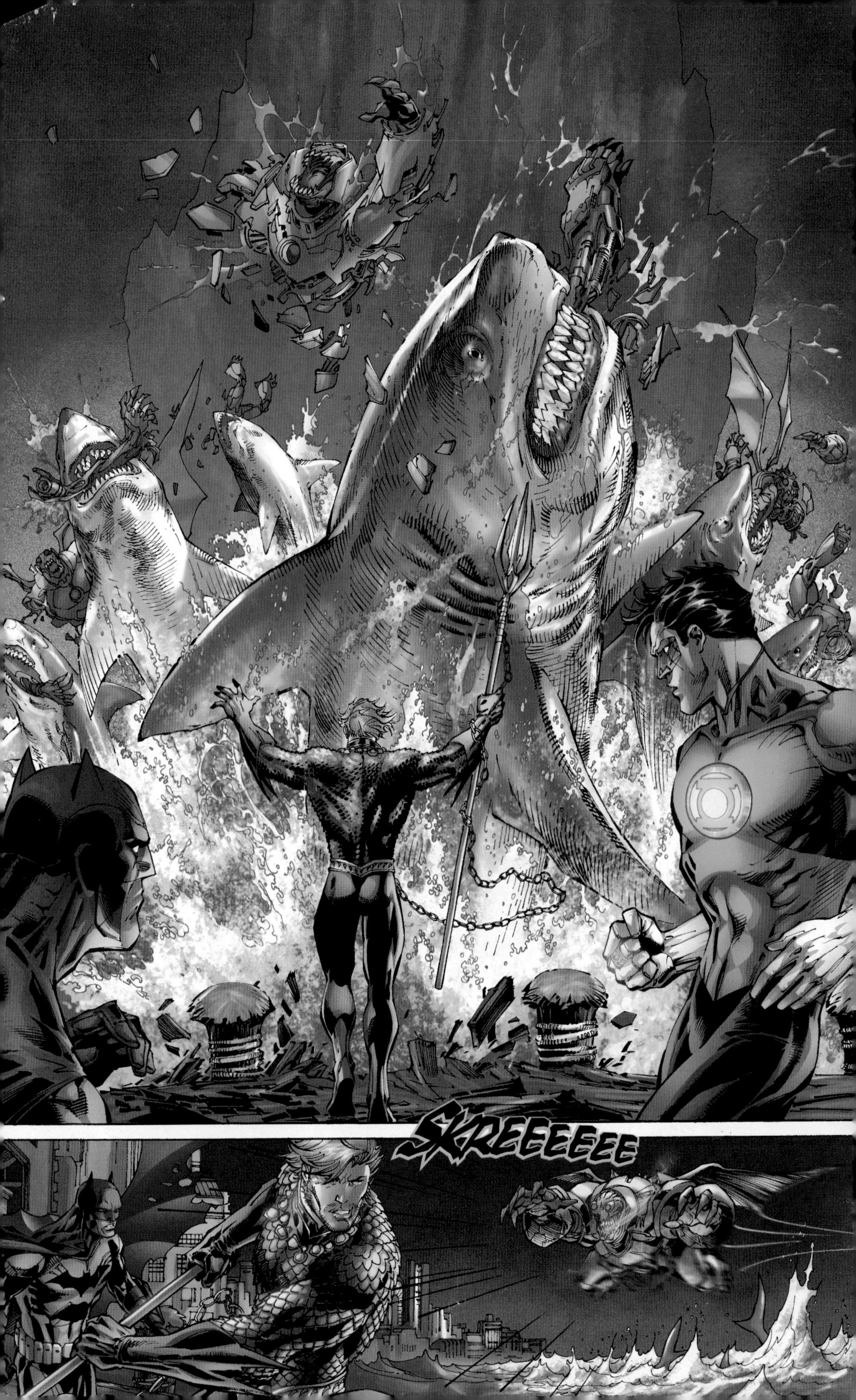
SKREEEEEEE

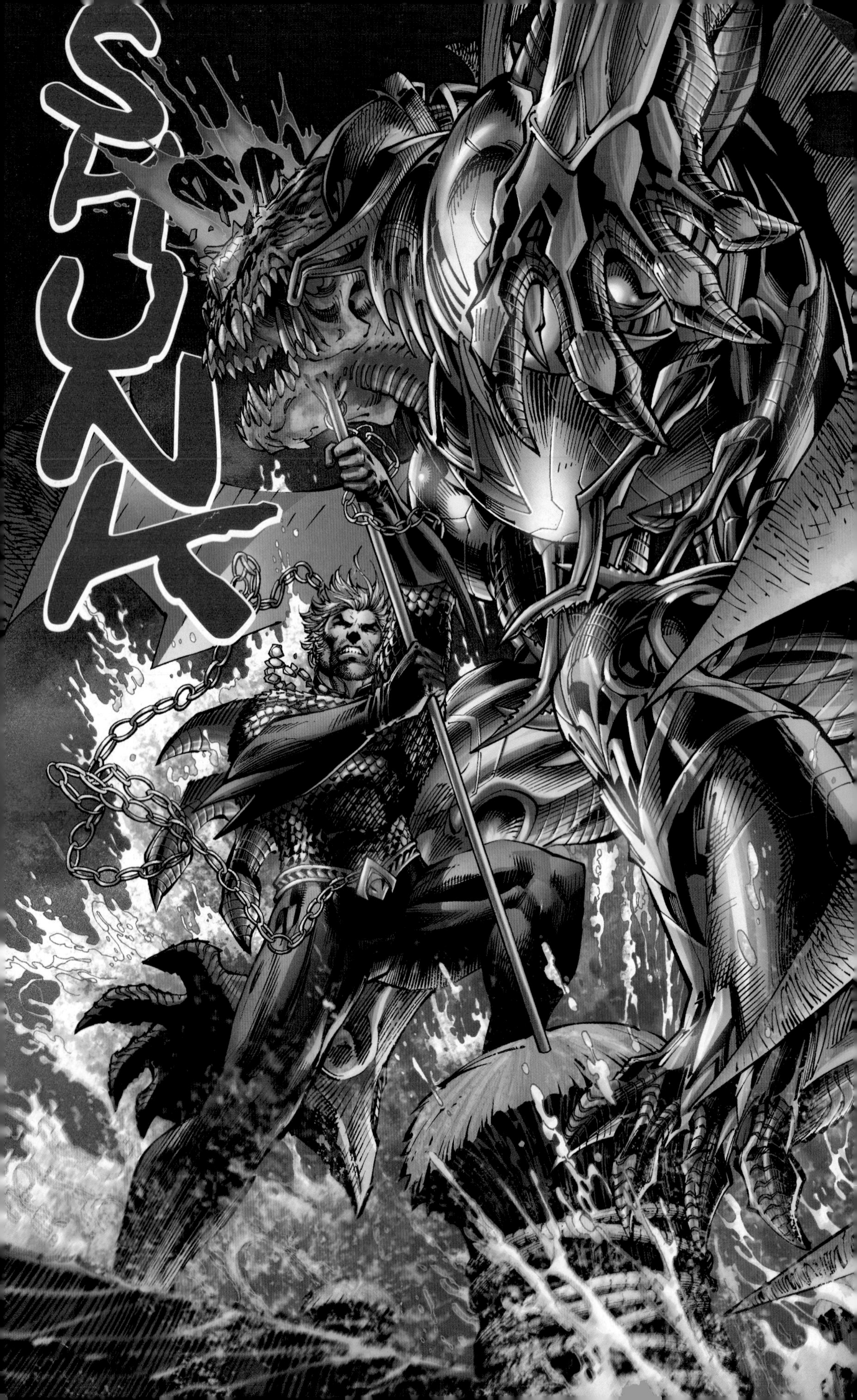
SHUNK

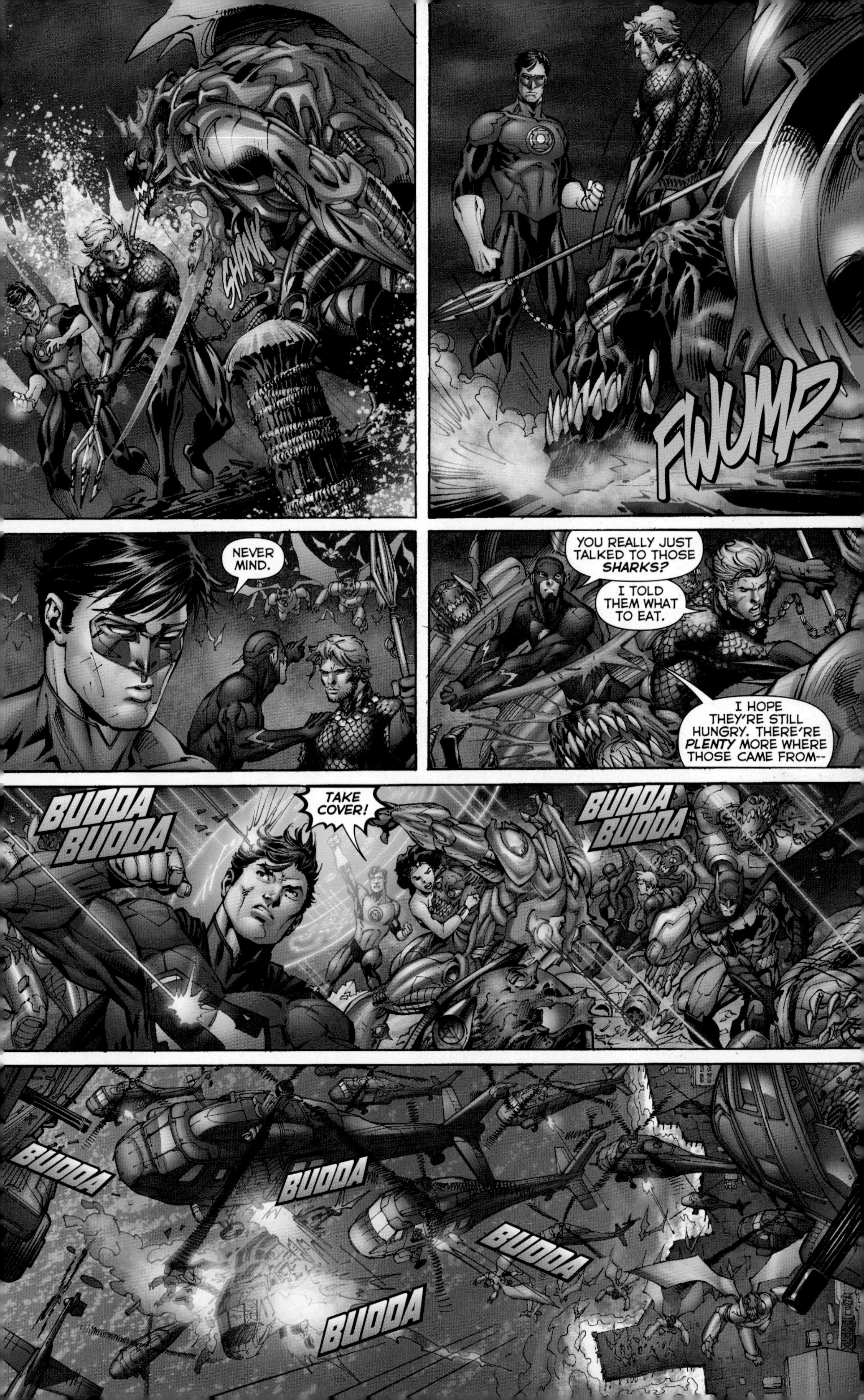
SHANK
FWUMP
NEVER MIND.
YOU REALLY JUST TALKED TO THOSE SHARKS?
I TOLD THEM WHAT TO EAT.
I HOPE THEY'RE STILL HUNGRY. THERE'RE PLENTY MORE WHERE THOSE CAME FROM--
BUDDA BUDDA
TAKE COVER!
BUDDA BUDDA
BUDDA
BUDDA
BUDDA
BUDDA

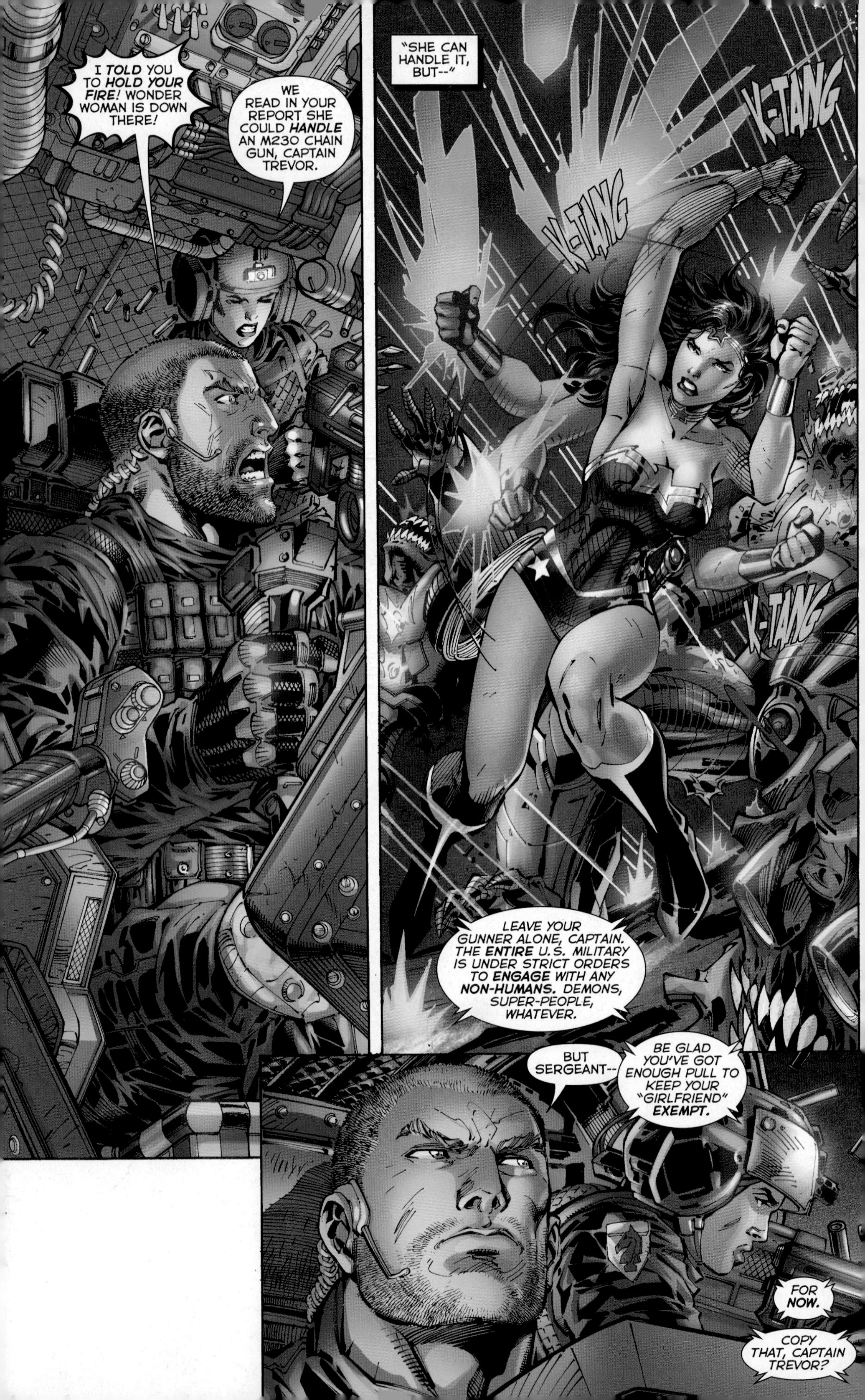
I TOLD YOU TO HOLD YOUR FIRE! WONDER WOMAN IS DOWN THERE!
WE READ IN YOUR REPORT SHE COULD HANDLE AN M230 CHAIN GUN, CAPTAIN TREVOR.
"SHE CAN HANDLE IT, BUT--"
K-TANG
K-TANG
K-TANG
LEAVE YOUR GUNNER ALONE, CAPTAIN. THE ENTIRE U.S. MILITARY IS UNDER STRICT ORDERS TO ENGAGE WITH ANY NON-HUMANS. DEMONS, SUPER-PEOPLE, WHATEVER.
BUT SERGEANT--
BE GLAD YOU'VE GOT ENOUGH PULL TO KEEP YOUR "GIRLFRIEND" EXEMPT.
FOR NOW.
COPY THAT, CAPTAIN TREVOR?

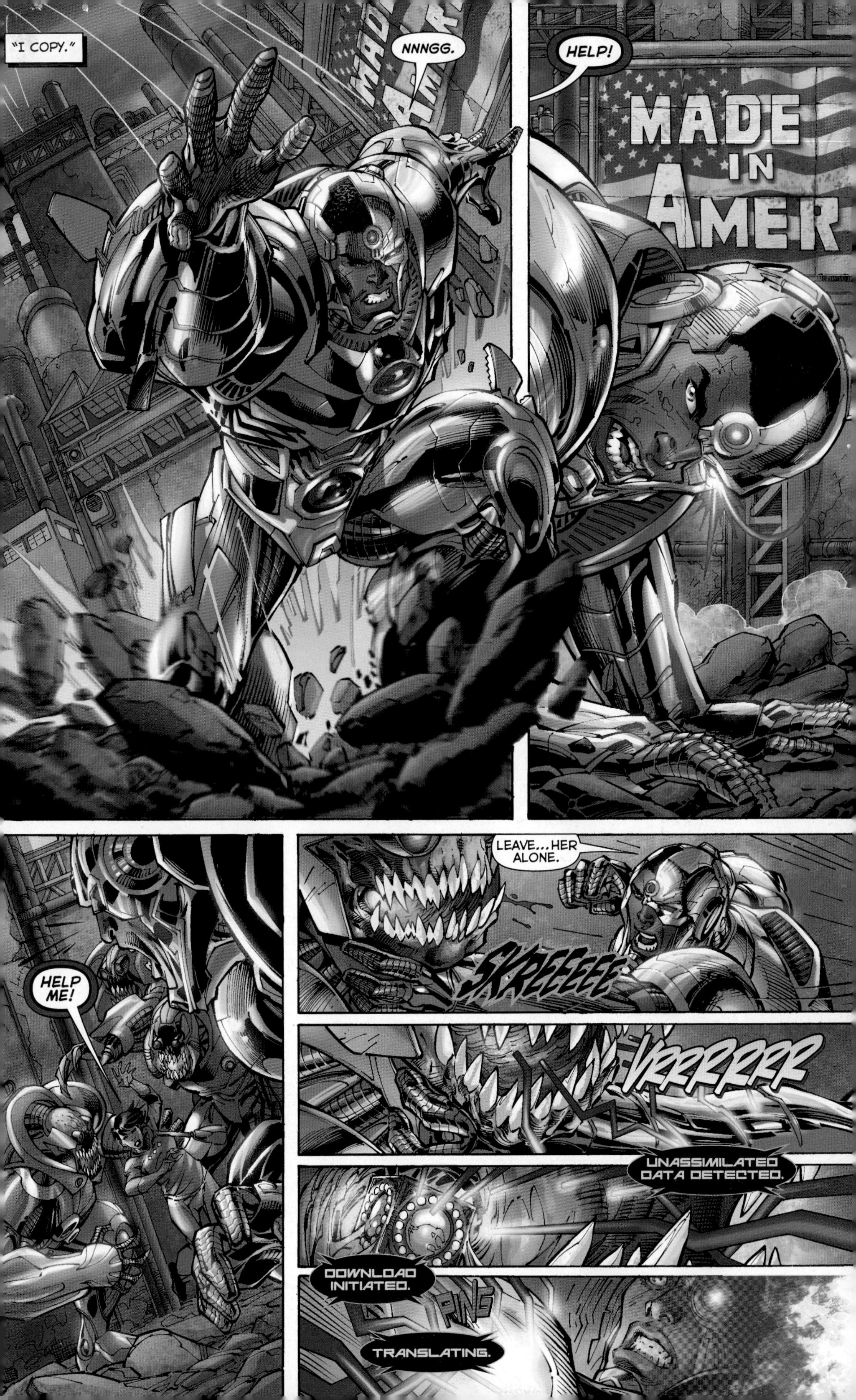
"I COPY."
NNNGG.
HELP!
MADE IN AMER
LEAVE...HER ALONE.
SKREEEEEE
HELP ME!
VRRRRRR
UNASSIMILATED DATA DETECTED.
DOWNLOAD INITIATED.
PING
TRANSLATING.

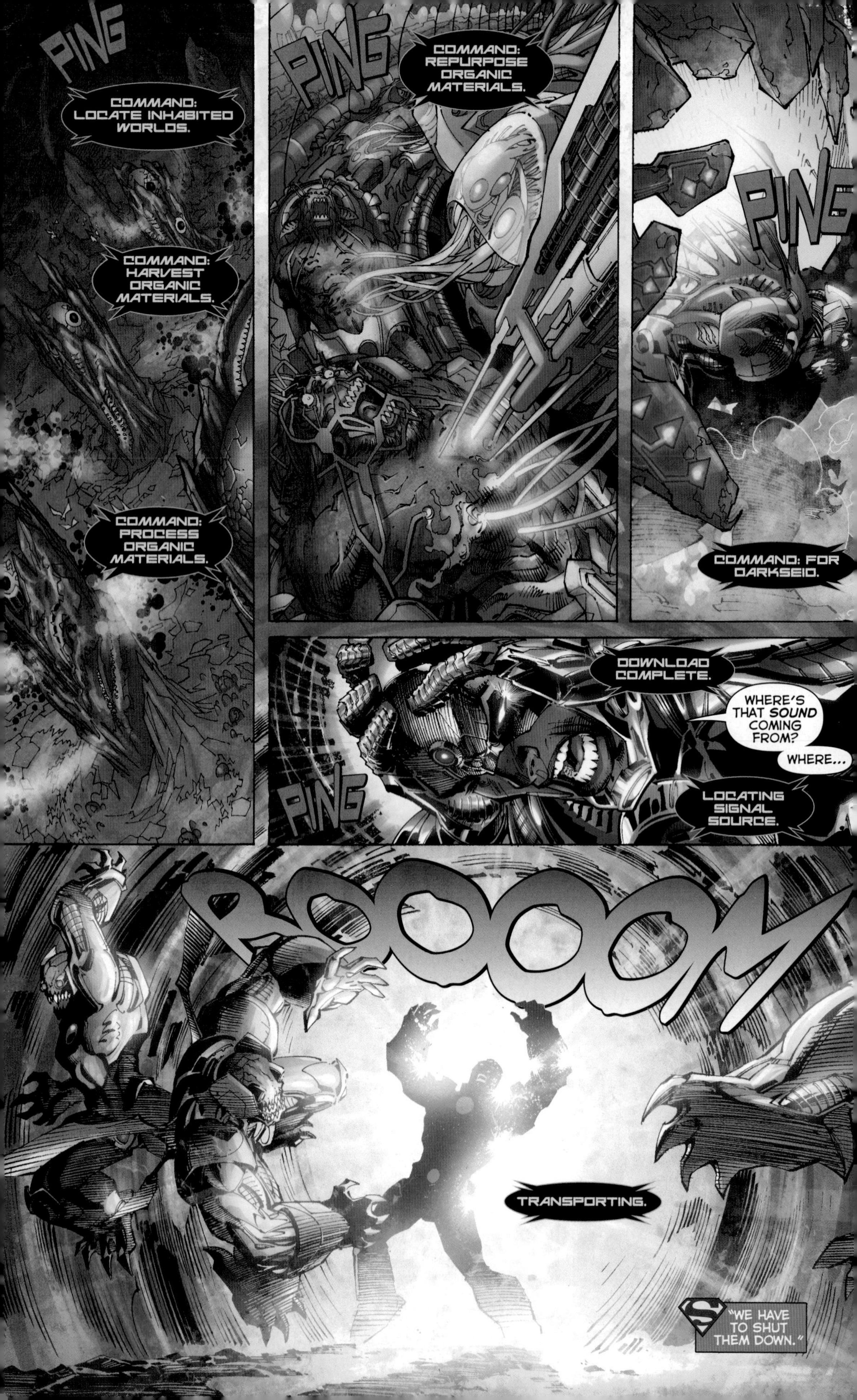
PING
COMMAND: LOCATE INHABITED WORLDS.
COMMAND: HARVEST ORGANIC MATERIALS.
COMMAND: PROCESS ORGANIC MATERIALS.
PING
COMMAND: REPURPOSE ORGANIC MATERIALS.
PING
COMMAND: FOR DARKSEID.
DOWNLOAD COMPLETE.
WHERE'S THAT SOUND COMING FROM?
WHERE...
PING
LOCATING SIGNAL SOURCE.
ROOOOM
TRANSPORTING.
"WE HAVE TO SHUT THEM DOWN."

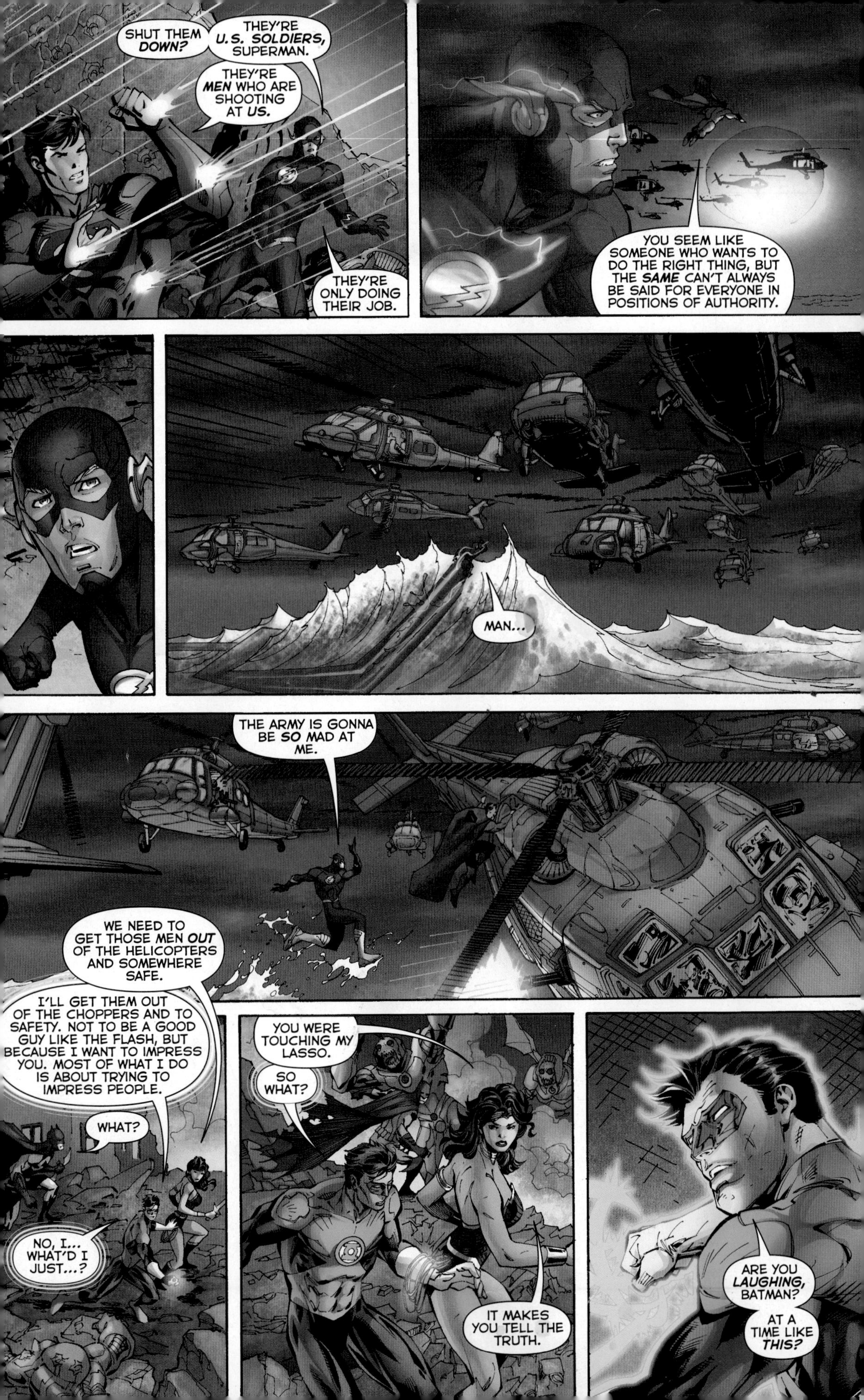
SHUT THEM DOWN?
THEY'RE U.S. SOLDIERS, SUPERMAN.
THEY'RE MEN WHO ARE SHOOTING AT US.
THEY'RE ONLY DOING THEIR JOB.
YOU SEEM LIKE SOMEONE WHO WANTS TO DO THE RIGHT THING, BUT THE SAME CAN'T ALWAYS BE SAID FOR EVERYONE IN POSITIONS OF AUTHORITY.
MAN...
THE ARMY IS GONNA BE SO MAD AT ME.
WE NEED TO GET THOSE MEN OUT OF THE HELICOPTERS AND SOMEWHERE SAFE.
I'LL GET THEM OUT OF THE CHOPPERS AND TO SAFETY. NOT TO BE A GOOD GUY LIKE THE FLASH, BUT BECAUSE I WANT TO IMPRESS YOU. MOST OF WHAT I DO IS ABOUT TRYING TO IMPRESS PEOPLE.
WHAT?
NO, I... WHAT'D I JUST...?
YOU WERE TOUCHING MY LASSO.
SO WHAT?
IT MAKES YOU TELL THE TRUTH.
ARE YOU LAUGHING, BATMAN?
AT A TIME LIKE THIS?

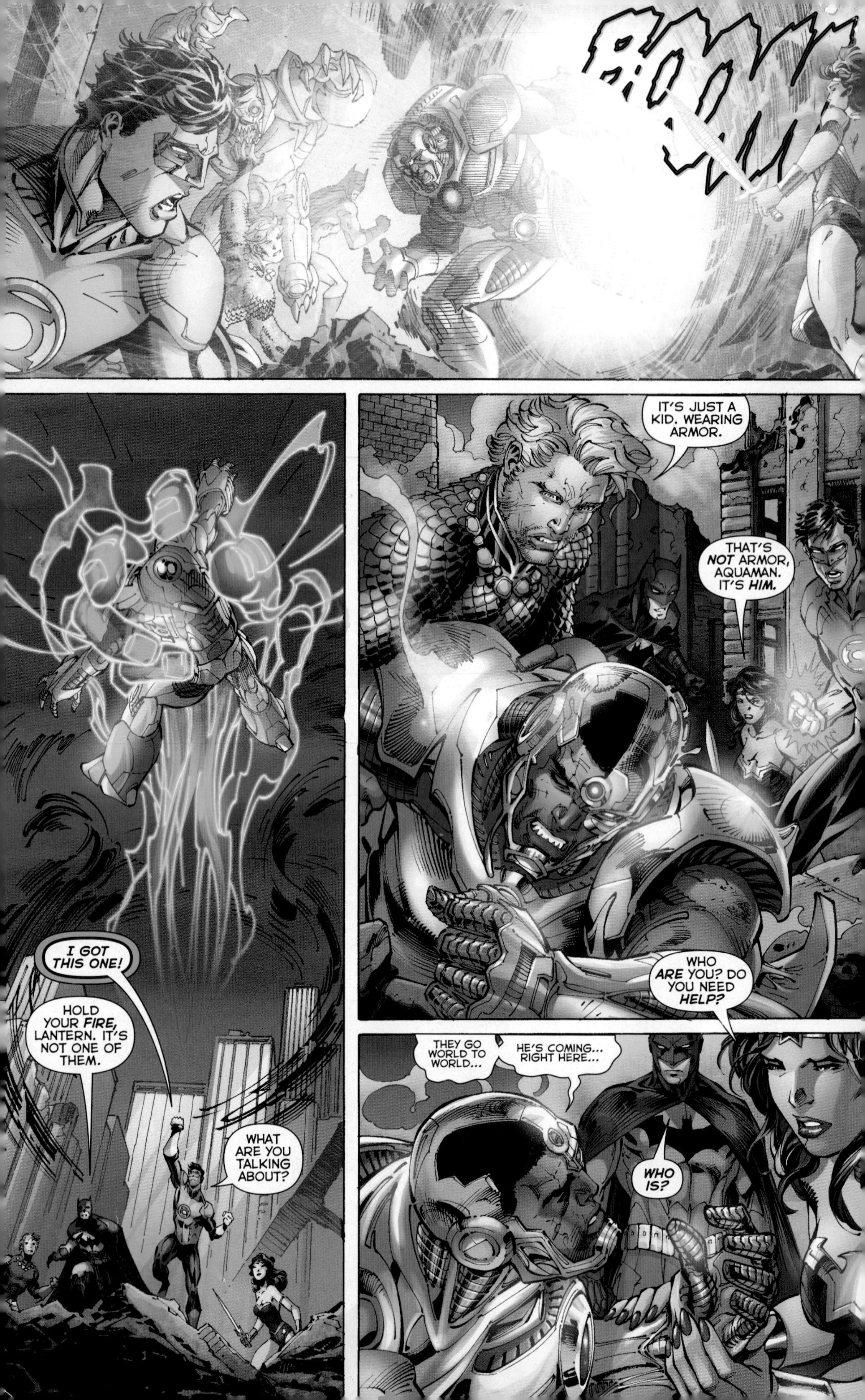
I GOT THIS ONE!
HOLD YOUR FIRE, LANTERN. IT'S NOT ONE OF THEM.
WHAT ARE YOU TALKING ABOUT?
IT'S JUST A KID. WEARING ARMOR.
THAT'S NOT ARMOR, AQUAMAN. IT'S HIM.
WHO ARE YOU? DO YOU NEED HELP?
THEY GO WORLD TO WORLD...
HE'S COMING... RIGHT HERE...
WHO IS?

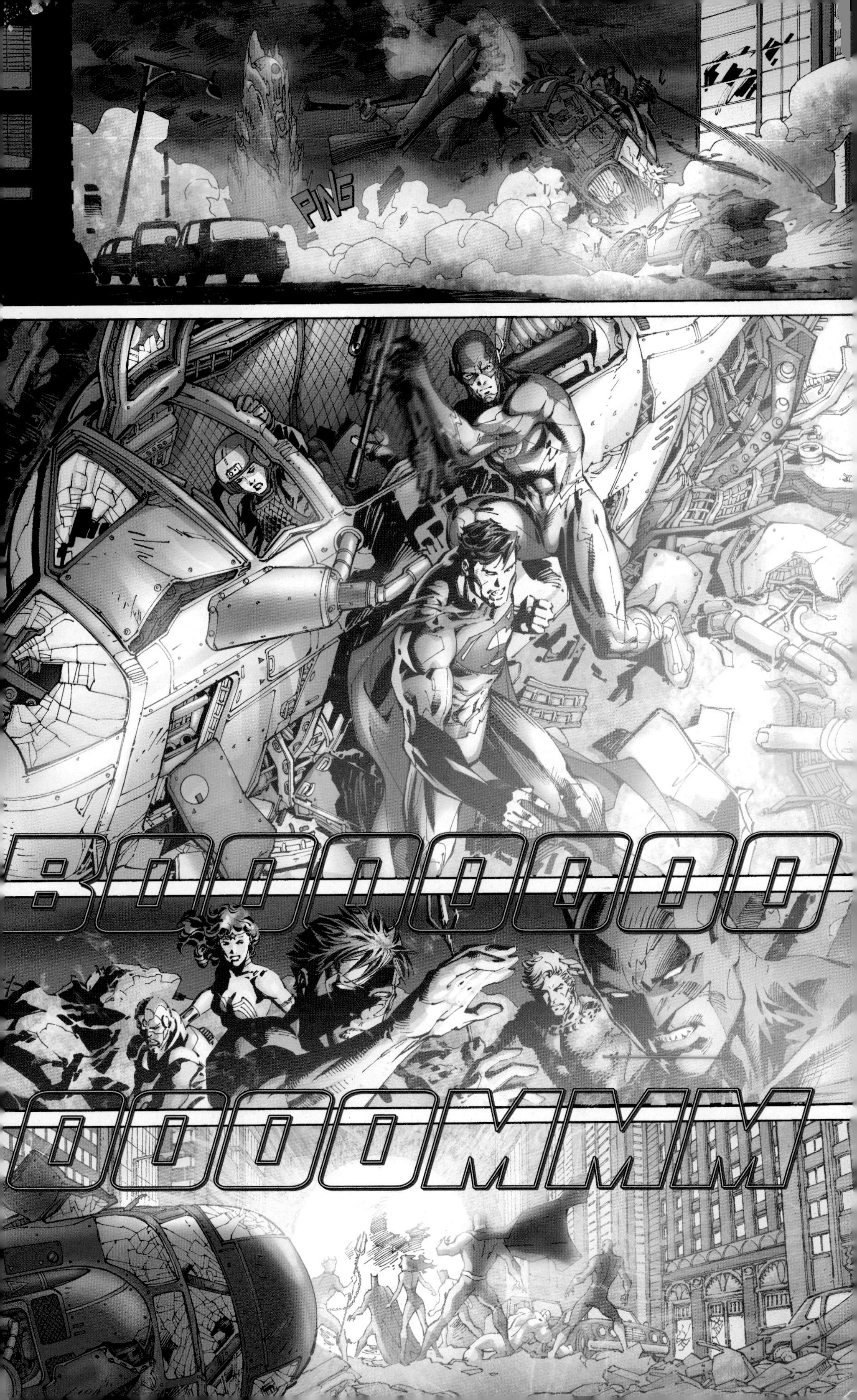
PING
BOOOOOOO
OOOOMMM

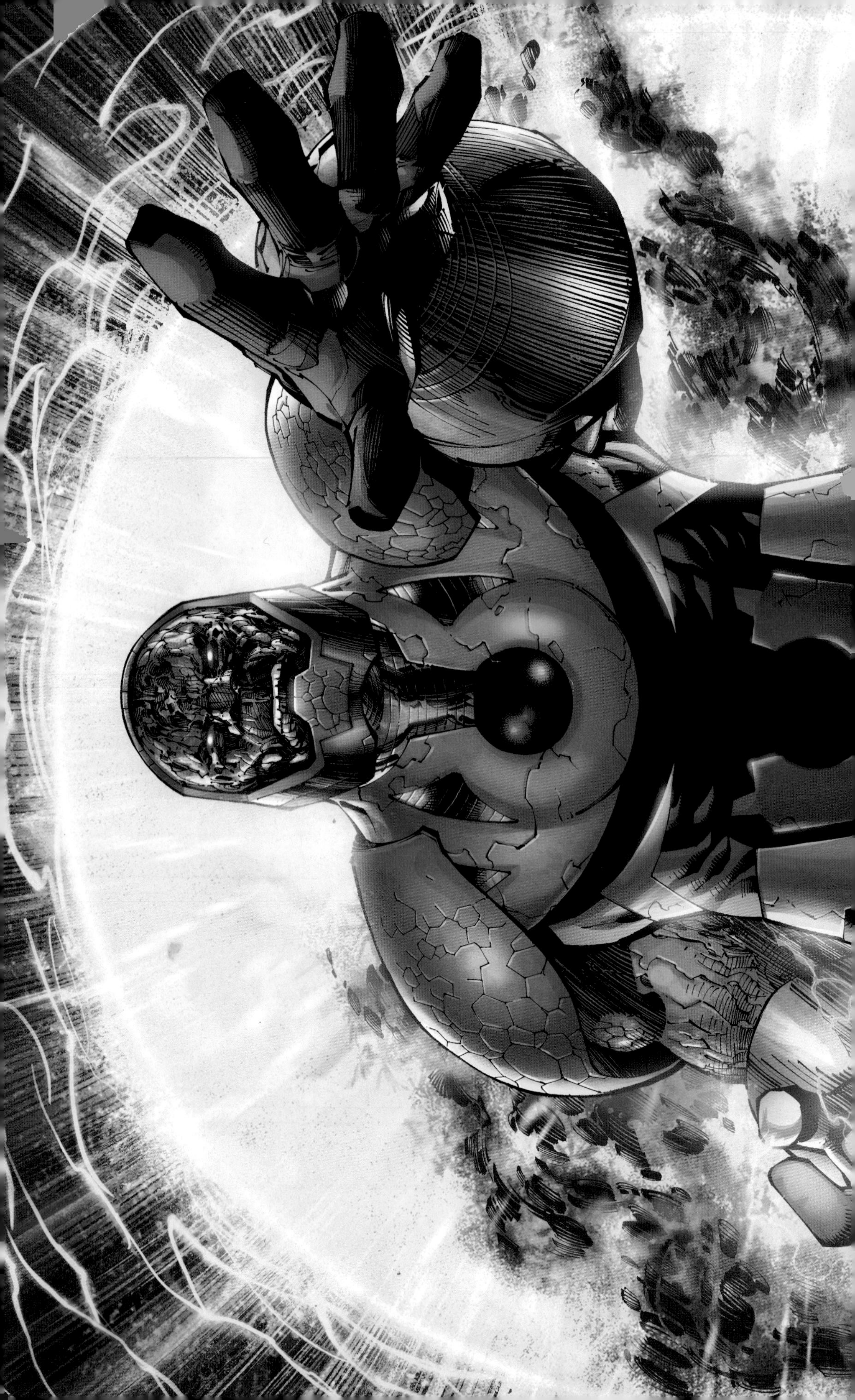

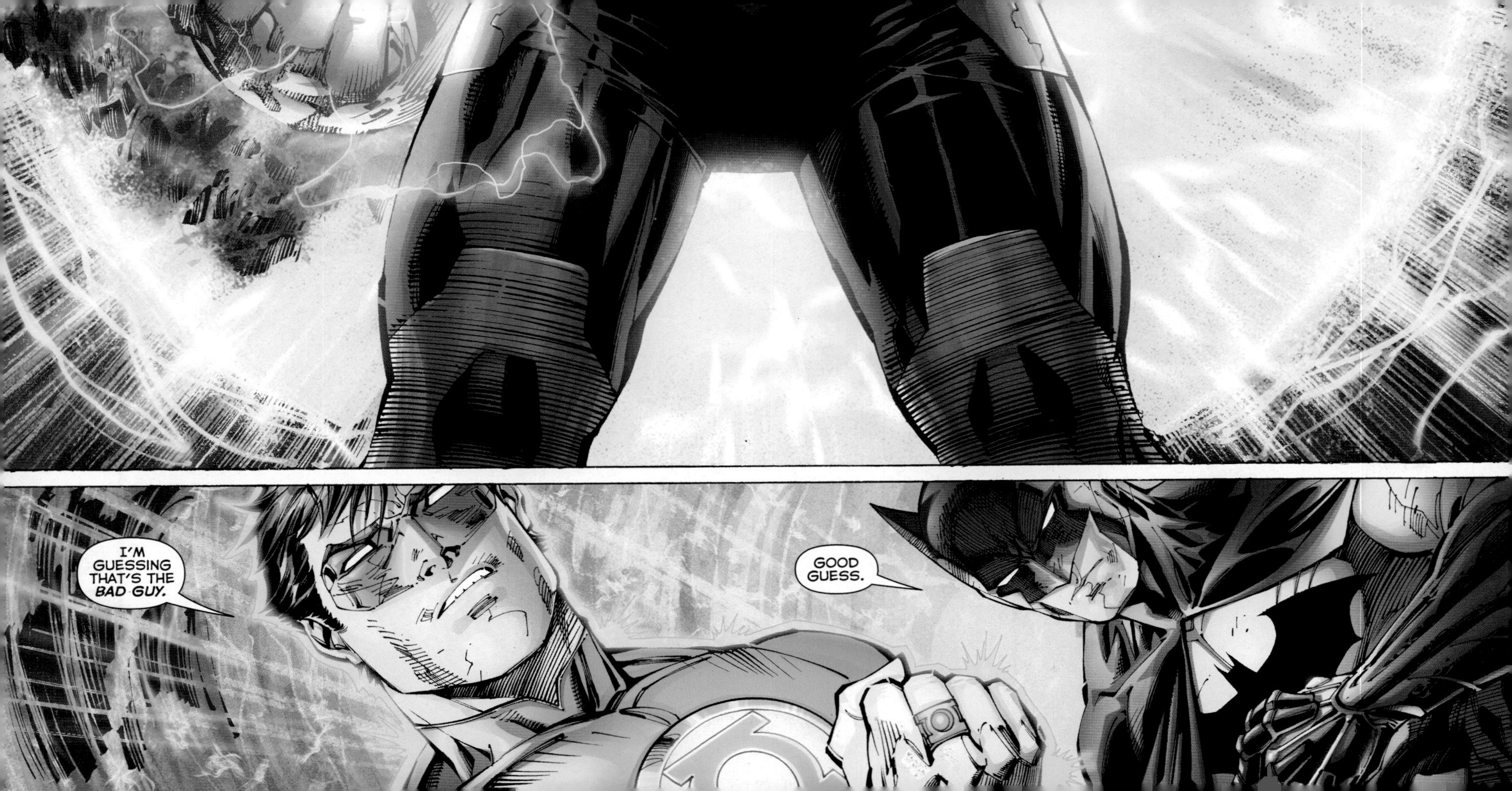
I'M GUESSING THAT'S THE *BAD GUY.*
GOOD GUESS.

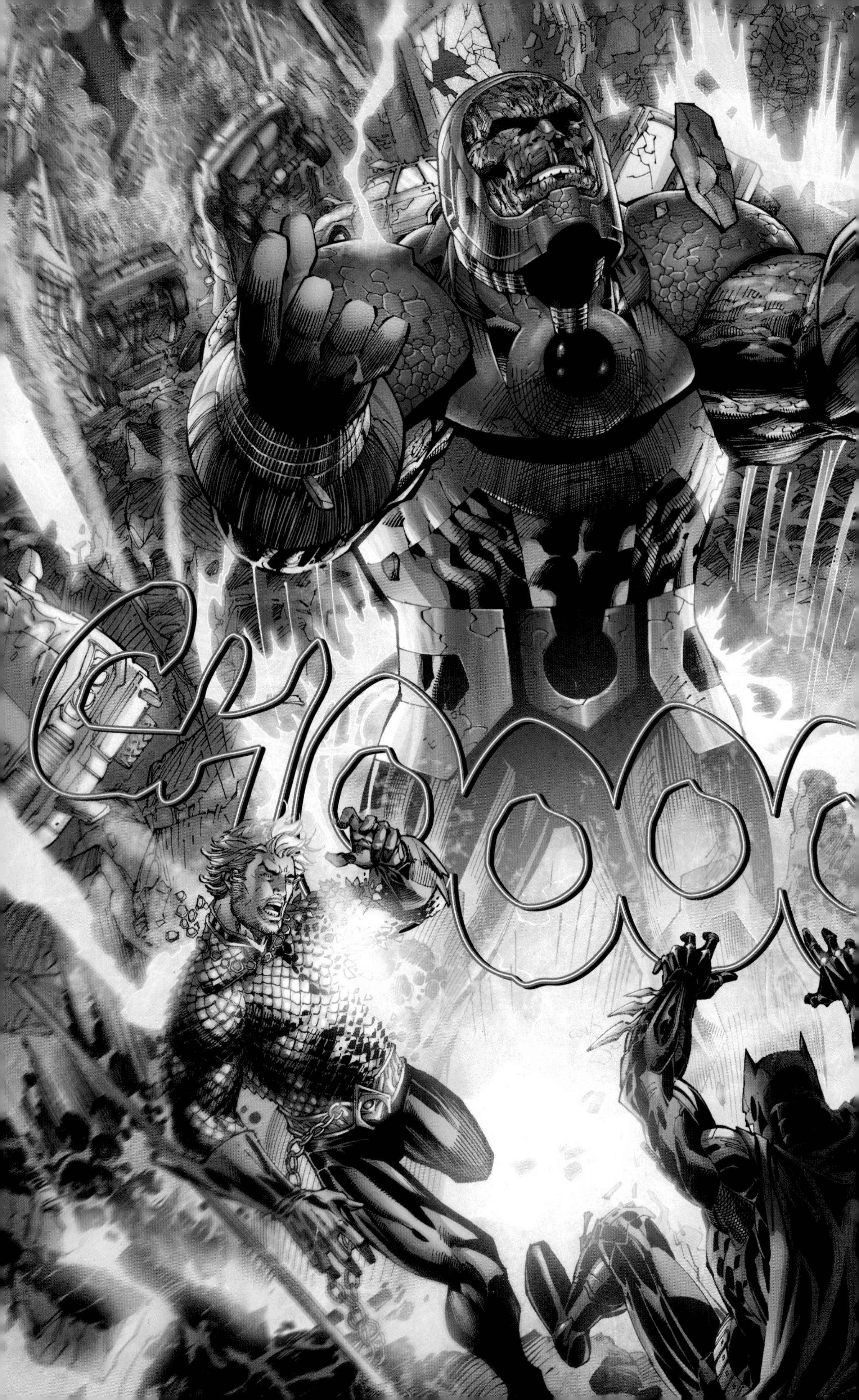
CHOOOO

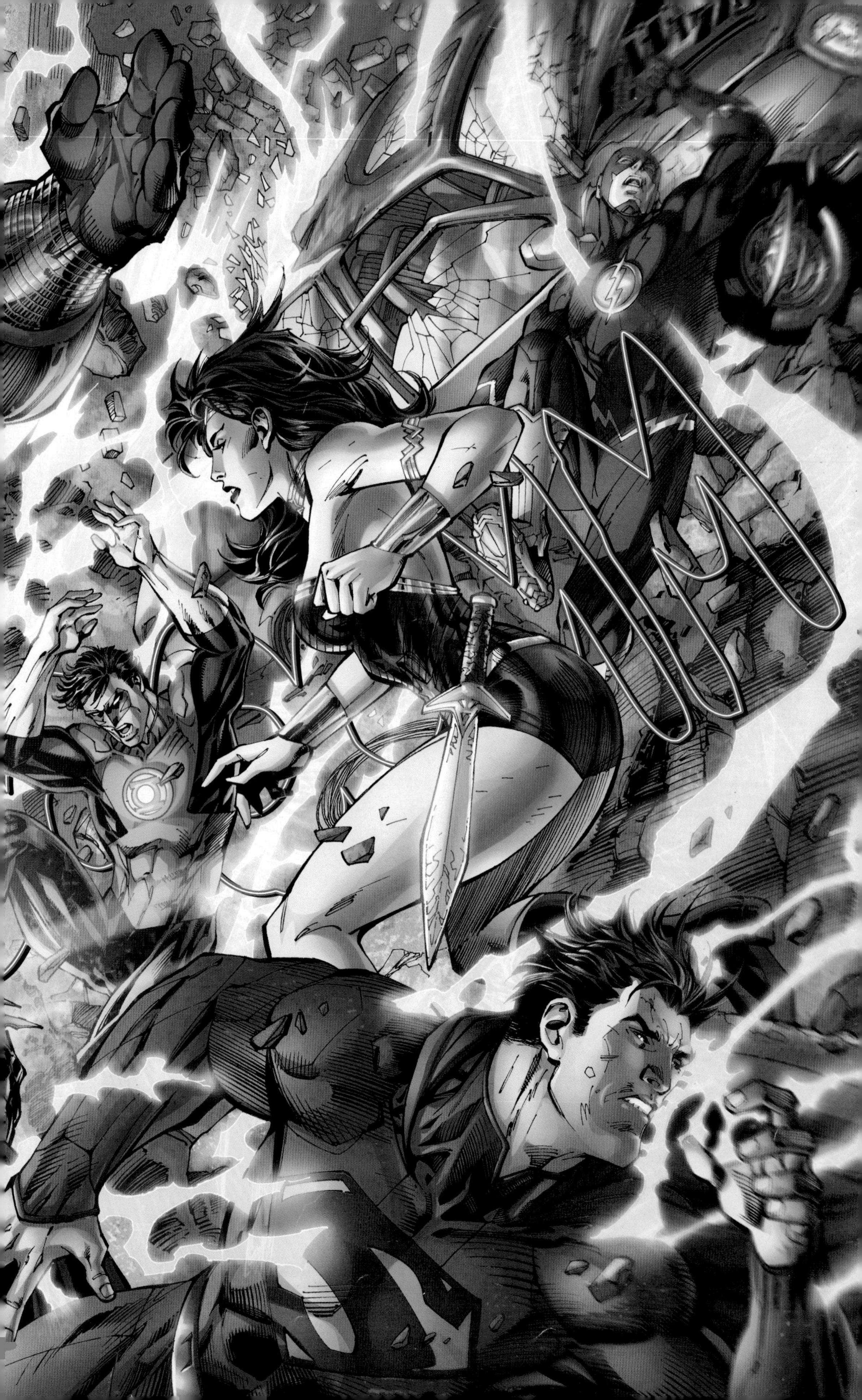

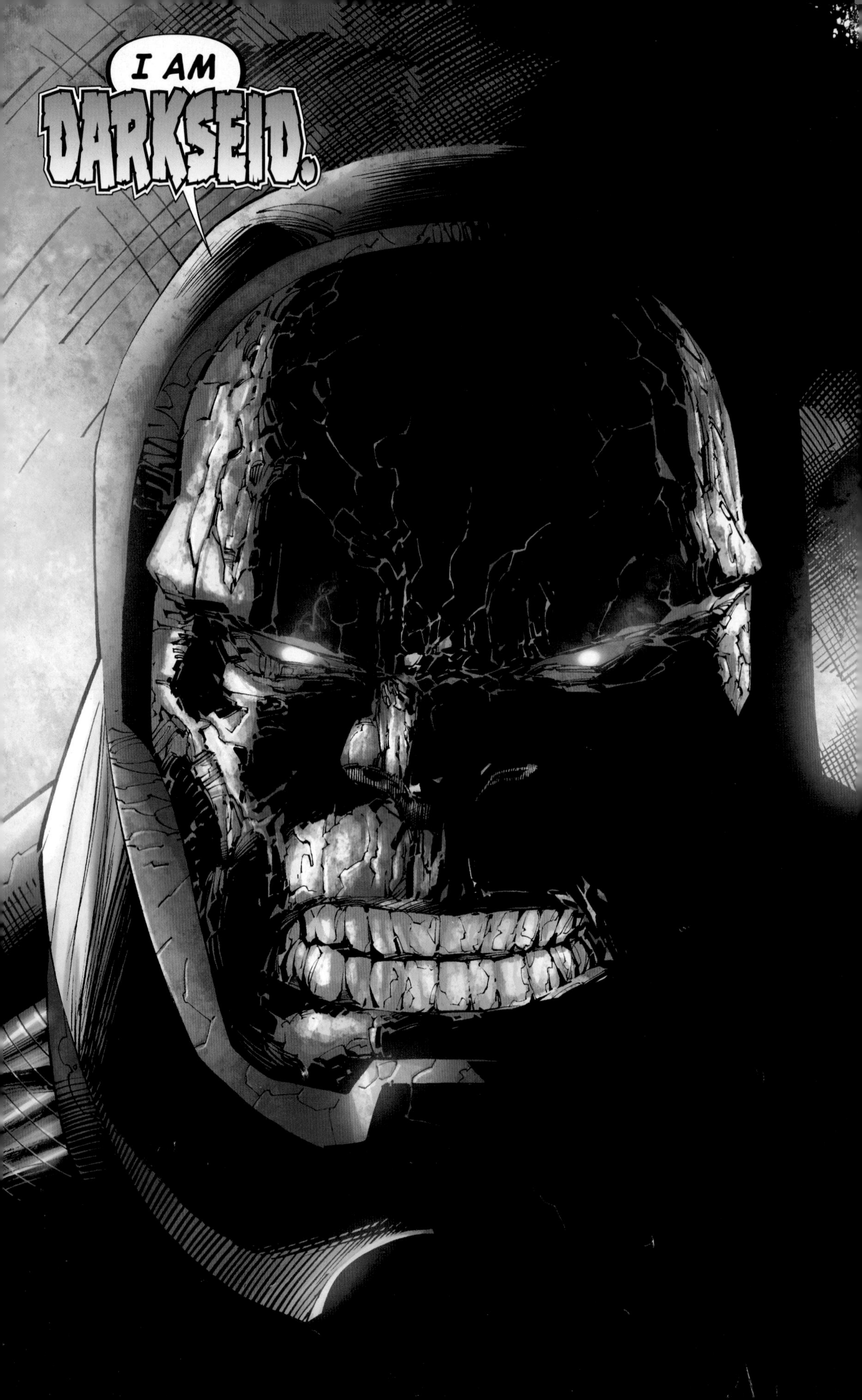
I AM DARKSEID.

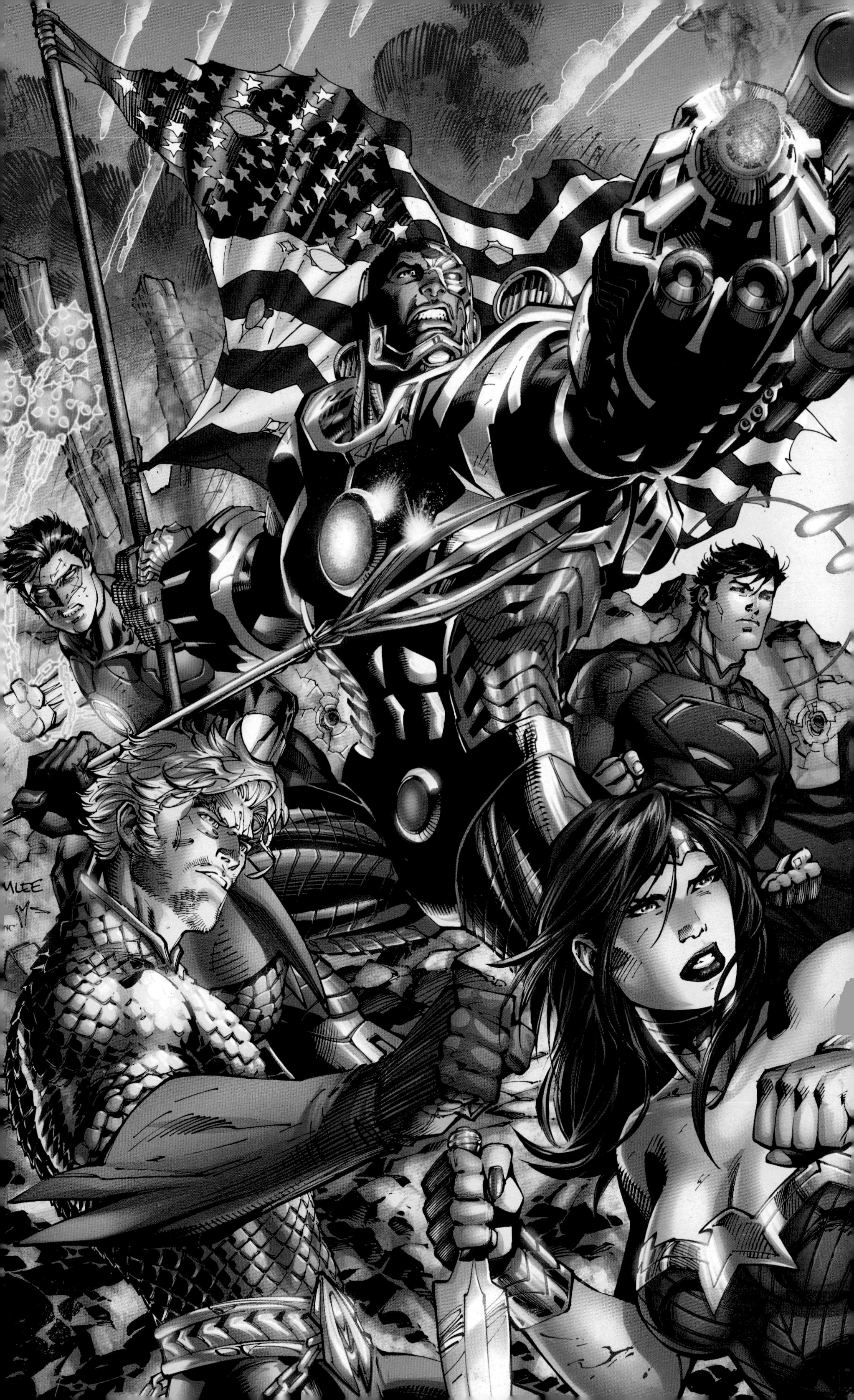

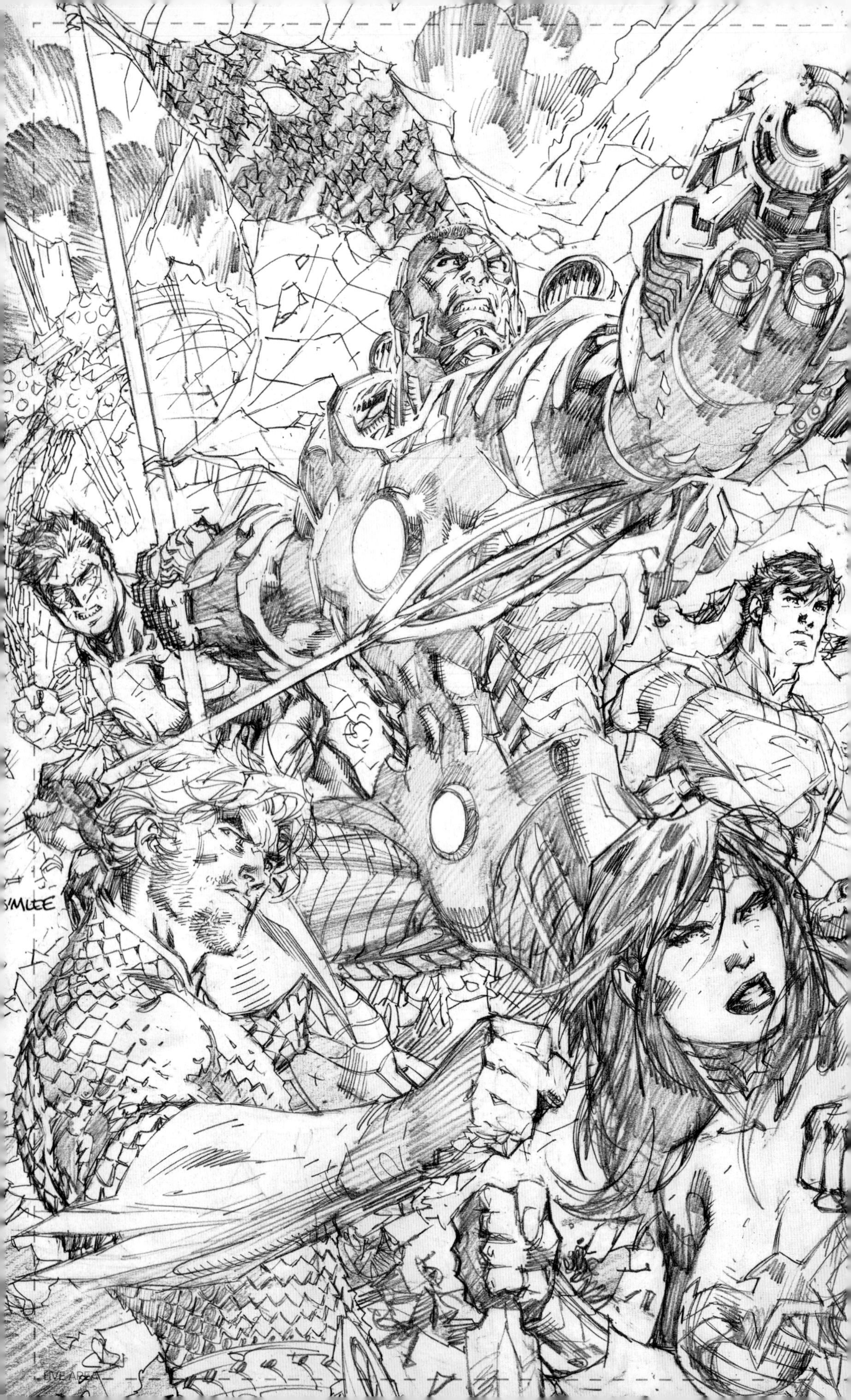
LIVE AREA

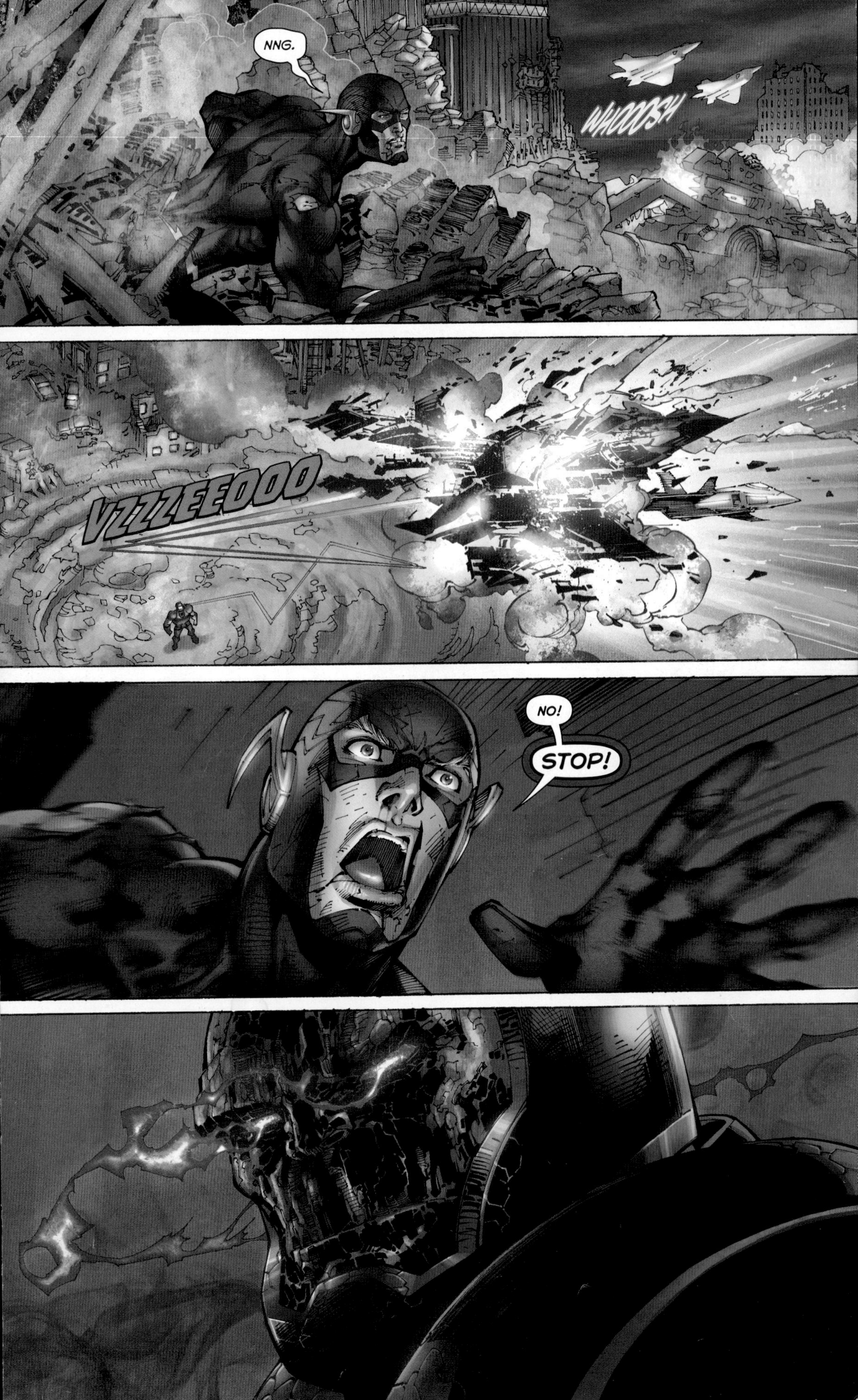
NNG.
WHOOOSH
VZZZEEOOO
NO!
STOP!

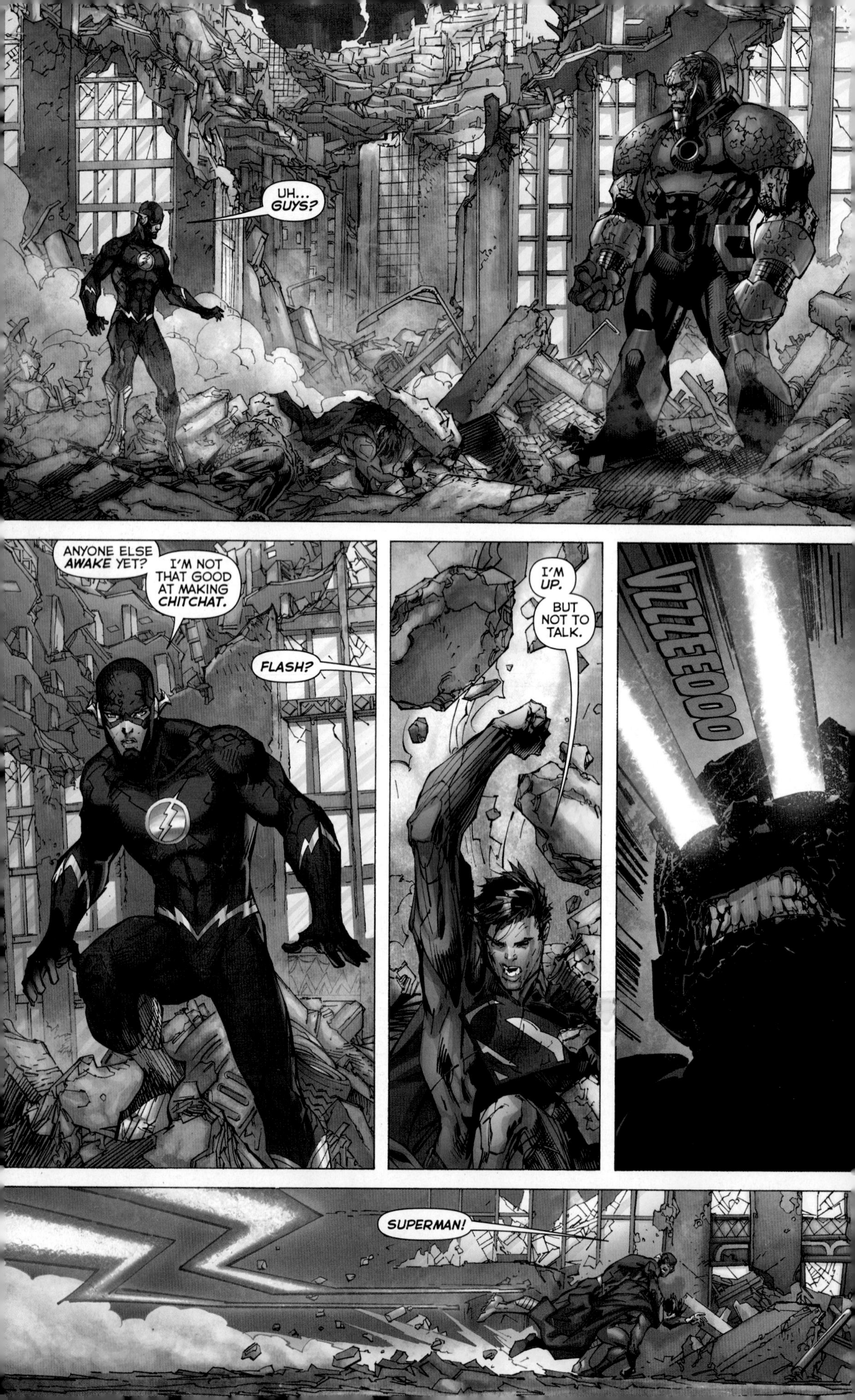

UH... GUYS?
ANYONE ELSE AWAKE YET?
I'M NOT THAT GOOD AT MAKING CHITCHAT.
FLASH?
I'M UP.
BUT NOT TO TALK.
VZZZEEOOOO
SUPERMAN!

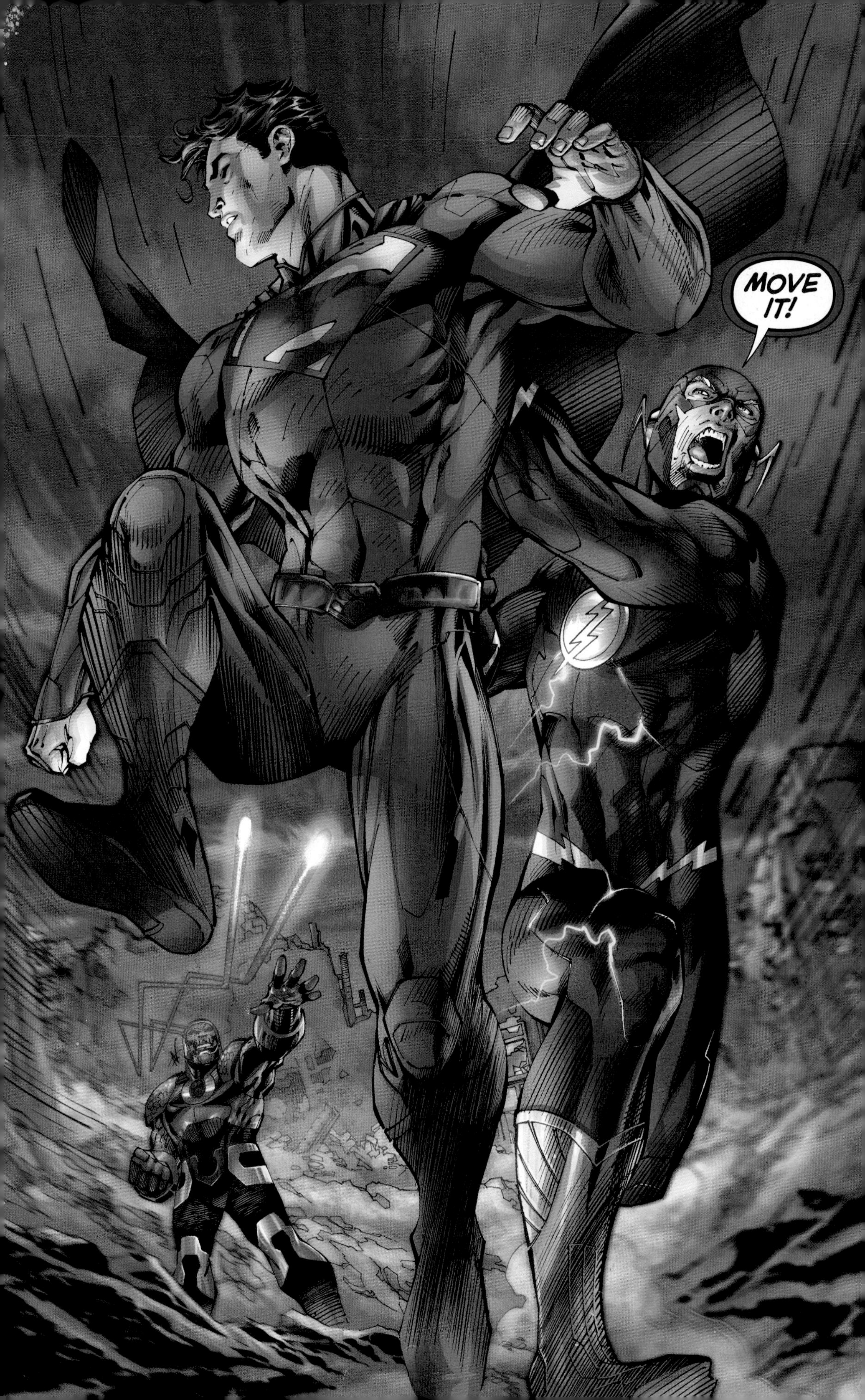
MOVE IT!

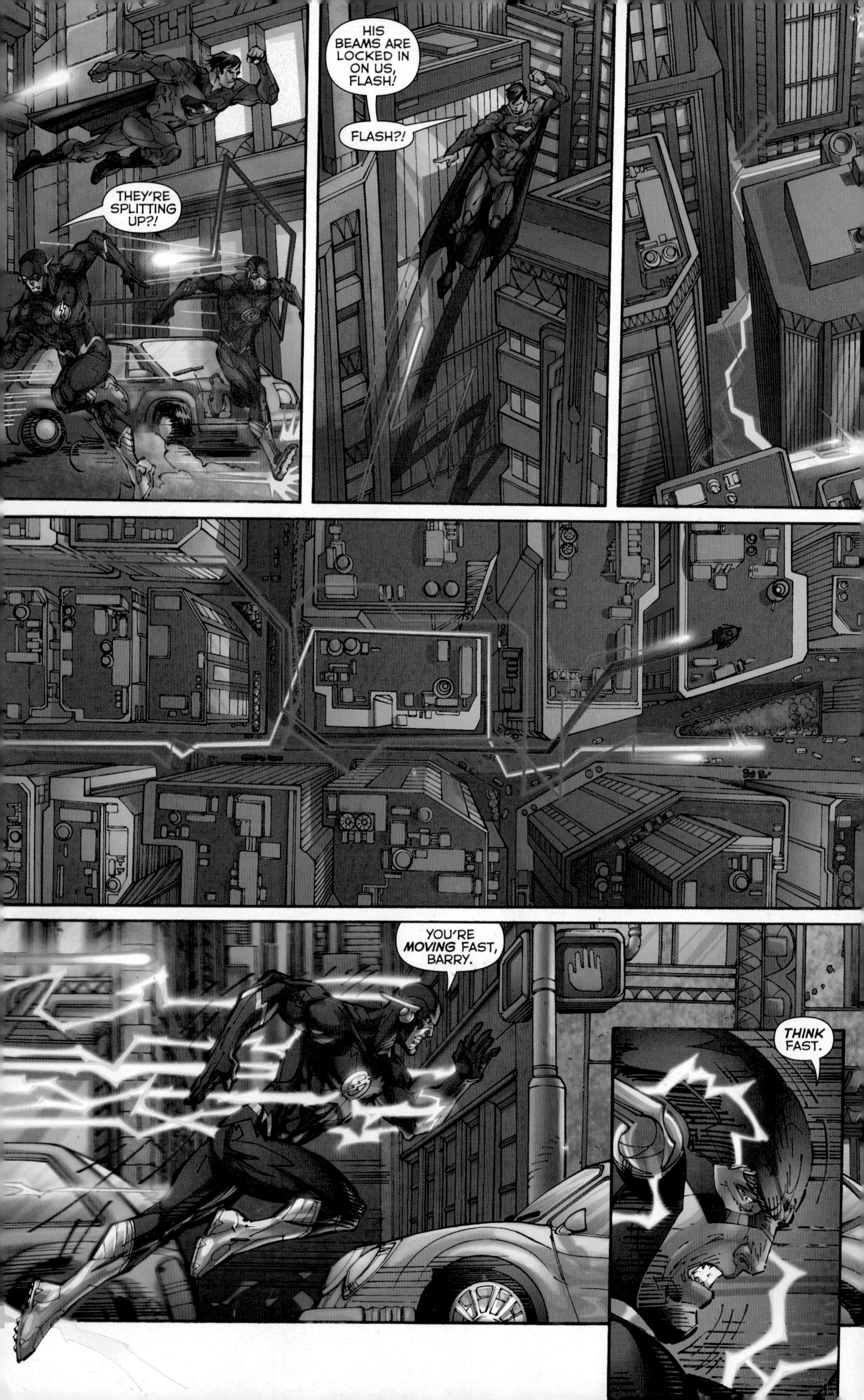
THEY'RE SPLITTING UP?!
HIS BEAMS ARE LOCKED IN ON US, FLASH!
FLASH?!
YOU'RE *MOVING* FAST, BARRY.
THINK FAST.

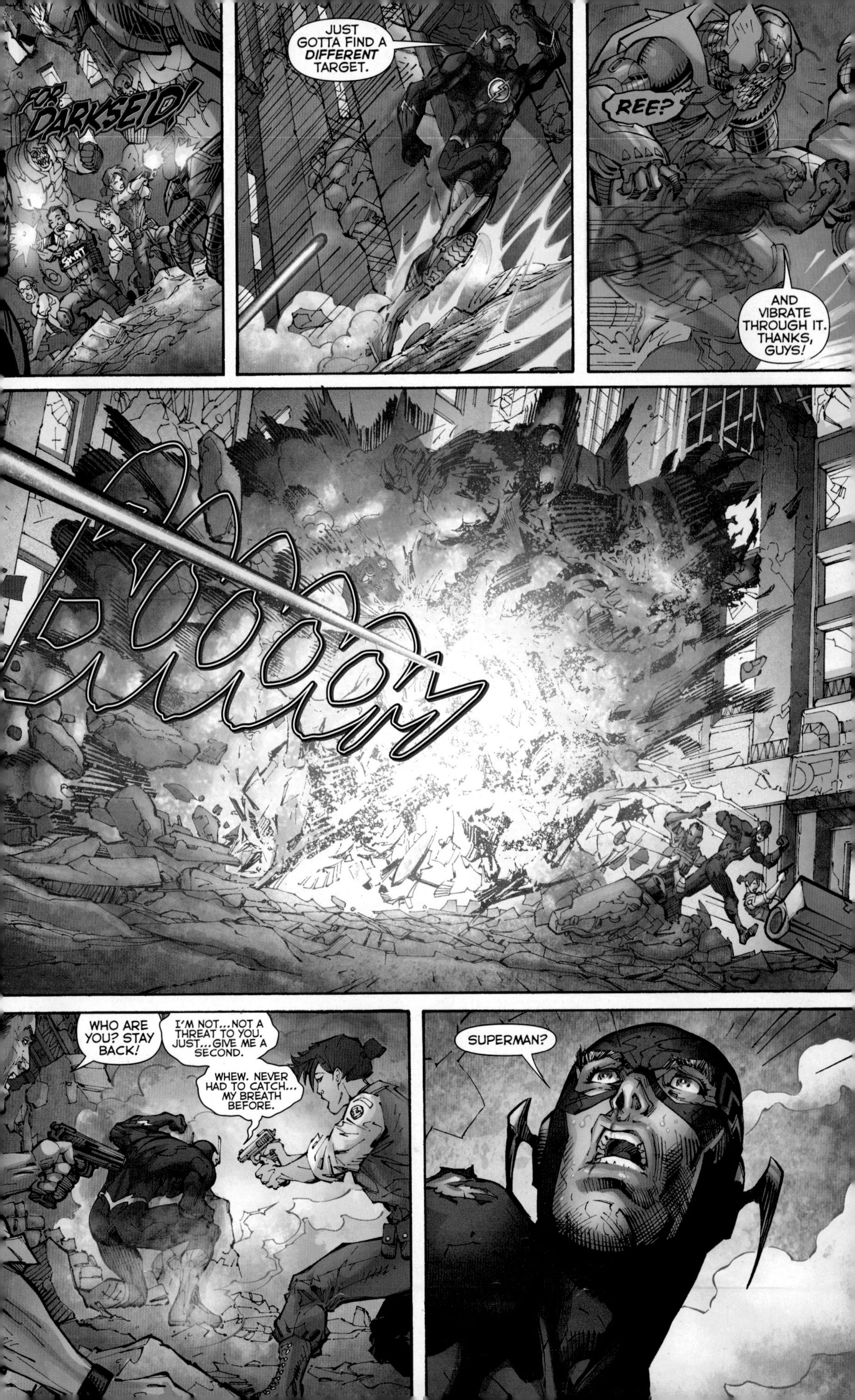
FOR DARKSEID!
JUST GOTTA FIND A DIFFERENT TARGET.
REE?
AND VIBRATE THROUGH IT. THANKS, GUYS!
BOOOOM
WHO ARE YOU? STAY BACK!
I'M NOT...NOT A THREAT TO YOU. JUST...GIVE ME A SECOND.
WHEW. NEVER HAD TO CATCH... MY BREATH BEFORE.
SUPERMAN?

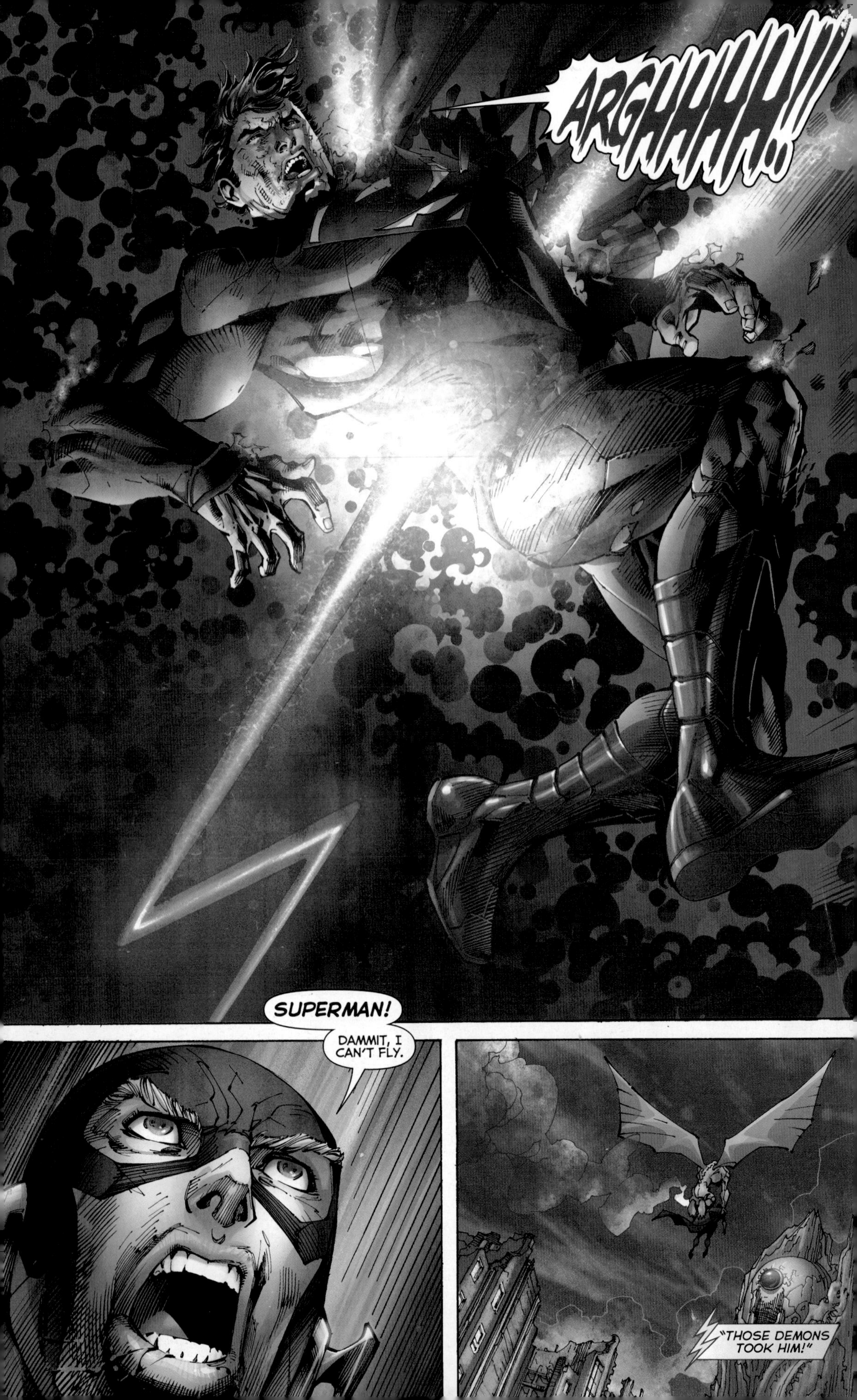
ARGHHHH!!
SUPERMAN!
DAMMIT, I CAN'T FLY.
"THOSE DEMONS TOOK HIM!"

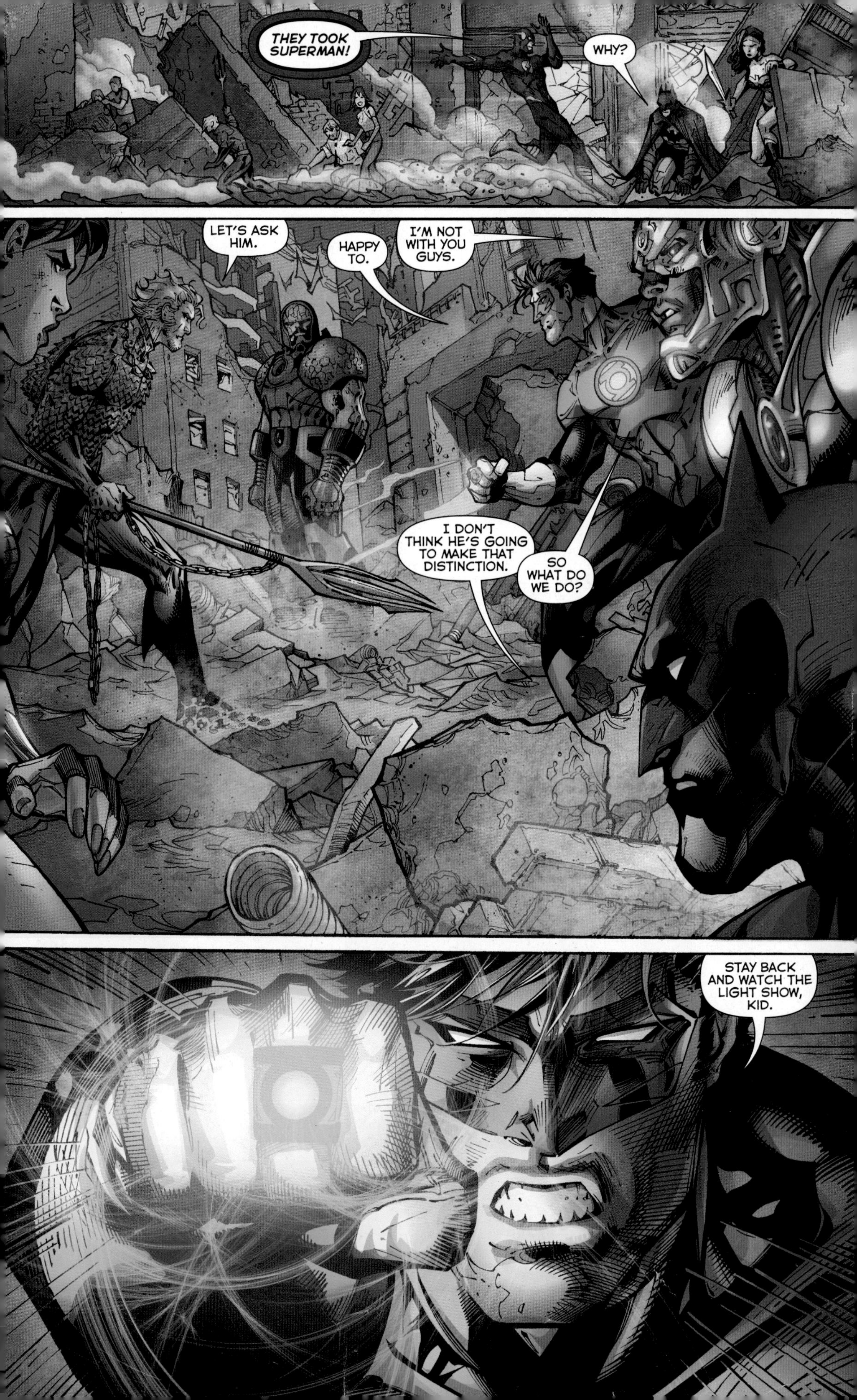
THEY TOOK SUPERMAN!
WHY?
LET'S ASK HIM.
HAPPY TO.
I'M NOT WITH YOU GUYS.
I DON'T THINK HE'S GOING TO MAKE THAT DISTINCTION.
SO WHAT DO WE DO?
STAY BACK AND WATCH THE LIGHT SHOW, KID.

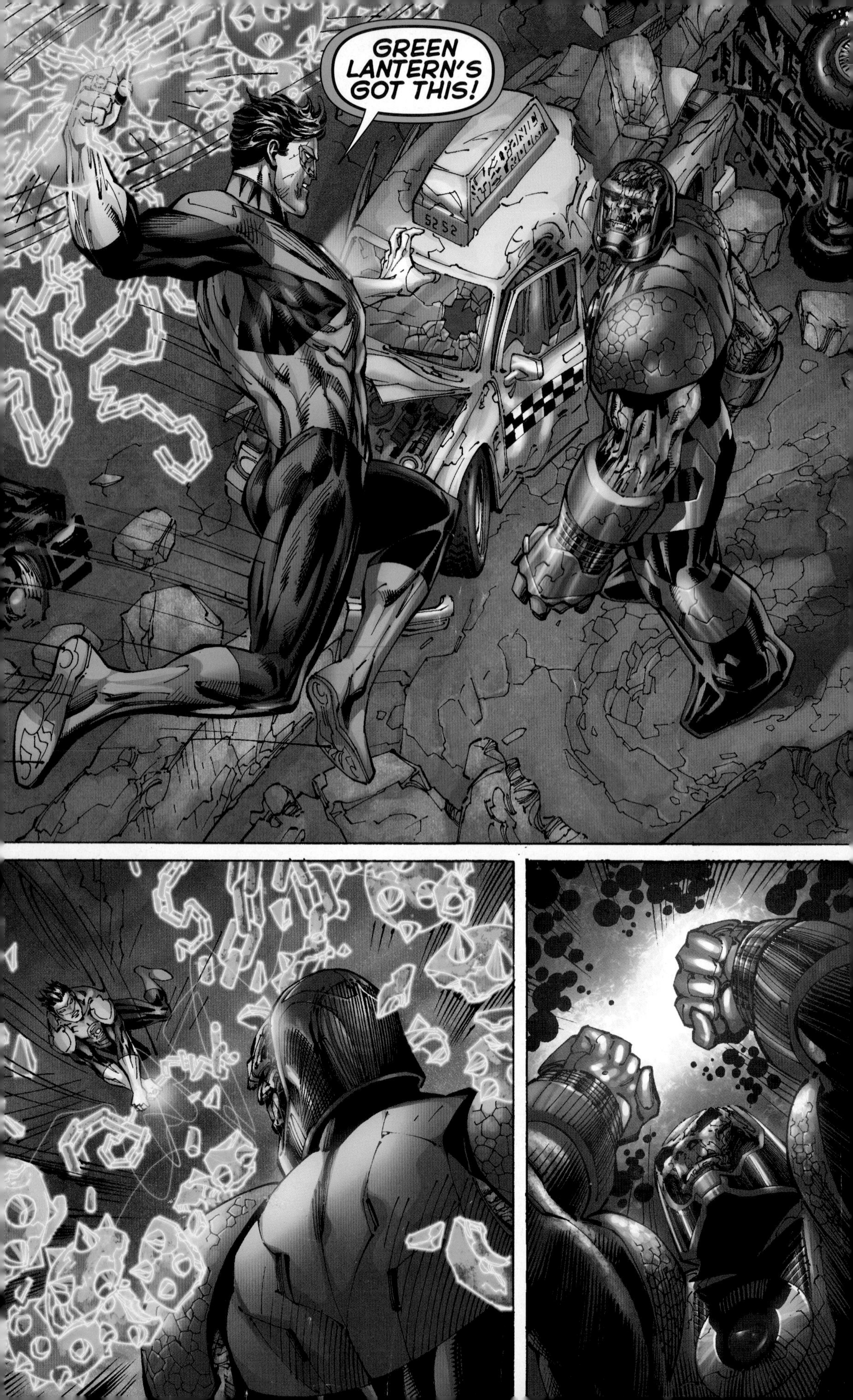
GREEN LANTERN'S GOT THIS!

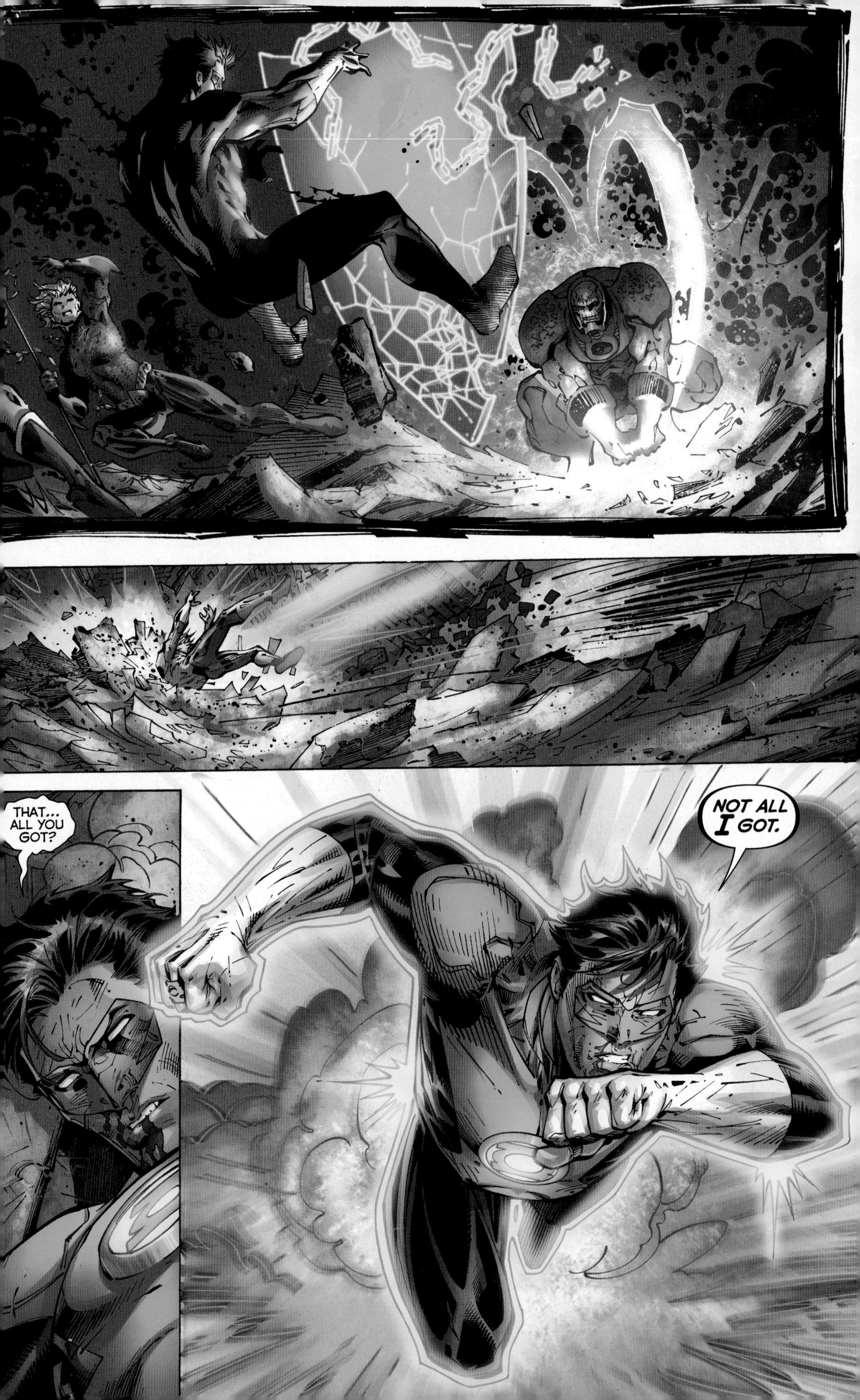
THAT... ALL YOU GOT?
NOT ALL I GOT.

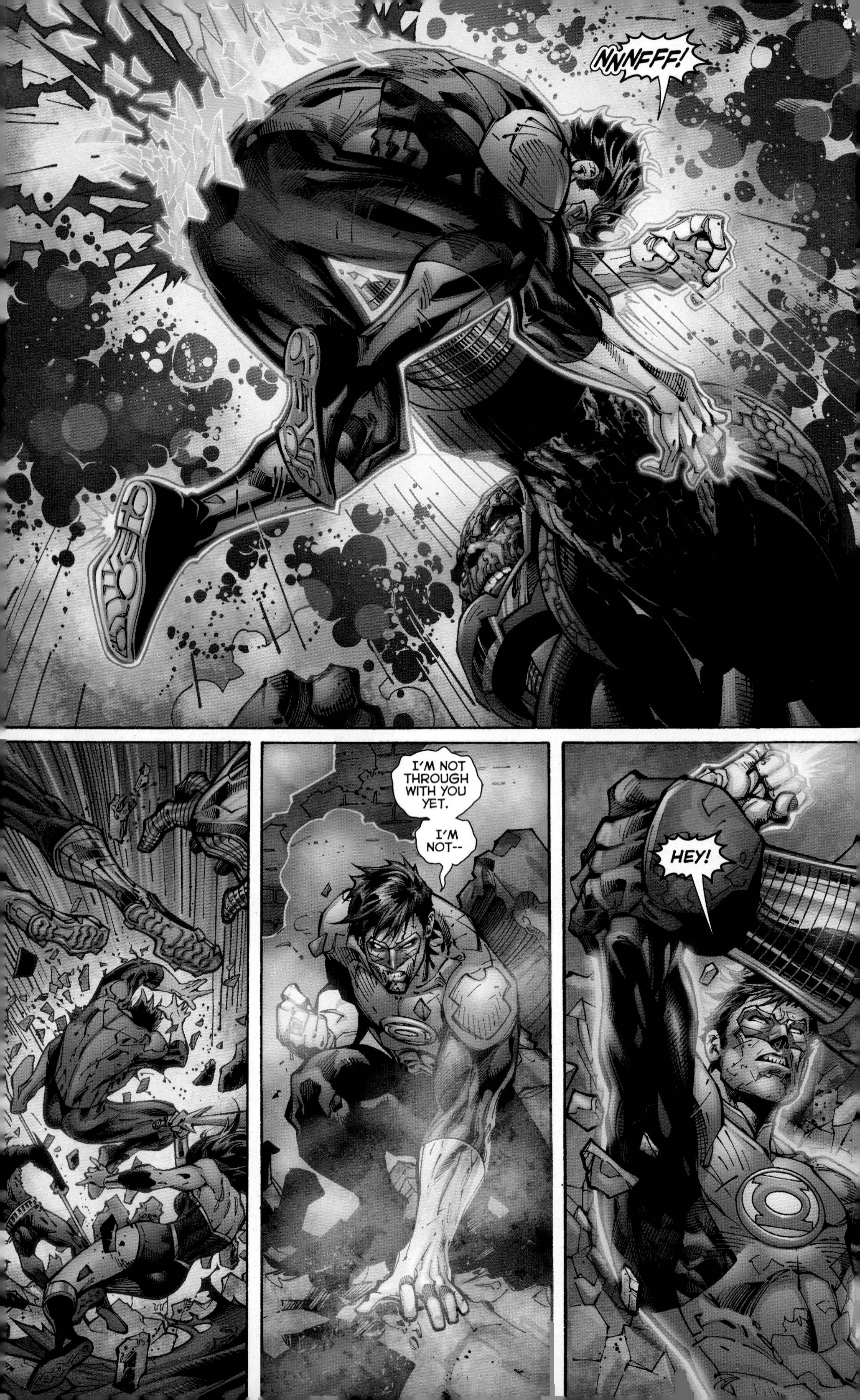
NNNFFF!
I'M NOT THROUGH WITH YOU YET.
I'M NOT--
HEY!

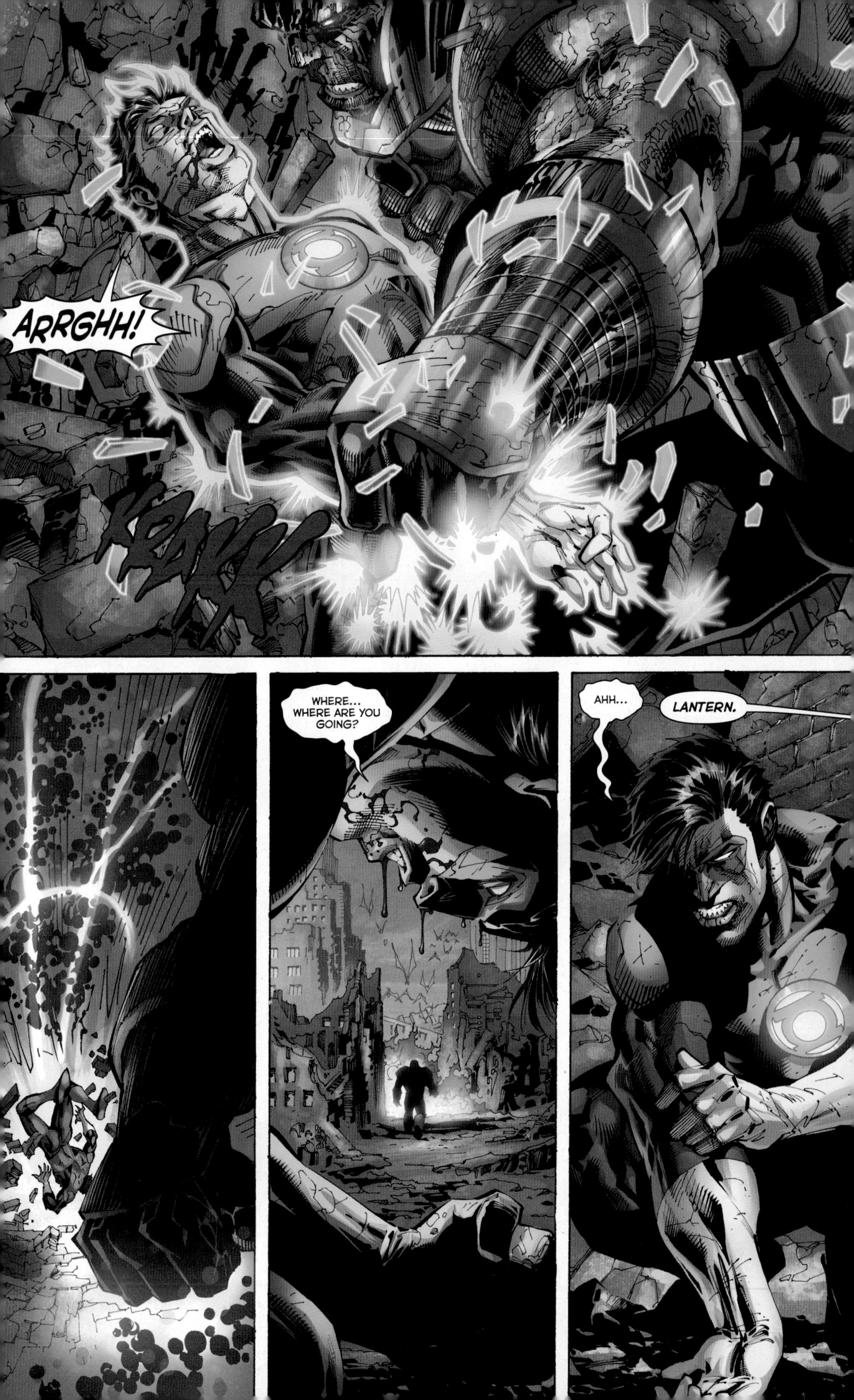
ARRGHH!
WHERE... WHERE ARE YOU GOING?
AHH...
LANTERN.

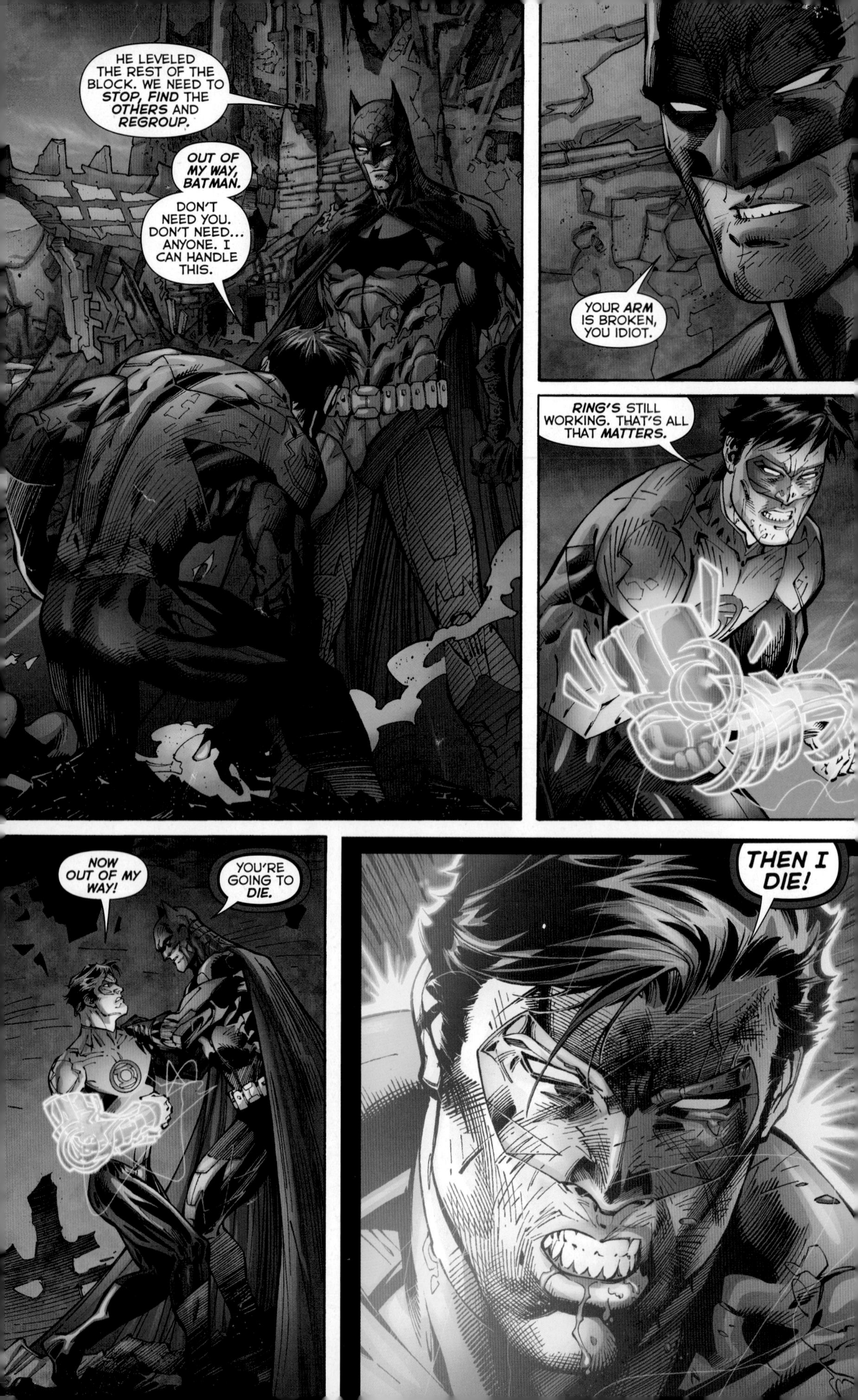
HE LEVELED THE REST OF THE BLOCK. WE NEED TO STOP, FIND THE OTHERS AND REGROUP.
OUT OF MY WAY, BATMAN.
DON'T NEED YOU. DON'T NEED... ANYONE. I CAN HANDLE THIS.
YOUR ARM IS BROKEN, YOU IDIOT.
RING'S STILL WORKING. THAT'S ALL THAT MATTERS.
NOW OUT OF MY WAY!
YOU'RE GOING TO DIE.
THEN I DIE!

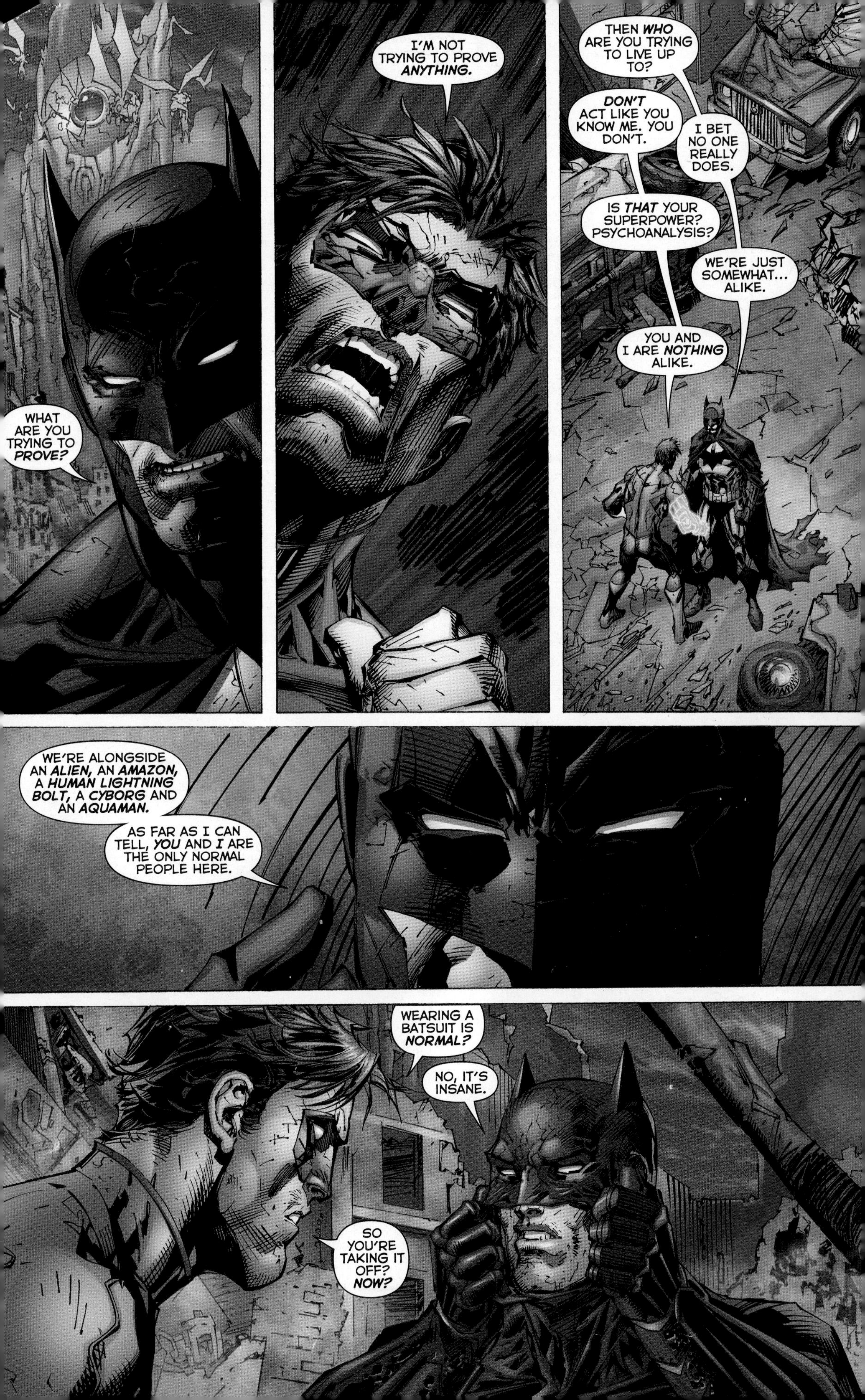
WHAT ARE YOU TRYING TO PROVE?
I'M NOT TRYING TO PROVE ANYTHING.
THEN WHO ARE YOU TRYING TO LIVE UP TO?
DON'T ACT LIKE YOU KNOW ME. YOU DON'T.
I BET NO ONE REALLY DOES.
IS THAT YOUR SUPERPOWER? PSYCHOANALYSIS?
WE'RE JUST SOMEWHAT... ALIKE.
YOU AND I ARE NOTHING ALIKE.
WE'RE ALONGSIDE AN ALIEN, AN AMAZON, A HUMAN LIGHTNING BOLT, A CYBORG AND AN AQUAMAN.
AS FAR AS I CAN TELL, YOU AND I ARE THE ONLY NORMAL PEOPLE HERE.
WEARING A BATSUIT IS NORMAL?
NO, IT'S INSANE.
SO YOU'RE TAKING IT OFF? NOW?

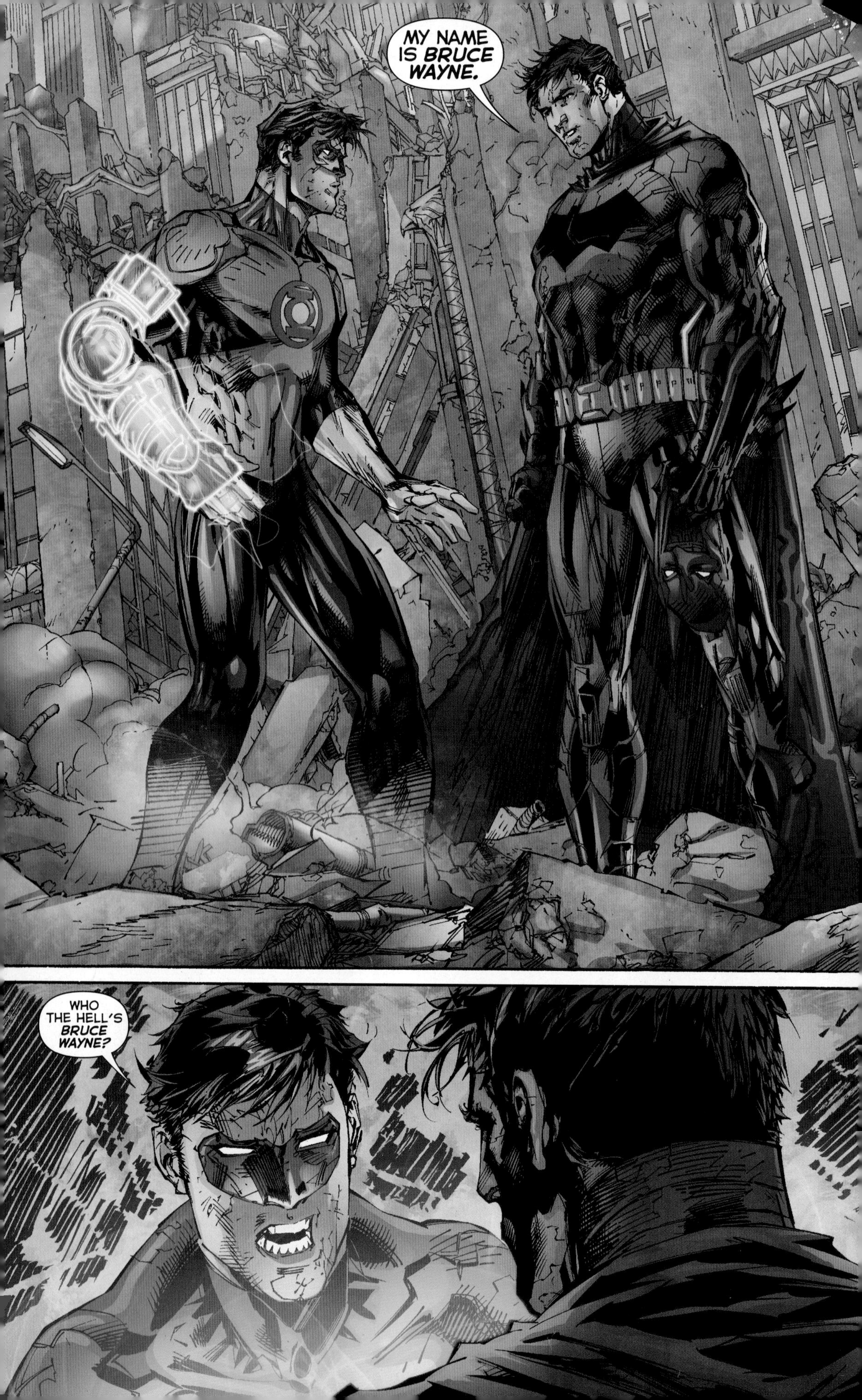
MY NAME IS BRUCE WAYNE.
WHO THE HELL'S BRUCE WAYNE?

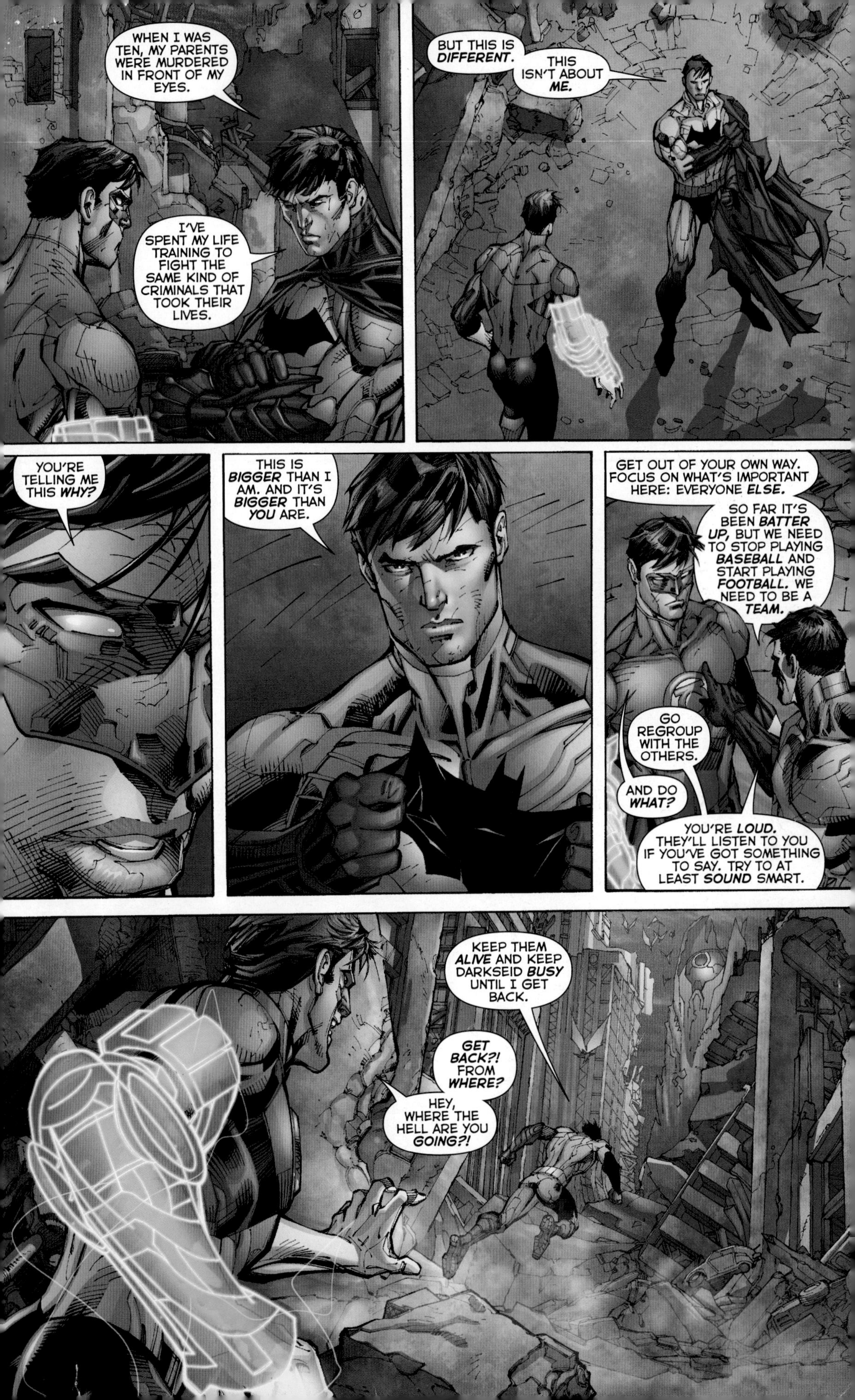
WHEN I WAS TEN, MY PARENTS WERE MURDERED IN FRONT OF MY EYES.
I'VE SPENT MY LIFE TRAINING TO FIGHT THE SAME KIND OF CRIMINALS THAT TOOK THEIR LIVES.
BUT THIS IS *DIFFERENT*.
THIS ISN'T ABOUT *ME.*
YOU'RE TELLING ME THIS *WHY?*
THIS IS *BIGGER* THAN I AM. AND IT'S *BIGGER* THAN *YOU* ARE.
GET OUT OF YOUR OWN WAY. FOCUS ON WHAT'S IMPORTANT HERE: EVERYONE *ELSE.*
SO FAR IT'S BEEN *BATTER UP,* BUT WE NEED TO STOP PLAYING *BASEBALL* AND START PLAYING *FOOTBALL.* WE NEED TO BE A *TEAM.*
GO REGROUP WITH THE OTHERS.
AND DO *WHAT?*
YOU'RE *LOUD.* THEY'LL LISTEN TO YOU IF YOU'VE GOT SOMETHING TO SAY. TRY TO AT LEAST *SOUND* SMART.
KEEP THEM *ALIVE* AND KEEP DARKSEID *BUSY* UNTIL I GET BACK.
GET BACK?! FROM *WHERE?*
HEY, WHERE THE HELL ARE YOU *GOING?!*

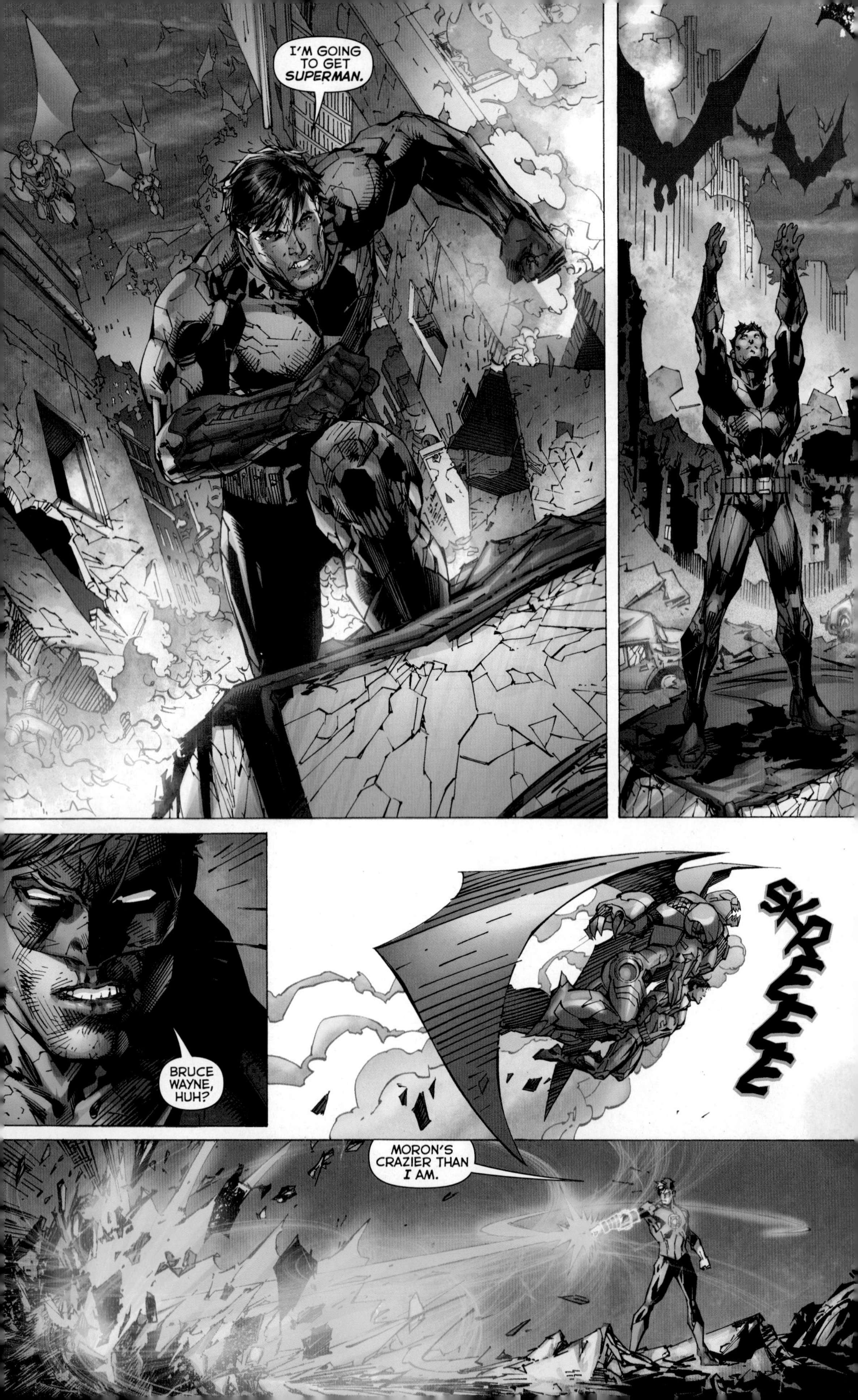
I'M GOING TO GET SUPERMAN.
BRUCE WAYNE, HUH?
SKREEEE
MORON'S CRAZIER THAN I AM.

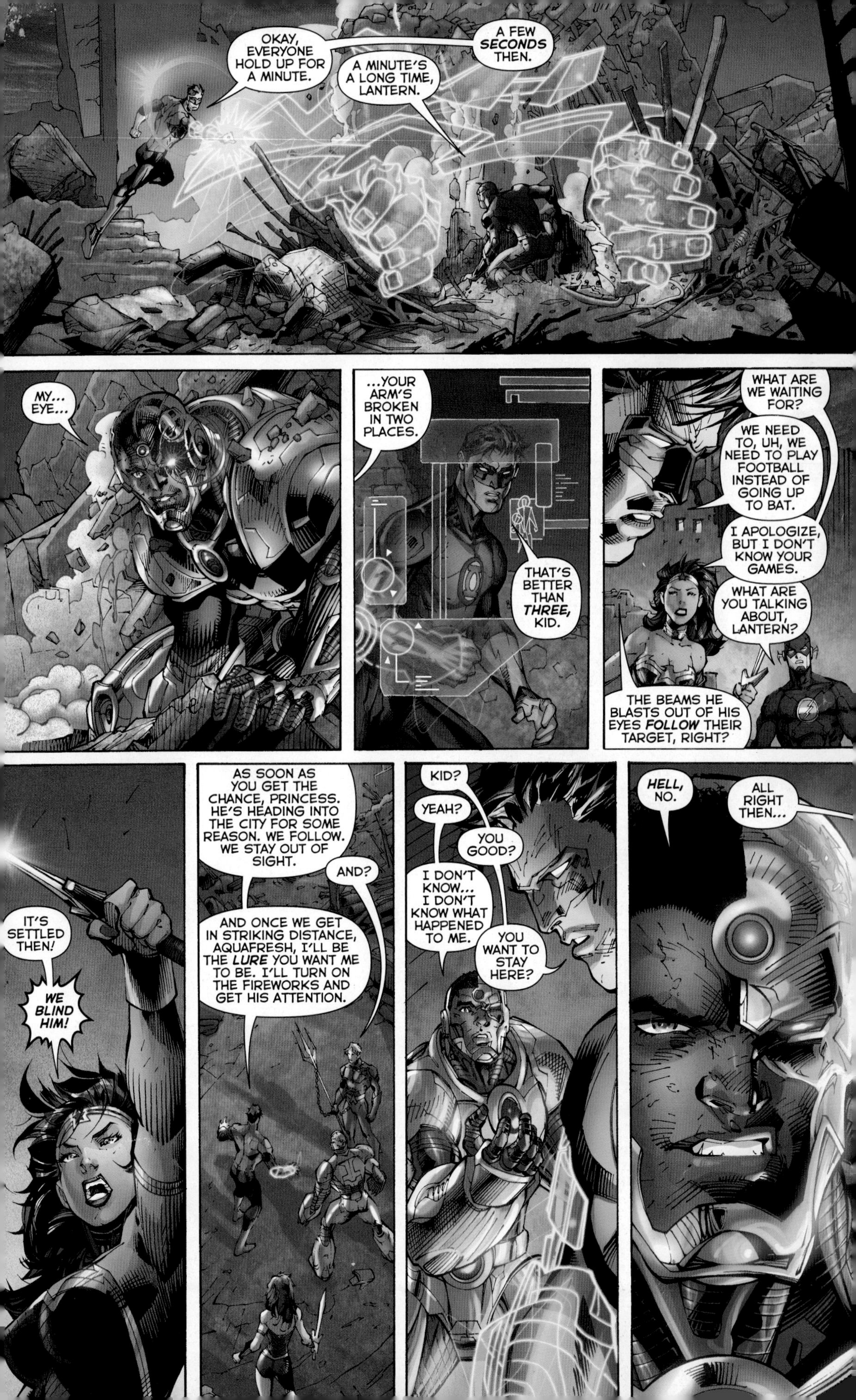
OKAY, EVERYONE HOLD UP FOR A MINUTE.
A MINUTE'S A LONG TIME, LANTERN.
A FEW SECONDS THEN.
MY... EYE...
...YOUR ARM'S BROKEN IN TWO PLACES.
THAT'S BETTER THAN THREE, KID.
WHAT ARE WE WAITING FOR?
WE NEED TO, UH, WE NEED TO PLAY FOOTBALL INSTEAD OF GOING UP TO BAT.
I APOLOGIZE, BUT I DON'T KNOW YOUR GAMES.
WHAT ARE YOU TALKING ABOUT, LANTERN?
THE BEAMS HE BLASTS OUT OF HIS EYES FOLLOW THEIR TARGET, RIGHT?
IT'S SETTLED THEN!
WE BLIND HIM!
AS SOON AS YOU GET THE CHANCE, PRINCESS. HE'S HEADING INTO THE CITY FOR SOME REASON. WE FOLLOW. WE STAY OUT OF SIGHT.
AND?
AND ONCE WE GET IN STRIKING DISTANCE, AQUAFRESH, I'LL BE THE LURE YOU WANT ME TO BE. I'LL TURN ON THE FIREWORKS AND GET HIS ATTENTION.
KID?
YEAH?
YOU GOOD?
I DON'T KNOW... I DON'T KNOW WHAT HAPPENED TO ME.
YOU WANT TO STAY HERE?
HELL, NO.
ALL RIGHT THEN...

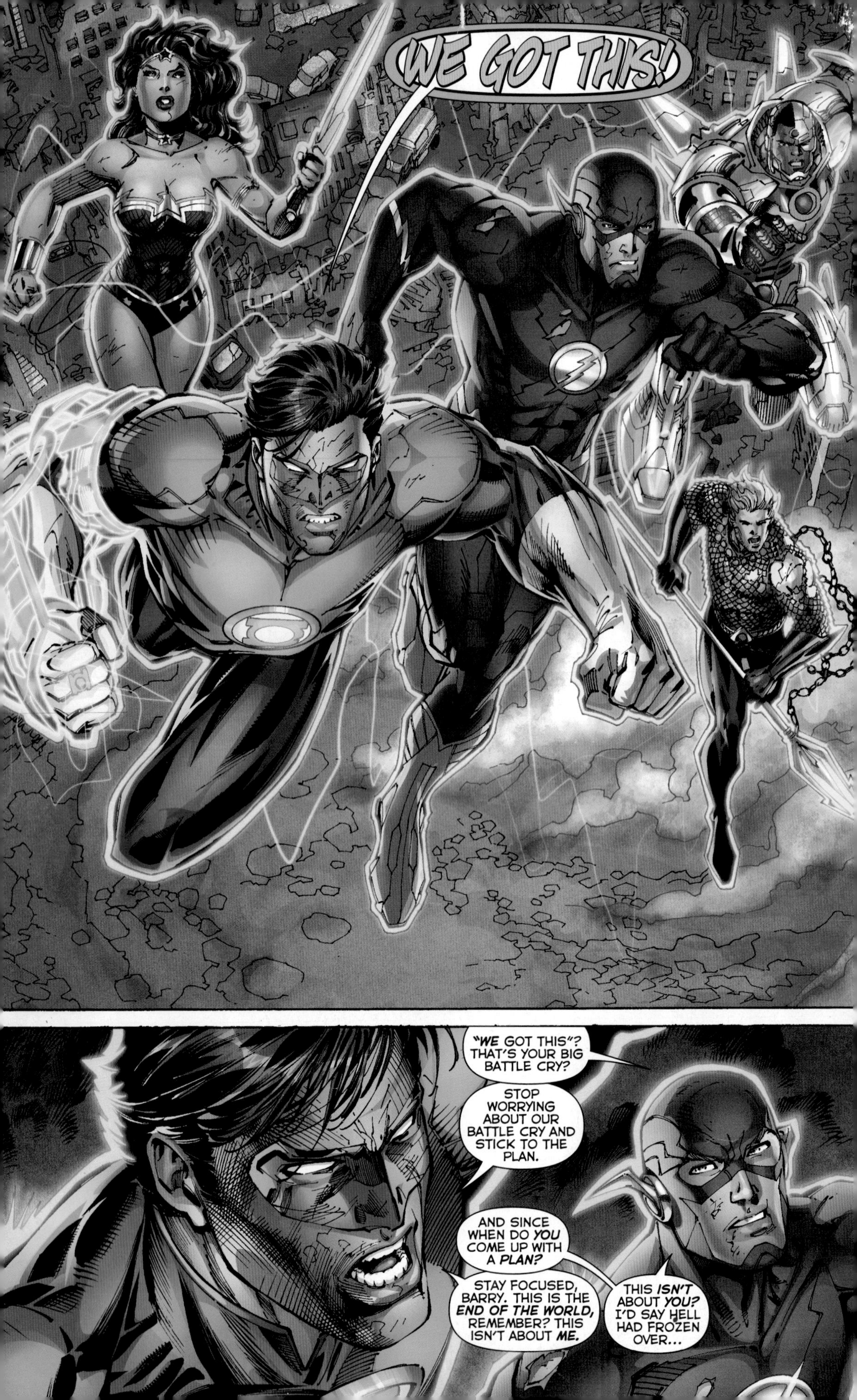
WE GOT THIS!
"WE GOT THIS"? THAT'S YOUR BIG BATTLE CRY?
STOP WORRYING ABOUT OUR BATTLE CRY AND STICK TO THE PLAN.
AND SINCE WHEN DO YOU COME UP WITH A PLAN?
STAY FOCUSED, BARRY. THIS IS THE END OF THE WORLD, REMEMBER? THIS ISN'T ABOUT ME.
THIS ISN'T ABOUT YOU? I'D SAY HELL HAD FROZEN OVER...

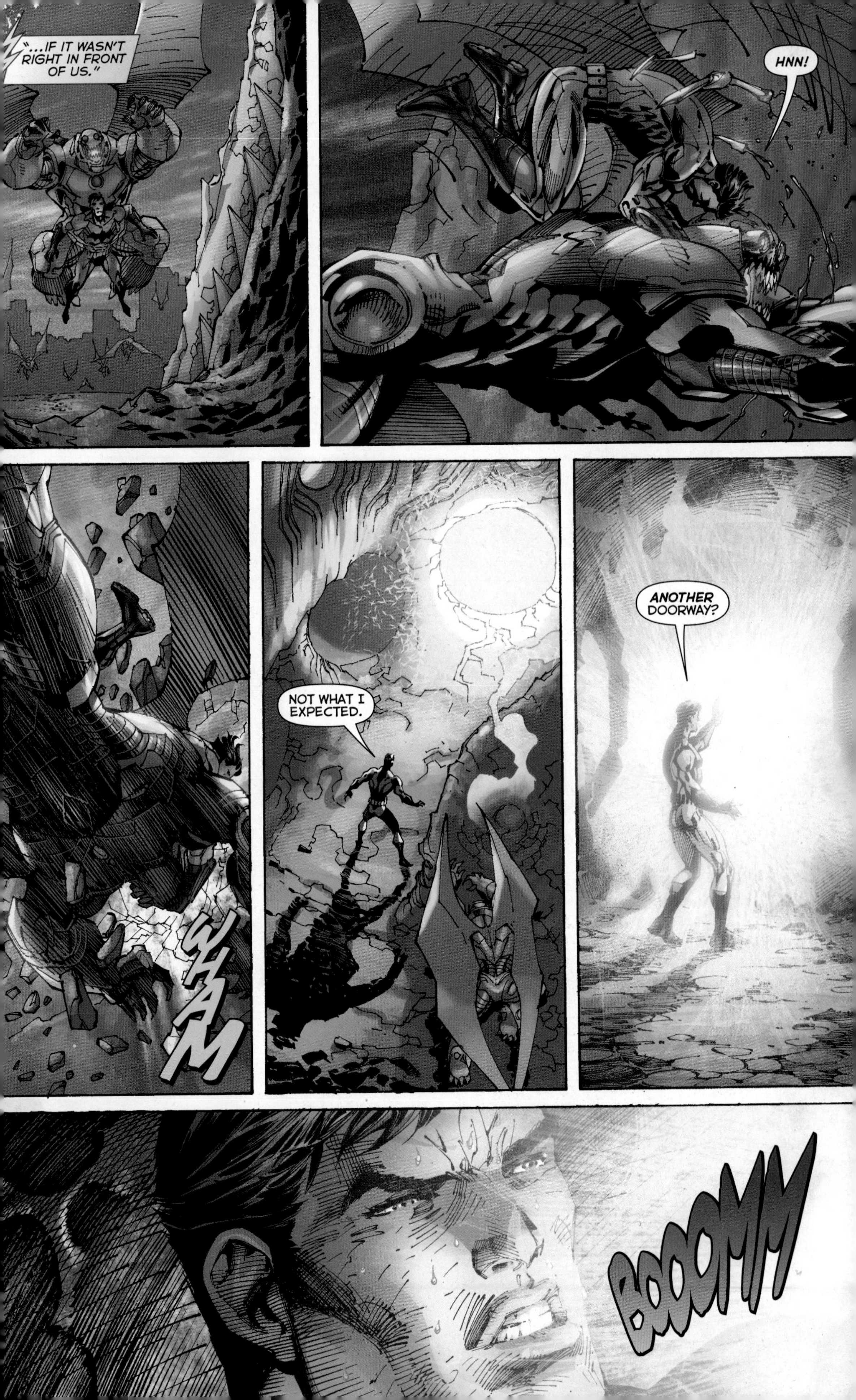
"...IF IT WASN'T RIGHT IN FRONT OF US."
HNN!
WHAM
NOT WHAT I EXPECTED.
ANOTHER DOORWAY?
BOOOMM

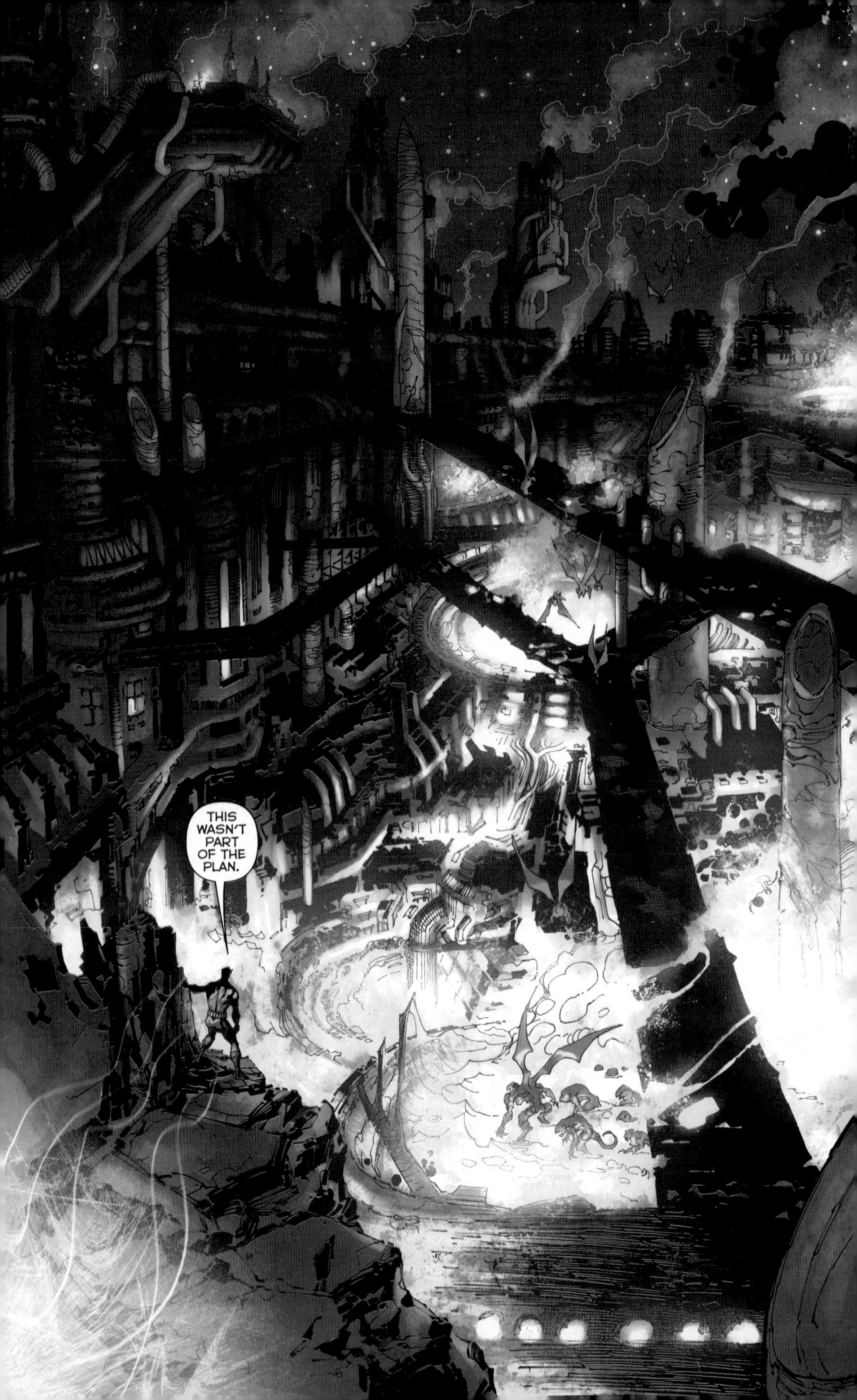
THIS WASN'T PART OF THE PLAN.

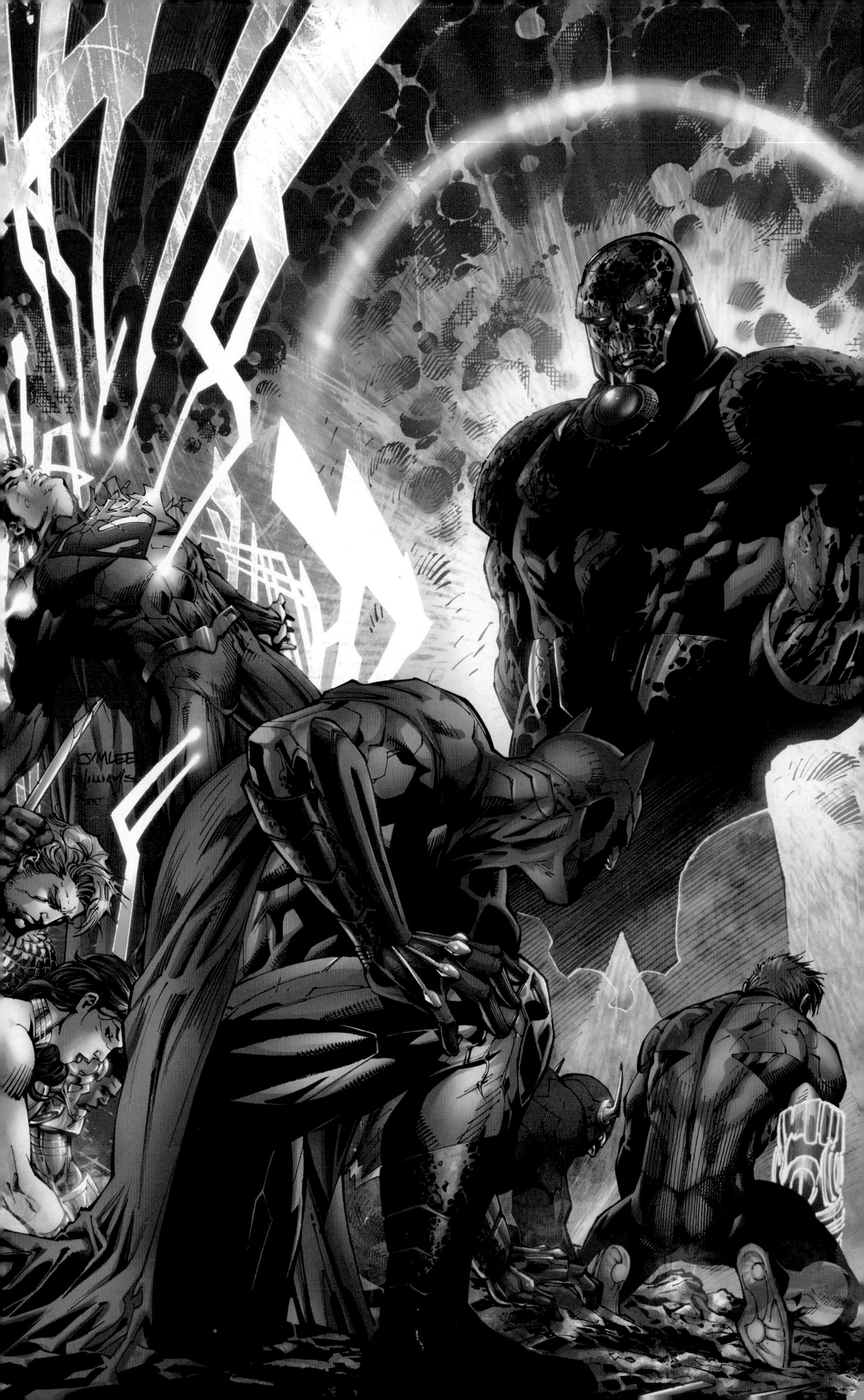

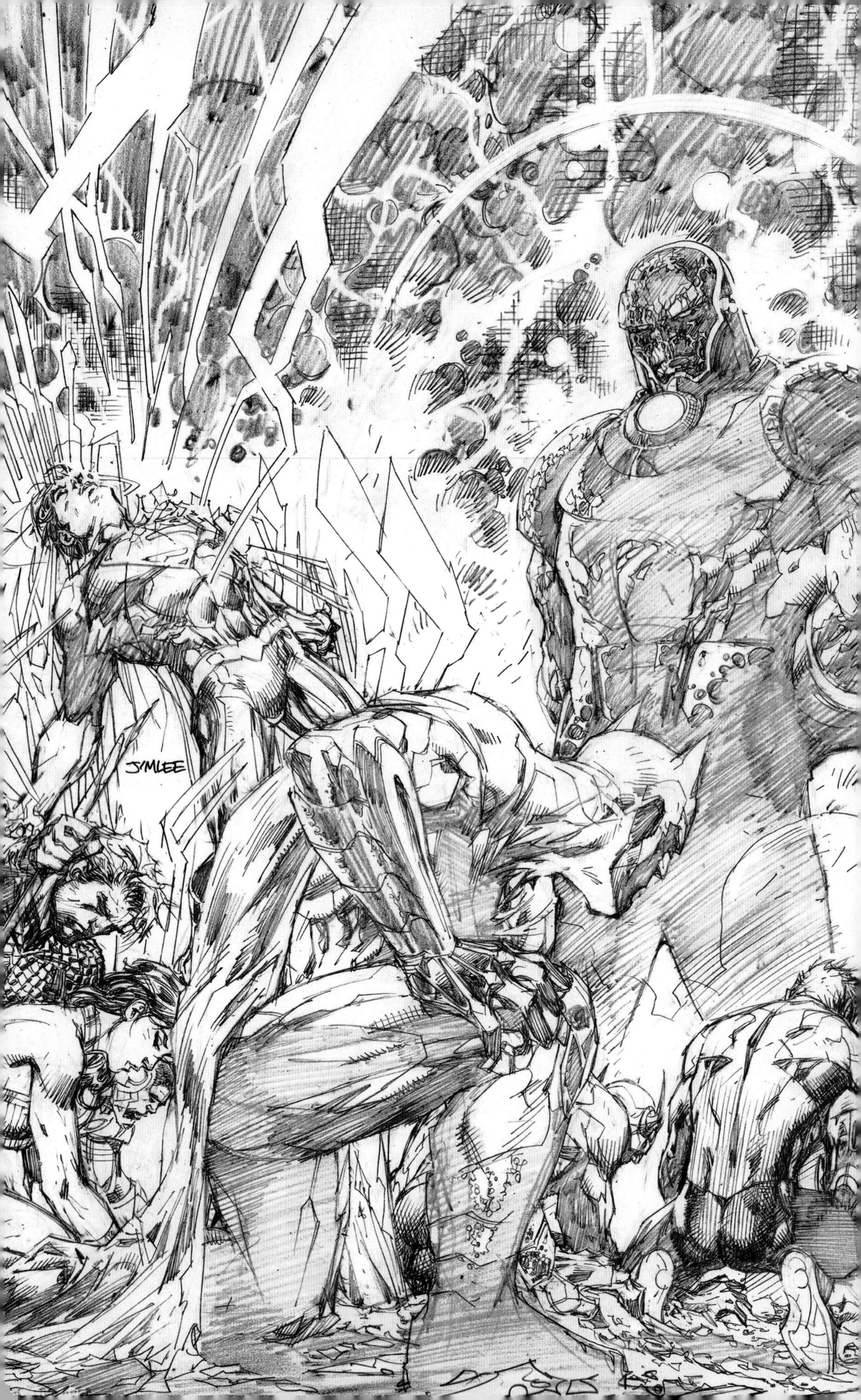
JIMLEE

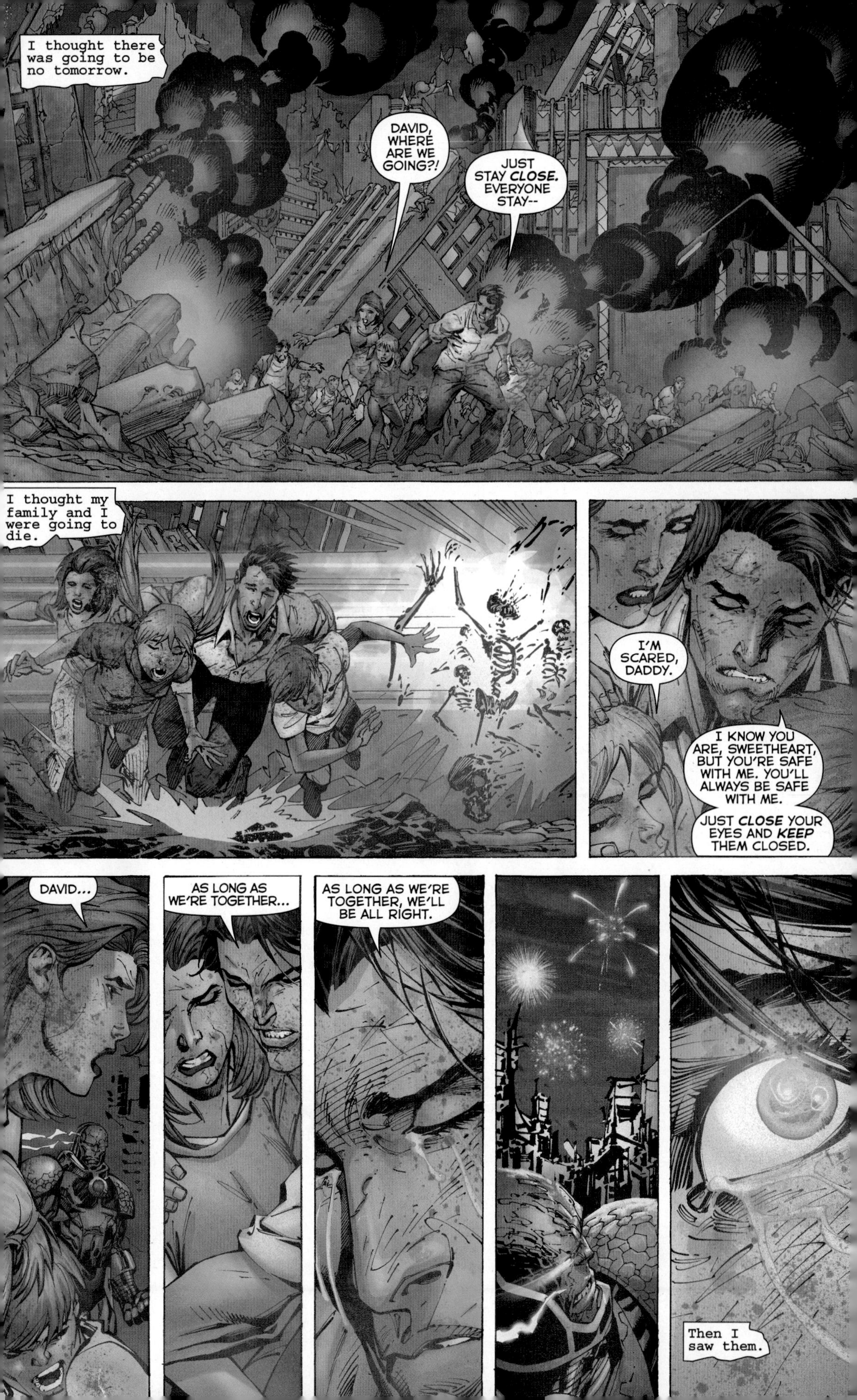

I thought there was going to be no tomorrow.
DAVID, WHERE ARE WE GOING?!
JUST STAY CLOSE. EVERYONE STAY--
I thought my family and I were going to die.
I'M SCARED, DADDY.
I KNOW YOU ARE, SWEETHEART, BUT YOU'RE SAFE WITH ME. YOU'LL ALWAYS BE SAFE WITH ME.
JUST CLOSE YOUR EYES AND KEEP THEM CLOSED.
DAVID...
AS LONG AS WE'RE TOGETHER...
AS LONG AS WE'RE TOGETHER, WE'LL BE ALL RIGHT.
Then I saw them.

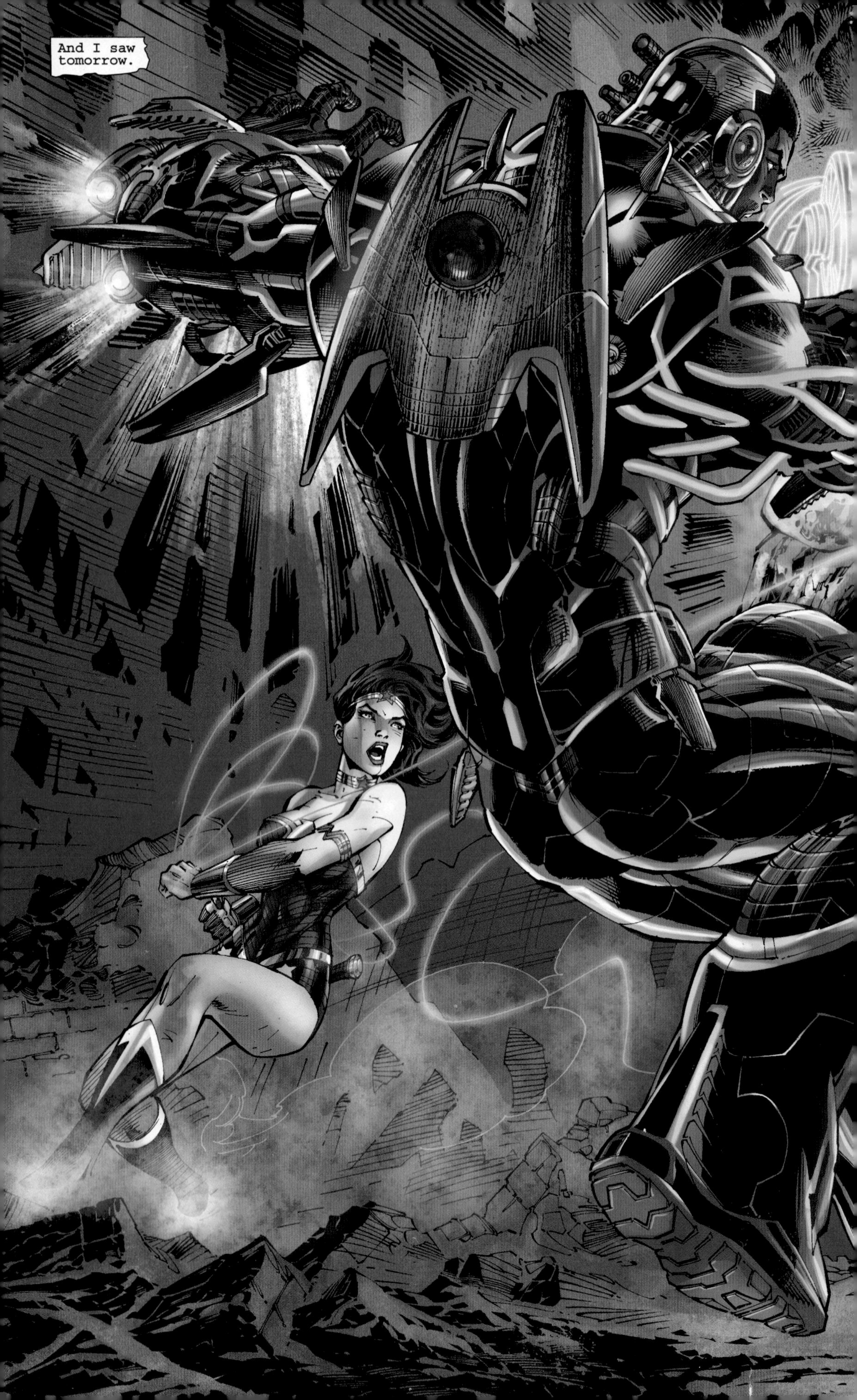
And I saw tomorrow.

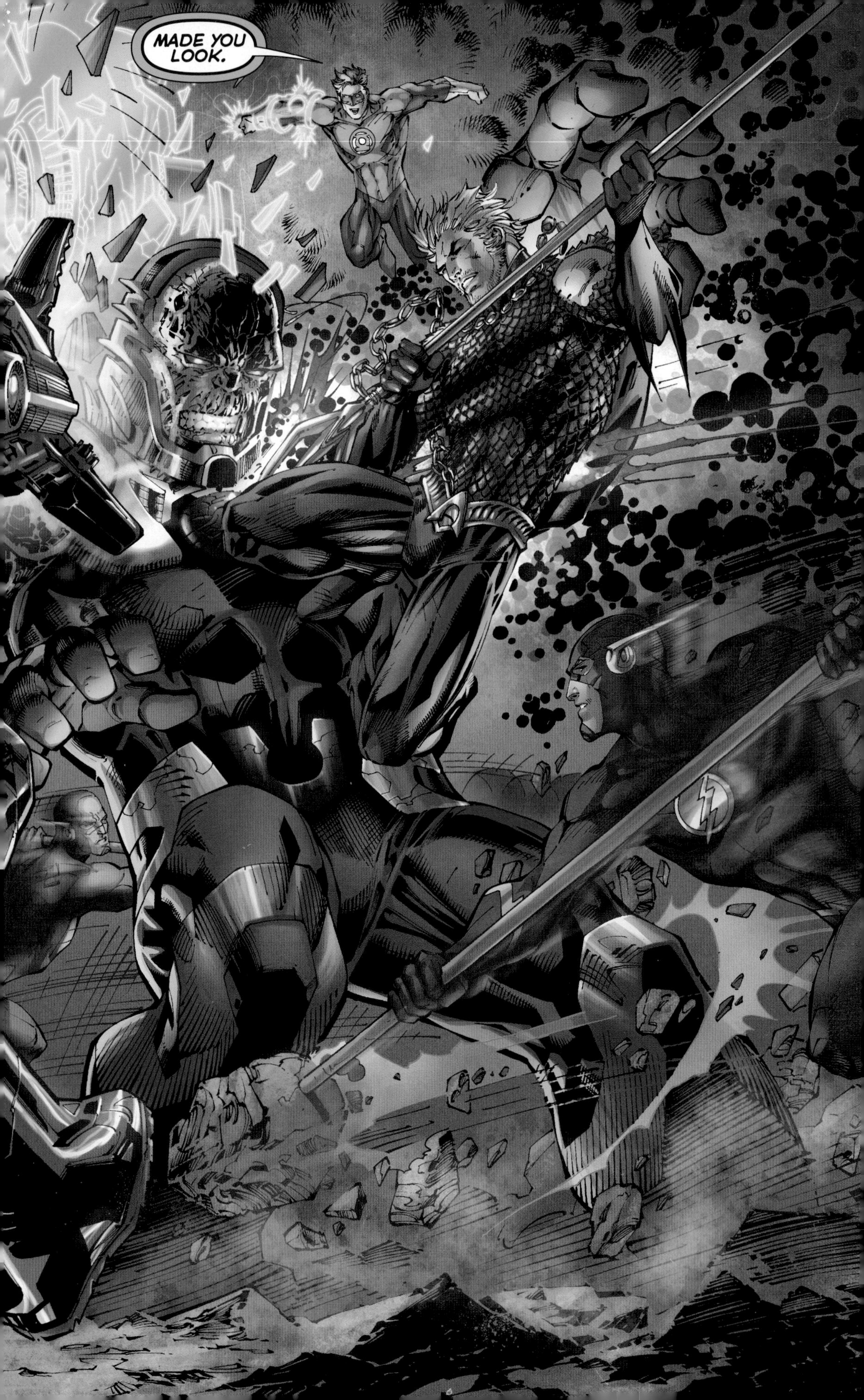
MADE YOU LOOK.

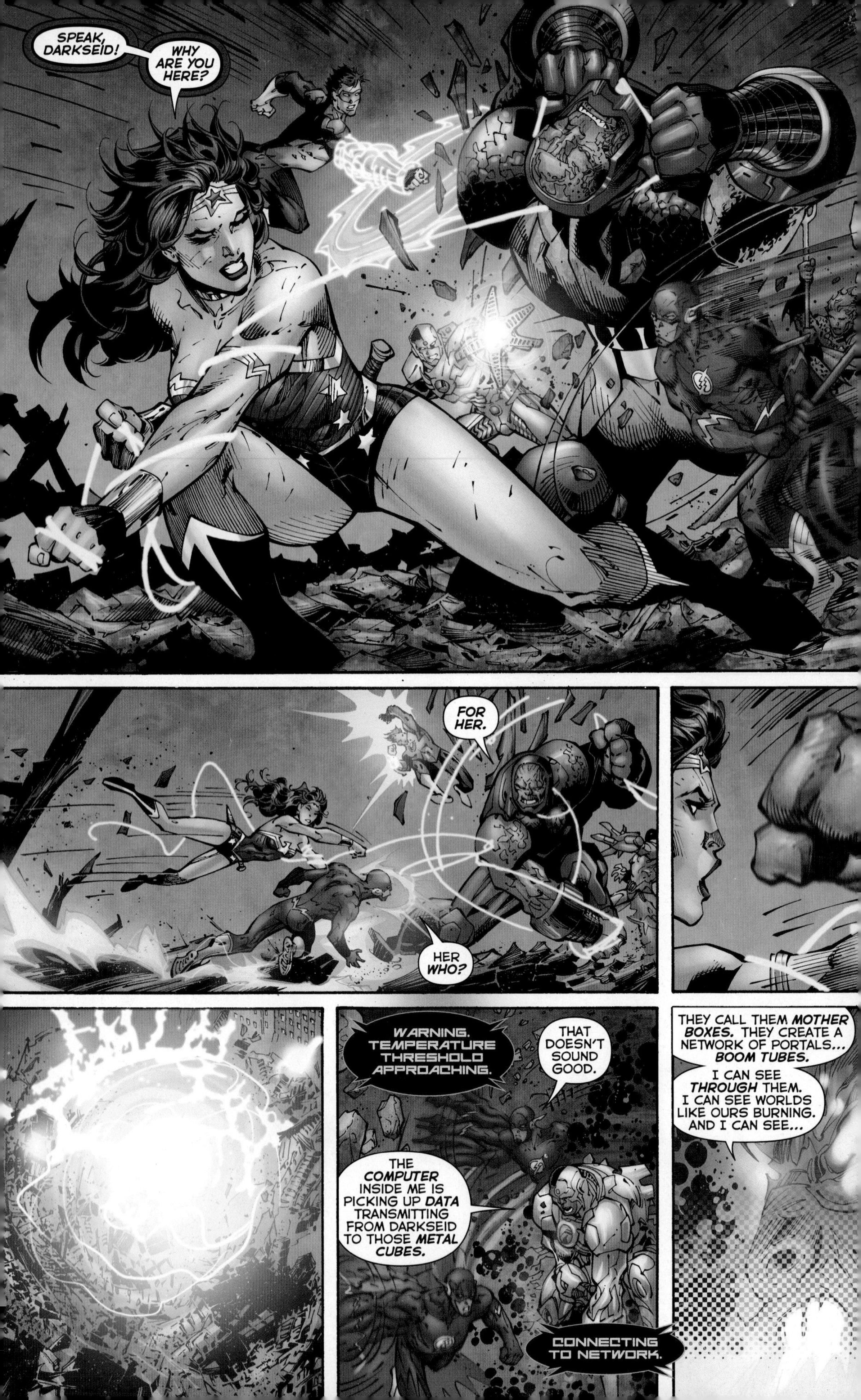
SPEAK, DARKSEID!
WHY ARE YOU HERE?
FOR HER.
HER WHO?
WARNING. TEMPERATURE THRESHOLD APPROACHING.
THAT DOESN'T SOUND GOOD.
THE COMPUTER INSIDE ME IS PICKING UP DATA TRANSMITTING FROM DARKSEID TO THOSE METAL CUBES.
CONNECTING TO NETWORK.
THEY CALL THEM MOTHER BOXES. THEY CREATE A NETWORK OF PORTALS... BOOM TUBES.
I CAN SEE THROUGH THEM. I CAN SEE WORLDS LIKE OURS BURNING. AND I CAN SEE...

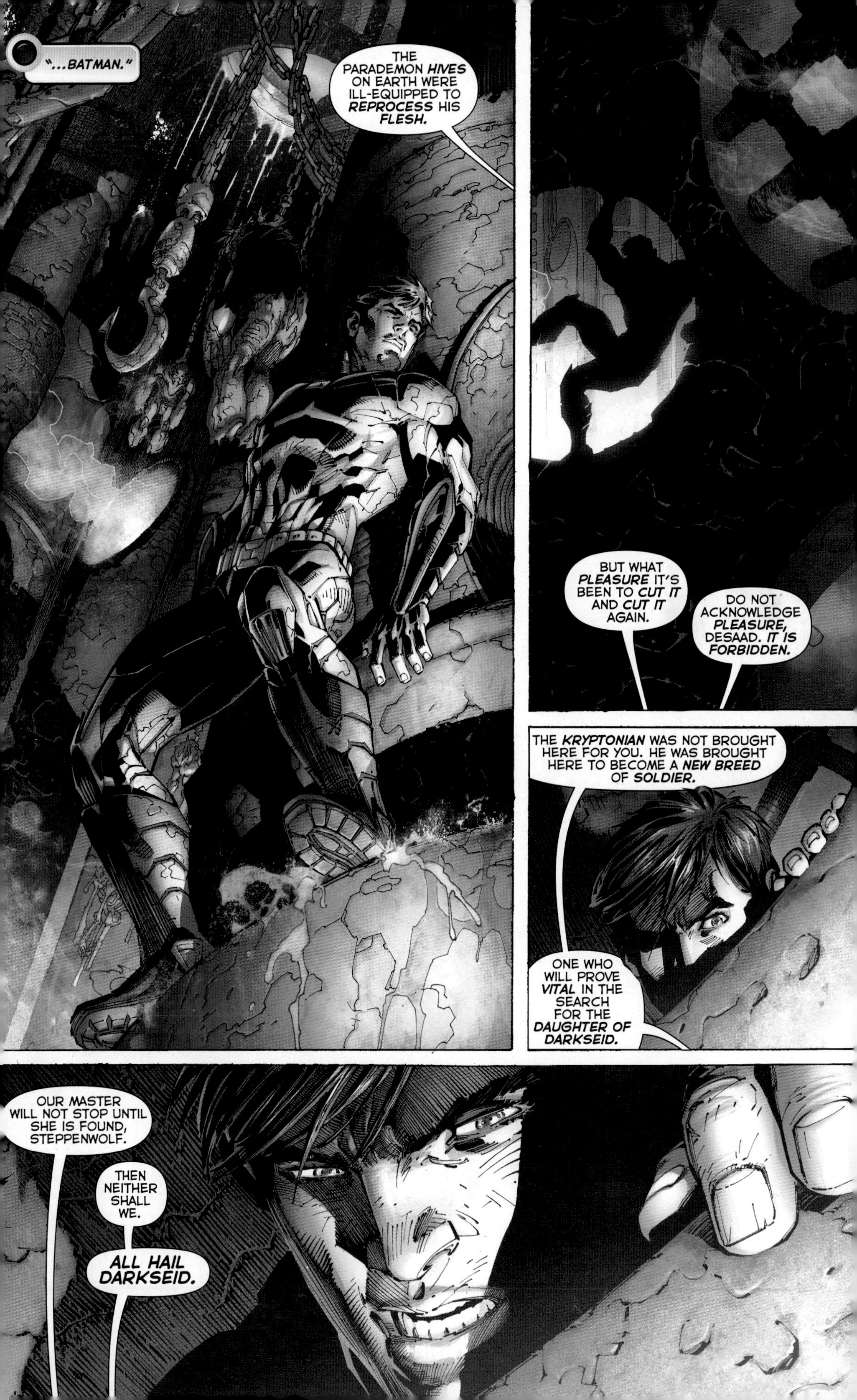
"...BATMAN."
THE PARADEMON HIVES ON EARTH WERE ILL-EQUIPPED TO REPROCESS HIS FLESH.
BUT WHAT PLEASURE IT'S BEEN TO CUT IT AND CUT IT AGAIN.
DO NOT ACKNOWLEDGE PLEASURE, DESAAD. IT IS FORBIDDEN.
THE KRYPTONIAN WAS NOT BROUGHT HERE FOR YOU. HE WAS BROUGHT HERE TO BECOME A NEW BREED OF SOLDIER.
ONE WHO WILL PROVE VITAL IN THE SEARCH FOR THE DAUGHTER OF DARKSEID.
OUR MASTER WILL NOT STOP UNTIL SHE IS FOUND, STEPPENWOLF.
THEN NEITHER SHALL WE.
ALL HAIL DARKSEID.

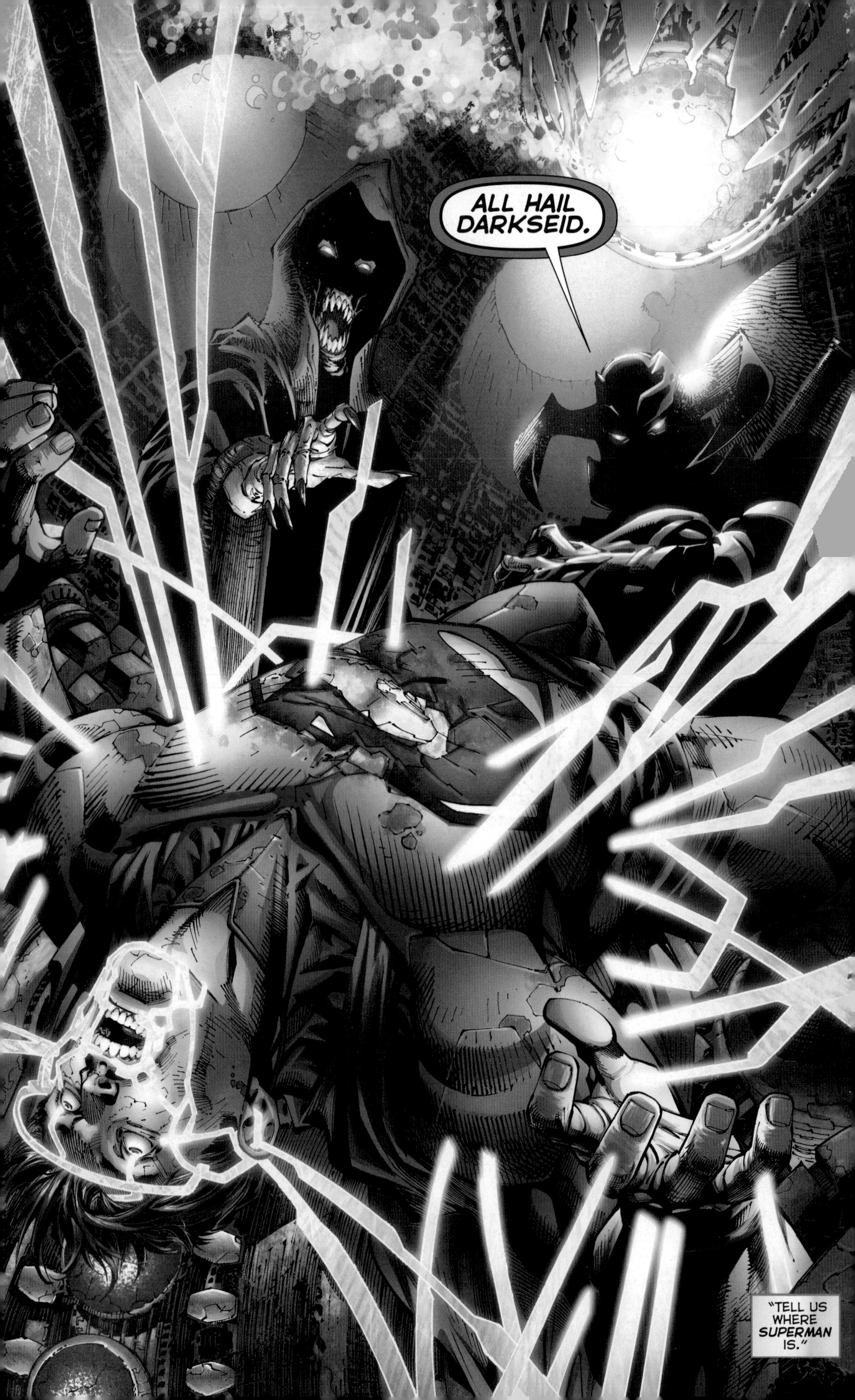
ALL HAIL DARKSEID.
"TELL US WHERE SUPERMAN IS."

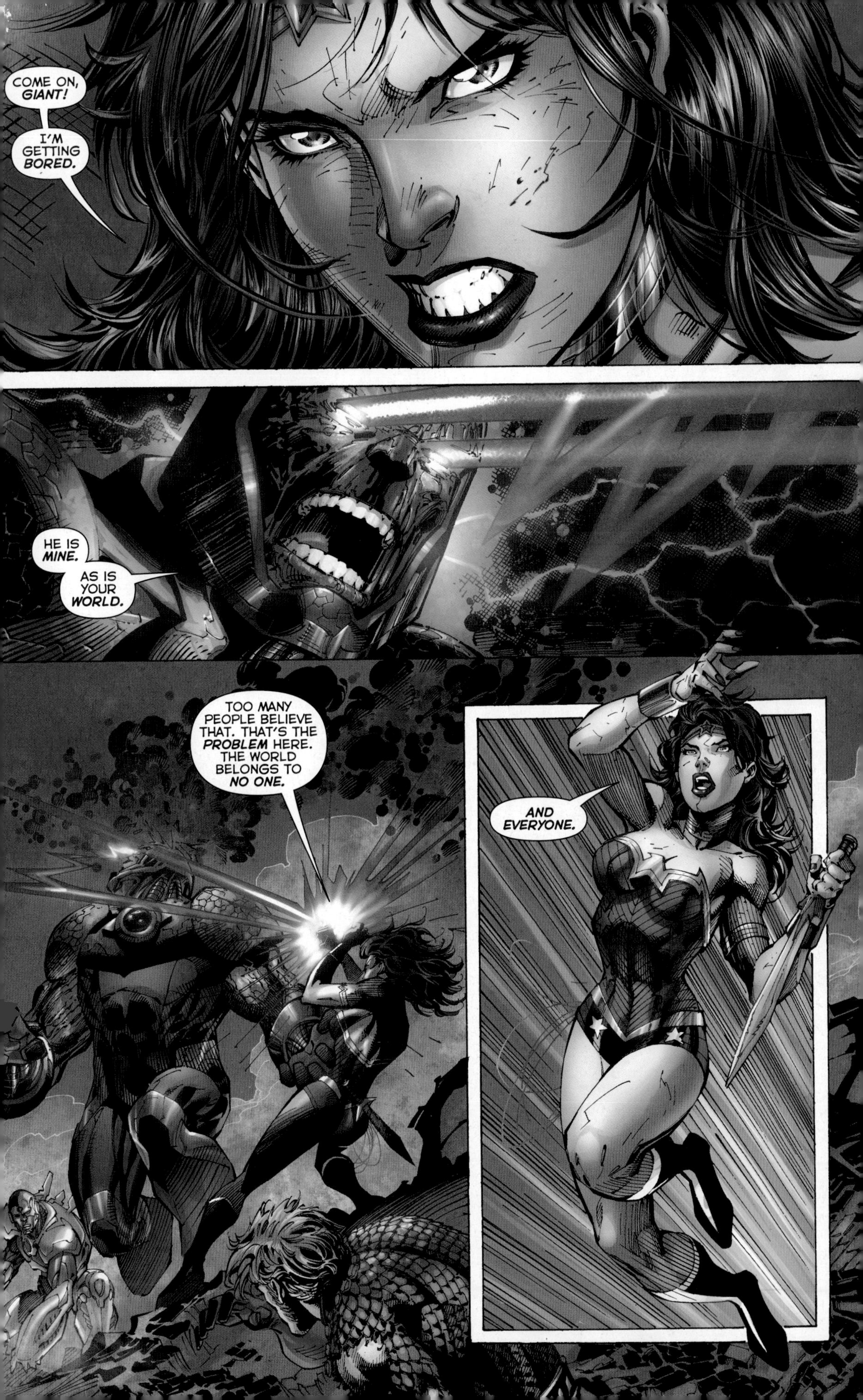
COME ON, *GIANT!*
I'M GETTING *BORED.*
HE IS *MINE.*
AS IS YOUR *WORLD.*
TOO MANY PEOPLE BELIEVE THAT. THAT'S THE *PROBLEM* HERE. THE WORLD BELONGS TO *NO ONE.*
AND EVERYONE.

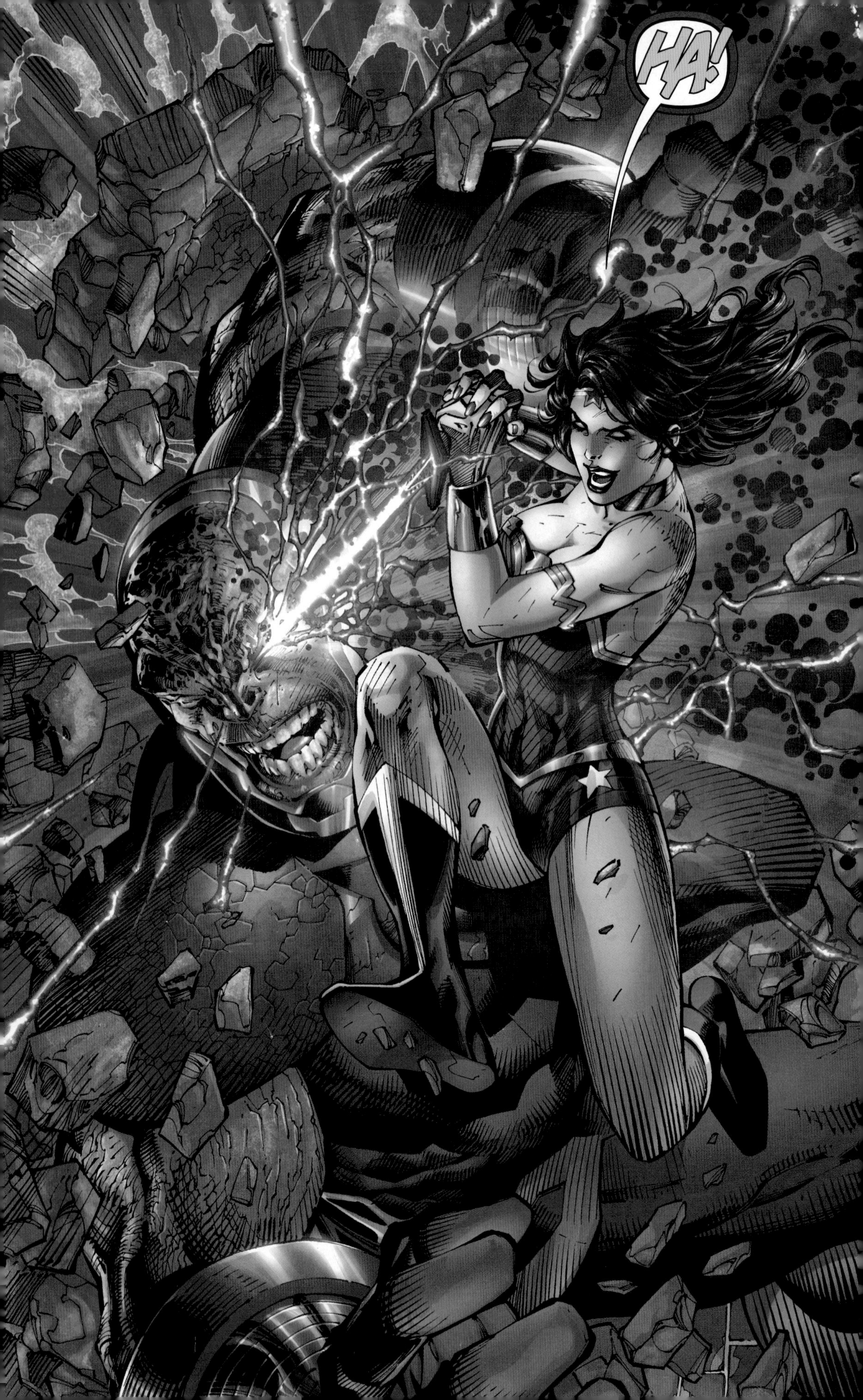
HA!

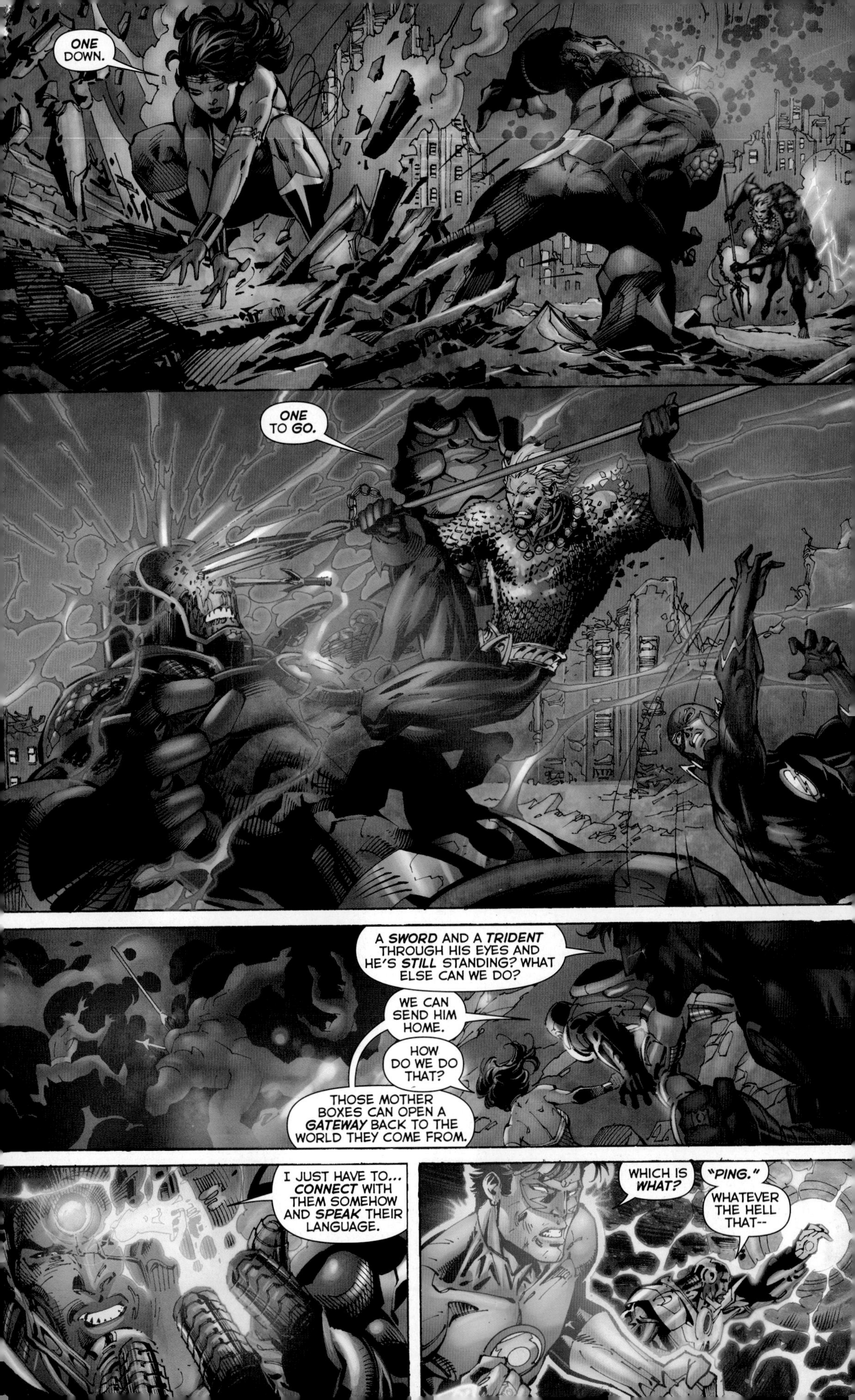
ONE DOWN.
ONE TO GO.
A SWORD AND A TRIDENT THROUGH HIS EYES AND HE'S STILL STANDING? WHAT ELSE CAN WE DO?
WE CAN SEND HIM HOME.
HOW DO WE DO THAT?
THOSE MOTHER BOXES CAN OPEN A GATEWAY BACK TO THE WORLD THEY COME FROM.
I JUST HAVE TO... CONNECT WITH THEM SOMEHOW AND SPEAK THEIR LANGUAGE.
WHICH IS WHAT?
"PING."
WHATEVER THE HELL THAT--

REE?

PING

BOOOOM

PING

BOOOOM

WHATEVER YOU'RE DOING, KID, KEEP DOING IT!

PING

BOOOOM

OUR MOTHER BOXES! THEY'RE ACTIVATING!

PING

PING

WE'RE UNDER ATTACK! SECURE SUPERMAN! SECURE--

BOOOOM

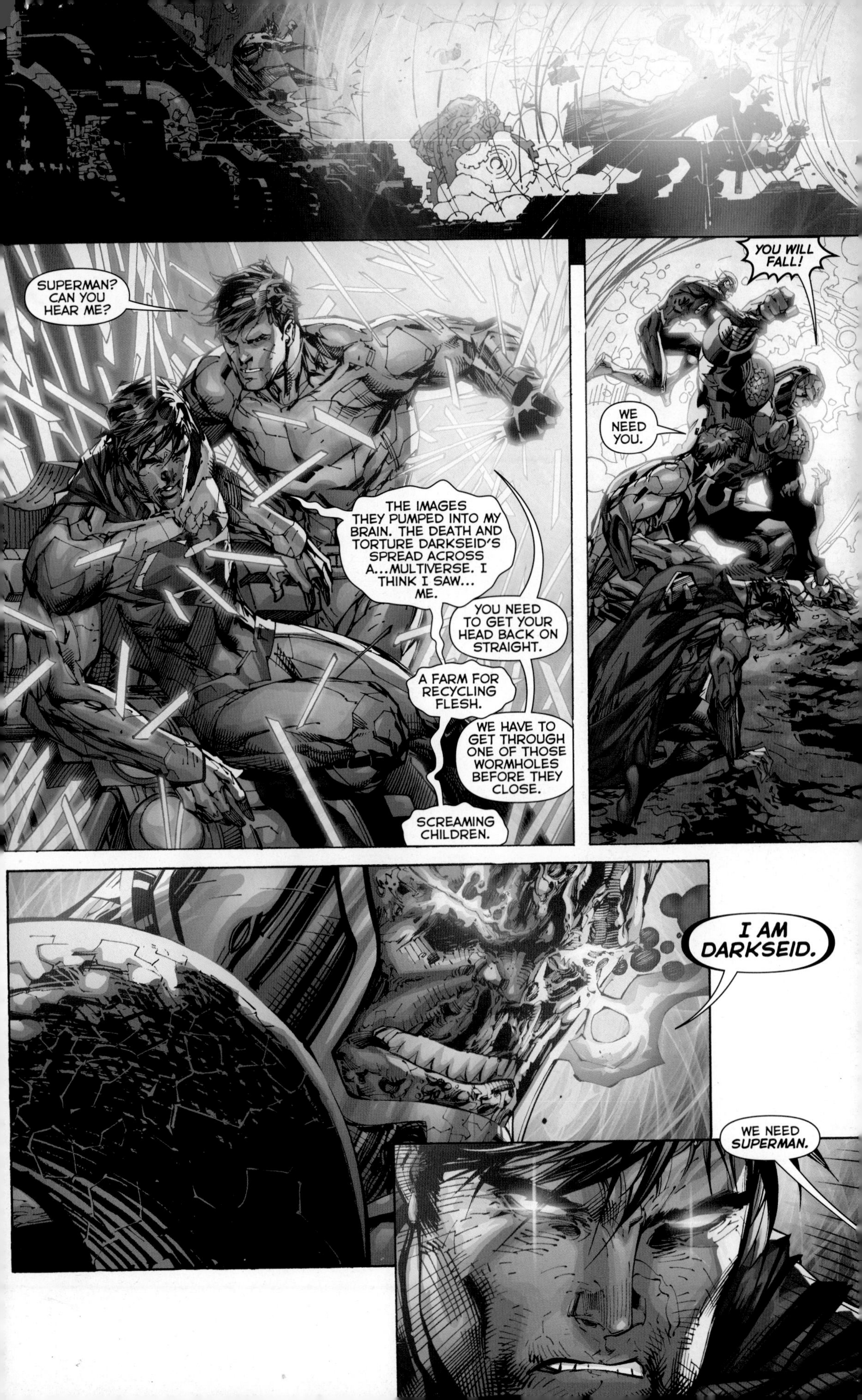
SUPERMAN? CAN YOU HEAR ME?
THE IMAGES THEY PUMPED INTO MY BRAIN. THE DEATH AND TORTURE DARKSEID'S SPREAD ACROSS A...MULTIVERSE. I THINK I SAW... ME.
YOU NEED TO GET YOUR HEAD BACK ON STRAIGHT.
A FARM FOR RECYCLING FLESH.
WE HAVE TO GET THROUGH ONE OF THOSE WORMHOLES BEFORE THEY CLOSE.
SCREAMING CHILDREN.
YOU WILL FALL!
WE NEED YOU.
I AM DARKSEID.
WE NEED SUPERMAN.

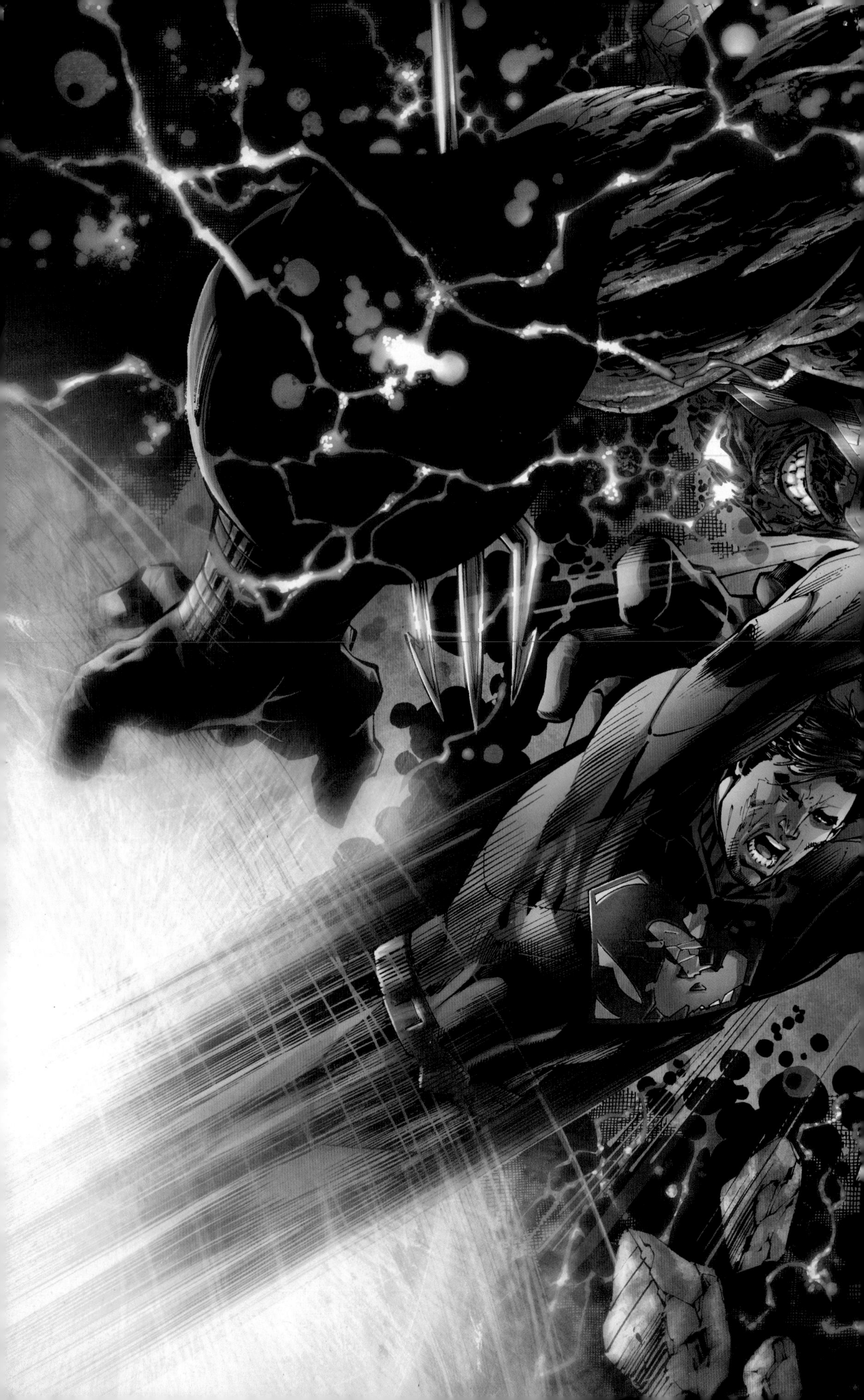

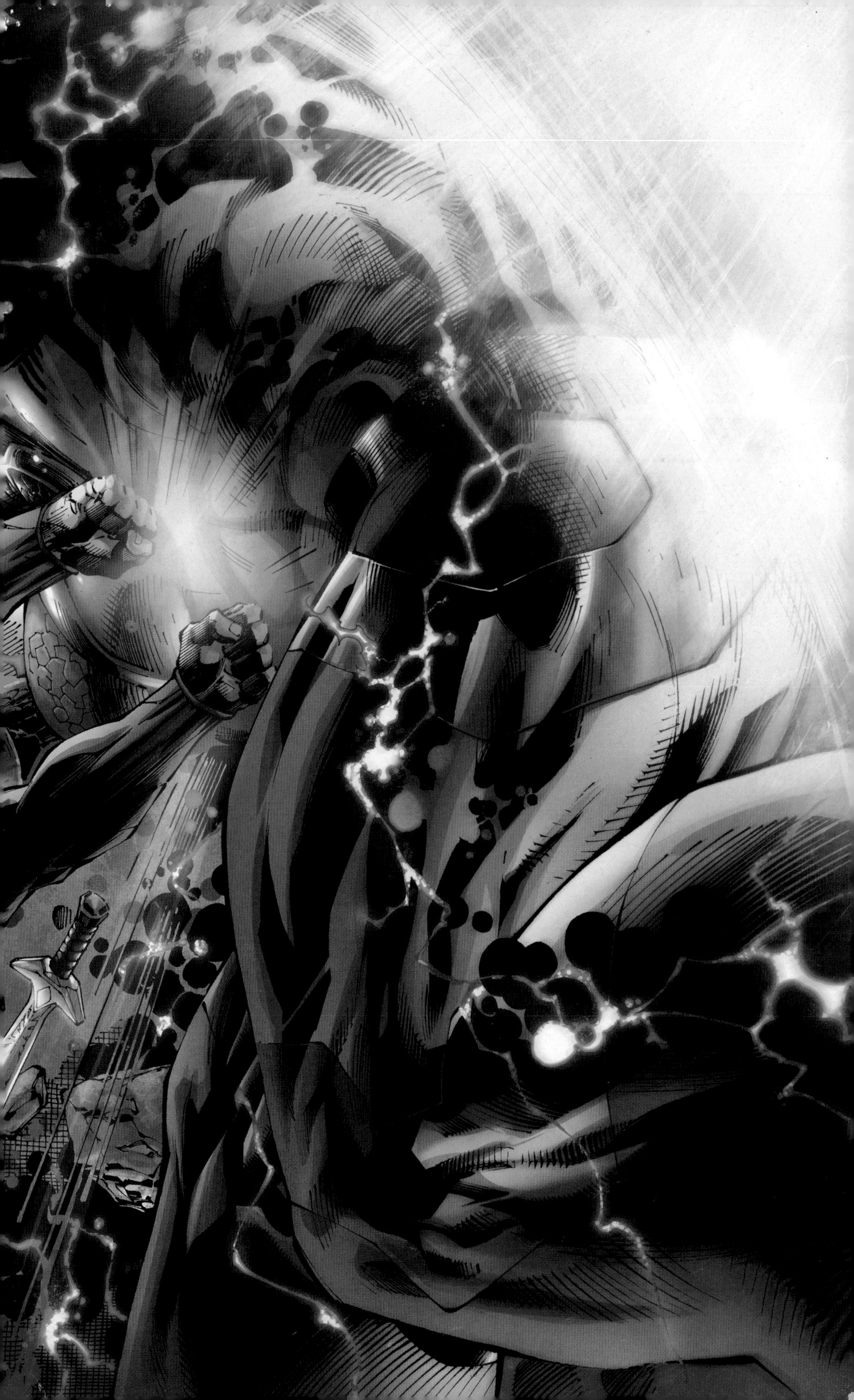

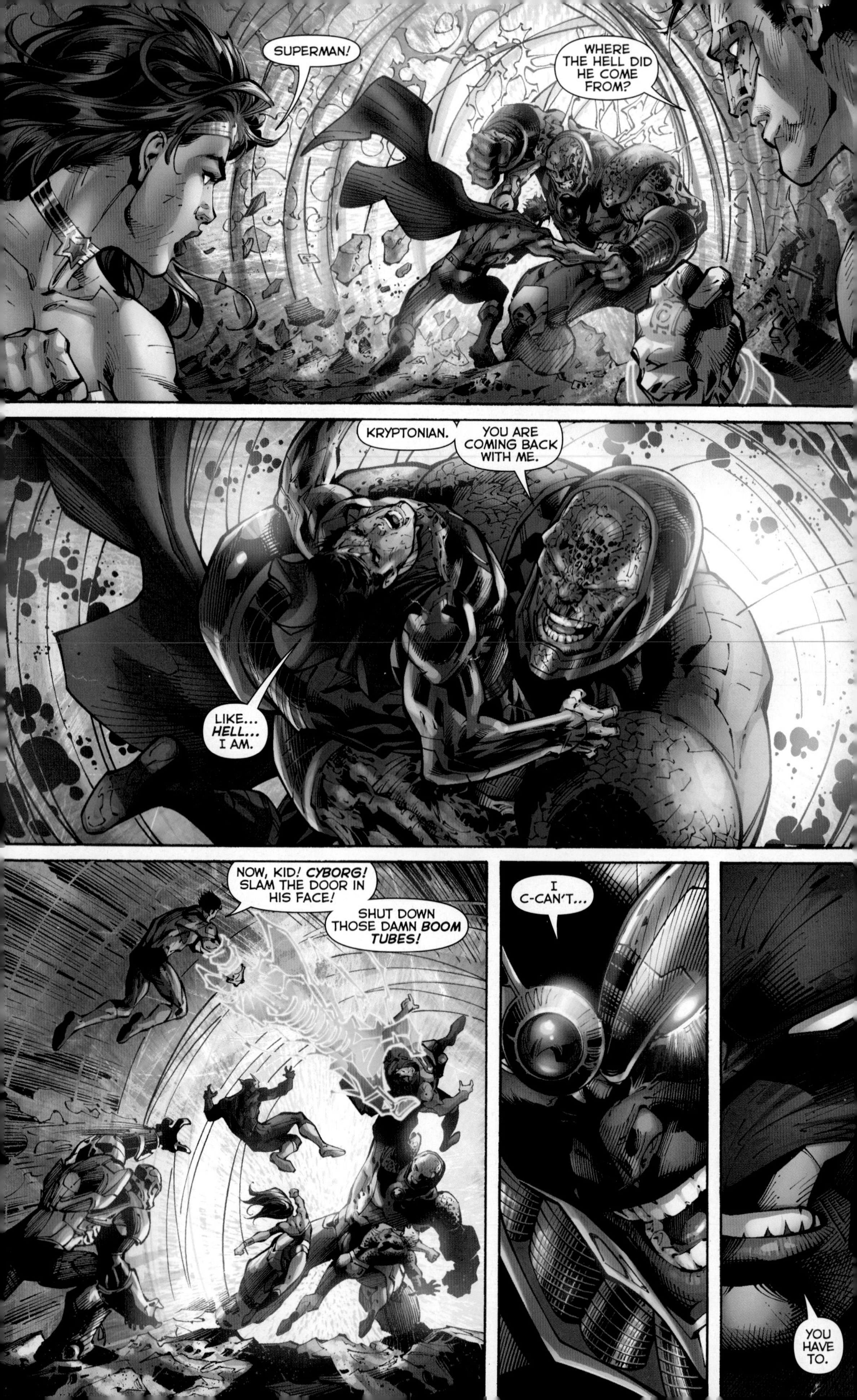
SUPERMAN!
WHERE THE HELL DID HE COME FROM?
KRYPTONIAN.
YOU ARE COMING BACK WITH ME.
LIKE... HELL... I AM.
NOW, KID! CYBORG! SLAM THE DOOR IN HIS FACE!
SHUT DOWN THOSE DAMN BOOM TUBES!
I C-CAN'T...
YOU HAVE TO.

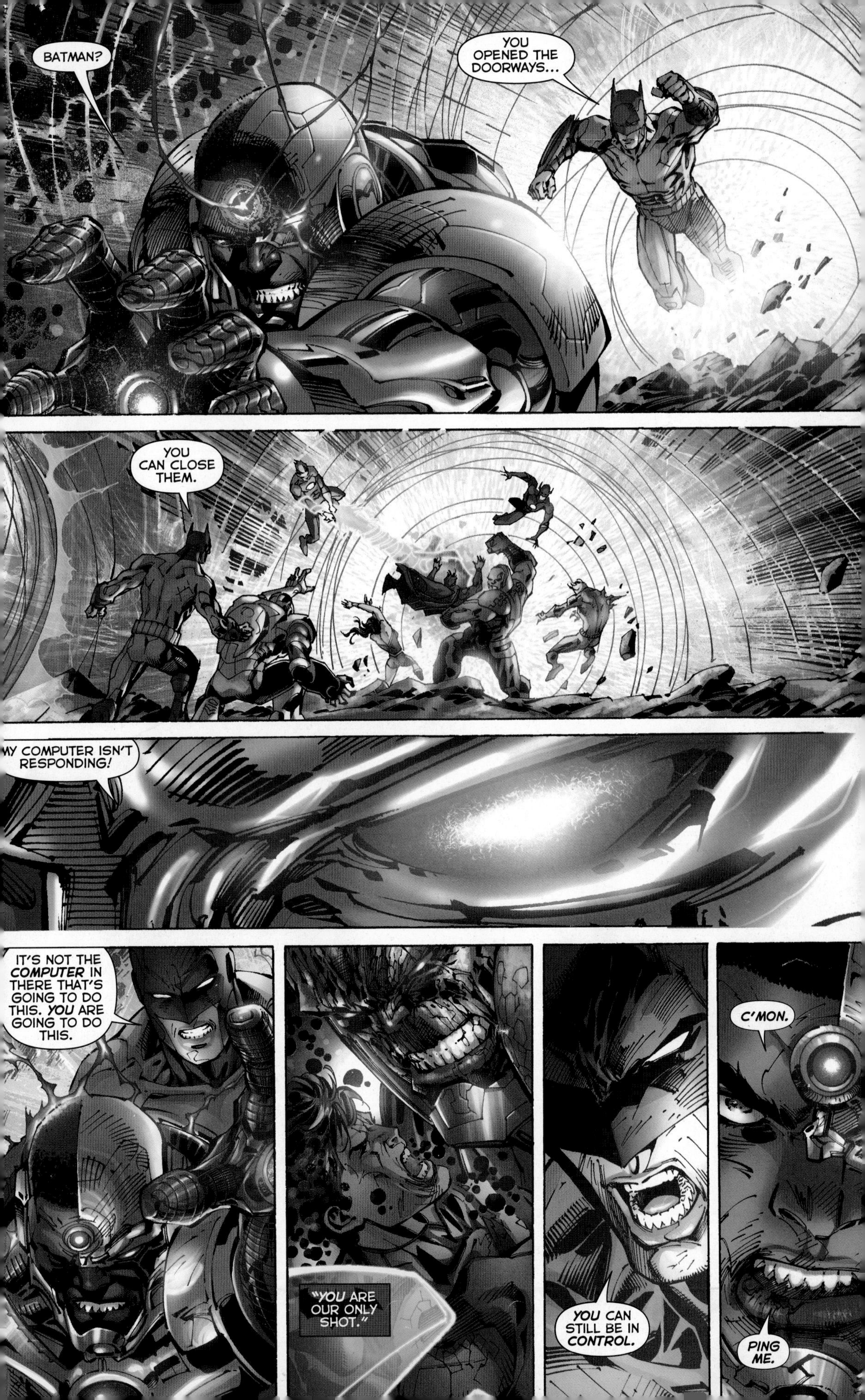
BATMAN?
YOU OPENED THE DOORWAYS...
YOU CAN CLOSE THEM.
MY COMPUTER ISN'T RESPONDING!
IT'S NOT THE *COMPUTER* IN THERE THAT'S GOING TO DO THIS. *YOU* ARE GOING TO DO THIS.
"*YOU* ARE OUR ONLY SHOT."
YOU CAN STILL BE IN *CONTROL*.
C'MON.
PING ME.

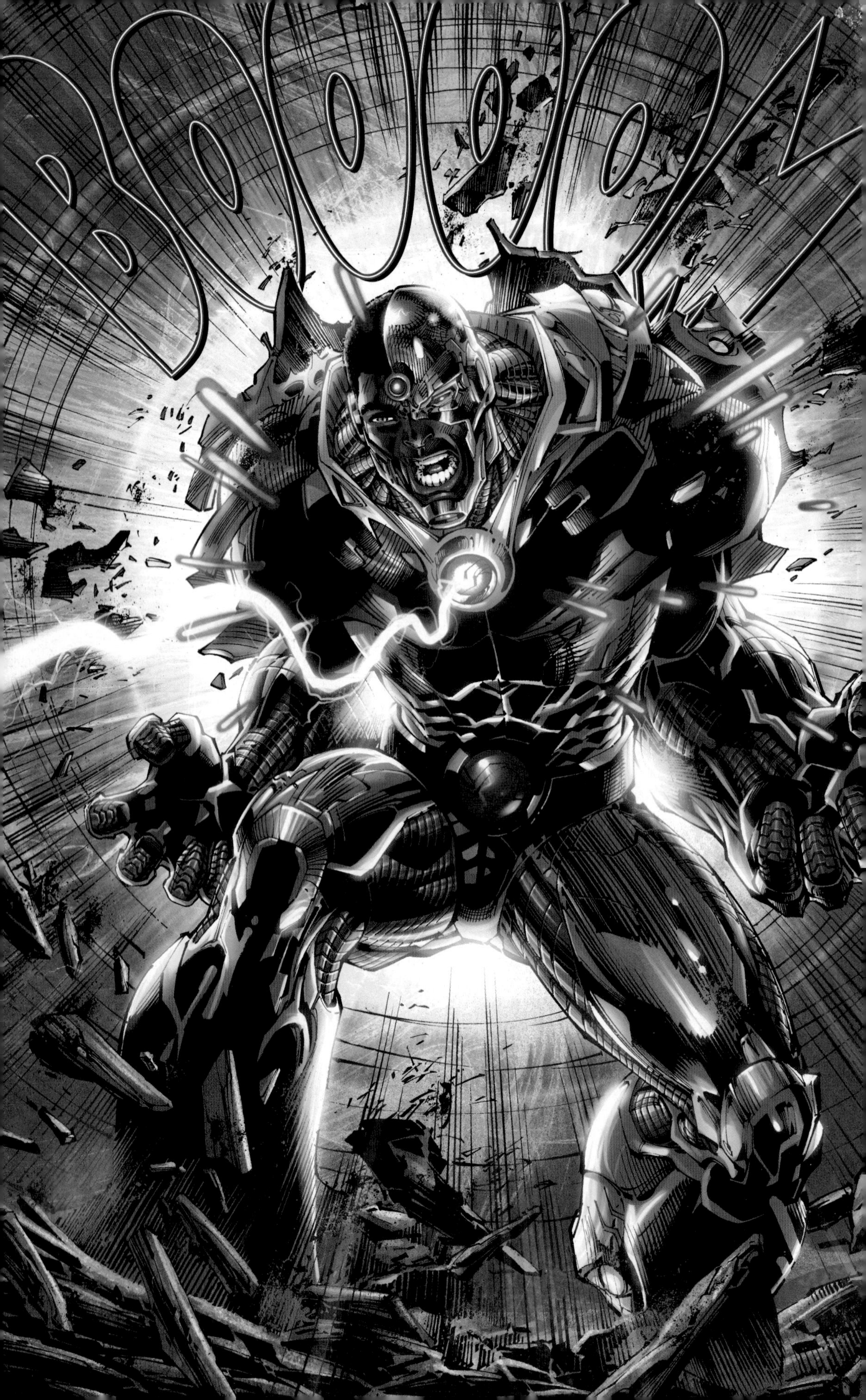
BOOOOM

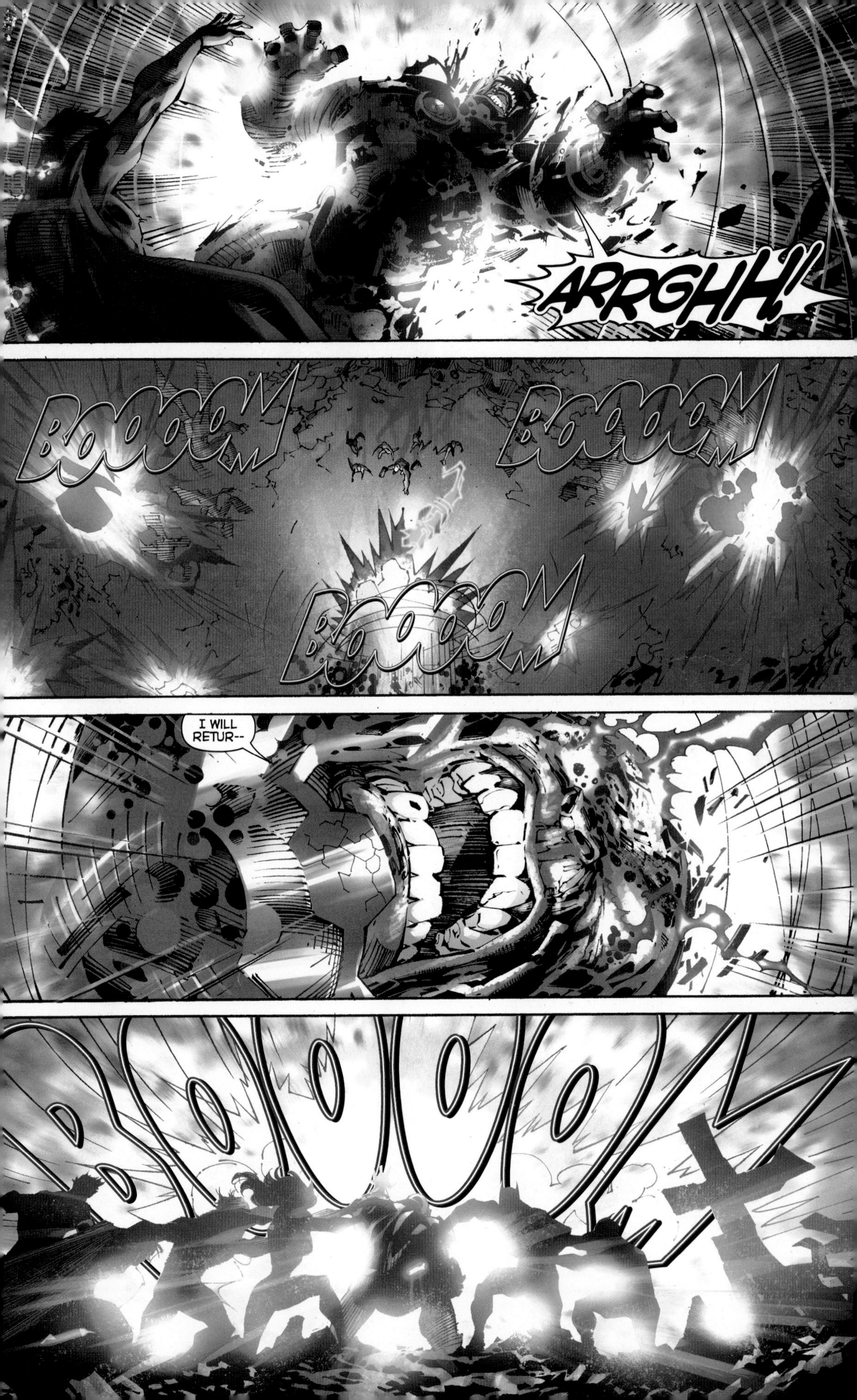
ARRGHH!
BOOOOM
BOOOOM
BOOOOM
I WILL RETUR--
BOOOOOOOM

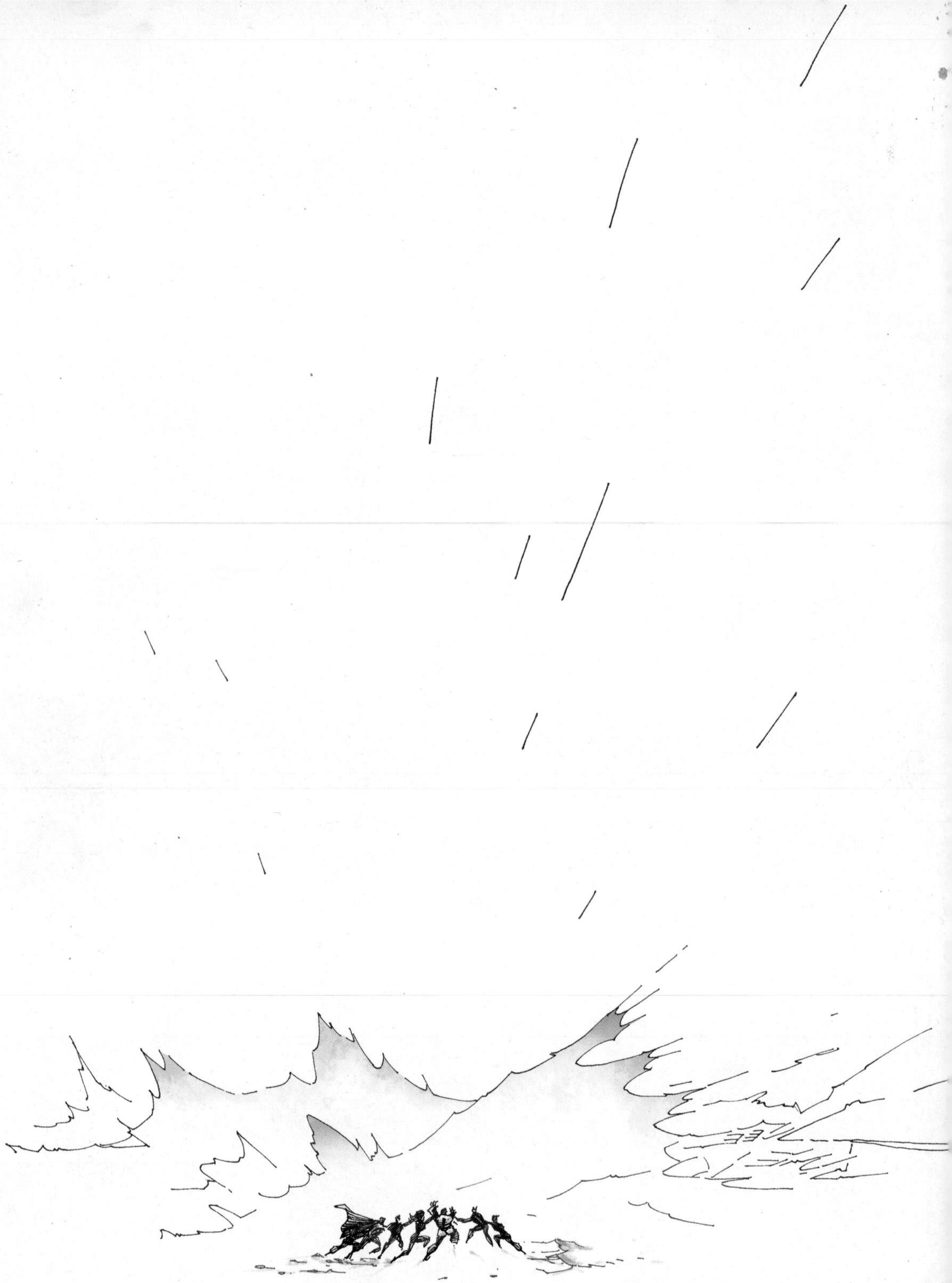

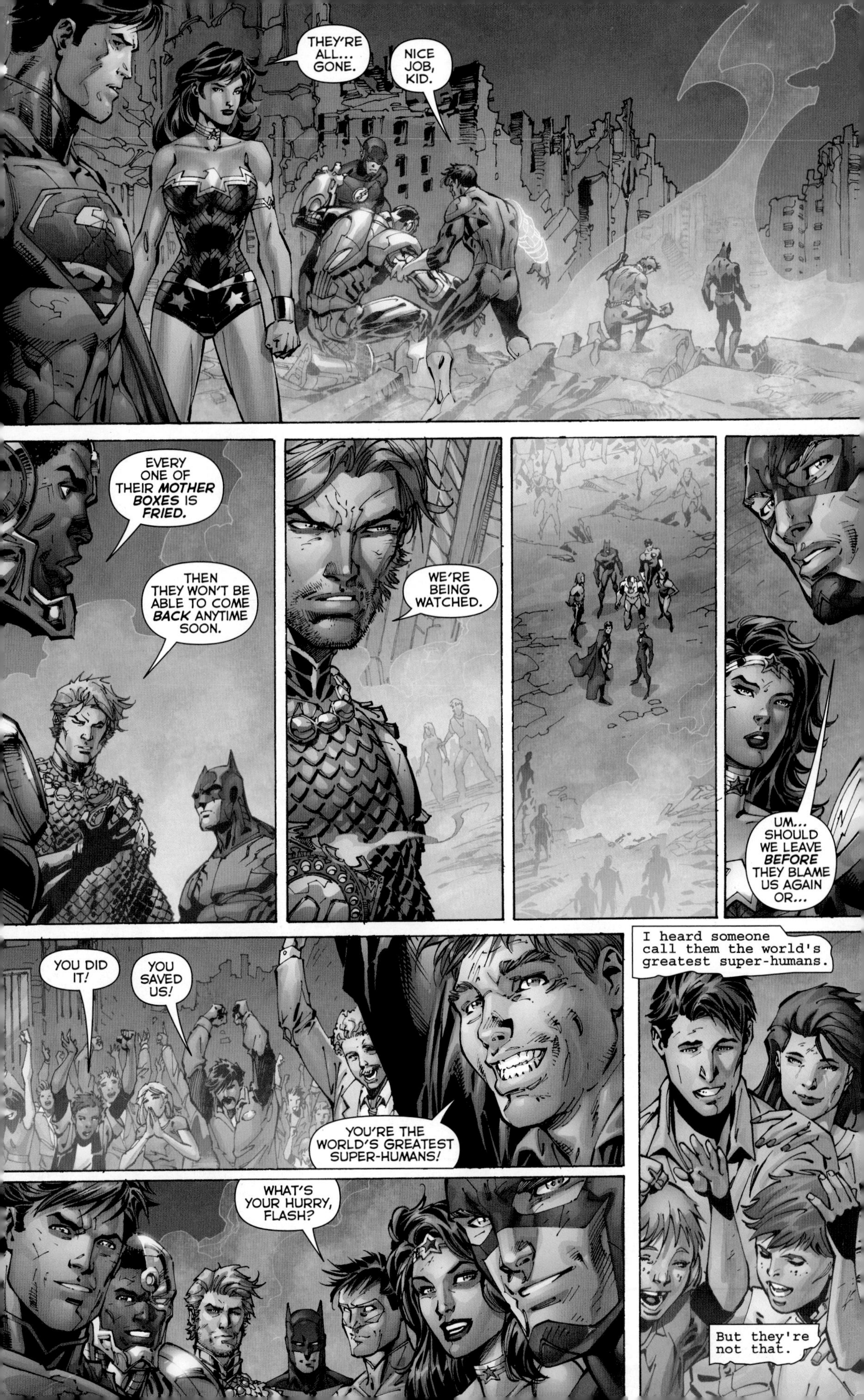
THEY'RE ALL... GONE.
NICE JOB, KID.
EVERY ONE OF THEIR *MOTHER BOXES* IS *FRIED.*
THEN THEY WON'T BE ABLE TO COME *BACK* ANYTIME SOON.
WE'RE BEING WATCHED.
UM... SHOULD WE LEAVE *BEFORE* THEY BLAME US AGAIN OR...
YOU DID IT!
YOU SAVED US!
YOU'RE THE WORLD'S GREATEST SUPER-HUMANS!
I heard someone call them the world's greatest super-humans.
WHAT'S YOUR HURRY, FLASH?
But they're not that.

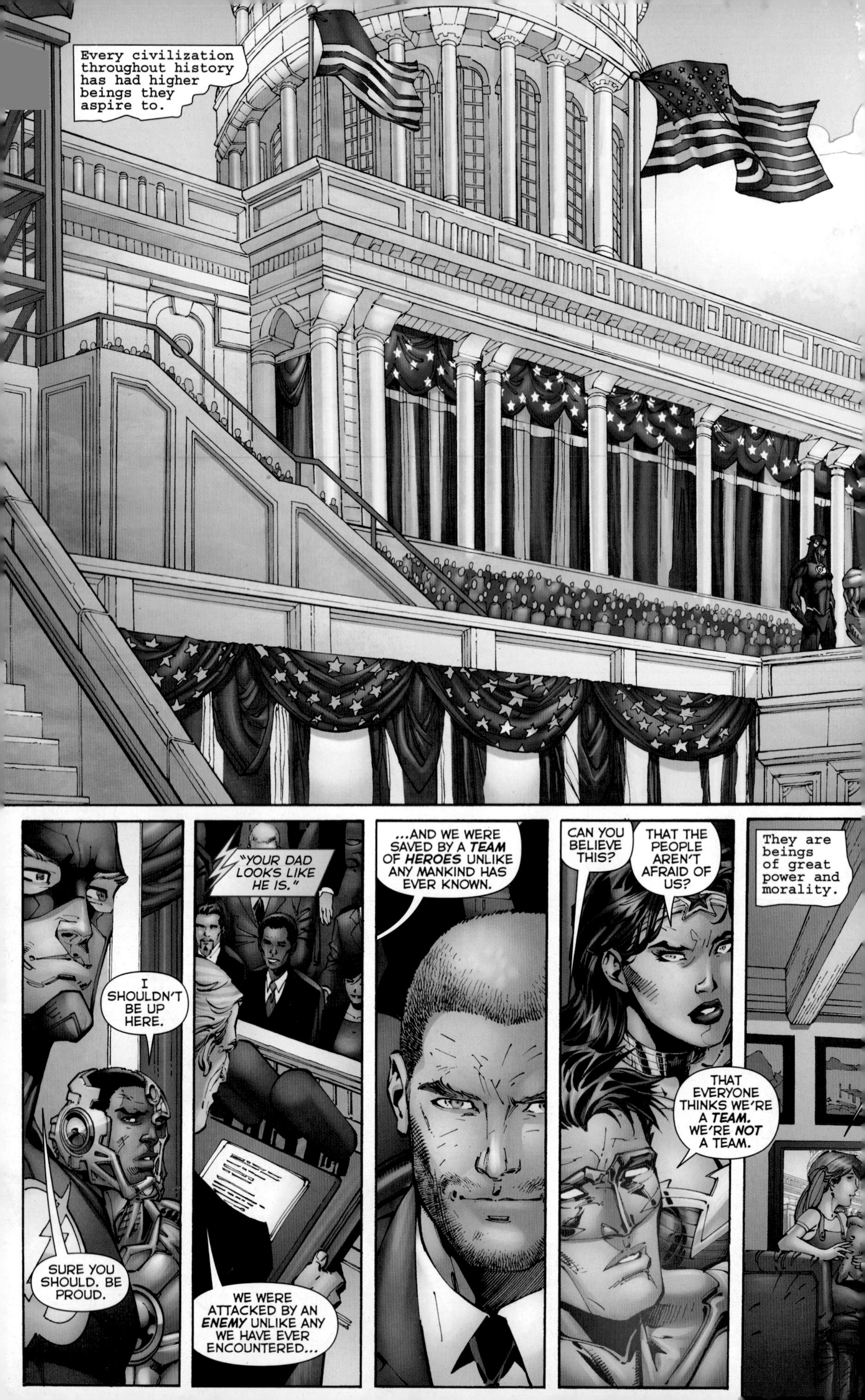
Every civilization throughout history has had higher beings they aspire to.
I SHOULDN'T BE UP HERE.
SURE YOU SHOULD. BE PROUD.
"YOUR DAD LOOKS LIKE HE IS."
WE WERE ATTACKED BY AN ENEMY UNLIKE ANY WE HAVE EVER ENCOUNTERED...
...AND WE WERE SAVED BY A TEAM OF HEROES UNLIKE ANY MANKIND HAS EVER KNOWN.
CAN YOU BELIEVE THIS?
THAT THE PEOPLE AREN'T AFRAID OF US?
THAT EVERYONE THINKS WE'RE A TEAM. WE'RE NOT A TEAM.
They are beings of great power and morality.

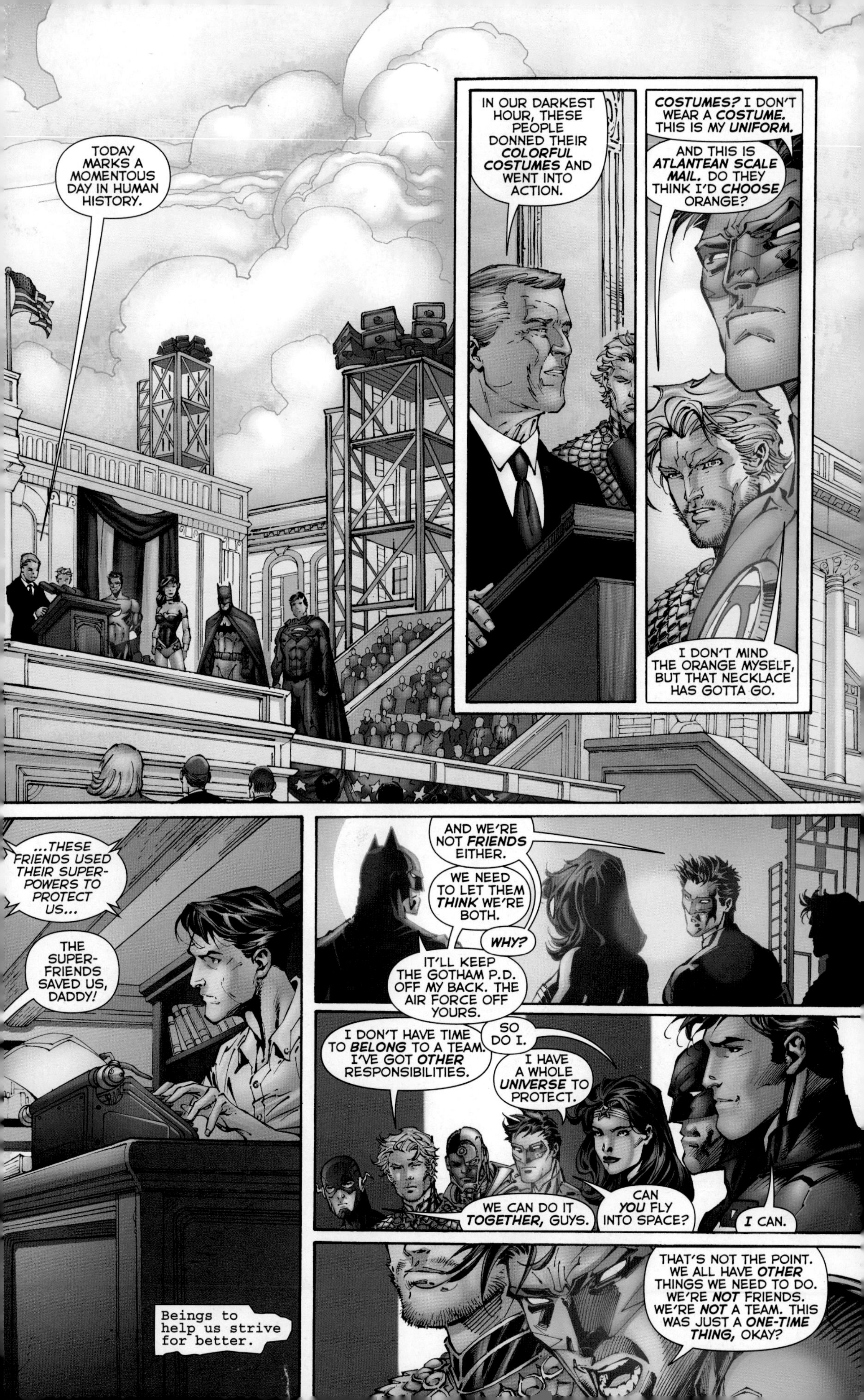
TODAY MARKS A MOMENTOUS DAY IN HUMAN HISTORY.
IN OUR DARKEST HOUR, THESE PEOPLE DONNED THEIR COLORFUL COSTUMES AND WENT INTO ACTION.
COSTUMES? I DON'T WEAR A COSTUME. THIS IS MY UNIFORM.
AND THIS IS ATLANTEAN SCALE MAIL. DO THEY THINK I'D CHOOSE ORANGE?
I DON'T MIND THE ORANGE MYSELF, BUT THAT NECKLACE HAS GOTTA GO.
...THESE FRIENDS USED THEIR SUPER-POWERS TO PROTECT US...
THE SUPER-FRIENDS SAVED US, DADDY!
Beings to help us strive for better.
AND WE'RE NOT FRIENDS EITHER.
WE NEED TO LET THEM THINK WE'RE BOTH.
WHY?
IT'LL KEEP THE GOTHAM P.D. OFF MY BACK. THE AIR FORCE OFF YOURS.
I DON'T HAVE TIME TO BELONG TO A TEAM. I'VE GOT OTHER RESPONSIBILITIES.
SO DO I.
I HAVE A WHOLE UNIVERSE TO PROTECT.
WE CAN DO IT TOGETHER, GUYS.
CAN YOU FLY INTO SPACE?
I CAN.
THAT'S NOT THE POINT. WE ALL HAVE OTHER THINGS WE NEED TO DO. WE'RE NOT FRIENDS. WE'RE NOT A TEAM. THIS WAS JUST A ONE-TIME THING, OKAY?

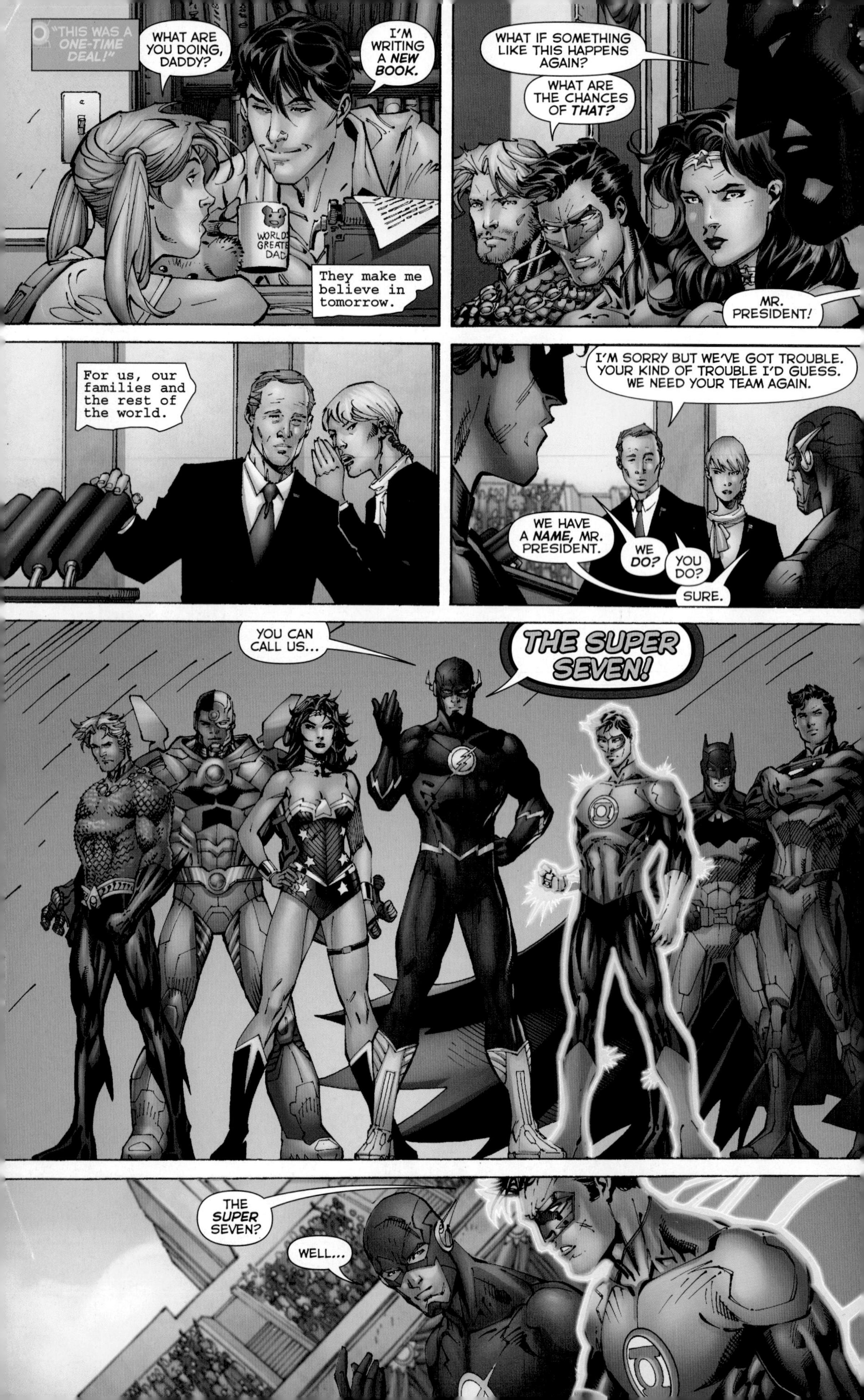

"THIS WAS A *ONE-TIME DEAL!*"
WHAT ARE YOU DOING, DADDY?
I'M WRITING A ***NEW BOOK.***
They make me believe in tomorrow.
WHAT IF SOMETHING LIKE THIS HAPPENS AGAIN?
WHAT ARE THE CHANCES OF ***THAT?***
MR. PRESIDENT!
For us, our families and the rest of the world.
I'M SORRY BUT WE'VE GOT TROUBLE. YOUR KIND OF TROUBLE I'D GUESS. WE NEED YOUR TEAM AGAIN.
WE HAVE A ***NAME,*** MR. PRESIDENT.
WE ***DO?***
YOU DO?
SURE.
YOU CAN CALL US...
THE SUPER SEVEN!
THE ***SUPER*** SEVEN?
WELL...

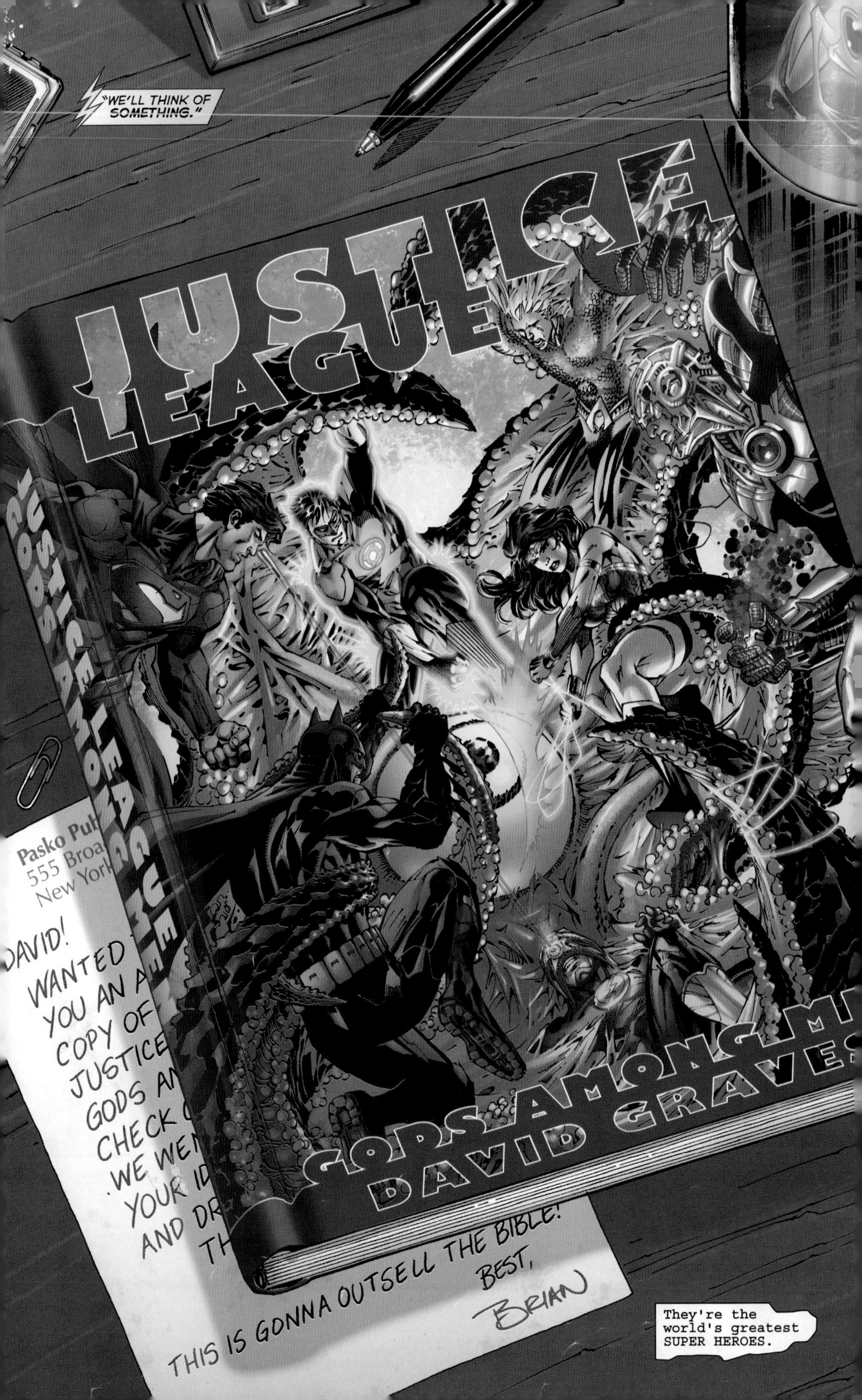

"WE'LL THINK OF SOMETHING."
JUSTICE LEAGUE
GODS AMONG MEN
DAVID GRAVES
JUSTICE LEAGUE GODS AMONG ME
Pasko Pub
555 Broa
New York
DAVID!
WANTED
YOU AN A
COPY OF
JUSTICE
GODS AN
CHECK
WE WEN
YOUR ID
AND DR
TH
THIS IS GONNA OUTSELL THE BIBLE!
BEST,
BRIAN
They're the world's greatest SUPER HEROES.

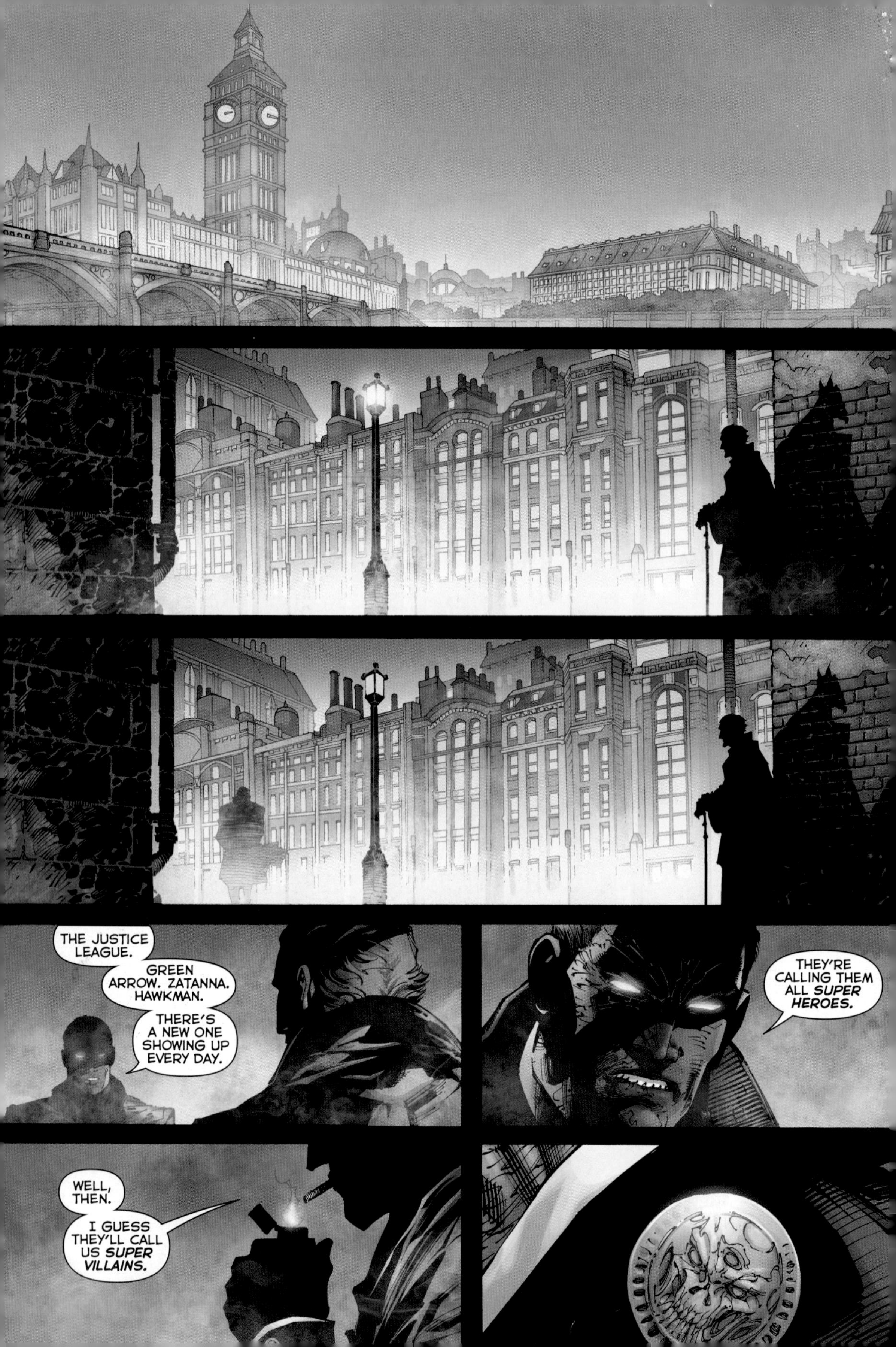
THE JUSTICE LEAGUE.
GREEN ARROW. ZATANNA. HAWKMAN.
THERE'S A NEW ONE SHOWING UP EVERY DAY.
THEY'RE CALLING THEM ALL *SUPER HEROES.*
WELL, THEN.
I GUESS THEY'LL CALL US *SUPER VILLAINS.*

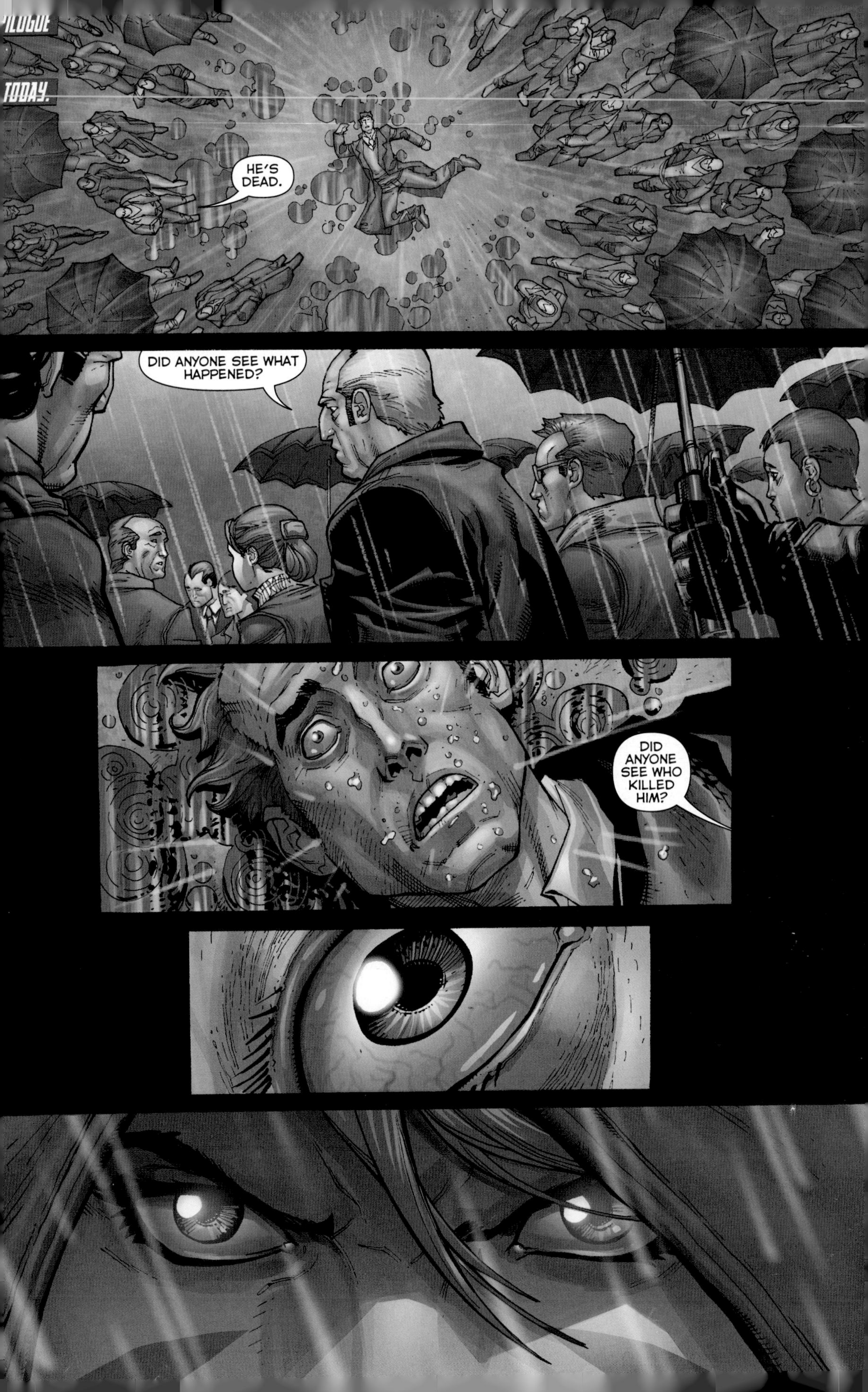
PILOGUE
TODAY.
HE'S DEAD.
DID ANYONE SEE WHAT HAPPENED?
DID ANYONE SEE WHO KILLED HIM?

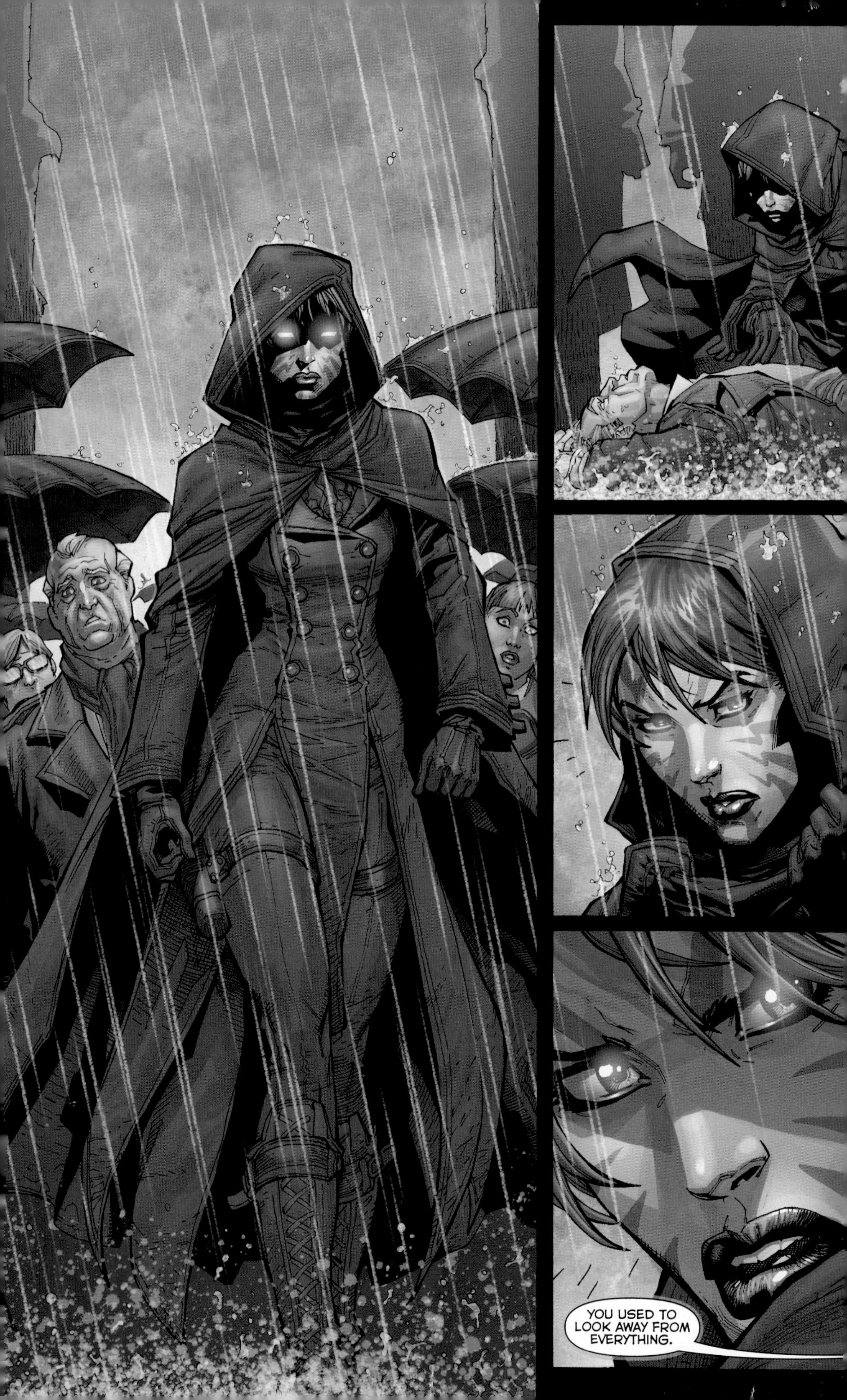
YOU USED TO LOOK AWAY FROM EVERYTHING.

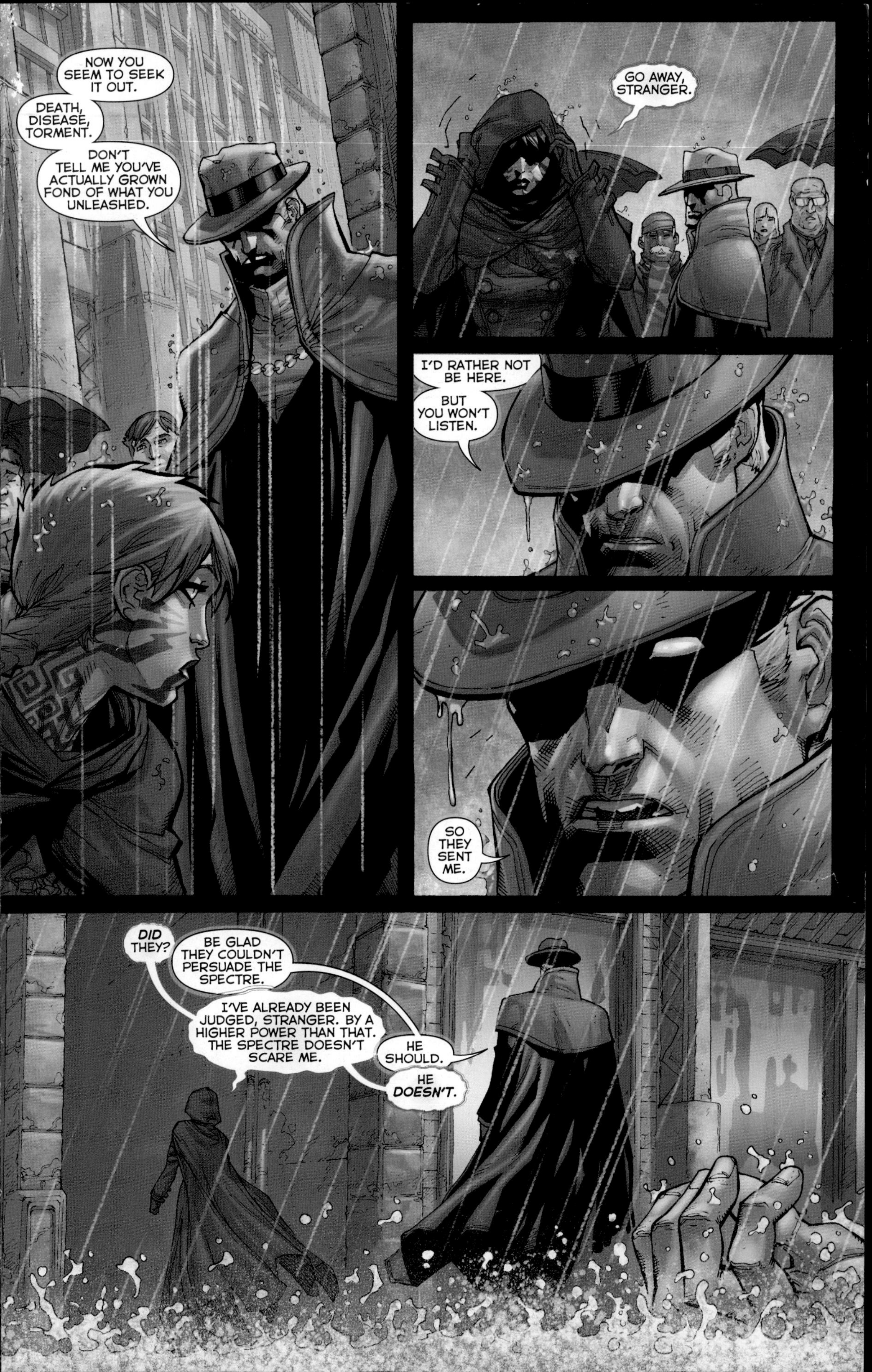
NOW YOU SEEM TO SEEK IT OUT.
DEATH, DISEASE, TORMENT.
DON'T TELL ME YOU'VE ACTUALLY GROWN FOND OF WHAT YOU UNLEASHED.
GO AWAY, STRANGER.
I'D RATHER NOT BE HERE.
BUT YOU WON'T LISTEN.
SO THEY SENT ME.
DID THEY?
BE GLAD THEY COULDN'T PERSUADE THE SPECTRE.
I'VE ALREADY BEEN JUDGED, STRANGER. BY A HIGHER POWER THAN THAT. THE SPECTRE DOESN'T SCARE ME.
HE SHOULD.
HE DOESN'T.

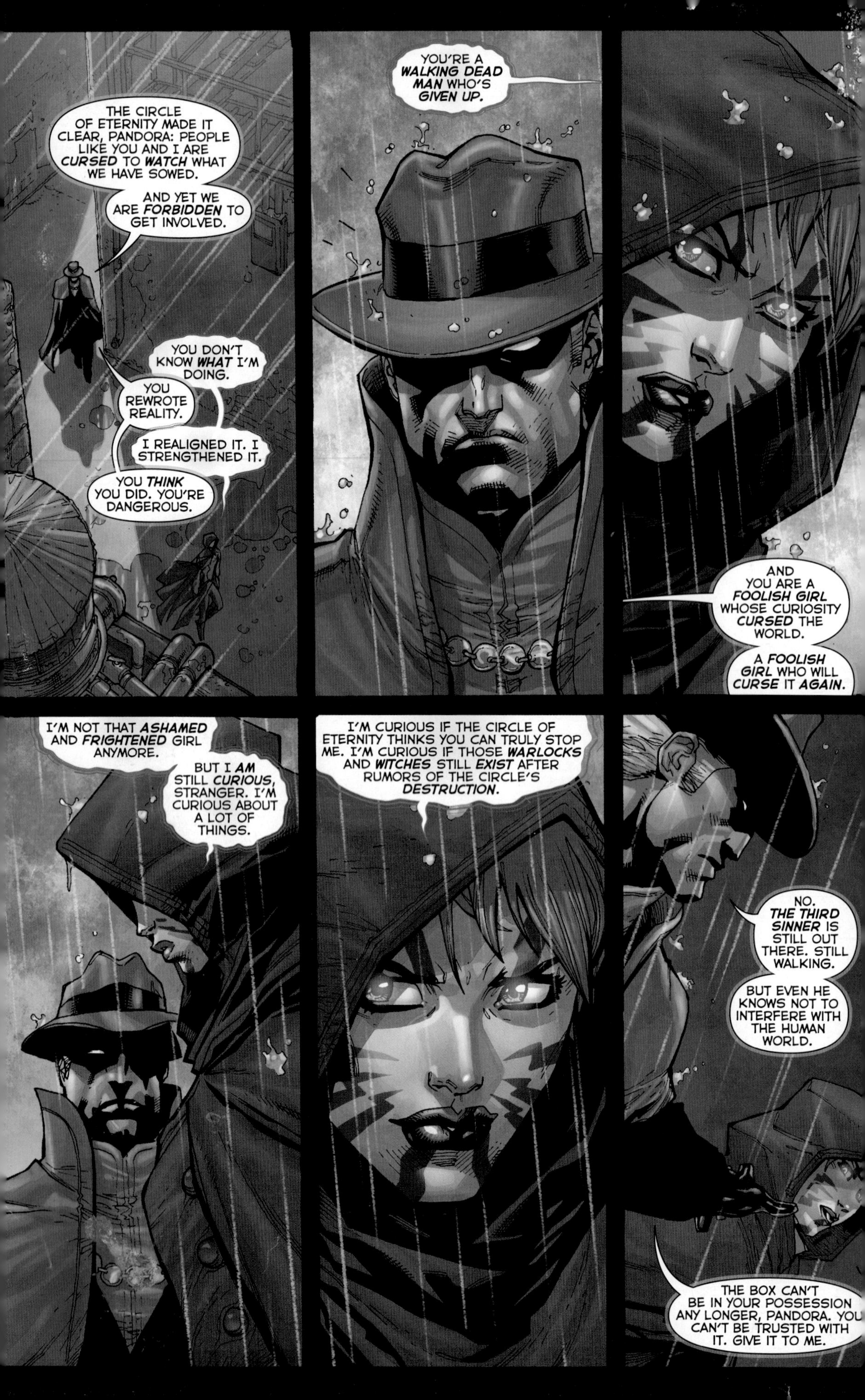
THE CIRCLE OF ETERNITY MADE IT CLEAR, PANDORA: PEOPLE LIKE YOU AND I ARE CURSED TO WATCH WHAT WE HAVE SOWED.
AND YET WE ARE FORBIDDEN TO GET INVOLVED.
YOU DON'T KNOW WHAT I'M DOING.
YOU REWROTE REALITY.
I REALIGNED IT. I STRENGTHENED IT.
YOU THINK YOU DID. YOU'RE DANGEROUS.
YOU'RE A WALKING DEAD MAN WHO'S GIVEN UP.
AND YOU ARE A FOOLISH GIRL WHOSE CURIOSITY CURSED THE WORLD.
A FOOLISH GIRL WHO WILL CURSE IT AGAIN.
I'M NOT THAT ASHAMED AND FRIGHTENED GIRL ANYMORE.
BUT I AM STILL CURIOUS, STRANGER. I'M CURIOUS ABOUT A LOT OF THINGS.
I'M CURIOUS IF THE CIRCLE OF ETERNITY THINKS YOU CAN TRULY STOP ME. I'M CURIOUS IF THOSE WARLOCKS AND WITCHES STILL EXIST AFTER RUMORS OF THE CIRCLE'S DESTRUCTION.
NO. THE THIRD SINNER IS STILL OUT THERE. STILL WALKING.
BUT EVEN HE KNOWS NOT TO INTERFERE WITH THE HUMAN WORLD.
THE BOX CAN'T BE IN YOUR POSSESSION ANY LONGER, PANDORA. YOU CAN'T BE TRUSTED WITH IT. GIVE IT TO ME.

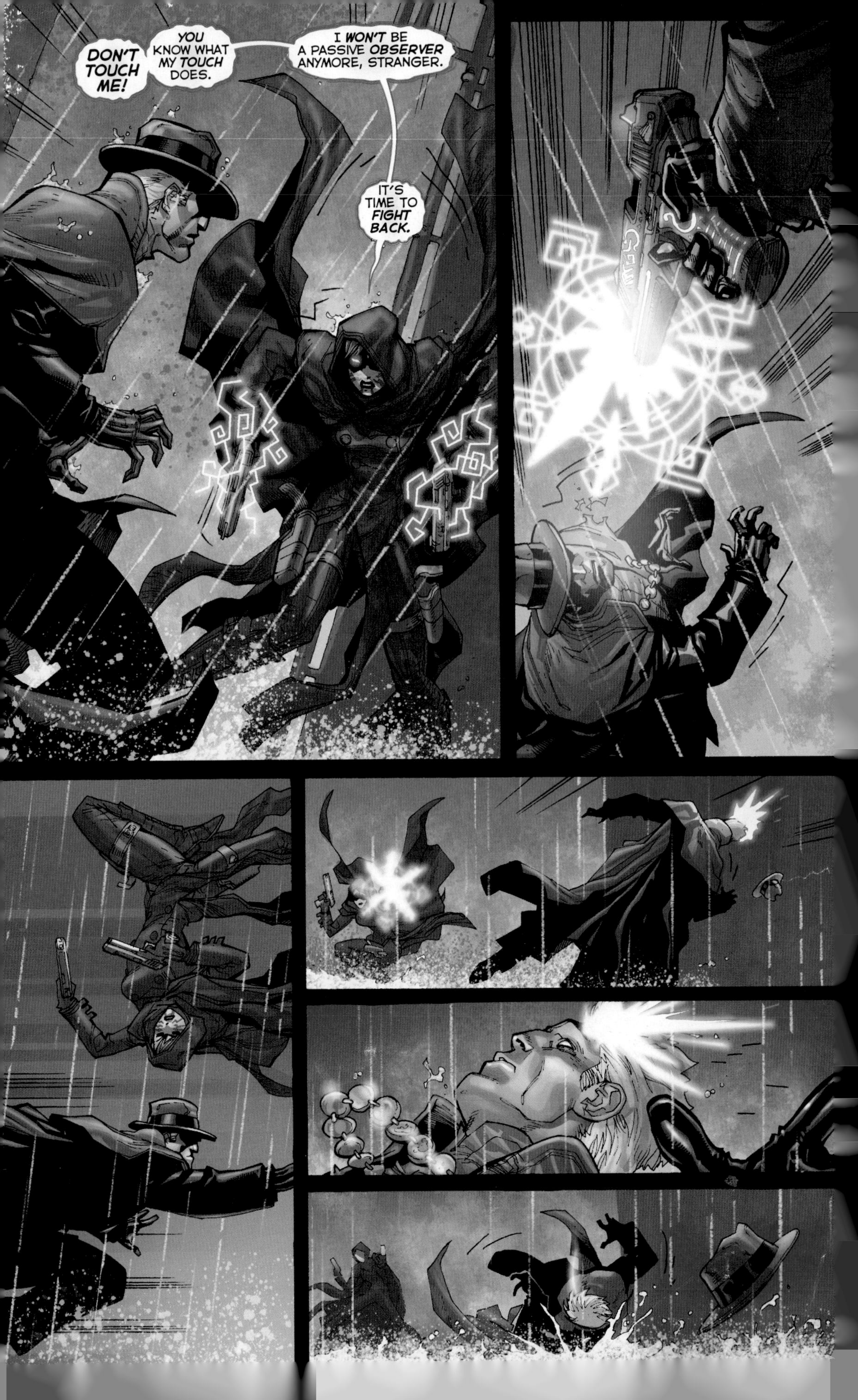
DON'T TOUCH ME!
YOU KNOW WHAT MY TOUCH DOES.
I WON'T BE A PASSIVE OBSERVER ANYMORE, STRANGER.
IT'S TIME TO FIGHT BACK.

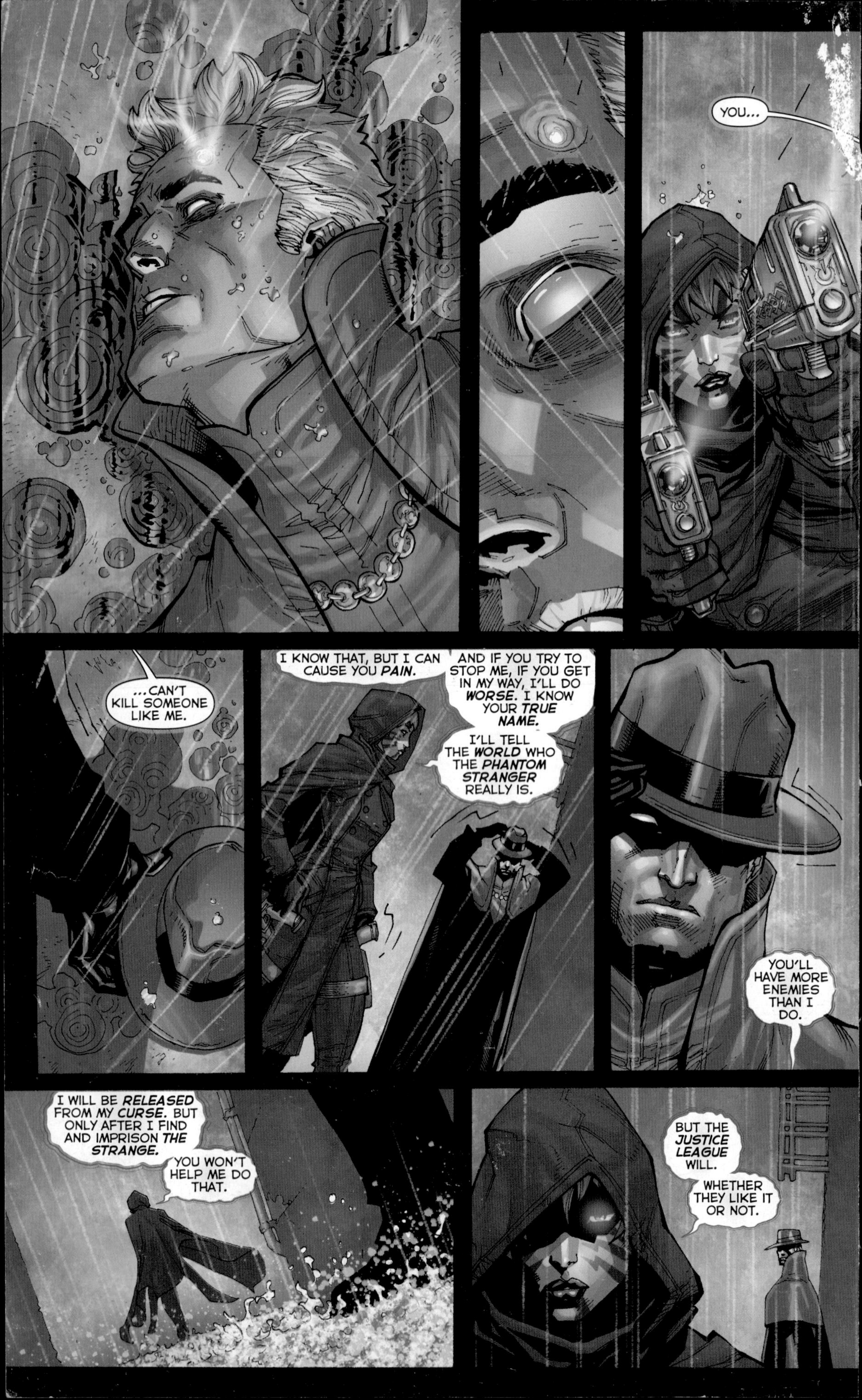
YOU...
...CAN'T KILL SOMEONE LIKE ME.
I KNOW THAT, BUT I CAN CAUSE YOU PAIN.
AND IF YOU TRY TO STOP ME, IF YOU GET IN MY WAY, I'LL DO WORSE. I KNOW YOUR TRUE NAME.
I'LL TELL THE WORLD WHO THE PHANTOM STRANGER REALLY IS.
YOU'LL HAVE MORE ENEMIES THAN I DO.
I WILL BE RELEASED FROM MY CURSE. BUT ONLY AFTER I FIND AND IMPRISON THE STRANGE.
YOU WON'T HELP ME DO THAT.
BUT THE JUSTICE LEAGUE WILL.
WHETHER THEY LIKE IT OR NOT.

U.S.A.F.

XD-4224

CONFIDENTIAL INFORMATION

TRANSCRIPT OF INTERVIEW WITH CAPTAIN
STEVE TREVOR, U.S.A.F. — PROJECT:
FLIGHT TO PARADISE

TRANSCRIBED BY GEOFF JOHNS

1) ENTER ON FORM 997 YOUR NAME AND DATE YOU HAD
ACCESS TO THE DOCUMENT(S).

2) EXERCISE THE NECESSARY SAFEGUARDS TO PREVENT
UNAUTHORIZED DISCLOSURE BY NEVER LEAVING THE
DOCUMENT(S) UNATTENDED EXCEPT WHEN PROPERLY
SECURED IN A LOCKED SAFE.

3) TRANSFER THE DOCUMENT(S) ONLY TO PERSONS WHO
NEED TO KNOW AND WHO POSSESS THE REQUIRED
SECURITY CLEARANCE.

4) OBTAIN A RECEIPT WHENEVER RELINQUISHING CONTROL
OF THE DOCUMENTS.

WARNING: SPECIAL ACCESS REQUIRED

TRANSCRIPT OF INTERVIEW WITH CAPT[illegible]R,

U.S.A.F. PROJECT [illegible] TO PARADISE

CONFIDENTIAL INFORMATION

TREVOR: I already answered that, Agent Waller.

WALLER: Yes, but I still find it hard to believe that a decorated pilot in the U.S. Air Force, one of the American "heroes" who took part in Operation: Pandora's Box and survived, an expert in search and rescue who saved over twenty-three lost ships, some the size of a rowboat --

TREVOR: For the record, I've never failed a rescue.

WALLER: Yet you couldn't point on a map and give us the location of the island you crashed on. And you have no idea how to return.

TREVOR: You want to know how I got there, ask the people who sent me into that storm.

WALLER: You were sent looking for a missing U.S. Coast Guard ship.

TREVOR: Except there was no missing boat.

WALLER: There was no missing boat?

TREVOR: I checked the records when I got back. There was no missing boat. It was a lie.

WALLER: Your superior officer lied to you?

TREVOR: More likely someone lied to them. They sent me into the eye of that hurricane knowing --

WALLER: Knowing you'd "fly through a circle of golden light and crash on an island full of Amazons"? That's a direct quote from your written account.

TREVOR: That's what happened.

WALLER: What also happened is that the missing Coast Guard ship was never found, and the crew was declared lost at sea.

TREVOR: There was no ship.

WALLER: Tell that to the grieving families, Captain Trevor. And I guess we should note here you have failed a rescue. For the record. How does that feel? To fail someone?

TREVOR: Are you a psychiatrist or a government bogeyman?

WALLER: A bit of both.

CONFIDENTIAL INFORMATION

TRANSCRIPT OF INTERVIEW WITH CAPTAIN STEVE TREVOR,
U.S.A.F. -- PROJECT: FLIGHT TO PARADISE

WALLER: Can Wonder Woman take us to the island?

TREVOR: She wouldn't, even if she could.

WALLER: That's unacceptable.

TREVOR: She can't get home. Look, they're not a problem. She's not.

WALLER: Try telling that to the rest of the world. After what Wonder Woman did to that kidnapper --

TREVOR: He was going to kill those children.

WALLER: She slit his throat with her sword. Right in front of those kids. Is that what Amazons do? Kill unarmed men?

TREVOR: He wasn't unarmed.

WALLER: But she is an Amazon. And there are more.

TREVOR: Yes.

WALLER: What do they want?

TREVOR: They want to be left alone.

WALLER: And what does Wonder Woman want? What motivated her to come here? Why does she have no interest in even trying to go home?

TREVOR: If you have any questions, let me ask her. She'll talk to me. Just don't provoke her.

WALLER: Provoking people lets me see what they're capable of. That's my job.

TREVOR: She's only doing what she was raised to do.

WALLER: Which is?

TREVOR: Fight.

CONFIDENTIAL INFORMATION

TRANSCRIPT OF INTERVIEW WITH CAPTAIN STEVE TREVOR, U.S.A.F. — PROJECT: FLIGHT TO PARADISE

WALLER: Is your relationship romantic?

TREVOR: What? No.

WALLER: That question makes you uncomfortable.

TREVOR: Nothing makes me uncomfortable.

WALLER: I don't believe that, and neither do you. Do you believe in U.F.O.'s?

TREVOR: Do I believe in U.F.O.'s? What's that have to do with anything?

WALLER: Humor me. Do you believe in U.F.O.'s?

TREVOR: They're saying Superman's an alien, right? I guess.

WALLER: And Atlantis? Do you believe in Atlantis? A new super-human, the one they're calling Aquaman, says it exists.

TREVOR: Aquaman? The guy who talks to fish?

WALLER: And there are these strange reports from several men and women across the world. People with absolutely no connection to one another who claim to have been abducted by a wizard and tested. Tested to see if they were worthy of something called "Shazam." They're calling them magical abductees.

TREVOR: Why are you telling me all this?

WALLER: I'm making a point here, Captain Trevor. In this world of super-humans, nothing can be counted out. Nothing can be trusted. Myth is fact. Rumor is nonfiction. Things like Amazons exist.

TREVOR: Tell me something I and everyone else on this planet doesn't know.

WALLER: No one's prepared for what's coming next. It's as if everything David Graves wrote has come true.

TREVOR: Who's David Graves?

WALLER: The author of a dozen books on the mysteries of the world. You should read more, Captain Trevor. Now let's move on. Tell me about this lasso.

THE SECRET HISTORY OF
ATLANTIS

BY DAVID GRAVES

► HISTORIC PUBLICATIONS ◄

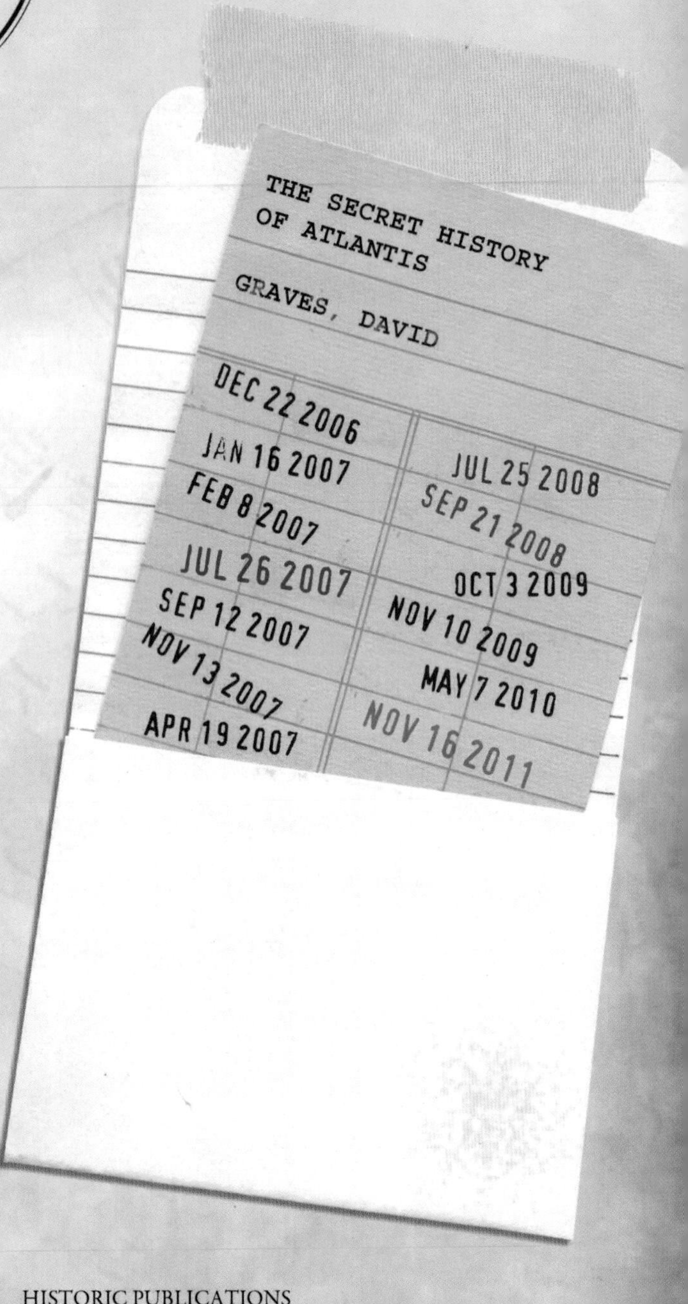
THE SECRET HISTORY
OF ATLANTIS
GRAVES, DAVID
DEC 22 2006
JAN 16 2007
FEB 8 2007
JUL 26 2007
SEP 12 2007
NOV 13 2007
APR 19 2007
JUL 25 2008
SEP 21 2008
OCT 3 2009
NOV 10 2009
MAY 7 2010
NOV 16 2011

HISTORIC PUBLICATIONS

ABOUT THE AUTHOR

DAVID GRAVES is the best selling world-renowned writer of some of the most popular books on the paranormal, supernatural and mythical, but he became the most important author of our time when he wrote his firsthand account of the formation of the Justice League and their role in saving him and his family. It is with great pride that Historic Publications rereleases Graves' line of World-Mystery ™ books in conjunction with the release of *THE JUSTICE LEAGUE: GODS AMONG US.*

Available at bookstores and e-book sellers everywhere:

THE YONAGUNI PYRAMID: CIVILIZATION UNKNOWN (1999)

STONEHENGE DECODED (2000)

THE SECRET HISTORY OF ATLANTIS (2002)

THE FATIMA PROPHECIES (2002)

ENTERING THE KALIASA CAVES (2003)

THE NEW SEVEN WONDERS OF THE WORLD (2004)

THE BELMEZ FACES AND BEYOND (2005)

THE TRUTH BEHIND THE TUNGUSKA EVENT (2005)

THE JUSTICE LEAGUE: GODS AMONG US (2006)

DEDICATION

David would like to dedicate this new edition of
THE SECRET HISTORY OF ATLANTIS
to his best friend and wife, Jennifer, his son, Jason,
and his ever-imaginative daughter, Emma.

He loves them more than *any* world mystery.

FOREWORD

How powerful is a story? That all depends on the author.

There's one reason that people believe Atlantis was real. Plato wrote about it. In times long before ours, Atlantis was commonly thought nothing more than a myth, a warning that no empire will last forever. It's only recently that Plato's tale of Atlantis began to be believed. Plato's name validated everything he wrote. But should we believe everything we read from Plato? Do we think an entire continent, home to a utopian society and ultimately a violent empire, was destroyed and washed away in but a day? Did Atlantis sink into the ocean to be forever lost? Are Plato's words fact or fiction?

I believe fact. I believe Atlantis was real. And I believe it still exists in some form today. And I believe after you read this book, you'll feel the same way.

I've gathered together historical accounts from the first travelers to the New World and the pirates that plagued them of encounters with aquatic humanoids who rose from the oceans and vanished just as quickly. I've spoken to Dr. Stephen Shin, the famed oceanographer and marine biologist who spent his life searching the seas for signs of the lost empire and even claims there's an Atlantean now living among us. I've traveled across the world myself to take part in Dane Dorrance's expeditions to the deep, uncovering what I believe are the remains of a path to the central city of Atlantis on the ocean floor.

The evidence is here. Believe.

David Graves
April 13, 2002

WRITTEN BY GEOFF JOHNS · DESIGN BY BRIAN WALTERS

A NEW WORLD ORDER

At the center of DC COMICS—The New 52 is the JUSTICE LEAGUE, and in the way that Geoff Johns had to structure a story that would reintroduce the World's Greatest Heroes, Jim Lee had to establish the look that would set the tone for what would be a younger and more contemporary set of heroes.

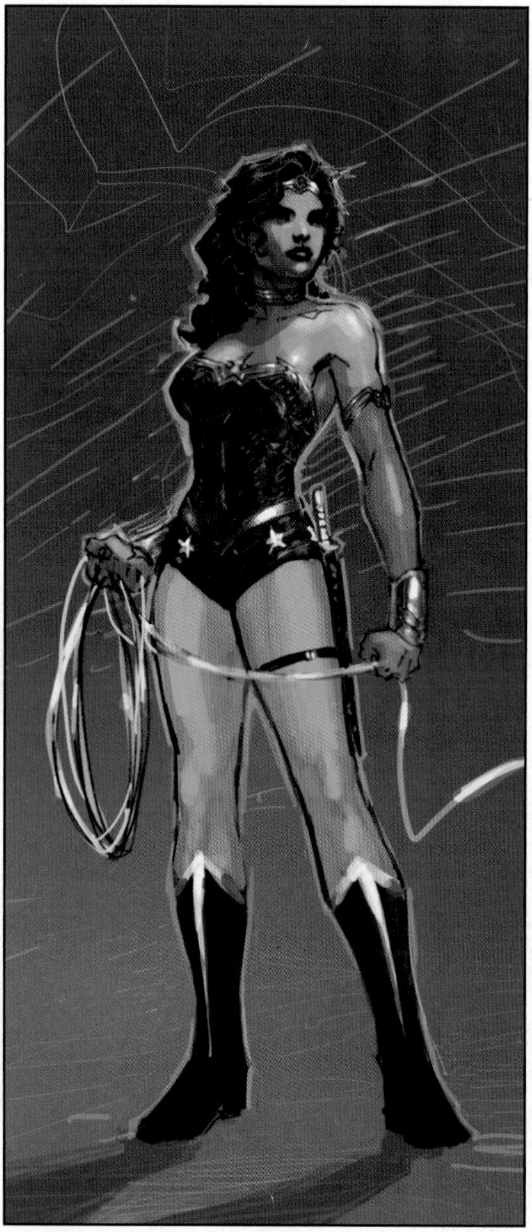

WONDER WOMAN: There was much debate on Princess Diana's legwear. This one denotes some deadly accessories.

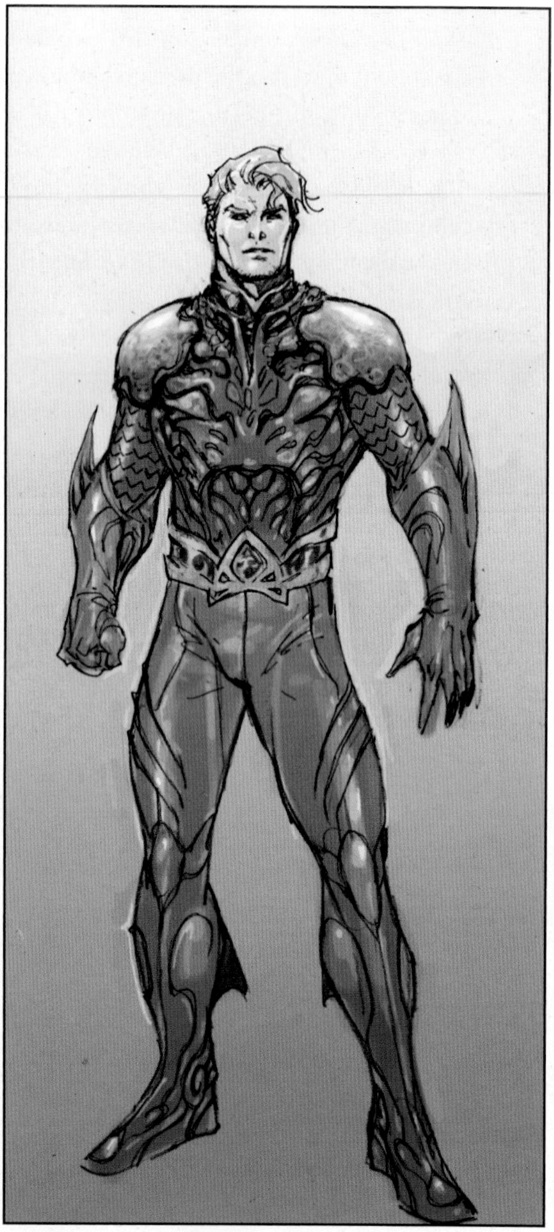

AQUAMAN: A more crustacean-looking armor was considered but ultimately deemed to be too detailed and "crusty" a look for the regal, majestic King of the Seven Seas. Maybe an Atlantean foot soldier will carry this mantle...

EMPLOYEE DOSSIER
RESTRICTED ACCESS
FILE FORM 778M REQ

COMPILED BY
GEOFF JOHNS

DESIGNER/ARCHIVIST

ARAM R. ISAACS

S.T.A.R. LABORATORIES

DR. SILAS STONE

OCCUPATION:
Project Director: The Red Room

AGE: 42
HEIGHT: 5' 9"
WEIGHT: 155 lbs.
EYES: Brown
HAIR: Black/graying

BACKGROUND:
Dr. Silas Stone graduated top of his class from the University of Michigan in Synthetic Biology and Technical Cybernetics. Although heavily pursued by LexCorp, Stone was recruited by S.T.A.R. Labs to participate in the recovery of [redacted]. Stone was the team leader in the successful reverse engineering of [redacted]. Although replication of [redacted] has so far failed, the technology involved led to the creation of promethium. With promethium, Stone established the Red Room: a level nine S.T.A.R. Labs facility in Detroit built to collect and analyze foreign, extraterrestrial and sentient technology deemed too dangerous to share with the world.

The death of Dr. Stone's wife, Dr. Elinore Stone, remains clouded by controversy. Although not held responsible legally, Stone continues to blame himself for her death. Thorough investigation confirmed that no one was at fault and that no one could have saved her. Stone is not convinced.

DR. THOMAS MORROW

OCCUPATION:
Project Manager: The Red Room

AGE: 31
HEIGHT: 5' 11"
WEIGHT: 187 lbs.
EYES: Blue
HAIR: Black

BACKGROUND:

Dr. Thomas Morrow earned master degrees in Emerging Technologies, Strategic Foresight and Future Studies from Harvard University. From a young age, Morrow exhibited a strong interest in future technology, citing influence from science fiction, specifically the works of H.G. Wells. Originally Morrow dedicated himself to the study of the possibility of time travel, but he abandoned it after an accident in particular FTL (faster-than-light) travel nearly took his own life and that of his former colleague Dr. Will Magnus. This event resulted in the resignation of Will Magnus who now works for the U.S. military on an unknown program called Project: Metal Men.

After his recovery, Morrow was recruited by Dr. Silas Stone to assist in the establishment of the Red Room located in the S.T.A.R. Labs facility in Detroit, Michigan.

There has been some criticism leveled at Morrow recently. Complaints have been filed for his lack of transparency on his projects and his sarcastic and demeaning attitude towards his fellow scientists, save for Dr. Stone. Additionally, Morrow is under investigation by the F.B.I. for reasons that are unclear.

SARAH CHARLES

OCCUPATION:
Intern

AGE: 17
HEIGHT: 5' 5"
WEIGHT: 112 lbs.
EYES: Brown
HAIR: Black

BACKGROUND:

Sarah Charles applied to the S.T.A.R. Labs internship program while studying for her master's degrees at the University of Michigan. Her father Daniel Charles is the current C.C.O. of Motor City Automotive while her mother is Congress-woman Sasha Charles representing Michigan's 9th District. Although Sarah Charles was moved to the top of the list because of her parents' involvement in the support of S.T.A.R Labs, Dr. Stone maintains that her credentials made her the prime candidate regardless.

Charles skipped several grades at a very young age, showing an intelligence level and learning capacity far beyond the other children around her. Charles graduated from Marion High School in Bloomfield Hills, Michigan at the age of 15. She received numerous awards for her scientific papers and projects, most notably her thesis on cyberware and its potential emotional impact on society.

Despite her parents' initial encouragement of Charles' internship at S.T.A.R. Labs, they have requested she end the program early because of the changing political climate and the recent controversies surrounding the existence of S.T.A.R. Labs and its shifting focus to the study of super-human biology and technology. With her 18th birthday weeks away, that decision will soon rest in Charles' hands. We expect her to not only remain at S.T.A.R. Labs, but to soon become an integral part of the team overseeing the Red Room.

PROF. ANTHONY IVO

OCCUPATION:
Project Director: A-Maze Operating System

AGE: 37
HEIGHT: 5' 10"
WEIGHT: 185 lbs.
EYES: Blue
HAIR: Black

BACKGROUND:

Professor Anthony Ivo served as head of the Cellular and Structural Biology department at Ivy University for over a decade until he was recruited by Dr. Silas Stone to oversee the biotechnology efforts of S.T.A.R. Labs. Professor Ivo has pioneered the organic pattern process: the means of creating technology to mimic organic life down to the cellular level. Although Ivo has had great success in developing the A-Maze Operating System that mimics cellular regeneration in trial tests with mice, he remains one of the most unpredictable members of Dr. Stone's team. Ivo has been known to disappear for days at a time, often consumed by his own personal projects which have been consistently frowned upon by S.T.A.R. Labs. Consequently, a parallel support program based on Ivo's designs, the B-Maze Operating System, was built without his knowledge. It has, thus far, showed results comparable to those of A-Maze OS.

Ivo suffers from thanatophobia: a fear of death. This often manifests in panic attacks and drug use and has led to several confrontations with Ivo's fellow team members.

Stone is currently looking to replace Ivo, calling him "a bomb waiting to go off."

Concept art by Cully Hamner
Based on designs by Jim Lee

Character Chest Emblem

Costume Details & Call-outs

Glove Details: Three recessed louver-like shapes are located on both topside and palm side of gloves. Gloves are a dense but malleable leather with ribbing on fingers (palm side), raised piping and convex metal knuckles (topside). Mesh detail appears just beneath the palm and inside the louver shapes. The fins can be released from gloves and are made of a razor-sharp, beveled metal that can penetrate solid rock surfaces. They are only used to assist Batman in his crimefigthing but never to maim or kill.

Boot Detail: Recessed louver-like detail on both sides of calves; Beveled knee pads in shape of bat heads are gray.

Convex metal ampules form belt and contain many of Batman's secret and useful gadgets. The buckle is made up of beveled metal platelets.

Character Name: Batman
Real Name: Bruce Wayne
Height: 6' 2"
Weight: 210 lbs

Eye Color on Cowl: White
First Appearance:
Batman: Justice League #1
(2011)

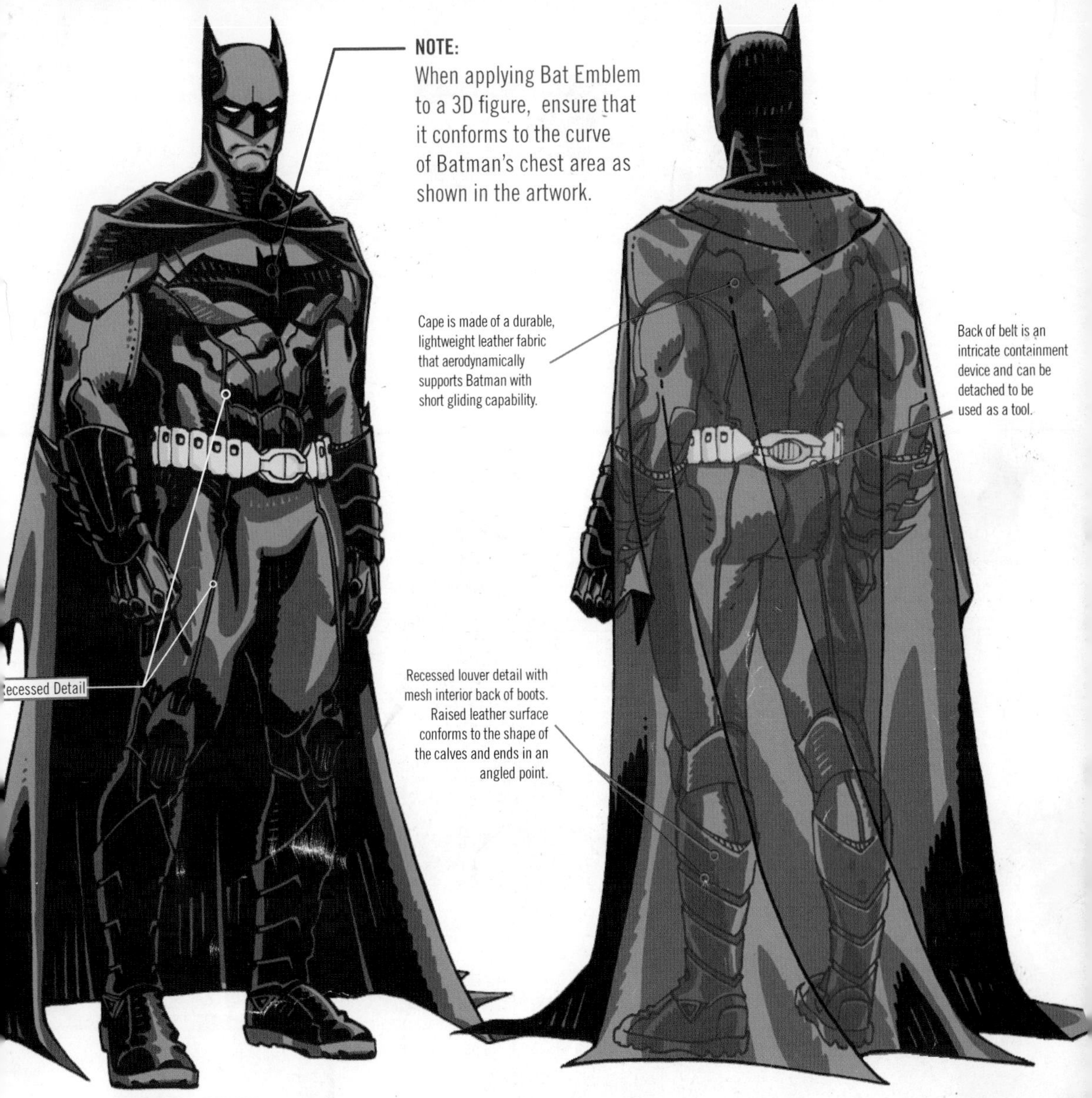
NOTE:
When applying Bat Emblem to a 3D figure, ensure that it conforms to the curve of Batman's chest area as shown in the artwork.
Cape is made of a durable, lightweight leather fabric that aerodynamically supports Batman with short gliding capability.
Back of belt is an intricate containment device and can be detached to be used as a tool.
ecessed Detail
Recessed louver detail with mesh interior back of boots. Raised leather surface conforms to the shape of the calves and ends in an angled point.

Front

Back

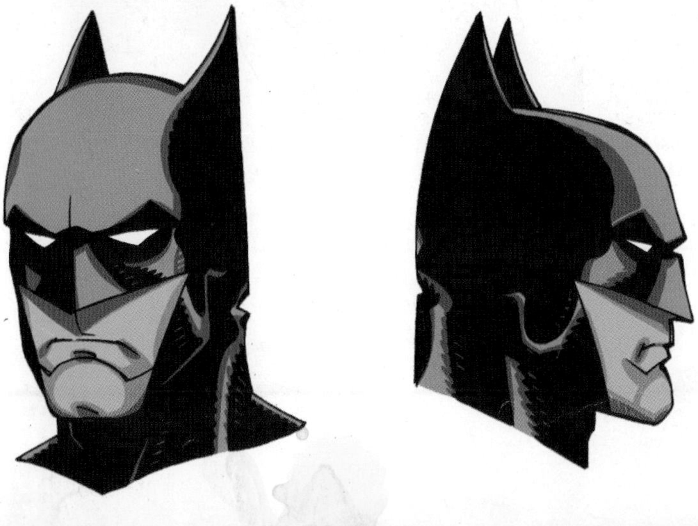

Head & Neck Details
Cowl is completely black when sculpted (3D).

Concept art by Cully Hamner
Based on designs by Jim Lee

SUPERMAN

Character Chest Emblem

Early sketch by Jim Lee

SUPERMAN: The red underwear is gone, and in this version the cape is directly attached to the armor itself. The full story of this costume will be played out in ACTION COMICS.

Costume Details & Call-outs

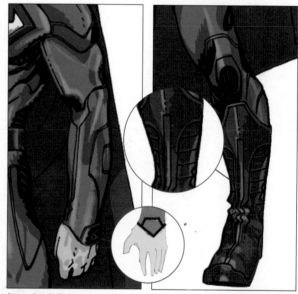

Sleeve Detail: Elaborate recessed detail runs along the arm and other areas of costume. Piping on sleeve should be red (see inset).

Boot Detail: Five horizontal seams at sides; raised piping at center and along edges.

Recessed areas of belt (buckle and on strap) should be beveled on 3D product.

Character Name: Superman
Real Name: Kal-El
AKA: Clark Kent
Height: 6' 3"
Weight: 235 lbs

Eye Color: Blue
Hair Color: Black
First Appearance:
Justice League #1
(2011)

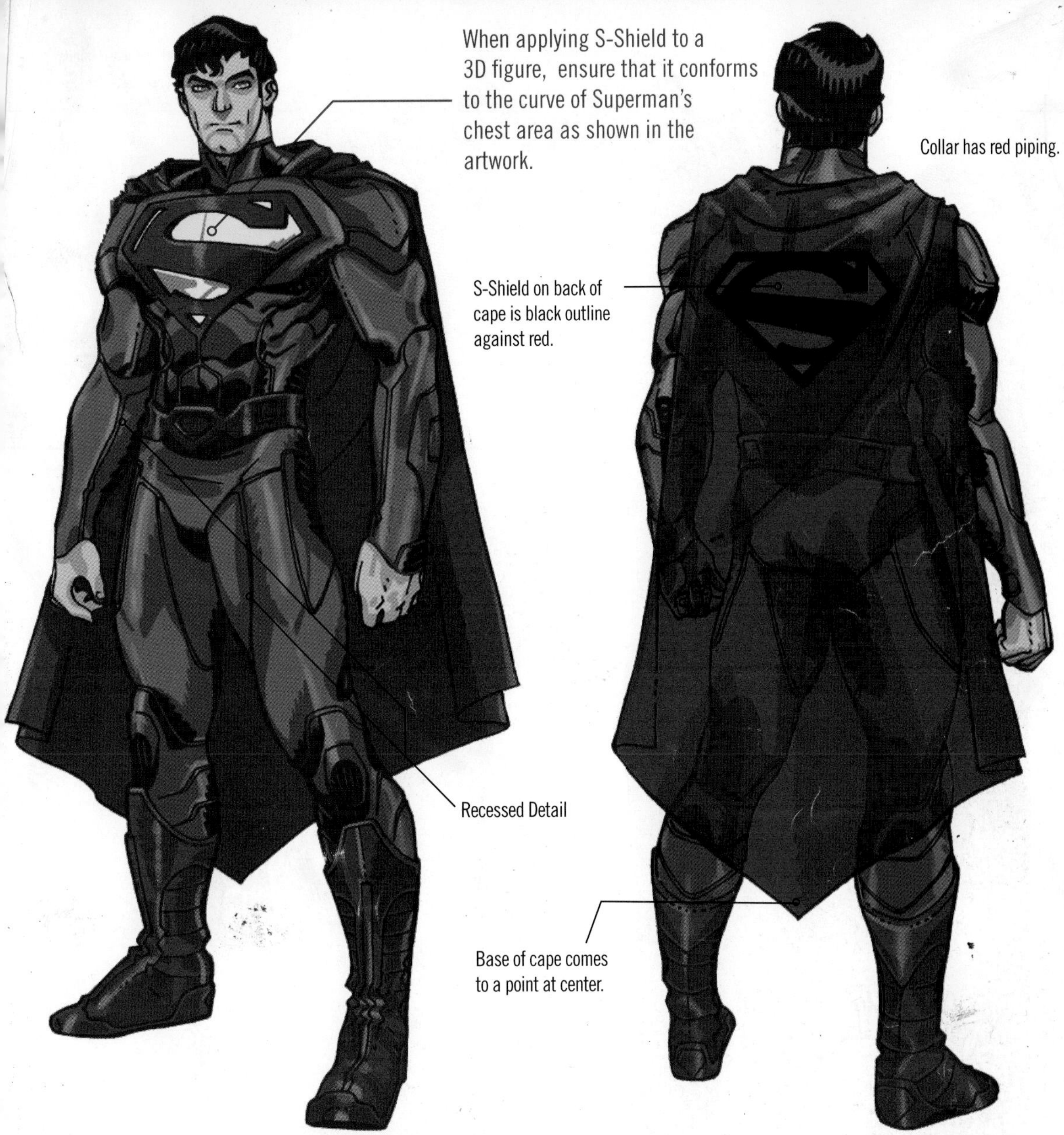
When applying S-Shield to a 3D figure, ensure that it conforms to the curve of Superman's chest area as shown in the artwork.
Collar has red piping.
S-Shield on back of cape is black outline against red.
Recessed Detail
Base of cape comes to a point at center.

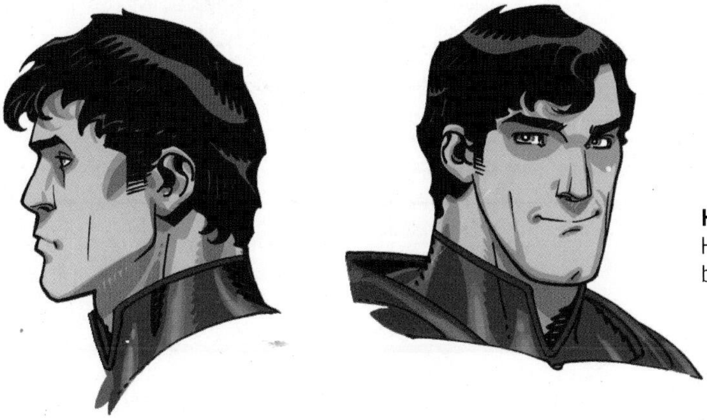

Head & Neck Details
Hair should be completely black when sculpted (3D).

GREEN LANTERN

Early sketch by Jim Lee

Character Chest Emblem

Concept art by Cully Hamner
Based on designs by Jim Lee

Note that on costume, the ring surrounding the emblem is the same thickness as the emblem.

Costume Details & Call-Outs

Ring: Negative area in the center of the ring glows continuously and more intensely when active.

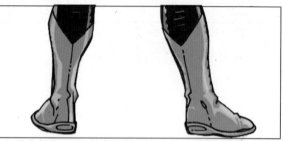

Boots: Hal's boots are made of a soft, lightweight leathery material and feature rubber sneaker-like soles.

Chest Area: The chest emblem on Green Lantern's costume glows continuously even when inactive. It radiates a green plasma-like energy when active or engaging in combat. The lines running through the upper shoulders and the chest also glow like the emblem although with slightly less intensity since there is less surface area. The linear detail maintains a faint glow when Hal's powers are inactive.

GREEN LANTERN: Here's an earlier, far more complicated version of the suit that was rejected earlier on. Design elements made their way into other non-Justice League characters.

Character Name: Green Lantern
Real Name: Hal Jordan
Height: 6' 2"
Weight: 186 lbs.

Eye Color: Brown
Hair Color: Brown
First Appearance:
Justice League #1 (2011)

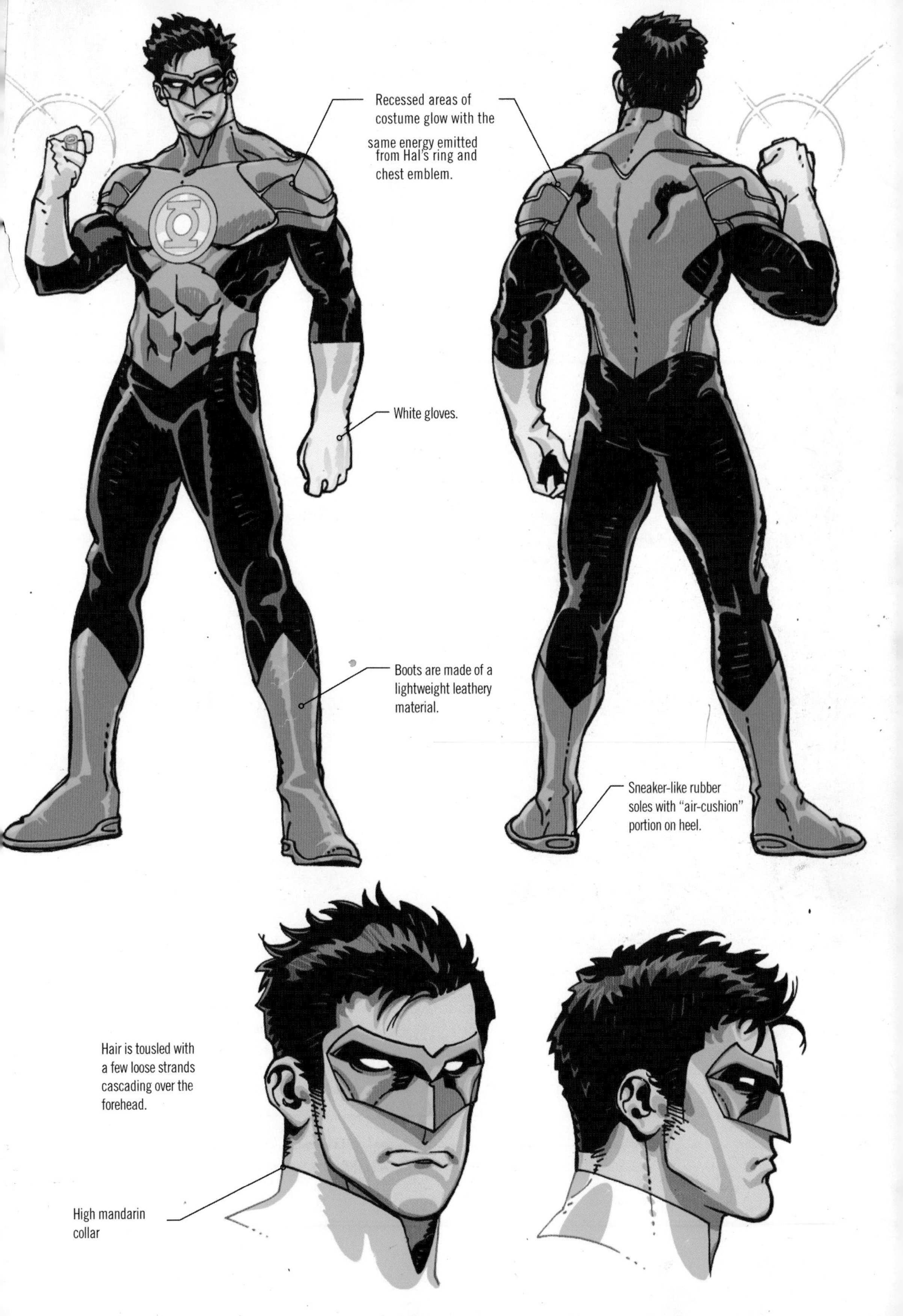
Recessed areas of costume glow with the same energy emitted from Hal's ring and chest emblem.
White gloves.
Boots are made of a lightweight leathery material.
Sneaker-like rubber soles with "air-cushion" portion on heel.
Hair is tousled with a few loose strands cascading over the forehead.
High mandarin collar

Pulsating LED power gauge

Costume Details & Call-outs

Sonic Canon Disruptor (Standby): The robotic arm is synced with Cyborg's nervous system. It generates and releases intense high-pressured sonic blasts and frequencies.

Sonic Canon Disruptor (Active): When active, the canon opens and releases concentric blasts.

Cyborg has the ability to transform parts of his robotics into technologically-advanced tools and weapons.

Hands are made of a refined kevlar material that providing a vise-like grip and durability.

Character Name: Cyborg
Real Name: Victor Stone
Height: 6' 5"
Weight: 385 lbs

Eye Color: Brown
Hair Color: Black
First Appearance:
Justice League #1 (2011)

NOTE:
Cyborg's robotic body has a chrome finish with a slightly recessed black metal over his pecs and shoulder blades. The ribbed detail along the sides of his body, inner thighs, calves and hands are a gun-metal grey color.

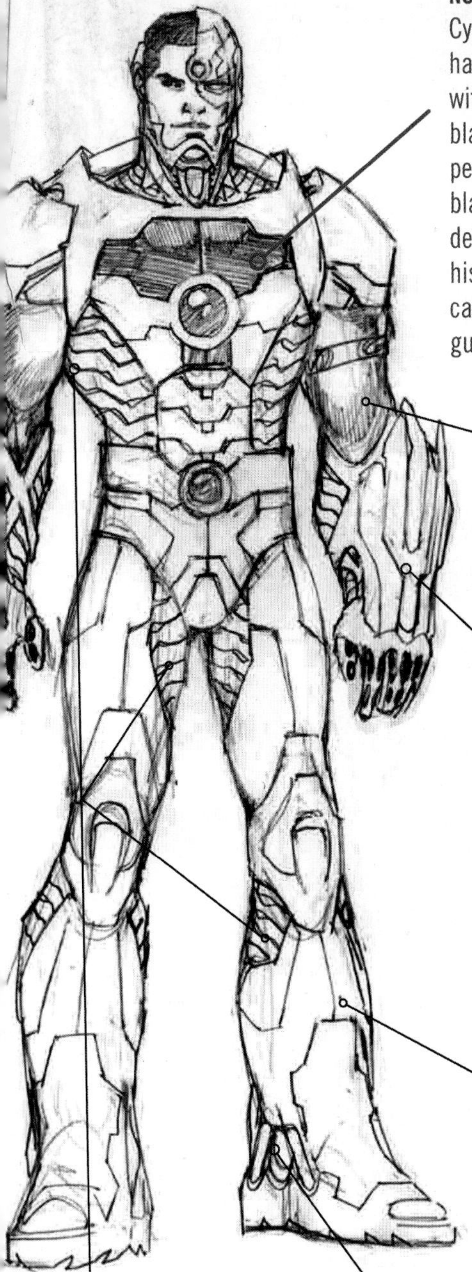

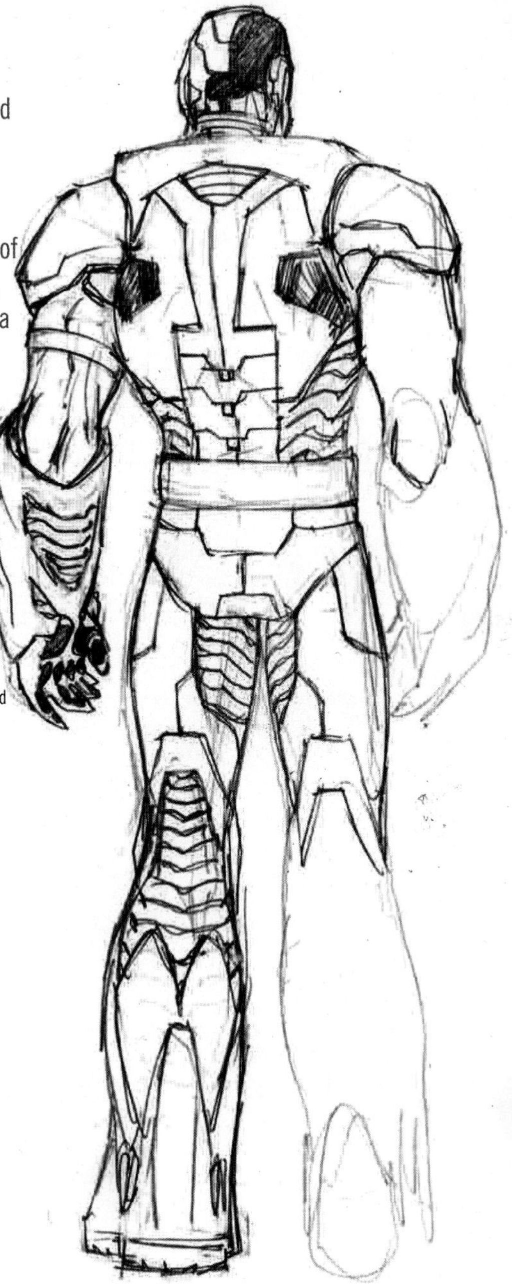

In standby mode, Cyborg's human flesh is visible on upper arms. With the exception of 3/4 of his head and upper arms, Cyborg's body is covered by a titanium alloy and carbon-fiber composite.

When activated, this 3-dimensional fork-like device projects outward and downward to form another one of Cyborg's powerful weapons.

Metal plates are pieced together to form the boots and other areas of the body.

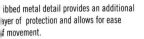

ibbed metal detail provides an additional ayer of protection and allows for ease f movement.

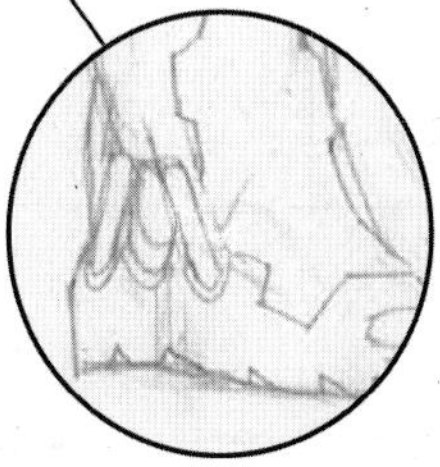

Recessed detail supporteded by two metal cylindrical pins. Soles of boots have metal treads.

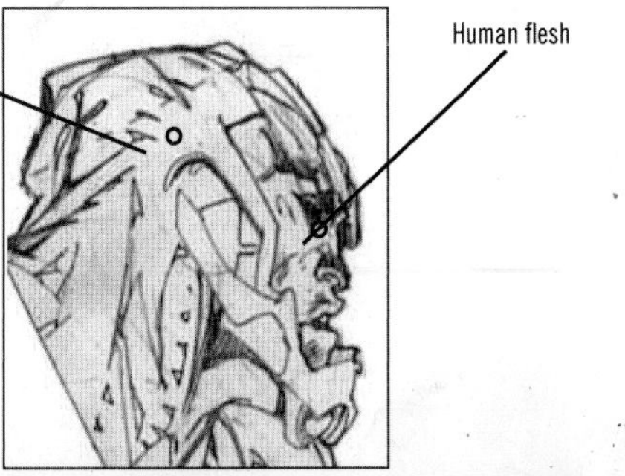
Metal
Human flesh

The Flash

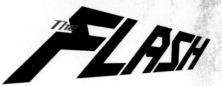

Concept art by Francis Manapul
Based on designs by Jim Lee

Character Chest Emblem

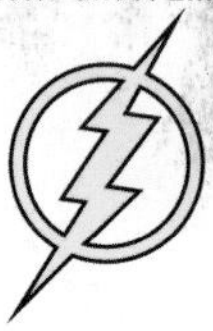

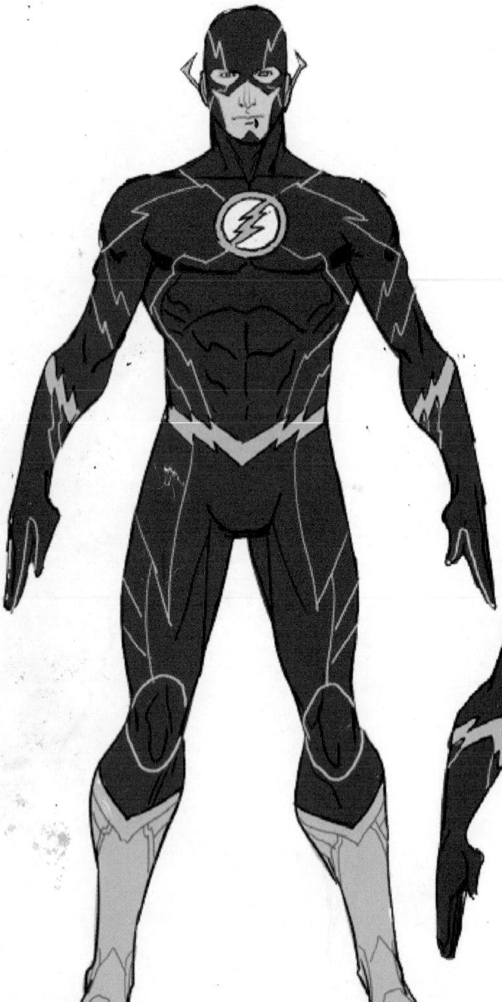

Electric Seams
When running at super speed, the black seams of The Flash's costume light up and pulse with electricity. When standing still or walking, the seams remain as black linear detail and do not light up.

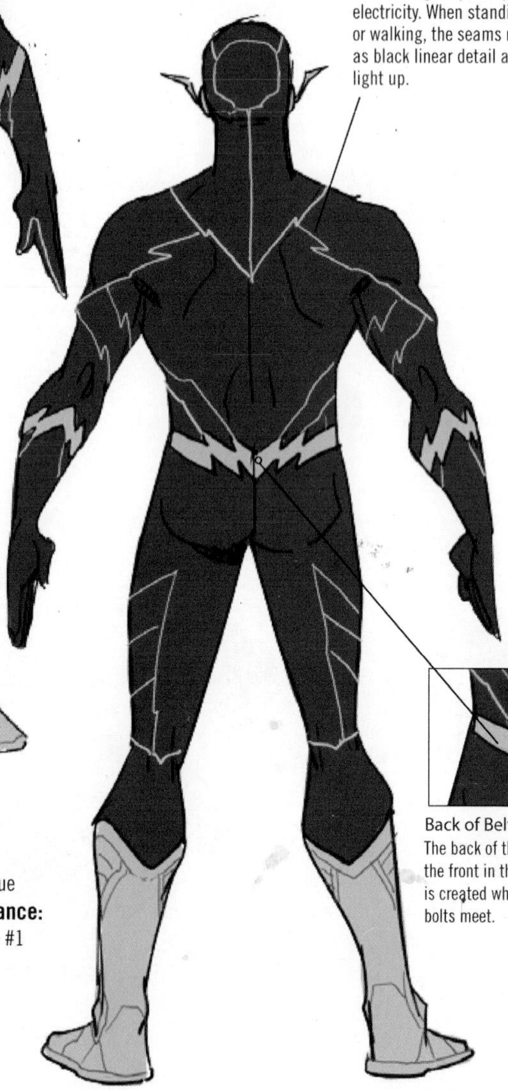

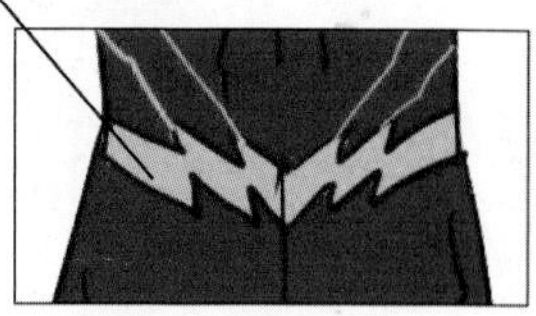

Back of Belt
The back of the belt differs from the front in that a narrow V-shape is created where the lightning bolts meet.

Character Name: The Flash
Real Name: Barry Allen
Height: 5' 11"
Weight: 179 lbs.

Eye Color: Blue
First Appearance:
Justice League #1
(cover 2011)